Urban Future 21

Urban Future 21

A Global Agenda
for Twenty-First Century Cities

Peter Hall and Ulrich Pfeiffer

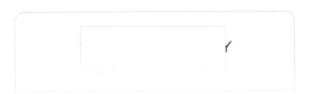

Federal Ministry of
Transport, Building
and Housing

Urban Future 21

First published 2000 by E & FN Spon
11 New Fetter Lane, London EC4P 4EE

Simultaneously published in the USA and Canada
by E & FN Spon
29 West 35th Street, New York, NY 10001

Reprinted 2002 by Spon Press

Spon Press is an imprint of the Taylor & Francis Group

© 2000 The Federal Ministry of Transport, Building and Housing
of the Republic of Germany

This book was designed and edited by Alexandrine Press, Oxford
Typeset in Sabon and Frutiger by NP Design & Print, Wallingford
Printed and bound in Great Britain by St Edmundsbury Press Limited,
Bury St Edmunds, Suffolk

British Library Cataloguing in Publication Data
A catalogue record for this book is available from the British Library

Library of Congress Cataloging in Publication Data
A catalogue record for this book has been requested

ISBN 0-415-24075-1

Contents

Contents

Foreword

Our world is becoming increasingly characterized by cities. The proportion of the world's population living in cities is growing permanently. This trend entails serious demographic, economic and social changes. For this reason, cities are the focal point of present-day problems. And that is why it is in the cities that the future quality of people's lives will be determined. Urban policy – as a global, national and local task – will thus assume increasing and crucial significance. This applies to all regions of the world – to the developing and newly industrializing countries, in which urban growth is racing ahead, and to the industrialized countries, in which urban growth has in many cases come to a standstill. The question is the same everywhere: how can we influence the development of towns and cities in such a way that all their inhabitants have a share in economic, technological and social progress, enjoy cultural diversity and a sound environment, and can participate democratically in shaping where they live?

To give new impetus to the discussion on the future of towns and cities, Germany, together with its partner countries of Brazil, South Africa and Singapore, seized the initiative for a Global Conference on the Urban Future (URBAN 21), which is to be held in Berlin from 4 to 6 July 2000 within the framework of the EXPO 2000 World Exhibition. At the same time, the German Federal Government entrusted a World Commission comprising renowned experts from all over the world with the task of drawing up a 'World Report on the Urban Future' as a basis for the subject matter of this conference. To assist them in this task, the members of the World Commission were provided with an extensive background report – *Urban Future 21* - written by the Moderator of the Commission, Sir Peter Hall, and Ulrich Pfeiffer from the empirica research institute. *Urban Future 21* is based on expert opinions on individual aspects of global structural change and its impact on the way in which cities develop; these opinions were drawn up by internationally acknowledged experts on behalf of the Federal German Government.

I am delighted that, thanks to this publication, the informative background report is accessible to all those who are interested in the urban future. For *Urban Future 21* enables them to better understand the World Report published by the German Federal Ministry of Transport, Building and Housing.

I would like to take this opportunity to thank all those who were involved in the production of the World Report and *Urban Future 21*, which provide profound analyses and valuable recommendations for action regarding sustainable urban development. I would like to thank the World

Commission and the authors of the expert opinions for their thorough work. Special thanks go to the two authors of *Urban Future 21* for the excellent way in which they have analysed the trends towards urbanization and the associated problems in their numerous and diverse dimensions, fields of action and manifestations throughout the world, and developed useful proposals for a future course of action. I would also like to thank the publishers who made publication possible.

Reinhard Klimmt
Minister of Transport, Building and Housing
of the Federal Republic of Germany

Preface

This book has come out of the work of the World Commission URBAN 21 and its Expert Group, which worked together over two years to prepare the Commission's report to be submitted to the Global Conference on the Urban Future URBAN 21, held in Berlin in July 2000. Originally, the intention was that this text should constitute the report. But the Commission unanimously decided that a shorter and more accessible version should be prepared for the conference itself. In order that the richness of the original material should be made widely available to the conference and to scholars and policy-makers outside, they agreed that this longer version should be prepared for final publication as the individual responsibility of the two authors.

Our first debt is to the German Federal Ministry of Transport, Building and Housing (BMVBW), which commissioned and provided support for the entire project; and in particular to Dr Klaus Töpfer, the former Minister, who originally conceived of the idea. We are delighted that, translated to the United Nations Commission on Human Settlements as its Director, he has been a valued member of the Commission and now sees the results of his enterprise.

Our second thanks go of course to the Commission itself and to the work of the Expert Group, which laboured so hard over many months to prepare the report that bears their name. Many of the latter reported directly in their daily work to individual members of the Commission, and so were able effectively to prepare the ground for the critical decisions of the Commissioners when they took over the project in March 1999. Their names are set out in Appendix 1. Also shown here are the names of participants at Expert Group and Commission meetings, including officials of BMVBW, who played a major role in smoothing our path.

Our third acknowledgements are to the many authors who produced working papers on specialist topics for the Expert Group and Commission. Some but by no means all of these have been published in a special volume by the German Federal Office for Building and Regional Planning (Germany BBR, 1999). A full list of these published reports is at Appendix 2.

Finally, our thanks go to present and past members of the staff of empirica, who did an heroic job in collating and preparing the materials for the meetings and for our work on the report and on this book: in particular, David Weltzien, Julia Krakau and Maggie Schriner. We also want to pay particular thanks to Ann Rudkin, who edited the text with superb efficiency against an almost impossibly tight deadline.

Peter Hall
Ulrich Pfeiffer
London/Bonn, May 2000

The World Commission

Dr. Ela Bhatt: Former Indian Member of Parliament; founder of the Self Employed Women's Association (SEWA), which has campaigned in India for women's social security and has helped many of them with loans from its own bank.

Professor Luiz Paolo Conde: Mayor of the City of Rio de Janeiro, and an internationally-recognized architect and planner whose priorities are the revitalization of public space in the city, the promotion of culture, social integration and slum rehabilitation.

Ovídio de Angelis: Special Undersecretary of State for Urban Development of the Federal Brazilian Government since July 1999; a lawyer, who previously held leading positions in the Federal State of Goiás and was then in charge of regional policy in the Brazilian Federal Government.

Professor Sir Peter Hall: Moderator of the Commission; Bartlett Professor of Planning in University College London, member of the British Academy and honorary member of the Royal Town Planning Institute; previously planning advisor to the British government and member of the Deputy Prime Minister's Urban Task Force.

Professor Thomas Herzog: An architect who lectures on design and building construction at the Technical University of Munich, he has received many awards for his work on resource-saving construction and the integration of solar energy into architecture and town planning.

Professor Tommy T. B. Koh: Ambassador-At-Large of the Ministry of Foreign Affairs of Singapore, Executive Director of the Asia-Europe Foundation, and earlier chair of the preparation and main committees of the United Nations 1992 Rio Conference for Environment and Development, he teaches law at the National University of Singapore.

Professor Vladimir R. Krogius: Deputy Director of the Scientific and Design Institute of Historic Towns in Moscow, he plays a major role in developing the scientific basis of urban renewal and architectural conservation in Russia.

Mark Malloch Brown: Administrator of the United Nations Development Programme (UNDP) in New York, previously (1996-99) Vice-President of the World Bank, and particularly committed to dealing with aid for refugees and the worldwide fight against poverty.

Sankie D. Mthembi-Mahanyele: Minister for Housing of the Republic of South Africa; under apartheid, spent several years in exile, where she was official representative of the African National Congress (ANC) in Germany and Austria.

Lord Rogers of Riverside: World-famous British architect, whose work has set new standards for a more environmentally-compatible and resource-saving type of construction; he gave the BBC 1996 Reith lectures which formed the basis of his book *Cities for a Small Planet*.

Dr. Ismail Serageldin: Vice-President of the World Bank, chairman of the World Commission for Water in the 21st Century and of the Consultative Group to Assist the Poorest; an Egyptian economist, who previously lectured in Cairo and at Harvard University and worked as a planning consultant; has received many awards for his work.

Professor Klaus Töpfer: Chief Executive of the office of the United Nations in Nairobi, Executive Director of the United Nations Environment Programme (UNEP) and of the United Nations Centre for Human Settlements (Habitat); earlier (1987-94) German Minister for the Environment, Nature Conservation and Nuclear Safety and (1994-98) Federal Minister for Regional Planning, Building and Urban Development.

Professor Ernst-Ulrich von Weizsäcker: President of the Wuppertal Institute for Climate, Environment and Energy, founded in 1991, and (since 1998) Member of the German Parliament; earlier Professor of Biology in Essen, University President in Kassel, Director at the Center for Science and Technology of the United Nations in New York and Director of the Institute for European Environmental Policy in Bonn.

Zhang Xinsheng: Former Mayor of Suzhou, a Chinese city which has particularly devoted itself to achieving a harmonious balance between the environment and urban development; is now studying business management and its application to city planning.

Secretariat of the Commission: Ulrich Pfeiffer, Manager Director of empirica, Bonn; an economist who has extensive experience as consultant for the German Federal Government, for Länder and local authorities as well as for international companies and organizations; has recently published *Germany: Development Policy for a Developed Country*.

CHAPTER I

The Millennial Challenge

I. The Millennial Challenge

This book opens with a city that was, symbolically, a world: it closes with a world that has become, in many practical aspects, a city.

Lewis Mumford (1961) *The City in History*

The First Urban Century

Two great milestones follow one another: two or three years after the millennium, for the first time in the history of humankind, a majority of the world's six billion people will live in cities (UNCHS, 1996*b*).[1] Already, the world's cities are growing in total by more than 60 million – equivalent to the entire population of the United Kingdom or France – each year. Between 2000 and 2025, according to UN projections, as the world's urban population doubles from 2.4 billion (in 1995) to 5 billion, the proportion that is urban is expected to rise from 47 per cent to over 61 per cent (UNCHS, 1996*b*).

But this growth will be unequally distributed: the explosive growth is occurring, and will occur, in the cities of the developing world, in Asia, in Africa, in Latin America. In the developed world, the great period of urbanization has already been and gone: here, 76 per cent of the population already live in urban places, and people and jobs are moving out away from the big cities to smaller places. Eastern Europe and the Commonwealth of Independent States have actually experienced a recent decline in their urban growth rates as people move back from city to farm, for the first time in half a century.

In sharp contrast, at the millennium less than 41 per cent of the population of the developing world live in cities. And here, the process of urbanization is still in full flood. There will be a doubling of the urban population, between 2000 and 2025, in Latin America, in Asia and in Africa – above all in Africa. Caio K. Koch-Weser, then Managing Director of the World Bank, advised Habitat II in Istanbul that 'By the time of Habitat III in 2015, 27 cities will have passed the 10 million mark, 516

3

cities will have passed the one million mark and the urban population will have passed the 4 billion mark. Populations will spread beyond metropolitan borders to secondary centers, and far into what are now largely rural areas' (Koch-Weser, 1996).

But the developing world, too, exhibits huge differences: already, nearly three quarters of the population of Latin America and the Caribbean is urban, and in some key countries the figures are higher: Argentina (89 per cent urban), Chile (85 per cent urban) and Uruguay (91 per cent urban). In contrast, less than one-third of the populations of Africa and Asia lives in urban areas. The central challenge lies here, in the exploding cities of some of the poorest countries of the world. For it is here that the great urban transformation has recently been occurring, and will continue to occur. In Asia, between 2000 and 2020 the urban percentage will rise from 38 to 50; in Africa, the expected increase is from 38 to 49 (table I.1). Africa – the latecomer to the process of urbanization, with the least urban tradition and the most recent experience of city life – is currently urbanizing at an estimated 4 per cent annually. In Asia the corresponding rate of urbanization is around 3 per cent. China reports up to 130 million surplus workers in the rural areas, a number expected to increase to 200 million by the year 2000. During the 1980s and 1990s, this surplus labour, plus higher-wage jobs in China's urban areas, especially in the south-eastern provinces, has created one of the most massive migrations in world history; perhaps 100 million have moved from farm to city (*Migration News*, 1994).

Already, the largest urban agglomerations of all are no longer in the developed world but in the developing world; and here, the scale of

Table I.1. Urban population.

	Urban Population in %			Urban Population Growth Rate in %		
	1980	2000	2020	1980-85	2000-05	2020-25
World	39	47	57	2.6	2.2	1.7
Africa	27	38	49	4.4	4.0	3.0
Europe	69	75	80	0.8	0.3	0.1
North America	74	77	82	1.2	1.0	0.9
Central America	60	67	73	3.1	2.0	1.5
South America	68	80	85	3.1	1.8	1.1
Asia	27	38	50	3.6	2.8	2.0
Oceania	71	70	72	1.4	1.3	1.3
Developing Countries	29	41	52	3.8	2.9	2.1
Developed Countries	71	76	81	0.9	0.5	0.3

Source: WRI, UNEP, UNDP, World Bank (1998).

urbanization is beyond anything conceivable even in 1950, let alone 1900. During the century just passed, especially in its second half, the cities of the developing world have seen dizzy rates of growth. São Paulo, which in 1900 had a mere 205,000 people, has grown to 16.5 million; Lagos, which as late as 1931 numbered only 126,000, has swollen to over ten million in 1995, though no one is really sure about the true number. By the year 2015, the UN predict that there will be 358 'million cities', cities with a population of one million or more: no less than 153 will be in Asia. And of the 27 'mega-cities', with ten million people or more, predicted for the year 2015, 18 will be in Asia (table I.2).

Urban experts now identify a new phenomenon among these mega-cities: an agglomeration of perhaps a score of cities of different sizes, formerly separate, still retaining a physical identity, but constituting a population mass of 20, even 30 million people, and highly networked. The Pearl River Delta between Hong Kong and Guangzhou is one such cluster that began to emerge in the 1980s; the Jakarta-Surabaya corridor another; Japan's Tokaido corridor, between Tokyo, Nagoya and Osaka, is perhaps the archetypal example. In several of these, the sheer logistical problems – of supplying services, of handling transportation, of waste disposal – are already daunting; they could reach crisis point between 2000 and 2025. Humanity has not been down this road before; there are no precedents, no guideposts.

But significant as is the growth of the mega-cities, we would do well not to be mesmerized by them: in truth, throughout the world, smaller cities grow faster than larger ones, for the quite basic reason that very large organisms can never grow as fast as smaller ones. We will do better to concentrate not on size but on function. Some of the biggest problems occur in relatively small cities in these countries, many of which – above all in Africa – have lower per capita GDP than thirty years earlier, thus compromising the ability of urban managers to provide infrastructure and services to new urban populations.

A Networked Urban World

The new millennium marks yet another urban milestone: not only is this the first urban century, it is the first century in which the world's city dwellers will form part of a single networked globe.

Three great forces have forged the explosive growth of cities in the century just passed. First, *industrialization* and its concomitant *deindustrialization*, which transformed the now-developed world before 1950 and has transformed the developing world since then. In the already-developed world, the proportion of manufacturing workers has dropped throughout the twentieth century, falling around 1990 to between 17 and 32 per cent in advanced countries, and absolute numbers have fallen since

Table I.2. Mega-cities 1995 and 2015.

Urban Agglomeration	Population (thousands)		Annual Growth Rate %	
	1995	2015	1985-1995	2005-2015
Africa				
Lagos	10,287	24,437	5.68	3.61
Cairo	9,656	14,494	2.28	1.97
Asia				
Tokyo	26,836	28,701	1.40	0.10
Bombay	15,093	27,373	4.22	2.55
Shanghai	15,082	23,382	1.96	1.85
Jakarta	11,500	21,170	4.35	2.34
Karachi	9,863	20,616	4.43	3.42
Beijing	12,362	19,423	2.33	1.89
Dacca	7,832	18,964	5.74	3.81
Calcutta	11,673	17,621	1.67	2.33
Delhi	9,882	17,553	3.80	2.58
Tianjin	10,687	16,998	2.73	1.91
Metro Manila	9,280	14,711	2.98	1.75
Seoul	11,641	13,139	1.98	0.32
Istanbul	9,316	12,345	3.68	1.45
Lahore	5,085	10,767	3.84	3.55
Hyderabad	5,343	10,663	5.17	2.83
Osaka	10,601	10,601	0.24	–
Bangkok	6,566	10,557	2.19	2.51
Teheran	6,830	10,211	1.62	2.30
South America				
São Paulo	16,417	20,783	2.01	0.88
Mexico City	15,643	18,786	0.8	0.83
Buenos Aires	10,990	12,376	0.68	0.50
Rio de Janeiro	9,888	11,554	0.77	0.84
Lima	7,452	10,562	3.30	1.32
North America				
New York	16,329	17,636	0.31	0.39
Los Angeles	12,410	14,274	1.72	0.46

Source: UNCHS (1996*b*), pp. 451-456.

1970; service workers now everywhere constitute a majority, accounting for between 60 and 75 per cent; and informational workers have risen from 20-25 per cent in 1920, to between 35 and 50 per cent around 1990

(Castells, 1996, pp. 209, 282-301);[2] in the developing world, conversely, the proportion of farmers and other primary producers has fallen and the proportion of factory workers has risen. In both cases, with a few sad exceptions, this new international division of labour has brought advantages to everyone: per capita incomes have risen several times in the half century. Second, the *transportation* revolution, successively in the form of the humble bicycle (still the basic mode of movement in much of the developing world), mass transit and the private automobile; and third, the parallel *telecommunications* revolution which has dramatically extended from the telephone to the fax and the internet. We could add a fourth factor, *political* transformation: though less momentous in its urban impacts, decolonization has fostered the growth of new national capitals.

The great transforming force of the twenty-first century can already be seen: it is the *informational revolution*, uniting previously separate technologies – the computer, telecommunications, television – into a single medium for the generation, storage and exchange of information. Already, as this new economic revolution gathers pace, cities worldwide are increasingly networked in complex systems of global interaction and global interdependence, which produce a new international division of urban labour: the largest cities of the advanced world shed manufacturing and goods-handling in favour of advanced services; the largest cities of the newly-industrializing world take on these manufacturing functions; large cities in the barely-developed world, which are still only weakly connected to the global networks, subsist largely by informally exchanging basic services. In the networked world, we can distinguish a few global cities which provide the core nodes of this global exchange of information and control, and a larger group of perhaps forty or fifty aspirant cities – call them 'sub-global' – which compete with them and which provide global-level services in selected fields. Below these, but overlapping with them, are 'regional cities': large cities performing similar functions for small countries or for regional parts of larger countries. And below them, in turn, there is a host of what we can call 'county towns': medium-sized cities which act as service centres for their surrounding areas, but which may also provide some specialized services (such as health care or higher education or tourism) for national or international customers.

All of these masses of urban humanity thus have one common characteristic: they are cases of global networking, in which information and goods are exchanged over limited distances of a few hundred miles or kilometres, and in which a principle of local agglomeration holds true. Mega-cities show that even in the new world of cyberspace, the old economic principle of agglomeration still holds true: people still need face-to-face contact to do business, and so communication is easier and cheaper over shorter distances than over longer ones. And this is doubly true, because demand begets supply; thus the larger cities in these regions

7

become major global air hubs and also the key points on the fast-emerging continental high-speed train systems.

By 2025, we can confidently predict that the whole world will be one urban network using automatic production, transportation and communication systems to free people to work in soft human services, in education, training, consultancy, community services plus an active citizenship – the ideal of all urban life since the Ancient Greeks. The great cities of the world, in particular, will be totally networked, forming a cyberspace version of the old Hanseatic League.

Thus, the twentieth century brought the urban transformation; the twenty-first century will transform the urban experience. The twentieth-century industrial and transportation revolutions freed millions of people from their lifelong bondage to the land – though too often, its first impact was to move them into equally degrading and exhausting forms of self-exploiting labour in the city. We can now see the real prospect for the coming century, which is that the informational revolution can potentially free them from this burden too.

But not inevitably or easily: indeed, one of the central questions, for the twenty-first century as for the one just ended, will be how we can consciously shape technological advance so that it liberates rather than exploits us. The experience of the twentieth century has been a very mixed one: in the cities of the developed world, millions have made better lives in more satisfying and less degrading work, but others have lost their work to machinery or to competitors in the developing world, where conditions all too often resemble those in London or New York a century ago.

The Urban Challenge

It is here, in the burgeoning cities of the developing world, that the real challenge lies. For there is a paradox: people are still coming into those cities, children are being born in those cities, because people believe that a better life lies in front of them. But in many cases these expectations are being cheated and may continue to be cheated. The disparities of income and wealth, both between cities and within cities, are not decreasing; they are increasing. The quality of the environment is not improving; in far too many cases, it is deteriorating. Crucial natural resources, vital to the future subsistence of these people, are not being conserved; on the contrary, despite solemn conference resolutions, they are actually disappearing.

An important word of warning: throughout this chapter and the rest of the book, we use the terms 'developed cities' (or 'cities in the developed world') and 'developing cities' (or 'cities in the developing world'). This is a commonplace division, found in much of the development literature. But we fully recognize that today, increasingly, it represents a massive oversimplification. Cities in the 'developed world' show some characteristics of 'developing cities' (for instance, a substantial and increasing informal sector); even more importantly, many cities in middle-income 'developing countries' closely resemble their 'developed' counterparts in their economic and social and political structures – in particular, the presence of a significant modern economic sector, integrated into the global economy – and need to be distinguished carefully from other cities where the development process is still at an early stage and is still slow or fitful. And even at any given level of development, we also find significant differences – for instance in the relationship between the formal and informal sectors, or in kinds of housing and infrastructure provision – between different countries and continents; thus there is a Latin American model, an African model and more than one Asian model, all significantly different in important respects. Throughout the book, wherever necessary, we shall emphasize such important qualifications and distinctions.

However, such distinctions can easily lead us to lose sight of important generalizations; it is too easy to conclude that every city is significantly different from every other. So we think that the basic developed/developing distinction still has some value, especially in this broad opening overview. And we make no apology for the fact that our book concentrates heavily on the challenge presented by growth in the developing cities. Experience in the already-developed world may be relevant for these cities equally, it may be misleading. The point is to learn from best practice, wherever it can be found.

Forecasts of Urban Lives: 1900, 2000, 2025 . . .

If we think about the lives of typical city people in the year 2000, how do we try to predict the equivalent lives of the year 2025, 2050, 2100? One way to start is to look at the century just gone. Observers in 1900 were daunted by the scale of the problems they found in the then-great-cities of the world. These cities were all in what we now term the advanced or developed world: London, Paris, Berlin, New York City. They had grown very rapidly, typically doubling their populations in the preceding half-century or even less. They had reached sizes never before recorded: six and a half million in London, four million in New York. Their poor people, including most of the recent arrivals, were packed into sordid inner-city slum tenements; with very few exceptions, land was too scarce, and too controlled, for informal housing solutions. They could not leave, because they depended on casual work in the centre of the city, and because there was no effective means of transport that would allow them to live at any distance from their work. The streetcar and the underground railway had just been invented, London, Glasgow and Budapest already had subways, Paris was just about to open one, and New York would follow in 1904.

9

The motor car, too, was a recent invention, and was still a rich man's toy, quite beyond the capacity of even middle-class people.

The people of these cities, especially the poor people, lived lives that were very similar from city to city. In some ways – the basic poverty, the insecurity, the total dependence on casual earnings – they were very like the lives of poor people in the cities of the developing world today. In others – particularly their housing – they were different. And, above all, like their richer brethren, they depended on available technology. They had no bathrooms, no telephones, no television. Nor did the rich.

Yet, within the following thirty years, first metro or subway systems completely transformed life and work of both rich and poor in these cities, allowing people with modest incomes to escape to villa suburbs; then, Henry Ford and his competitors democratized the motor car, permitting and even encouraging further spread and sprawl. Technology was not the only agent, of course; it was aided by rising incomes, particularly among a new middle-class salariat, and by new institutional arrangements that allowed people to buy houses with mortgages. But, without the technology, these developments could not have transformed the city. Thus, the twentieth century marked a process that had barely begun in the nineteenth: the urban glue, that had constrained cities over centuries, quite suddenly dissolved.

With a few remarkable exceptions, such as the novelist and science fiction writer H.G. Wells, most people in 1900 could never have foreseen, did never foresee, most of these developments. Most were convinced that cities and city life would remain much the same: city slums for the majority, horse-drawn buses and trams, and a majority of all urban workers in factories. Still less could they have predicted the vast movement from the land and into the cities. Even in countries like France and Germany, fully half of the population in 1900 was rural, mainly farmers. Elsewhere, the great majority of all humankind were small peasant farmers dependent on their subsistence plots, completely cut off from the wider world. It would not have seemed possible to run a global economy in which only a small minority could produce all the food and raw materials the rest of the world needed.

So we should be very bold in our predictions of technological progress and its possible effect on cities. Just as the twentieth-century farming revolution has made it possible for a small number of farmers to feed hundreds of millions of people, so another revolution – currently in progress – will surely make it possible to meet the world's demand for most mass-produced consumer goods (even homes) on the same basis. Many service functions, too, will be transformed by technologies such as voice recognition and automatic response, making it possible to shrink hugely the numbers employed in call centres and similar routine tasks. In education, interactive technologies will replace many of today's teachers, although some may find alternative roles in designing software or in distance learning. Health services will be partly automated, allowing self-diagnosis and remote medical care.

The question is, what then is the role for people? Of course, it has been asked throughout history: in 1800 people in England could have talked about de-agriculturalization, but what was really happening was the Industrial Revolution. There are going to be jobs after de-industrialization and de-tertiarization too, but we have only faint inklings of some of them: in personal services, in managing complex organizations, in developing technology, in the creative and cultural sectors. It could even be true that by 2100 the world's basic economic problem will be solved, as Keynes forecast in 1930, and people will at last be free to cultivate their minds and their sensibilities.

Many of these developments will also extend to the cities of the middle-income countries in Asia and Latin America. The big question mark is how many are likely to spread to the least-developed cities of Africa and South Asia, and how fast. There are some positive signs: consider the extraordinary diffusion of everyday consumer durables, like air conditioners and refrigerators and mobile phones, among the urban poor of China and Latin America. But other parts of the urban world, as in Africa, seem to be sinking back on the scale of economic development and wealth diffusion. There is a risk that technological progress may have the perverse effect of further increasing the disparities between the haves and the have-nots.

The new technologies will reduce both the time and the cost involved in exchanging information, whether by electronic means, or by actual travel. They could imply the 'death of distance' and the end of agglomeration, hence the decline and decay of cities: by 2025, information technology may allow us all to flee the city and communicate from telecottages, as Alvin Toffler has predicted (Toffler, 1980). But there are real reasons for doubting this. More than a century of modern telecommunications and automobiles has seen no weakening of the agglomerative position; rather the reverse. It seems that more telecommunication simply increases the demand for face-to-face contact, which most readily takes place in the cores of cities. So we should expect that by 2025 cities, and city cores, will still be significant parts of the urban landscape. The change will be that there will be more of them, and above all that they will be even more intensively networked. Workers in the burgeoning informational service economies are likely to work in more than one place: at home, on the move, in remote hotels and conference centres, and in 'hot desk' offices where they occupy space for a few hours at a time. Their 'product' will be non-material, embodied in words that are exchanged face-to-face, by telephone or over the global information superhighway of which today's Internet is the precursor.

As a result, it is almost certain that employment structures will radically change. One primary reason is the globalization of the economy. In 1965 nearly three-fifths of the world's workers worked in agriculture, by 2000 less than half do; in 1965 less than a quarter worked in services, now well over a third do, and sometime in the early twenty-first century most will work in services. In many developed countries, manufacturing workers make up only about 20-25 per cent of total employment; we should expect that proportion to fall further, to between 5 and 10 per cent, by 2025 (table I.3). But for the future, we should expect that information handling, too, will show declines in employment as software substitutes for people, and as some kinds of activity follow manufacturing into the cities of the developing world.

Table I.3. Structure of world employment (in per cent), 1965 and 1989-91.

	Agriculture		Industry		Services	
	1965	1989-91	1965	1989-91	1965	1989-91
World	57	48	19	17	24	35
Industrialized Countries	22	7	37	26	41	67
Developing Countries	62	61	11	14	17	25
East and South Africa	73	50	9	18	18	32
Sub-Saharan Africa	79	67	8	9	13	24

Source: ILO (1995), p. 19.

More likely, the twenty-first century will see a big increase in personal services, ranging from restaurants to old people's care – particularly because of the spectacular growth of older people in advanced countries. However, there are limits to this process. Services have to be paid for out of net income after tax, so that average-income people cannot afford to consume many of them. And there are limits to the use of labour-saving technology in education and health care; the quality of these services depends fundamentally on labour inputs, especially labour time, so that a constantly-increasing demand for these services implies more and more labour, more and more time. Higher and higher percentages of GDP will therefore be absorbed by education, health care and other personal services. Much will depend on the ability of these societies to cope with the increasing burden of dependency caused by the ageing of the population. Though having children is very expensive in advanced societies, the irony might be that not having them turned out to be even more expensive in old age. There may be answers, which we discuss in Chapters III and IV.

In the burgeoning cities of the developing world, the picture will be in some respects similar, in some respects very different. Here, too, the advanced sector of the economy has evolved parallel to that of the developed world, for essentially this sector – subject to global economic forces – is part of that developed world. And developments in the coming century should be no different, in particular the ageing of the population because of the sharp fall in birth rates that has recently characterized most (but not all) of these countries. This could hugely ease the flow of migrants from countryside to city, but it will force these societies to confront the problem of increasing numbers of old people coupled with a diminution in the numbers of active adults needed to support them.

The real question to probe here will be the evolution of the other part of the economy, that part that employs the immigrant poor. We cannot simply project the twentieth-century history of Western Europe or North America on to Eastern Europe and the Middle East and Asia and Latin America and Africa, because technology continues and will continue to evolve. The most likely scenario we shall explore, already evident in some Asian mega-cities, is a very rapid set of changes: core cities (like Singapore and Hong Kong and Shanghai) shed manufacturing employment to become high-level information-handling service centres, controlling and financing production in their own lower-income peripheries, but – just as on the global scale – producing a new spatial division of labour that brings rising incomes for everyone. Yet this process may not happen everywhere in the developing world, because it needs to be driven by the rapid technological and economic evolution of the core cities; and the ultimate challenge is posed by those who come to the city without education or skills, for whom the future may remain precarious and bleak.

Because cities will survive, conventional urban problems like sanitation, transport and housing will continue to dominate the lives of city dwellers, especially these poorer inhabitants, and the minds of urban policy-makers – even though technology may powerfully have affected the shape of these problems. But they will be overlaid increasingly by a new range of environmental concerns. There will be huge challenges: to rebuild cities so as to conserve energy and recycle waste, to reorganize urban transport systems so as to use less energy, to provide personal care for increasing numbers of old people, to conserve and recycle historic urban areas to carry new activities that do not need space and can flourish in such surroundings. These will make use of new technologies, but they will also demand big human inputs – some highly expert and highly skilled, some consisting of people's own hands and muscle power. There will be plenty of work to do; the question, at least for the foreseeable future in these cities, will be how to find the resources to pay for it.

The World of the Urban Poor

Urban growth has brought a sharp rise in urban poverty: according to United Nations Development Programme estimates, at the present time, more than half the world's poor are living in urban areas. Approximately

90 per cent of poor households in Latin America, 40 per cent in Africa and 45 per cent in Asia will be in urban areas by the year 2000 (UNDP, 1995, p. 4). And in the cities of Latin America and Africa and Asia, the overwhelming problem is not urban growth in itself, but the fact that city administrations lack the will, the competence or the resources to manage that growth. As a result, all too many of the incoming migrants find themselves without adequate jobs or housing or urban services – often, all three. It is this failure that produces the glaring disparities between the lives of the urban rich (including the large and fast-growing numbers of the urban middle class) and the urban poor. Despite the proliferation of cheap consumer goods, too many of the poor lack the luxury of air conditioners or even the option of closing windows against leaded-fuel emissions, smoke and dust that make up the air in many cities; nor can they afford bottled water or proper sanitation. And the gap is widening dramatically because so many of the poor get pushed out to the peripheries, where they cannot find transport. The poor suffer disproportionately from lack of basics – health care, schools, job opportunities, food, transport, training, adequate housing, security, information, access to justice.

In Latin America, the highest level of urbanization in the developing world has brought a host of problems: one in three households is run by a single parent; homicide rates are the highest in the world; street children are more prevalent than anywhere else; and alcoholism, drug abuse and domestic violence are part of everyday life for many people.

In Asia, too, Jeremy Seabrook concludes that:

... with increasing convergence in the policies of all the governments in Asia, there is no doubt that pressure on the infrastructures of all the cities will grow ... City life is bound to become more polluted, more dangerous, more violent. The fateful line when more than half the world's people become urban is always on the point of being crossed. It may be that they will demand something better than either of these majestic, appalling, energetic and pitiless places at present offer.

(Seabrook, 1996, p. 251)

Still, we have to reflect that people come into cities voluntarily: the buses that bring so many of them run in both directions, but they often run back empty. When Jeremy Seabrook talked to some of the most wretched workers of the urban world, the cycle rickshaw drivers of Dhaka, they reflected on the difference between poverty in the village and poverty in the city:

There is a difference, they acknowledge. Village life is better, but if you don't have enough to eat, there is no remedy. In the city, you can find some labour, some form of income, and if you don't you can beg or even steal. To some extent, the poor try to re-create the social relationships of the village; and there are little oases ... of mutual help and protection.

(Seabrook, 1996, p. 41)

And he found the same of the young and equally-exploited women garment workers in Dhaka:

> The destiny of migrants is usually not to go back. They do not see the journey to the city as readily reversible (although some certainly will go home). Going to the city is seen as a success by the family, and the move as a kind of commitment. They feel compelled to like the place where they must now make their life, and to show they are successful.
> These people are intelligent and their choices are rational. But they are rational choices taken at very near the margin of existence, a margin that has been ever-present for the great bulk of humankind throughout their history.

(Seabrook, 1996, p. 123)

That is the point: cities are quintessentially places that offer opportunities and risks, obscene inequalities and extraordinary opportunities. A century ago Ebenezer Howard, in his famous diagram of the Three Magnets, summarized this dilemma: cities offer employment and social opportunity, but also degraded environments and brutal squalor. In the language of the 1990s, even though they are potentially the most sustainable form of settlement, they are at present too often unsustainable. The conditions he described in the London of the 1890s could be reproduced, with little change, in many developed cities and in all developing cities in the 1990s. The key question is whether these cities can make the transition more rapidly and with less intervening pain.

But there is a special and central difference between Howard's time and ours. The urban poor of the year 2000, far more than their equivalents of 1900, depend on the informal economy of the city. They get by, somehow or other, by doing odd chores and performing odd services: running errands, selling a few things by the roadside, finding any odd job that comes along. And they live overwhelmingly in informal settlements, some of them vast,[3] on land that they have themselves occupied, without benefit of legal title or any official permission, and in houses that they have created and then improved with their own hands. They depended on absolutely no one but themselves. They have built their own city, without any reference whatsoever to the whole bureaucratic apparatus of planning and control in the formal city next door, and they are rightly proud of what they have achieved.

But all too often, because they were not allowed to defy the authorities in any place that mattered, they have occupied the worst pieces of land, the places no one else ever contemplated developing: the sides of main traffic streets, the borders of railway tracks, perilous hillsides prone to mudslides, alluvial flats prone to flooding. They are prone to all kinds of hazard: their children may all too easily be killed or maimed by passing trucks or trains, their homes may be swept away by mudslides or destroyed by floods or buried under earthquake rubble, they may fall prey to the diseases that come from primitive sanitation and polluted water and from nearby toxic sites, they may suffer robbery and violence because the city police do not recognize their existence. They know these risks, but they have no option. Though they have never heard of Howard's Three Magnets, they know from their own experience that the urban magnet exerts an irresistible attraction for them.

Urban Needs and Urban Expectations

The quality of life for a majority of humankind, therefore, will – some catastrophic event excepted – be the quality of the life they lead in cities. They will doubtless want what people have wanted throughout history: satisfying work that yields sufficiency of income and freedom from poverty; taking a part in well-integrated societies with stable social networks; living in a society that recognizes the force of tradition and preserves its links with the past, yet is poised to adjust to new challenges; acting as citizens within a political system that offers balanced representation of interests and values; served with adequate public services from sewers to schools, respecting basic needs of all people living in a city; and dwelling in a built environment that preserves tradition but serves the needs of modern economic life and modern lifestyles.

On present indications, they are unlikely to get anything near what they would wish. On the contrary: those that have made the long trek from countryside to city may find themselves severely disappointed. That is partly because the speed of urban growth makes it difficult, almost impossible, to develop the social capital that is essential to any kind of decent social life. It is compounded because so many of the new arrivals – and indeed the locally-born residents – are unaccustomed to the constraints and difficulties of urban living. In China and India, the majority of new arrivals come from the villages; in Sub-Saharan Africa, the astonishing fact is that there was hardly any urban tradition at all – certainly, at best, a very weak one. Sociologists have come to recognize that sociable urban living requires generations of inculcated habit. Yet waiting all that time is a luxury these cities and their people cannot afford. They have very definite expectations of what they want from urban life, though these may not always be realistic. And this is a central challenge to urbanists worldwide.

Urban Essentials: Dimensions of the Sustainable City

We must now turn to prescription. What are all the world's urban millions going to want in the first half of the twenty-first century? What will be their principal and most basic concerns? It may seem presumptive that a group of experts should seek to lay down priorities in this way. But these principles are not at all abstract or academic. They have been developed out of vast experience of working in cities across the world, including many of the poorest cities.

We start with the most basic principle of all: sustainable urban development, a principle easy to state in general terms, much harder to make operational in terms of everyday decisions. The central principle is well-known: in the often-quoted words from the 1987 Brundtland report:

Humanity has the ability to make development sustainable – to ensure that it meets the needs of the present without compromising the ability of future generations to meet their own needs.

(World Commission on Environment and
Development, 1987, p.8)

This means that, put most simply, we must not rob the generations that come after us; rather, we should seek to leave them a larger and a better legacy than we have had ourselves. Part of it was always explicit in the old notion of economic growth and wealth creation: it is a thoroughly good thing that we are richer than our grandparents and that our grandchildren should be richer still. But the notion of sustainability carries with it many other dimensions, and we cannot afford to ignore any of them; from the start – since the original Brundtland formulation of 1987, but particularly since the adoption of Local Agenda 21 at the 1992 United Nations Conference on Environment and Development – the term has been extended from the environmental sphere, with which many people associate it, to the economic, the social and even the cultural areas of policy. A society could become richer in material terms yet poorer in its culture and quality of life; as the Nobel prize-winning economist Amartaya Sen memorably put it: '. . . a society or an economy can be Pareto-optimal and still be perfectly disgusting' (Sen, 1970, p.22). Or it could get richer by mining irreplaceable natural resources, as many frontier economies have done throughout history and are still doing in many parts of the world. Or it could enjoy affluence while producing negative effects, like global warming, which threaten the lives of all future generations.

The notion of sustainability is thus inherently multi-dimensional; in particular, economic growth often comes at a price, and that price has to be factored in. Further, a stronger and more limiting principle, that price will not be worth paying if it actually entails a loss of the total resource base of the world – a base that includes not merely the physical environment, important as that is, but social and cultural dimensions as well. The United Nations Development Programme has promoted the notion of Sustainable Human Development: development that centres on people's choices and capabilities, that generates economic growth but distributes its benefits equitably, that regenerates the environment rather than destroys it and that empowers men and women rather than marginalizing them. It is precisely the notion that we want to capture and develop in this book. We are arguing that there is a huge paradigm shift: development until now has been seen largely as a process of saving labour in the production process, but this century will see it as conserving and maintaining irreplaceable natural and human resources.

It is not an easy notion to operationalize, of course. Even within the environmental sphere, it is not always easy to achieve a set of common yardsticks or measures which will encapsulate such diverse objectives as the maintenance of non-renewable resources, the preservation of endangered species, the maintenance of biodiversity and a worldwide reduction in greenhouse gases. This is, of course, not to say that it is either impossible or undesirable; only that it represents a formidable intellectual challenge. Extended into the other dimensions, it becomes more challenging still.

But there is a positive message too: all over the world, the transition to the informational economy is bringing a revolution in the way cities and urban economies relate to each other. Big accountancy firms in New York and London subcontract a lot of their work to Bangalore in India, where it gets done efficiently and cheaply over the ether. This is potentially a huge gain in terms of sustainability. And it could be a model for the way the world does its business in the informational economy of 2025.

We return to this problem below. First, we actually want to extend this argument about multiple sustainability: we propose that, applied to the city, sustainability has a number of key dimensions or aspects. To be called properly sustainable, a city must score on all of them. The dimensions we set out below represent our analysis; other observers could well produce slightly different lists. (They might, for instance, want to include mobility under environment.) Our argument is that these dimensions are among the most important ones that experts have discussed over the past decade.

A Sustainable Urban Economy: Work and Wealth

The basic problem, as throughout human history, is the fundamental economic one that many of the world's urban populations lack the resources to lead decent and satisfying lives. The most basic poverty problem of all, that of getting enough to eat, may have actually been solved; but too many other problems – access to employment, to adequate shelter, to good public health, to public safety, to adequate childcare – still afflict hundreds of millions of poor city people. Of Bombay's 12 million people, nearly 2 million live on the pavements; another 5-6 million people, probably more, live in slums, nearly half squatting on public land, the others on privately-owned land. About 95,000 families live as squatters around the city's two airports, another 35,000 along railroad tracks. Dharavi, 'the largest slum in Asia', houses half or three-quarters of a million people.

Box I.1. Dharavi: 'The largest slum in Asia'.

Buses merely skirt the periphery. Autorickshaws cannot go there, because, anomalously, Dharavi is part of central Bombay, where threewheelers are banned.

Only one main road traverses the slum, the miscalled '90-foot Road', which has been reduced to less than half that for most of its length. Some of the side alleys and lanes are so narrow that not even a bicycle can pass. Whole neighbourhoods consist of tenement buildings, two or three storeys high with rusty iron stairways to the upper part, where a single room is rented by a whole family, sometimes twelve or more people; it is a kind of tropical version of the industrial dwellings of Victorian London's East End.

But Dharavi is a keeper of more sombre secrets than the revulsion it inspires in the rich, a revulsion, moreover, that is in direct proportion to the role it serves in the creation of the wealth of Bombay. In this place of shadowless, treeless sunlight, uncollected garbage, stagnant pools of foul water, where the only nonhuman creatures are the shining black crows and long grey rats, some of the most beautiful, valuable and useful articles in India are made. From Dharavi come delicate ceramics and pottery, exquisite embroidery and zari work, sophisticated leather goods, high-fashion garments, finely wrought metalwork, delicate jewellery settings, wood carvings and furniture that will find its way into the richest houses, both in India and abroad . . .

But extraordinary though it is, the production of such articles is not the real wonder of Dharavi. The true marvel is the ability of the poor to reclaim and to reuse almost any item of consumption that has been discarded: used-up papers and rags, metals, glass, plastic, cardboard, to save and to conserve, to keep and to mend. In this sense, Dharavi is a model of recycling. Only the spectacle of children burrowing through heaps of fetid garbage, the women, arms stained with filth, cuts festering where they have injured themselves on pieces of glass and jagged tin, infants who can scarcely walk hunting for an old bottle or a few stinking plastic bags to place on the rusty metal scales of one of the hundreds of dealers in precious junk for the sake of 25 paise, speak of the depths of destitution to which many have been brought. It is only people who are not recyclable; and this illuminates the most cruel secret of all: that here human beings are expendable. The energy, health and well-being of the people do not count in the ugly calculus of profit and loss that dominates not merely Dharavi, but Bombay and the world beyond . . .

Dharavi was an arm of the sea, that was filled in by waste, largely produced by the people who have come to live there: Untouchables, or Scheduled Castes as they are now known, and poor Muslims. It comprises rambling buildings of corrugated metal, 20 metres high in places, used for the treatment of hides and tanning. There are pleasant parts, but rotting garbage is everywhere.

(Seabrook, 1996, pp. 50, 51-52)

These people overwhelmingly work in the informal economy: a term that covers a huge range of activities, from child prostitution and petty crime to micro-entrepreneurship, and that almost loses its meaning in a country like India, where nearly 93 per cent of all employment and 64 per cent of all the savings come from the informal sector. The people who find their living in it are seen as completely marginalized, and indeed they are getting poorer; yet essentially, they are the real economy of India. They live in the cities but they are not really of the cities: they have no status; they command no economic power; they are too often harried bureaucratically and treated merely as an urban nuisance; to all intents and purposes they still belong to the villages they have left. They are not free to move away, as skilled workers or international capital are free; they remain at the mercy of competition from even poorer people in poorer cities far away. As long as this remains true, Indian cities and other cities like them are not developed, are not developing. Recognizing the central importance of the urban informal economy, building policies on that recognition, must surely be a first step.

In the richer cities of the now-developed world, primary poverty can be overcome, has largely been overcome, by economic growth. Here, few indeed of the world's urban population are truly poor compared with fifty or a hundred years ago. But the problem simply changes its shape: here, against a background of general prosperity and even affluence, it becomes one of relative deprivation. Today, even poor people in advanced cities enjoy a standard of material life that was unattainable by the rich a century ago (bathrooms, colour TVs), but they still are poor in relation to the people around them, or to the array of goods and services they see in the shop windows or in the TV commercials; and they suffer the stigma of feeling different.

Therefore, economic growth is not enough as an objective: we need also to consider income distribution, democratic participation, empowerment. A fierce debate has raged between right and left, between free-marketeers and economic interventionists, as to the desirable policy trade-off between policies to encourage growth, which may increase inequalities, and policies to equalize incomes, which (it is argued) may stifle growth. There is no axiomatic answer: it depends on political ideology and it also seems to vary between different forms of capitalism. In recent years, the USA and the UK seem to have been willing to tolerate a widening income gap in order to achieve faster overall growth. But the historical evidence shows that it is possible to have both growth and equity: Germany in 1965, after a period of high growth, was much more equal than the Germany of 1995 after a period of low growth; Taiwan has achieved long-term growth while maintaining relative equality; in the 1990s, the Netherlands achieved the same result. The reason was almost certainly investment in human capital and in research and development: an economy based on large numbers of well educated people will be both richer and more equitable.

But there is a major problem: both in the developed and the developing world, large sectors of employment are simply disappearing. A century ago in New York, the legend was that when an Italian son reached the age of 21, his father presented him with the image of manly security: a shovel. That shovel could immediately be put to use in digging the city's first subway line. But, in the typical giant city of 2000 – be it London, Tokyo or Rio de Janeiro – the subways are dug by giant machines, and the demand for strong young men is much reduced. The same is true of many of the basic components of the urban economy of 1900: manufacturing, port activity, warehousing. They have either disappeared altogether, replaced by machinery, or they have been moved to other cities in other countries, generally at an earlier stage of economic development, where however they are filled mainly by young women.

Here is the real significance of that much-overworked word, globalization. In older-industrialized cities, the effect is often long-term structural unemployment, especially of men. In developing cities, though ambitious migrants may continue to be attracted, the prospect awaiting them may be drastically different from what they expect. Here, across the cities of the developing world, a central question concerns the fate of the huge numbers of unskilled and desperately poor migrants and the still growing numbers of young people with minimal education.

True, falling birth rates, in cities and even the countryside, could greatly diminish the flows of new inhabitants; and we have to assume that lower birth rates will allow parents, together with urban school systems, to produce new generations better equipped for satisfying and rewarding work. But the biggest threat will always be that global forces and new technologies will strip out large sectors of work, displacing them to other lower-cost cities or substituting increasingly sophisticated machinery for labour power. Up until now, the informal sector has absorbed a large part of the urban population increase, and has done a remarkably good job in generating work and incomes for those with few urban skills. But the question is whether this can continue, or whether over time the informal sector in developing countries could become increasingly uncompetitive with the formal economy, displacing its members or grinding them into even more desperate poverty. This is one of the bigger dilemmas to be considered in this book.

Cities can and do adapt, by converting themselves into service-industry cities. In the developed world, this is the story of Glasgow and Birmingham, Rotterdam and Dortmund, Boston and Baltimore. It is becoming the story of the most advanced cities of the developing world – Singapore, Hong Kong – which have themselves passed beyond the manufacturing phase to become service cities. But in many old industrial cities of Europe and North America, the men are unemployed while the women – now, a majority of the workforce – work in the retail stores and the call centres that have taken the place of the cotton mills and the blast furnaces. As the economists put it, the rent paid to muscle-power has sunk nearly to zero, while the rent paid to secondary and tertiary education and cultural knowledge has – despite a vast growth – become extraordinarily high.

But technology is making inroads into service employment, too, and this will continue: voice-recognition software could replace much call centre employment; multimedia 'morphing' could replace live actors and actresses; neural computers could provide personal digital assistants; and computer instruction could displace many forms of teaching. Yet there will always be limits to this process: labour-intensive personal services like gardening, haircutting, cooking and serving in restaurants, poodle-clipping, psycho-analysis, teaching and preaching, and a thousand and one other kinds of job, which are expanding hugely and will continue to do so because they are income-elastic: as people become richer (and more short of time, the unique non-expandable commodity), they will want proportionally more of them. The same goes for the creative and cultural industries, which have burgeoned with the growth of disposable incomes, and which are now more important than many manufacturing industries in advanced countries.

One key source of demand for personal services is demographic: in every advanced country, rising numbers of old people – in Germany there are roughly four workers to service every pensioner today, by 2040 less than two – create huge demands for health and care services, while an equally sharp decline in the traditional nuclear family means that many of these people cannot depend on the informal unpaid care of their families. But there is a big question of how these labour-intensive services are to be paid for: because they are not very susceptible to capital substitution, they are likely to become increasingly expensive in relative terms.

Another area of growth could well be in the environmental services. Already a few cities in Europe – Freiburg, Basle, Zürich, Copenhagen, Bologna – have become famous for the quality of their urban sustainability policies. A few places in the middle-income countries, such as Curitiba in Brazil, have joined them. The question is whether such cities could export their expertise. Already, in Germany, the Dortmund Science Park in the Ruhr, an old industrial area suffering from historically high levels of pollution and contamination, has established an important niche role in exporting environmental treatment products and services. The combination of such industries, with management expertise derived from model cities, could prove a huge economic driver in the twenty-first century.

Open Questions. In thinking about the consequences of these trends for urban policy-makers, some central questions occur. Is it possible, or desirable, to slow the process of globalization and the growth of labour-saving technology, with all their momentous consequences? If not – the most likely answer – how can cities and their inhabitants remain one short step ahead of the action? Can they anticipate the next shift in their local economies and prepare for it? And what form would these preparations take? For those already overtaken by the wave, is it possible to re-educate or re-train so as to remain useful and productive urban citizens? There is an answer, long ago provided by cities like New York and London: flexible cities with a diversified, adjustable economic base. But can these cities emulate those good examples from the past? What might be the role of new industries – managerial, cultural and creative, environmental? Can we imagine environmentally-benign cities exporting their expertise to other cities across the world, and how might this happen? Or are parts of urban populations doomed to continuing and increasing social poverty, cut off from the urban mainstream? Does the informal sector have a continuing long-term role – and if so, what is it?

A Sustainable Urban Society:
Social Coherence and Social Solidarity

The problem of work thus relates to another, deeper phenomenon: social and political exclusion. In the cities of the developed world, it is related to income distribution, but is subtly different; recently, policy-makers and analysts have come to see it as an additional dimension. Low incomes can be addressed through welfare policies which subsidize the poor, protecting them from the most direct results of poverty, but leaving them in a state of permanent dependence; even stigmatized; isolated from the mainstream society and without hope of re-integrating with it. The evident result is that in cities across the world, from Latin America to the Middle East, from the United States to Europe, some young men and increasingly women also employ their talents and energies in illegal activity of all kinds, from drug dealing to kidnapping. More police, more draconian punishments, even the death penalty, prove no answer.

There is thus a social dimension of sustainability: a city that prospers economically, but fails to distribute the wealth with some degree of equity, runs the clear risk that it disintegrates into a civil war between the haves and have-nots, a war in which both sides are the losers. Indeed, some see that situation occurring in some major cities of the developing world. This means that there really is no substitute for an inclusive city with supportive neighbourhoods and integrative labour markets.

Such exclusion, we would argue, is fundamentally bad both for the excluded minority and for the included majority; a society will experience severe tensions if it experiences such fundamental social divisions. It is exacerbated by the political dimension: in some societies, ranging from

South Africa under apartheid to the Federal Republic of Germany, significant sections of the population lack fundamental political rights. But even in the most inclusive societies, the excluded populations may cease to have any interest in the political process: they may not vote, and may increasingly regard themselves as outside civic society.

Social exclusion has been a concern in American cities and is spreading now to Europe; it is clearly a problem affecting most cities of the developing world, where millions of urban poor live almost invisibly in their informal settlements, eking out an existence in the informal economy. The answer is seen not in distributing more money income to the poor in the form of social welfare payments, but in reinstating them into the mainstream social fabric; this is the inspiration for the experiments in 'workfare' which are being widely introduced in the USA and the UK, and which seem destined to be repeated elsewhere.

But how could such policies be relevant to the cities of the south, where welfare is still a dream? As Seabrook says of the people of Dharavi, they are as excluded from the consciousness of their fellow-citizens as any human beings could be anywhere: 'a city within a city, dark heart of a gaudy Bombay . . . 'a blot on the landscape of India's richest city'; it is surprising, he observes, how many well-to-do Bombay people, who travel freely to London or Vancouver, have never set foot in Dharavi. And the astonishing fact is that the people of the slum, widely perceived as idle and workless, spend their days slaving to create things of rare beauty (Seabrook, 1996, p. 49). In fact, in the cities of the developing world, the informal sector and informal living do not imply true social exclusion. The people in places like Dharavi are forgotten by their fellow-citizens, and they do suffer fairly massive exclusion from basic services: health, good schools, easy access to clean water. But they enjoy intimate, even intensive, social contacts; they are socially integrated and intensively networked.

The United Nations Development Programme, out of forty years of experience, has developed the concept of sustainable human development: a vision that centres on people's choices and capabilities, that does not undermine the well-being of present or future generations. It entails development that not only generates economic growth but that also distributes its benefits equitably, that regenerates its environment rather than compromising it, and that empowers people rather than marginalizing them. That is a vision that we share and that we try to develop in Chapter IV.

Open Questions. Here, too, there are very basic questions. How can policy-makers combat social exclusion? Is it simply an economic matter – of finding remunerative and meaningful employment for those who are mired in long-term unemployment? Or do other questions – family structure, education, cultural values – play a part? If so, what can be done to increase children's motivation to learn and to network effectively? How can different agencies and policy streams be brought together in multi-dimensional programmes? What is the role of political inclusion, and how can urban societies integrate their new immigrant communities into the mainstream political process? What is the role of education in all this, and how can education most effectively aid social inclusion?

Sustainable Urban Shelter: Decent Affordable Housing for All

There is a third basic question, and it concerns shelter: how shall all these additional millions be housed? Simplifying, we can say that in the last thirty years of the twentieth century, cities in the developing world took two sharply contraposed views of housing policy. Some, especially in Eastern Asia, took it upon themselves to provide basic public housing to all who needed it, even though they may later have encouraged their tenants, by now relatively prosperous, to buy their own homes; they also took care to cluster this housing at relatively high densities along public transport routes, so as to offer fast and convenient journeys to work and other destinations. Others, especially in Latin America and Africa, made a virtue out of necessity, turning a blind eye to illegal occupations of the land by squatters, and later on trying to provide basic services and legal title to these clandestine high-density low-rise settlements.

But even though this latter prescription has been born of necessity, and has provided a minimal solution in terms of the resources directly used to provide the shelter, it has hardly been a sustainable solution, for three basic reasons. First, these areas were inadequately provided with basic services like water and sewerage, so they were polluting, sometimes grossly so; and retrofitting these services has often proved difficult and expensive. Second, although this housing seldom needed large resources to build or to run, most of it has been very simple and far from the technical ideal – attainable now – of the zero-energy house. Third, much of this development has taken place at the periphery of the city, and it very seldom proved possible to retrofit effective public transport; so workers in these cities have often faced extremely long and inconvenient journeys to work and other destinations, via buses and informal vehicles which share the congested highways with the private car. Indeed, the irony is that when the authorities tried to rehouse the slum dwellers of Dharavi they gave them smaller homes more distant from the city; many have gone to commercial uses, while the owners have gone back to the slum (Seabrook, 1996, p. 55). In Bangkok, forced removal of the poor from central slum areas caused them to commute over much longer distance to their work (Seabrook, 1996, p. 249). The poor of the developing world, like their equivalents in the developed world a century ago, have a desperate need above all to be near their work.

Just as the informal economy is the real economy of poor cities, so does informal housing constitute their real housing stock. This, too, has been ignored: informal housing tends to be treated as an aberrant fact, to be either ignored or eliminated. The first step in many such cities has to be to recognize informal housing, to give the people who live in it security of tenure, a sense of stakeholderhood and pride in their home and their neighbourhood, so that they can begin to work individually and collectively to improve both. They need this and they want it and they are even willing to pay out of their meagre earnings and savings to get it. We know from hundreds of cases, all over the world, that people can upgrade their own shelter and massively improve their own quality of life, transforming slums into middle-class villa suburbs. The clue is to diffuse these lessons, to show other people in other cities how it can be done.

Open Questions. In the developing world, where the most intractable problems are concentrated, the basic question is how to generate huge numbers of homes for the urban poor, with at least minimal services in terms of public health, but affordable by those on minimum incomes; and to upgrade the millions of substandard homes that already exist. That immediately raises the question of agency. In these countries, the poor invariably provide their own shelter, albeit with some help from friends and perhaps some supplies bought in the market. They have infinite energy and enthusiasm, and often they have time too. How best to harness these resources, making them work more effectively? How to bring them, as they and their settlements become richer, into collaborative ventures to upgrade their own environments, retrofitting the services that they could not afford to provide at the beginning?

A Sustainable Urban Environment: Stable Ecosystems

A further and basic dimension of sustainability is the problem of the environmental deficit: in every city but especially in the most advanced cities, there is concern with the depletion of non-renewable resources; negative externalities arising from pollution and contamination; and, most potently, the threat of fundamental and irreversible damage to the global ecosystem. These three concerns can be regarded as quite distinct: natural resources have been consumed throughout human history, so far without major disasters; negative externalities can be controlled and taxed; only the third danger represents an absolute downside risk that could potentially lead to the destruction of the human race.

How exactly to resolve this dilemma? The resolution is bound to differ from one part of the world to another. For, in the developing world and in the short run, unsustainable forms of development may continue, because of dire poverty. Here, people will cut down forests and pollute streams, because they have to live. City authorities will allow untreated sewage to seep into rivers and back into the slum areas where people live, because they lack the resources and the technical competence to do anything else. In Bombay, a report prepared in co-operation with the World Bank revealed that sewage is not treated before discharge into the Arabian sea at any of the city's three sites; all sewers overflowed into coastal waters, making them unfit for recreational use at any time in the year; hundreds of septic tanks overflow into the ground, causing flies and mosquitoes to breed; two million people live with no toilet facility; drinking water has to be supplied in tankers to supplement piped water; over 5.5 million live in slums where enteric and respiratory disorders are common and gastro-enteritis, tuberculosis, malaria and filaria are 'rampant' (Seabrook, 1996, pp. 45-46).

The message cannot be too often repeated, and will be repeated more than once in this book: In the developing cities *poverty is the greatest threat to achieving a good environment*. We have to stress that it need not be; indeed, in some respects the poor are naturally respectful of the environment, because it is in their interests. Poor people do not consume very much, so they produce little waste; they have a natural incentive to behave sustainably, for instance (as in Cairo) by recycling waste that can be sold. So, to achieve sustainable development, the first essential is to discover a way out of poverty that will protect the environment. By using new wealth to provide the services necessary to maintain public health, it might be possible to maintain ecological balance. It can be done: Serat, the dirtiest city in India, where plague broke out in 1996, was voted second-cleanest city in India only one year later.

The problem comes in the transition to affluence, where most middle-income countries have demonstrated an insatiable appetite for ways of life that produce environmental problems – above all, for car ownership. Here, we believe, is one of the most acute dilemmas, shared by the world's most highly developed cities: people know the problem and they know what is right, but there is an acute dichotomy between their sentiments and their behaviour. And it also comes because in some middle-income countries, large corporations can acquire disproportionate clout which allows them to exploit natural resources and despoil the environment – at least for a time.

In the most highly-developed cities (and in many middle-income cities) the enemies are a curious combination of ignorance, vested interests, sunk capital and trade-offs between private goods and environmental goods, which have to be attacked in sophisticated ways. Across all these cities, the answer seems to lie in a form of technical progress based on resource conservation which reduces the trade-off problem; in the conclusion to this chapter we will discuss just such a solution. But as long as people perceive economic scarcities, the basic problem will not disappear: there is a permanent tendency for economic progress to solve some problems of environmental management, while creating others.

Open Questions. In the developing world, the most basic challenge is therefore how to achieve a satisfactory compromise between wealth creation and overcoming environmental poverty. Put crudely, for poor people the two appear irreconcilably opposed; but is this really so, or is there an approach which can bring increased incomes and environmental improvement? In the middle-income cities and the cities of the developed world, the challenge is subtly different: how can more affluent people be persuaded to change their lifestyles, consuming less energy and other resources, and generating less pollution and waste? Is there some new formulation, that would persuade them that it is actually in their interests to do so? Can we do this through the economic principle of 'internalizing the externalities', by making the polluter pay and by subsidizing good behaviour? And if so how?

Sustainable Urban Access: Resource-Conserving Mobility

Mobility is a special case of the dilemma of environmental sustainability, but such an exceedingly important one that it deserves to be treated by itself. In essence it is this: many cities in the developing world are just beginning to experience rapid and sustained economic growth, which – on all previous evidence – is likely to lead to an explosion in car ownership and use, multiplying total car travel by fifty or one hundred times over the next quarter century. Thus, virtually all experts argue, they are likely to produce totally unacceptable levels of congestion and pollution: the car has produced a mobility revolution that has transformed cities worldwide, but it is now driving the city into a dead end, from which it cannot escape.

As *The Economist* has put it: 'The world has gone car-crazy, and the measure of a metropolis is the size of its traffic jams'(Levinson, 1998, p.3). As families become more prosperous, one of the first things they want is a car. The income elasticity of car ownership is roughly two: each 1 per cent increase in average household income means a 2 per cent increase in the number of cars.

Thus, there can be dramatic traffic growth in a short time: in Mexico City, the number of vehicles has grown 30 per cent since 1991; in Seoul, traffic more than doubled between 1990 and 1996; in Bangkok, before crisis struck, 300 new vehicles a day went on to the streets (Levinson, 1998, p. 4). These transport experts point to the example of such Latin American mega-cities as São Paulo, Mexico City and Buenos Aires, where car ownership and use are already far higher than would be predicted from per capita income levels; citizens in such developing cities, it seems clear, have lower needs and thus lower expenditures for other basic items, such as housing and heating, and petroleum prices are often low there. And besides, the political pressures to provide for the car are often very great.

The conflict is dramatically illustrated by these developing mega-cities; but it is universal, and it has dimensions that go beyond the simple fact of car ownership and car use. For, as the experience of the twentieth century has shown, these have dramatic effects on urban form. First: people, as they become richer, want – and can afford – more space: separate rooms for their growing children, home office space (especially with the growth of telecommuting, or the 'electronic cottage'), for storage of consumer durables, for lounging around or playing games in the garden. Second: in the advanced countries, while population is not growing, household numbers are, and in many households two earners mean two cars. Third: they also want the convenience, the comfort and the flexibility that comes with car ownership, and so the no-car household becomes a one-car, a two-car, even an n-car household, n being the number of adults. But, if each individual and each household pursues these individual goals through market mechanisms – I can afford, therefore I buy – there is a classic case of the 'tragedy of the commons': they mutually destroy the quality of life that is most precious to them.

One key point about the middle-income mega-cities is that suburban car-based residential sprawl is associated with increasing concentration of commerce in the heart of the city, on the model first set by New York City in the early years of the twentieth century. The great majority of these cities – Buenos Aires and São Paulo, Hong Kong and Jakarta – illustrate this pattern all too well. It seems to confirm the traditional attractions of the urban core as a base for high-level contact activities, and it supports a galaxy of restaurants and cafes and bars and clubs where face to face encounters take place; thus, it can be said to underpin the quality of urban life. But it also leads both to long commuter journeys and congestion, and to the destruction of well-loved monuments in the heart of the city.

Here, the transport experts do not agree on the prescription: some argue for yet greater central concentration, on the basis that only such a pattern will support an adequate public transport network; others assert that policy should seek to disperse jobs and to reconcentrate them in suburban 'Edge Cities', where journeys to work will be shorter. So there is an urgent question: has the process of urban diffusion any limit? Can it, should it, must it, be ended and even reversed? And what does that say for the quality of lives in these cities? Perhaps the answer may be found in the pattern that is now appearing in some of the largest of these mega-cities: a polycentric city with multiple concentrations of employment, surrounded by informal high-density low-rise housing.

In highly-developed countries, above all in congested Western Europe, citizens and politicians have awakened to these problems and have begun to develop solutions to them. Thus, in cities like Karlsruhe and Freiburg,

Basle and Zürich, Amsterdam and Copenhagen, they have begun simultaneously to promote public transport and cycling, to restrain car traffic, and to promote more compact urban forms. Even here, though, population is dispersing as space demands per head continue to grow. And even here, the policies have never embraced systematic traffic management or congestion pricing based on information technology. The problem is that in the cities where the problem will shortly become most acute – the mega-cities of the middle-income developing world – there is very little consciousness of it. On the contrary: such cities are often actively promoting the growth of car traffic through the construction of vast expressways and downtown parking garages, while at the metropolitan periphery rampant land speculation brings new suburban development at huge distances – 40, 50, even 60 kilometres – from the core. This is the pattern that can be seen most clearly in Latin American cities like São Paulo, Rio de Janeiro, Buenos Aires and Lima, and in Asian cities like Jakarta, Taipei and Seoul. Cities such as Hong Kong and Singapore, that have followed a more sustainable path, are far rarer and seem to have arisen from an extraordinary conjunction of circumstances: a heavily constrained location on an island or peninsula, and a strong colonial or ex-colonial government with the courage to pursue unpopular courses of action.

So there is a real dilemma here: by the time the problem is recognized and action is taken, it may be too late. And the consequences could extend over far more than the limits of one city: by contributing to global warning, the explosion in car ownership and use, coupled with uncontrolled suburban sprawl, could threaten the ecological balance of the world.

The major question here is whether there is some magic bullet which would allow us the best of all worlds: unlimited mobility through a new type of technology based on zero-emission vehicles, electronically guided to their destinations. It is a vision that has haunted futurologists for years. But it looks as if it could translate from the science-fictional to the real world faster than most people now appreciate.

Open Questions. In the cities of the developing world, the key question is how to generate minimum-cost forms of effective mobility, sometimes necessarily over quite long distances, between low-income residential areas and workplaces. The relevant low-cost technologies are the bicycle and the bus: the challenge is how to allow them to operate rapidly and efficiently, particularly in relation to the fast-increasing fleet of cars which threaten to reduce all these cities to permanent gridlock. In the developed world, the challenge above all is to provide alternatives to the car which will be perceived as superior by an affluent public. This could be a very high-quality public transportation system, a successor to the motor car of today, or some combination of the two. But, in both developed and developing cities, there is likely to be no alternative to a politically-unpopular solution: to find ways of restraining car ownership and use.

Sustainable Urban Life: Building the Liveable City

These different aspects of land use and built form relate to yet another and more elusive question: the quality of urban life. Unlike some of the other dimensions of sustainable urbanism so far discussed, this one is quintessentially subjective; there is a quality of life on the great streets of the world's great cities, that people everywhere instinctively recognize – and indeed flock to experience as tourists – but that is not easily reducible to measurements and numbers. Urban designers spend a great deal of time trying to capture the essence of the attraction of the Champs Elysées, of Wenceslaus Square, of the Ginza. But to some extent, it is always elusive. Times Square and Piccadilly Circus and Shinjuku station are not great architectural experiences. But they are among the greatest magnets in the world; they have an almost electrical attraction for the thousands of people who are drawn there every day and night.

Traditional urbanists, that is to say most urbanists, associate these qualities with density and variety. They say that if we allow cities to disperse, we will destroy the very qualities that make them attractive to people: in the famous epitaph on Los Angeles, we shall have 'ten suburbs in search of a city'. (Or, in the even more famous verdict of Gertrude Stein on Oakland in California, 'There's no there there'.) The problem with this view is first that people continue to flock to live in such non-traditional cities, and second that they do manage to develop places that attract crowds of people: in Los Angeles, for instance, the ocean beaches and the suburban centres like Westwood or Santa Monica. The answer may be that in every successful city, people need such points of congregation and that they will naturally develop, though not always in traditional locations or traditional forms.

There is however another variant of this argument: that people need such qualities also in their everyday residential and working neighbourhoods. Not, of course, in the same measure: such areas demand a delicate balance of quiet, stress-free, safe and secure residential streets, but with access to nearby places that offer animation and sociability and within easy reach of shops and services and transport. American urbanists, in particular, point to the models of New York's Greenwich Village or San Francisco's Pacific Heights, as well as countless neighbourhoods in European and Japanese cities: Islington, Passy, Wilmersdorf, Akasaki. They could equally point to examples in the great middle-income cities: like Palermo and Belgrano in Buenos Aires, Ipagena in Rio de Janeiro, or La Zona Rosa in Mexico City. They emphasize that these correspond closely to the model set out by Jane Jacobs in her *Death and Life of Great American Cities*, nearly forty years ago (Jacobs, 1962): they have a mixture of medium-density row housing and higher-density apartment blocks set along short street blocks, with a good admixture of other land uses such as shops and local services, and they support high-quality public transport. They contrast such areas with the homogeneous low-density, car-dependent suburbs that have extended far around every American city since World War II, and are now extending around European cities and many cities in the developing world.

Very few serious urbanists would dissent from this view. The problem is that people *en masse* seem only too willing to desert the well-designed, liveable urban areas for their inferior suburban equivalents. The statistical evidence is very clear: throughout the world, over the last half-century, cities have been decentralizing. There is some counter-evidence, on which urbanists always eagerly seize; but it is invariably fitful and impermanent. One problem is socio-demographic: because household size tends to decline, a given density of housing supports a declining number of people. On top of that, people as they become richer demand more space for themselves and their possessions and their activities (including home work, a significant new element). And in fashionable inner-city areas, rich people can buy more space, squeezing out other people. But many ex-industrial cities seem not to be very attractive to anyone.

Further, the question – raised several times already in this chapter – must be whether the new service activities need an urban base, or more precisely a big-city base, at all. Some experts, like Alvin Toffler, believe that the urban glue is loosening (Toffler, 1980, pp. 200-204). Others, including such high priests of the information age as Bill Gates and Bill Mitchell of MIT, are more cautious: cities, they believe, will continue to prove attractive for all the face-to-face activity that cannot be adequately performed by phone, fax or e-mail. Thus there is a new question: the city of 1900 had to be dense, the city of 2000 has become less dense because the agglomerative glue has weakened, the city of 2025 will most likely see further dispersal as population continues to grow and space standards rise, but also some continuing agglomeration of some significant kinds of activity. Almost certainly, the next quarter century will see more and more cities becoming networked into mega-cities, physically separated by open space but functionally interlinked by complex and sophisticated systems of high-speed trains, motorways and advanced telecommunications. Such urban systems, properly planned, could be sustainable and efficient places to live and work in; but without such planning, they could prove highly problematic.

In such urban complexes, people may again come together to congregate in new Edge City gathering places like giant shopping malls or multiplex cinema complexes. But, the argument goes, these are inherently inferior to traditional places of congregation – as evidenced by the tourists who are drawn in such huge and increasing numbers to these latter places.

A related problem is the preservation of the built heritage. In many cities in the advanced world in the quarter-century after World War II, and in the fast-growing middle-income cities today, rapidly rising land values are associated with a shortened building cycle: in Eastern Asian or Latin American cities, expensive developments may be torn down and rebuilt in as little as fifteen or twenty years. Further, the dominant ideology in such places tends to be one of aggressive modernism, in which total rebuilding is seen as virtuous, and the preservation of older buildings as second-rate or wimpish. Often, only when it is too late do city administrations suddenly appreciate the horror of what they have been condoning, even encouraging: the production of a city without quality, without charm, without a memory. In a few such places – Buenos Aires, Georgetown, Kyoto – large parts of the patrimony remain, albeit threatened by commercial redevelopment pressures; in all too many – above all in Eastern Asia, where the modernist spirit has proved particularly strong – a change of policy has come only at the last moment, when much of the traditional built environment has already fallen to the bulldozer.

One can argue, fatalistically, that this is a phase that all cities must go through; and that the past can be restored, as after World War II in Warsaw and Gdánsk, much later in Frankfurt. But it is an odd policy that destroys the real thing, only to replace it by a Disneyesque replica a few years afterwards.

In some older cities of the developed world, affected in the last quarter-century by radical deindustrialization, the problem is the reverse. Here, as long evident in the American Midwest and more recently in northern England, we are seeing the abandonment of the cities by those capable of moving, a process that leaves a residual excluded population inhabiting a semi-ruined landscape full of abandoned buildings and gaping holes. This is one of the most intractable problems of all, since in some cases these places have simply lost their economic *raison-d'être*. But in other cases, areas of abandonment are found next door to vibrant city centres. The challenge here is to forge an urban renaissance that is simultaneously physical, economic and social: not an easy task.

Open Questions. The central dilemma here is to persuade not only policy-makers, but also the citizenry generally, that protection of the traditional built environment and built heritage is going to make sense in the not-far-distant future. This may be done, simply, by an elitist policy that recognizes the fact that most people will not easily grasp the point. But it needs to be set within a framework of democratic participation, because of yet another key issue.

Sustainable Urban Democracy: Empowering the Citizenry

The end of the twentieth century sometimes seemed like a political miracle:

democracy recaptured most of the ground it earlier lost to totalitarian or autocratic dictatorships. True, in some variants it is a peculiarly managed or manipulated kind of democracy, with restrictions on opposition candidates and a state-controlled media. But what is most remarkable, in the last quarter-century, is the restoration of democracy in a whole raft of countries ranging from Southern Europe and the Middle East to Latin America.

There are, however, two remaining dilemmas. The first is pressure-group politics. Democracies are more open than dictatorships to the ministrations of development groups, and also to the kind of local politics that have been labelled NIMBY (Not in My Back Yard). These two, it might be thought, will simply cancel each other, and life will continue as before. Not quite; because the evidence of the 1980s and 1990s clearly demonstrates an escalation in the number, length and expense of public inquiries or court hearings into the validity of planning decisions. The record to date is set by the public inquiry into Terminal Five at London Heathrow airport: four years to complete, £70 million spent, no resolutions so far.

The second and more general problem is the failure of local democracy in many cities of the world: however, it is compounded by the fact that in many cities, people generally – even the 'included mainstream' – are decreasingly interested in running their city: voting turnout falls to very low levels, and there is a general feeling that key decisions are made at other levels, by other agencies, often outside their control ('international big business'; 'bureaucrats in Brussels'). The basic reason is that city governments are seen as impotent in the face of larger economic and social forces: they have no power to decide the rate of growth or their economic strength, though they can improve their competitiveness by education, training and quality of life. It is as if the feeling of exclusion spreads to all levels of society – a potentially ominous threat to social and political cohesion. Here, though, there is immensely reassuring evidence from Latin America: the massive revival of democracy, in one country after another in the 1980s and 1990s, centred itself particularly on the cities, and has been associated with a major decentralization of power from the central governments to the city administrations and, beyond them, down into the neighbourhoods.

Open Questions: The questions here are among the most difficult. Is it possible to devise mechanisms that provide a resolution of the conflict between pro-development and anti-development interests, and to do so in timely fashion without bringing the entire machinery of planning to a halt? Is it possible to find ways of again involving the majority of the citizenry in active participation in local politics – and in particular, will this entail giving local government a more active and powerful role than it has enjoyed in many countries in recent years? If this happens, how can local government acquire the resources and the political and professional competence to discharge its new roles? And what will then, what should then, be the relationship between city halls and active neighbourhood groups, given that quite often they may be in mutual opposition? Is there a universal prescription, or do different countries and cities need to find different variants?

Summing Up: Key Dilemmas and Opportunities

These then are some of the key dilemmas for policy-makers in every city of the world. They are experienced equally in London and in Lima, in Stuttgart and São Paulo, in New York and Nairobi. But there cannot be any doubt that they express themselves most acutely in the fast-growing cities of the middle-income countries, for three key reasons.

- First, many of these cities are already bigger than their equivalents in the developed world, and are projected to become yet larger.

- Second, they are for the most part only recently embarked on their development process, so that in many if not most, the main consequences will emerge only in the next quarter-century.

- And third, with some conspicuous exceptions, neither their structures of local government nor their administrative traditions have equipped them to tackle the problems at all adequately.

Experience in the now-developed parts of the world at the time of their urbanization process, a century ago, is hardly encouraging; in some parts of the world today, the prospects are if anything worse. The United Nations reports that 'During the 1980s, the increase in the level of spontaneous, or informal housing in and around African cities reflected the almost total inability of most national or city authorities to provide adequate serviced land and infrastructure to their growing populations. The 1980s and early 1990s thus became, in common parlance, a period of "urban crisis" across the continent' (UNCHS, 1996*b*, p. 89). This crisis had three major components: a decline in formal employment, and corresponding increase in informal sector activities; a deterioration in the quality and distribution of basic services, and a decline in the quality of the urban environment, both built and natural. All adversely affected the quality of life for everyone, but particularly those on lower incomes. The same story could be told in many developing cities across the world.

What is needed is two parallel streams of transfer: first, of resources and skills from the developed to the developing world; second, just as significant, from the successful cities of the developing world, including the model middle-income cities, to the rest. The combination of these two is difficult but important: technological solutions can easily be exported from the developed to the developing world, but solutions that involve changes in the behaviour of people and institutions have to be adapted to the conditions of each individual city, and it is easier to achieve this locally, within the same country or at least within the same culture. New York and Berlin may have few lessons to teach Bogotà or Kinshasa or Phnom Pen, but American and German technology may achieve a lot if combined with experience derived directly from other cities in Latin America or Africa or Pacific Asia.

These are huge and daunting challenges. Nevertheless, we think that there are some grounds for optimism.

First, twentieth-century history has shown that technological developments can fundamentally alter patterns of urban life and work. True, these achievements have been uneven; many urban societies have been transformed, many others have not. The challenge is to learn how to emulate the successes and how to avoid the chains of circumstance that led to the failures. We do not doubt that the twenty-first century will be equally inventive. To be sure, technology will create new challenges, too; the surge in car traffic, in all the cities of the developing world, is ample testimony to that. Therefore, the challenge is to accept the advantages that technology brings, while seeking to regulate what the economists call negative externalities.

Second, we expect that the democratization of decision-making in cities, as in nations, will continue and make city governments more responsive. This is one of the most remarkable global trends of the last twenty years, and there seems no reason to expect a reversal, even if economic recession temporarily halts growth and brings political pressures to many countries for a few years.

Third, there is a real prospect that population growth, which is the source of many of the problems of ordinary city people, will soon slow down, producing a much more steady state. Indeed, in much of the developing world – in Eastern Asia, in Latin America – it is already happening; the big question is whether the trend will soon extend into Africa and the Muslim Middle East. It is true that this process will bring little relief in the first quarter of the twenty-first century, during which the urban population of the world will double in size. The challenge is to devise appropriate strategies thereafter, as the average number of children per family begins to sink.

Fourth, associated with this, we expect economic growth to continue, especially in the developing world, thus producing the resources to tackle the problems effectively. That is not certain, of course: one alarming counter-trend is that in much of Sub-Saharan Africa there actually seems to have been a sharp economic regression during the 1980s and 1990s, slashing per capita incomes to a fraction of their former levels. But we think this is a temporary problem resulting from extraordinary circumstances.

Fifth, in the developing world – at least for the next quarter-century, and perhaps for longer – there will be an increasing recognition of the need to accept the informal sector as an appropriate solution for poor people who lack access to global capital markets and interregional trade.

Sixth, it is surely significant that a host of cities, most of them in the developed world but many also in the developing world, have set standards for sustainable development, which are providing good practice benchmarks for other cities across the world. They have tried to tackle the problem of achieving economic growth in a sustainable way; of course they have not totally succeeded, but their efforts have set new standards of achievement not merely for other cities of the South, but for the entire world. The challenge is to diffuse the lessons of their experience more rapidly, and show how they can be improved upon.

Cities need, in a sense, to be able to export good urban governance as a service, just as they export manufactured goods or services. This is particularly crucial in the developing world, within which many cities are now making quite remarkable innovations in management and service delivery. The key is to spread the word about such innovations, and in turn to inspire other cities to invent their solutions to their own problems. But this will not be easy: experience shows that urban administrations are remarkably resilient to absorbing good practice, even from their close neighbours, let alone cities half way across the world. Clearly, then, learning from other places will be a central area of promotion.

To sum up this argument: we believe that technological progress and economic globalization will prove to be on balance benign forces, whatever short-term problems they bring in their wake. Technology and capital accumulation will together bring millions of people out of poverty into relative affluence, as John Maynard Keynes correctly predicted for the developed world at the end of the 1920s, and as can happen again for the people of the developing world. But the path will not be smooth or easy, not least because increasing wealth may also bring with it increasing disparities between countries and within countries; and the problem for policy-makers is to try to predict the deep long-term trends as far as it is possible to trace them, and then to seek to anticipate both the likely challenges, and the shifts in value systems that they will engender.

The Central Problem: Balance and Trade-off

The central objectives in each of these dimensions of sustainability may sometimes come in conflict, sometimes may positively reinforce each other. There may be difficult trade-offs, as where new industry may provide jobs and incomes for low-income people but nevertheless increase pollution, or where a buoyant economy multiplies car ownership or brings commercial pressures to redevelop traditional quarters of the city. There may be supportive strategies, as where economic growth allows a city to embark on long-delayed water supply and sewage treatment facilities, or where a better-quality physical and social environment helps a city generate new economic growth.

The fundamental problem is to develop a common framework, a common thread, that will allow us to analyse and compare these major facets of urban sustainability. We first propose that they can be treated within the framework of welfare economics, extended to embrace the new concept of sustainability which sits comfortably within it.

The aim of urban policy is to produce cities which are economically prosperous, culturally vibrant, socially equitable, clean, green and safe, and in which all citizens are able to live happy and productive lives. It follows from these objectives that cities should provide their citizens with jobs, affordable housing and health care, education for all children, potable water, modern sanitation, convenient and affordable public transportation, nature, culture and public safety. It shall also be an objective of good urban policy to give to the citizens of every city opportunities to participate in the governance of their city and to feel that they are their stakeholders.

We can seek in each case to measure the benefits and disbenefits of different policies and policy bundles, as far as possible using a common quantified framework, elsewhere employing whatever proxies we can find.

However, the traditional economic framework of trade-offs will no longer serve the purpose, because of the overriding concern for sustainability, which becomes in effect an economic meta-objective transcending the others. In particular, traditional economic development theory depends heavily on the notion that by substituting capital for labour, we increase productivity and thereby generate wealth; but if this has the result that the displaced labour sinks into long-term unemployment while the new capital-intensive technology has polluting side effects, the overall result might actually be negative in sustainability terms. The consumption patterns of the developed cities are of course very desirable: good education, high-quality healthcare, clean water, and so on. But if we calculate the land needed to provide all those services, calculations based on all people using the same amount of resources as Canadians suggest something like four hectares per person (Rees and Wackernagel, 1994). And if we then apply this not to the half-billion lucky citizens of the developed world but to the six billion people of the entire world, we find we need three planets Earth, which are unlikely to be available in the near future.

We need therefore a new economic paradigm that starts from this meta-concern for the maintenance of every kind of irreplaceable resource, but then combines it with acceptance of market forces and also with an indicative style of planning that can gently bend those market forces, thus producing a series of policy innovations. The outcome, we believe, could be a pattern of integrated urban growth that is flexible and adaptive, but that also respects the demand for sustainable urbanism. We believe that such a paradigm now exists. *Factor Four*, surely one of the few truly original political tracts of the twentieth century, argues – from strict economic principles – that the present system of production is massively sub-optimal and inefficient, and that by changing the rules we can develop a system which uses half the inputs to produce double the output (von Weizsäcker *et al.*, 1998). It gives many examples of how to quadruple resource productivity with no compromise on the quality of services, thus needing only one Earth to make six billion people or more happy. The clue is to start from labour productivity (the basis of our wealth), but adding resource productivity as a new critical feature. And this should become easier to achieve, because in the transition to the informational economy we find that the resource content of production progressively diminishes while what one can call the educational content progressively rises. True, affluent informational economies may become heavy consumers of resources, but this is not at all inevitable; it is a matter of conscious policy choice.

This, we believe, represents a major U-turn in orientation, which establishes new yardsticks for measuring economic development and new incentive systems for achieving them. But it is not currently recognized in the policies of many countries and cities, which perversely subsidize the use of resources and displace the use of labour. We return to it in Chapter IV, as a guiding principle for policy development.[4]

The Rest of this Book: A Quick Guide

Chapter II sets out the basic driving forces which will create new opportunities for the world's city dwellers, but will also set new and increasing constraints on their freedom to act. Then it sets out the likely outcomes, if present trends continue without positive policy interventions to bend or shape them.

On that basis, Chapter III presents a Business as Usual scenario, asking: if our cities continue as they have been going, on the basis of the trends that we know are almost certain to obtain, what will our urban world look like around the year 2025? What will be the problems that loom largest for policy-makers, and what will be some of the solutions that are being debated at that time? Then it presents an alternative scenario, based on 'Bending the Trends': suppose cities do act, how can they change for the better?

Assuming that is possible, Chapter IV sets out a vision of the principles that should guide them in developing these solutions, and applies them to the key areas of urban policy. Especially, it proposes that there are two key organizing and informing principles: *sustainable urban development* as a central policy objective, and *decentralized local empowerment* as the means of delivery.

Finally, Chapter V takes these principles and applies them in an action plan for the world's cities, showing what national and city governments will need to do.

Notes

1. Davis (1959), p. 63, quotes 9.2 per cent in cities above 20,000 for 1900, 20.9 per cent for 1950.

2. Japan, with just over 30 per cent, is an anomaly.

3. Latest estimates suggest that the third biggest city in Brazil is the informal city of São Paulo; with a turnover of $3 billion in 1998, its economy is as large as Israel's.

4. It should perhaps be remembered that Robert Solow's neoclassical model of total factor productivity (1957) incorporated technical progress which was both capital and resource saving, though the latter was not mentioned explicitly. 'Factor Four' thus signalizes and demands a reorientation of economic activities and a reorientation of intellectual efforts using analytical tools.

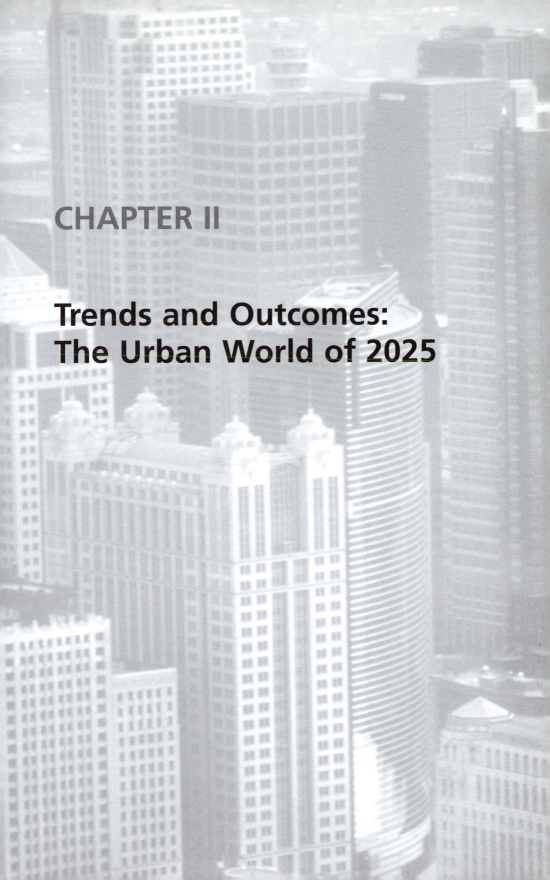

CHAPTER II

Trends and Outcomes:
The Urban World of 2025

II. Trends and Outcomes: The Urban World of 2025

Introduction: The Basic Driving Forces

Basic driving forces will shape the urban world of 2025: demographic, economic, social, environmental. In Chapter II we look at these forces and at the resulting pattern of cities and city life.

In the short and medium term, at least, urban policy-makers must accept these forces of change and these constraints as given; but they can bend and shape them, to serve their objectives. The political process, itself one of the drivers, can help shape the way the economy and society and technology and culture develop. It should do this, as suggested in Chapter I, based on the principles of *sustainable human development*, delivered through *good urban governance*.

Thus, urban governance will interact with the local economy and with the exogenous forces. And the driving forces themselves interrelate with each other in a complex way. This makes the task of urban governance exceedingly complex and demanding.

At least some of these interrelationships are predictable. High population growth reduces the possibility of rapid growth of income per head; conversely, rising per capita income is in general associated with falling birth rates and so with lower rates of population growth, increasing the chances to improve quality of life. Yet, at later stages of development, the relationships become less clear: increasing income disparities may be associated with divergences in fertility patterns, including high rates of pregnancy among lone teenage females. And advanced societies, in spite of low population growth, may display relatively high rates of household formation, with consequent effects on demand for housing and consumer durables. Other things being equal, increased rates of household formation in all cities with rising incomes are likely to create big demands for additional housing, decoupling population growth and spatial needs, which will lead to increasing dispersal from cities into surrounding suburban rings.

As already observed in Chapter I, rising incomes, most importantly, bring rising car ownership. And in developing cities, more people tend to own cars at a given income level than in developed cities: first because driving is often cheaper here, especially in oil-producing countries, and second because other costs, such as those for housing, are lower in tropical and subtropical cities. And higher car ownership, in turn, will tend to lead to increasing dispersal from cities into surrounding suburban rings. This is a prime illustration of the complexities of sustainable development: unless growth in income and wealth is accompanied by positive measures (such as enhancement of public transport) it can all too easily produce negative effects such as an increase in pollution.

For urbanists, these interrelationships between driving forces represent a challenge: it proves difficult to predict future paths of development. And this is especially true in the medium and long term, over twenty and more years. In 1950 it would have proved nearly impossible to forecast the economic miracle that transformed Munich from a provincial capital and central place for an agrarian hinterland, into one of the leading high-tech cities of Europe; or to guess at the economic development that would take some Asian cities to the ranks of the world's richest (but then threaten them again, as their economies went into crisis); or to credit the unravelling of the urban economies that followed the fall of communism in Russia.

Still more difficult, if anything, would have been to predict the fortunes of cities in the developing world. In 1952, Seoul had been virtually wiped out by the Korean War; its transformation into one of the great industrial power-houses of Eastern Asia would have been well-nigh unimaginable; the people of Nairobi, a charming colonial capital soon to experience the stresses and strains of the independence movement, could likewise never have envisaged its future as a city of 2.7 million, with a large majority living in abject poverty in ever-spreading shanty towns, as industrial development failed to keep pace with in-migration and population growth.

These examples show that driving forces are not inexorable or irreversible: they have to be translated and transformed into local growth preconditions. The secret is how to use the driving forces positively, to promote local development; and this must be done locally.

In the paragraphs that follow, we trace these driving forces and their impacts. There is one key question that will need to be raised each time: to what extent will the urban world of 2025 display common problems – and, conversely, to what extent are the developed and the developing world different, even contradictory?

Demographic Change

Demography and the Urban Explosion

In the world of demography we see two different and opposite imbalances, partly created by policies: rapid and burdensome population growth in many developing cities, equally problematic ageing in many developed cities.

In the *developing cities*, the problem is that the explosive growth of the recent past has left a very young population and thus a still rapidly growing number of young families. In these countries, seven major factors appear to be principally responsible for urban growth. The first five affect rural areas, producing powerful and even draconian incentives to move to the city:

1. Big productivity gains in agriculture due to mechanization, allowing fewer and fewer farmers to feed more and more city dwellers, and leading to rural over-population;

2. Coupled in some cases with lack of arable land and over-exploitation leading to soil exhaustion;

3. Lack of resources (technological inputs, access to credit) and social services in rural areas;

4. Natural disasters and environmental degradation in rural areas;

5. Growing civil unrest and internal conflicts in parts of Africa, Latin America and Asia.

But these are parallelled by trends in the cities to which the migrants go:

6. Better health care and consequent decreases in death rates, especially in the cities.

7. High birth rates in cities and increased life expectancy, mainly due to reduced infant mortality.

The cities offer the prospect of jobs, albeit precarious and poorly rewarded; they also offer an escape from traditional thoughtways and traditional practices, often irresistible to the young. Push factors and pull factors both reflect large and widening disparities between regions, between cities and countryside (UNCHS, 1996a). They produce the major global trends summarized by the Habitat II agenda:

- *Rapid urbanization:* the concentration of the urban population in large cities;

- *Urban spread:* the sprawl of cities into wider geographical areas; and

- *Hyper-urbanization:* the rapid growth of mega-cities.

In most developing countries, these forces focus on just one or two major cities; current estimates indicate that in some countries, migration to capital cities may be responsible for up to 80 per cent of all internal population movements. But increasingly the growth of cities depends on their own natural increase rather than migration.

Rapid population growth has at least two highly negative consequences, especially because of the very large numbers of children. First, it severely hinders the capacity of poorer cities to increase infrastructure per head, to provide an adequate number of jobs or homes or school places. Each individual needs a growing endowment for survival and much more than that for a decent standard of life in the urban environment. Without a certain definite minimum of education and training, such an individual is very unlikely to succeed in the modern urban economy.

Second, the survival problems of the rapidly-growing young generation tend to override all other considerations. The time horizons of the present generation shrink; their pressing needs compel a life of day-to-day survival. Only when their survival problems are solved will citizens and decision-makers be free to turn their attention to the survival and quality of life of future generations.

Sub-Saharan Africa offers a special and extremely nightmarish variant on the general pattern: here, more than 8 million children under 15 have lost one or both parents to AIDS, and by 2010 the number is expected to reach 40 million, 16 per cent of all children under 15. An enormous burden will fall on grandparents and other relatives, and there are growing numbers of street children.

But in many cities in the *developed* world, the problem is the ageing of the population. Here, birth rates are plunging below replacement rate, creating a skewed age structure where in the long run more and more elderly have to be fed and helped by shrinking numbers of active younger people: the proportion of people over 65 has increased from 7.9 per cent in 1950 to 13.5 per cent today and is expected to reach 24.7 per cent by 2050; the most rapidly ageing countries (which include Japan, Germany and Italy) will approach or exceed 40 per cent of their populations at older ages. The effects on urban society are hard to forecast; at present, we can only ask questions, such as:

- Will the slower renewal of human capital through ageing reduce innovative potential?
- How can urban systems stay flexible and innovative?
- Will people be capable of lifelong learning to overcome the ageing of knowledge?
- Will the family as producer of care and personal services for old people be replaced by new associations (of old people), who take over the role of families as provider of services?

- How do societies deal with a rising burden of dependency, whereby a diminishing number of younger working people have to generate more and more income to support increasing numbers of pensioners? If past trends continue, in 2030, public spending on old age security in OECD countries will be 16.5 per cent of GDP. How will these younger working people react politically to the growing social security taxes? How will they cope with the resulting reduced incentives to work, or with the possible flight of capital to other nations and other cities?

We cannot answer these questions now. But we need to find answers to them, and we return to these challenges in Chapter IV. Before we do this, however, we need to examine the trends in greater detail. For this, we need a slightly more sophisticated basis than the familiar binary contrast, developing versus developed; we need to add an intermediate category, countries and cities in demographic transition.

Table II.1. Age structure in selected countries.

	Percentage of Population in Specific Age Groups					
	1975			1995		
	<15	15-65	>65	<15	15-65	>65
France	23.9	62.6	13.5	19.6	65.5	14.9
Germany	21.5	63.6	14.8	16.1	68.7	15.2
Poland	24.0	66.4	9.5	22.9	66.1	11.0
South Africa	40.0	55.2	3.8	37.3	58.3	4.4
Côte d'Ivoire	45.8	51.8	2.4	49.1	48.2	2.6
Mexico	46.3	49.8	3.9	35.9	59.9	4.2
Brazil	40.1	56.2	3.7	32.3	62.5	5.2
Uruguay	27.7	62.7	9.6	24.4	63.3	12.3
Indonesia	42.0	54.8	3.2	33.0	62.7	4.3
Korea, Rep	37.7	58.6	3.6	23.6	70.8	5.6

Source: WRI, UNEP, UNDP, World Bank (1996).

The City of Hypergrowth

In the earliest stage of demographic development, as is well known, high birth rates are accompanied by reductions in death rates. They result in a high rate of natural population increase and a high proportion of young people. This demands large investment in human capital (high education costs). Because of high birth rates, the age structure of the population of these countries is generally young. In Kenya, for example, 52 per cent of the population are less than 15 and only 2.8 per cent are over 65. This is clearly an extreme case, but in most of the developing cities in the next ten to twenty years, the large numbers of the under-15s and those in their 20s entering the labour force and the housing market will still create enormous stresses on poorly developed education, health and housing systems, on infrastructure, on mass transit systems, and on hospitals.

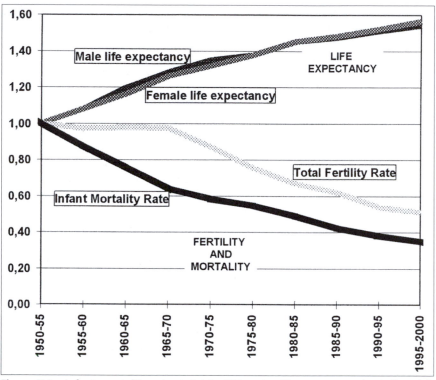

Figure II.1. Infant mortality rate, total fertility rate, life expectancy (male/female), 1950-2000 (as a ratio to 1950 levels), developing countries. (*Source*: UNFPA, 1998)

Cities in Demographic Transition

But there is one ray of hope in the cities of the developing world: although their high percentages of young people will automatically result in large numbers of children during the next twenty years, the number of births per woman is already shrinking and will shrink further, with improved education of women and urban living conditions. Urbanization and urban culture produce a sharp fall in birth rates; countries and cities enter into a phase of demographic transition. Contraceptive knowledge spreads and the economic value of children declines, particularly because of the costs of their longer and more intensive education. Thus, the next generation will be smaller, and will enjoy more care – especially time for their education.

Such demographic cycles are now often much more rapid than they were in developed cities at the equivalent point in demographic evolution, about 100-200 years ago. But they will become easier to manage, because – as we show later – many of these countries and cities are experiencing rapid economic growth. Thus the quality of population change will alter more than the overall figures signal.

And, in the more advanced among these countries, falling births are already producing a 'workforce bulge' which is a 'demographic bonus' to these countries; recent East Asian experience, where the ratio of working-age to non-working people will rise to a peak around 2010, shows clearly that it is likely to contribute quite strongly to economic growth. Over the next few decades there will be a demographic shift towards an older population in all countries; and by 2045-2050, no less than 97 per cent of the growth of the old age population will be in today's developing countries. However, the proportions of old people will still be relatively low compared with the developed world.

In a few cases (Singapore in the 1980s) governments may become concerned about this process, trying to raise the birth rate again among the more highly educated groups. However, such attempts have been rare.

Mature Developed Cities – Ageing and Implosion

Birth rates in developed cities generally remain low and in some cases (Western European countries in the 1980s and 1990s) fertility rates have fallen below replacement levels. Because of this, immigration – especially of workers to fill lower-skilled, lower-paid jobs – has become a critical element, subject to State control.

The other major factor is household 'fission' – the fall in average household size and the rapid increase in numbers of one-person households, resulting from both demographic and social change – more young people leaving parental homes for higher education; higher divorce and separation rates; more old people outliving their partners for longer periods; and, most startlingly, more young people choosing to live alone. There has been fierce debate, in some countries, as to the degree to which policy can control this process. In the United Kingdom the government has announced an end to 'predict and provide' housing policies, implicitly accepting the argument that household formation (e.g. by young people) depends at least in part on housing availability. However the best available evidence suggests that failure to provide housing will lead to real hardship (e.g. young people living involuntarily with their parents; separating couples forced to continue to cohabit).

Because of continuing medical advances in high-income countries, predictions show a huge increase of older (post-retirement) groups between 2000 and 2025. The pyramidical age structure thus changes into something resembling a tree.

Public social security services, especially provision of health care, will become extremely costly as labour costs will be high, particularly where

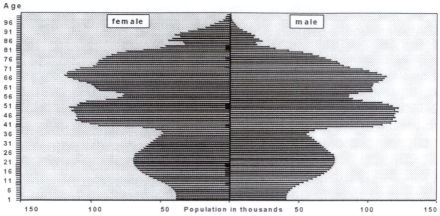

Figure II.2. Age structure in East Germany in 2030. (*Source:* German Federal Statistical Office)

those services have to be paid out of net income in economies with high tax burdens. To date no city with a rapidly-increasing elderly population has found a means to cope with and provide for growing service needs.

A significant proportion of the population will be in the 'old old' group (85+). They will impose a new, and so far unknown, economic burden through their needs for health and medical care in an economy with a declining proportion of working people. In particular, the 'old old' are likely to have special housing needs. One question here is the extension of retirement ages or the abolition of mandatory retirement, as has already occurred in the United States, to reduce the burden of dependency.

Falling birth rates in developed cities, as many surveys show, are in part a consequence of urban lifestyles, especially women's higher participation in the labour force and the high investment and time costs of rearing children and providing for their security. Today in cities, providing care, attention, supervision and services for children has become extremely expensive compared with the typical informal support systems earlier developed in villages or suburban environments, or as compared to past urban lifestyles. Housing which is adequate for families (quiet streets with low density of transportation, small houses with only one family per building) is expensive. Highly qualified working women pay a high price when they have children, as their careers can suffer. Work and the role of a mother are not easily compatible.

The overall shift is accompanied by a shrinking household size; in many cities 75 per cent of the people live in households with one or two persons. More than 30 per cent of urban dwellers will have no children. This means that the traditional role of the family in providing services for the elderly will break down, especially as the proportion of women who are in employment is still rising.

The consequences of this imbalance in age structure are hard to forecast, as we have no experience of it; we can only speculate. One risk is that because of ageing, human capital can depreciate in terms of a decline in technical knowledge, flexibility and mobility. Cities with high percentages of pensioners may run the risk of a flight of capital to 'younger regions' with higher growth rates and possibly higher increases in productivity. Saving rates, especially among people between 55 and 70 years, tend to be very low at the same time as competition for scarce capital is increasing and the urban systems become economically less attractive.

Box II.1. Pace of population ageing.

Most of today's developing countries still have a long way to go before they reach the proportions seen in European countries but they may reach these proportions more quickly because their demographic transition has been quicker. In Sweden, one of the earliest countries to complete the demographic transition, it took 84 years for the proportion of the population over age 65 to increase from 7 to 14 per cent. The increase from 7 to 14 per cent of the population over 65 will be dramatically faster for countries with the most rapid demographic transitions (18 years in Singapore, 20 years in the Republic of Korea, 28 years in Japan, 30 years in China).

(UNFPA, 1998, p. 17)

The Urban Economic Base

Cities: Engines of Economic Growth

After population growth, the most visible driving forces for urban change are rising productivity through new technology and higher capital per person and its corollary, rising income. This demands high savings. Transfers of capital and knowledge between regions can act – and, during the course of economic development, mostly have acted – as a mechanism to reduce inequality between one urban region and another. But rapid population growth tends to reduce the potential for increasing capital intensity, including investment in human capital. So reduction of population growth is still a precondition for wealth creation and sustainable development.

Everywhere, cities are the great engines of economic growth. Their share of national output, in almost every country, is much higher than their share of the labour force. Cities make their people productive. Two of the more extreme cases are São Paulo and Bangkok (figure II.3). Cities are concentrations of both physical and human capital. They are places of innovation – in production, lifestyle as well as consumption patterns.

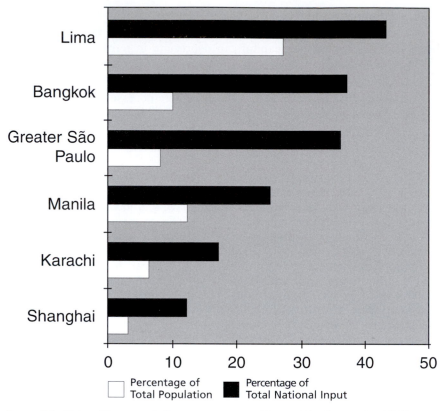

Figure II.3. Major cities: population versus output. (*Source: The Economist*, 1995)

Cities everywhere are highly and increasingly tied into a system of global competition – even though everywhere, most of their people work for local markets. So ruthlessly efficient is this global division of labour, that all cities have to run in order to keep still. As lower-cost locations compete in the production of goods and services, so do cities constantly need to seek new economic niches. Cities like nations need to travel up the learning curve, moving into activities needing higher investment in human capital – above all, advanced services. This is the history of the most successful cases of urban economic development in recent decades, such as Hong Kong and Singapore.

Markets and the Process of Accumulation

Urban economies everywhere work through markets. And, with the fall of the socialist command economy, markets – for goods, for services, for labour, for capital – now cover the globe. But this does not mean that all markets are global.

Global Markets and Local Markets

In fact urban markets are of two kinds: those connected with outside markets, exchanging tradable goods, and those providing local goods. In fact, even in the biggest and most globalized cities, much production and consumption is local. The local hairdresser usually does not export his/her services. The local greengrocer serves the local neighbourhood. Cities have strong and growing local markets (especially for labour) and a local accumulation process of capital, knowledge and networks. With increasing employment, they take part in constantly augmenting interregional and even international exchange. Without effective and flexible markets for local goods, from retailing to transportation, tradable goods cannot be produced efficiently. Without the contacts and technology transferred via international markets, productivity gains will be too weak – or income earned too low – to feed a differentiated local demand. Without a proper spatial division of labour, economic welfare cannot increase rapidly enough.

Markets in a Global Economy

Globalization increases and intensifies competition between urban economies. Markets limit the powers of cities; global markets widen the range of external influences and tighten their grip. But markets do not render cities helpless. Markets are both demanding and rewarding. The better a city plays the game, the higher the rewards. The 'winner takes all' principle can even be seen among cities as they compete in global markets. Success breeds success. Growing cities attract more investment. Investment and growth increase resources and attract more investment. In flexible global markets, economic miracles are quite common.

Globalization is not new. 'The modern world system' (Wallerstein, 1976), as a system of interrelated international markets, has existed for several hundred years. In the late nineteenth century, globalization was already making itself felt as the Lancashire textile industry lost its markets to Indian suppliers, or as new electrical manufacturing companies made Berlin the great high-tech city, the Silicon Valley, of that day. But recently, globalization has reached new dimensions. On the Mexican border, the *maquiladora* plants receive components from California or Texas and ship them back embodied into finished products; shoe plants in mainland China, managed from Taiwan, receive the latest Milan fashions turned into computerized lasts, and export their products through Hong Kong; clothes from low-wage Far East countries go through Italy to have designer labels sewn into them saying 'Made in Italy' (and indeed, the labels are).

The twenty-first century will see totally integrated capital markets and more and more integrated markets for tradable goods. Transport and

53

communication costs have sunk to an all-time minimum, bringing cities and nations into more direct exchange. The 'death of distance' (Cairncross, 1997) works in favour of innovative, creative and ambitious cities, allowing developing cities to fulfil the locational requirements of global markets. Rich cities, on the other hand, cannot shelter from competition behind monopolistic walls or high capital investment or superior knowledge. They become more international every day in their business and private life. A commuter driving in his Japanese car in an Italian suit to his New York office, where he will use a Taiwanese computer and the worldwide software of an American near-monopolist, sees his international equipment as perfectly normal. *Le défi americain*, Servan Schreiber's concern of the 1960s (Schreiber, 1967), has become *Le défi mondial*, yet it does not worry him. He is used to Asian and Mexican food. To him, globalization has an intense personal dimension: it influences lifestyle and competition in more and more workplaces. Markets have changed cities, and with them urban life is transformed permanently.

Markets, Accumulation and Poverty

The process of accumulation in market economies is a mechanism for wealth creation, but not for overcoming inequality; so far, the process of accumulation and economic growth has not eliminated poverty anywhere in the world. But importantly, markets – apart from creating small rich upper classes – have generated wealth that has propelled millions of ordinary people out of poverty into middle-class urban affluence, with lifestyles and income levels unimaginable by earlier generations.

That is fine in the aggregate and on the average. But global accumulation creates its own new inequalities: core cities that enjoy high income and accumulated wealth, and peripheral cities that are left way behind. Thus, a mere 28 per cent of the world population receives no less than 91.5 per cent of all Foreign Direct Investment (Hoogvelt, 1997). In Europe, the United Kingdom is by far the biggest recipient of FDI. Ireland and Sweden receive an even bigger share per thousand inhabitants. In the developing world, a disproportionate part goes into a few areas such as the Pearl River Delta of China, while large parts of Africa are almost completely ignored. International real estate investment tends to concentrate on an even smaller number of cities.

We might complain about the inequitable results of uneven accumulation, but we know that they can be remedied over time. In 1965, seven South Asian countries contributed a mere 9 per cent to world GDP; by 1975, 15 per cent; by 1995, no less than 25 per cent, equivalent to the USA and only exceeded by the EU's contribution of 29 per cent. The same can happen to other countries and other cities; the boundary between core and periphery has shifted, is shifting and will continue to shift. The fast-moving boundary within the Pearl River Delta is just one example: Hong Kong, once a peripheral colonial country, is now the dynamic core of one of the fastest-developing regions of the world. It is a matter of finding the appropriate new market niche at a particular point in time, and of making a city more profitable, more secure and more attractive for international investment. What seems a constraint may also prove to be an opportunity, because it can mean that the development potential is so much the greater.

Therefore, cities need to provide the necessary basic preconditions for private accumulation of capital, through a combined effort of good local governance and local markets. They need to demonstrate stable government, the right business environment (including more social equity) that will attract foreign direct investment, and the ability to harness the loyalties and enthusiasms of their people. In particular, in many of the less developed cities of the world, they need to exploit the fact that their people are often quite well educated and that they offer a remarkably attractive labour force for the information economy of the twenty-first century.

The argument then is that we need markets; but we need markets plus democracy, in order to channel scarce state and city resources for education, health and infrastructure. Poverty always enforces hard choices, for nations and cities as for individuals: whether to invest more in housing or in education, in decentralized energies, health care, in public transportation or in highways. Each time (in the short run), investment in one means less investment in another. As democracy necessarily means a multitude of goals and interests, urban democracy needs a clear vision in order to make adequate choices in the interests of the population, especially the poor people who make up the great majority of the population.

The Long March through the Sectors: Growth and Structural Change

General Trends

For more than a century, growth meant industrialization and a shift away from the agricultural sector. In the UK, the share of agricultural employment fell under 50 per cent in around 1780; in Germany and France in around 1870. As countries industrialized, they urbanized (table II.2).

This trend has not continued indefinitely though. In most cities, industrial employment began to decline during this century. Since then, deindustrialization has become the norm, both in advanced cities like London and New York and in middle-income cities like Buenos Aires. Today, only a few Asian and African cities are in an early phase of industrialization, with industrial employment still growing as a share of total employment – though recently some Sub-Saharan African cities seem

Table II.2. Employment structure (per cent) in selected countries, 1850-1990.

	1850			1900			1950			1980/90		
	I.	II.	III.	I.	II.	III.	I.	II.	III.	I.	II.	III.
Great Britain	22	48	30	9	51	40	5	49	46	2	29	69
Germany	56	24	20	40	39	21	19	45	36	3	40	57
France	52	27	21	41	29	29	27	36	37	6	30	64
USA	55	21	24	40	28	32	12	30	58	3	26	71
India				67	10	23	74	8	18	70	13	17

I. = Agriculture, II. = Industrial Sector, III. = Services
Source: Buchheim (1994).

also to have deindustrialized. In cities of the economically more advanced world, heavy manufacturing and goods-handling jobs have almost disappeared. Yesterday's growth industries have become the declining sectors and locations of today, while different locations are becoming new growth centres. Thus shipbuilding has migrated from Europe to Japan, Korea, Brazil, and then China.

Urban economies are still changing dramatically, but these changes follow stable rules. As economists tend to say: economies change but not economics. While the form and sectoral composition of urban economies may differ between cities, they are nevertheless the result of common driving forces:

- Continuous internal search for new products and more efficient production processes for growing markets;

- Continuous search for locations with cheaper yet productive labour and other low costs of production;

- Continuous search for access to new markets.

These factors are reflecting a tireless process of profit-oriented accumulation, and a continuous need for innovation. Together they create patterns of constant economic restructuring which have not changed much since the Industrial Revolution two hundred years ago. Schumpeter's 'Creative Destruction' still describes these transformation processes very accurately (Schumpeter, 1942, pp. 80-86). Growth and innovation are their strength. Inequality and degradation, as well as waste of natural resources, are their weaknesses.

Urban industrial development still shows striking contrasts. For example, automated factories for integrated circuit production, located in greenfield business parks in suburban areas, exist alongside labour-intensive shoe production in small backyard workshops in the middle of high-density urban neighbourhoods. The latter may still constitute the most typical kind of urban production. Worldwide, there are more backyard sweatshops than superclean, sterile, automated suburban factories. Nevertheless, sweatshops should not be discarded: they generate jobs and incomes for poorer, less productive and less educated workers, who would otherwise remain mired in rural poverty.

The advanced high-income cities are now largely dependent on the service sector, especially information processing and related labour-intensive 'multiplier services'. In recent years, research has become a new growth industry, very often located in attractive outer areas of big agglomerations. Information has become the production factor which symbolizes the end of the twentieth century and the start of the twenty-first. Many growth-oriented activities depend on information, accessed either electronically or face-to-face. In theory, electronic communication is becoming cheaper. Thus the 'opportunity surface' is getting flatter, with activities spreading across the globe.

Yet, as seen in Chapter I, it appears that demand for face-to-face contact is also growing rapidly, creating high-access points in the cores of the major global cities. Although often small in itself, the direct employment base in advanced information services is likely to generate a disproportionately large linkage effect to low-tech, high-touch services, especially personal services (food and drink, hairdressing, cleaning, public services). Employment serving purely local needs (retailing, education, construction, health care, repair and catering) is on the increase. Capital, information, knowledge and goods are produced and traded on increasingly global markets, with productivity gains resulting in expanding output and employment remaining static or shrinking.

Another frontier of the urban economy is the management of financial flows and financial wealth. These frontiers are moving. Developing cities have had their own forms of industrial revolution, lagged in time and differing in style. The Taiwan type of industrial revolution, for example, carried out by thousands of small companies, is remarkably different from the neighbouring Korean *chaebols*. At present, industry's share of total employment is declining in Rio de Janeiro, Hong Kong and Bangkok and the 'urban' economies of the largest cities are going to depend less on manufacturing throughout the world.

The Industrial Sector

In developed cities, because of ever-increasing productivity and use of modern technology, the industrial sector still contributes a substantial share of output, despite its declining employment share. Urban industry in developed cities is increasingly high-tech and knowledge-based. Spatially, high-tech industry is declining as a core city activity, while smaller cities and suburban centres are increasing their share of high-tech production.

At the new century begins, the percentage of employment in the manufacturing sector in many developing cities has already started to decline, while in others it is only just beginning to grow. The resulting differences are enormous: in 1996, manufacturing accounted for 24.5 per cent of total employment in Mexico and 23.7 per cent in Singapore, but for only about 13 per cent in Indonesia.

In most developing cities, the present state of the industrial sector bears only a small resemblance to the image promoted by the development policies of the 1960s. Concentrating essentially on large, capital-intensive plants, designed to implement export substitution, industrial strategy was based on an ideal of industrialization borrowed from the advanced economies. In reality, industry in developing cities is dominated by small companies with few workers, which are very often producing for local markets.

In Rio de Janeiro, more than 80 per cent of industrial workers are employed by small firms. In contrast, less than 5 per cent of the industrial labour force works in large firms which produce 80 per cent of the industrial output. The number of registered employees in mining, manufacturing and construction fell from 400,000 in 1991 to less than 350,000 in 1996. In Mexico, 75 per cent of manufacturing firms employ less than five workers. In the informal manufacturing sector, about 65 per cent of the firms are operating with one owner and no employees. This percentage rises to 77 per cent in the textile and leather industries.

These fourfold structural differences have far-reaching consequences for urban economic policy. For example, small firms owned by one person tend to be unstable. Indeed, very often they are quasi-informal enterprises which experience great difficulties in obtaining credit. In developing cities, small firms suffer much stronger negative effects from credit barriers than in developed cities. Permanent turnover and rearrangement of credit becomes an urgent task for them.

In their capacity as purchasers, large cities with centralized administrations are not natural partners of small companies and make it difficult for them to participate in formal bidding procedures. Not all cities provide the right supportive environment, especially for small companies, as the World Bank observes:

In other parts of the world, Rio included, access to raw materials, machinery, assistance with managerial and technical skills, marketing and, of course, capital present hurdles for smaller firms . . . The registration and licensing requirements a potential new entrant must fulfil in Rio municipality can involve six months of red tape and an exhausting paper trail. Credit is expensive, technological spillovers from the research establishment are few and industrial networking is not the developed art form it is in Third Italy.
Some entry barriers such as registration and regulatory requirements can

be solved by determined administrative or legislative action. Certain other barriers related to marketing, information gathering, debugging and servicing equipment and replenishing inventory are being brought down by the access to Internet. This is especially advantageous for small businesses for whom the transaction costs are burdensome.

(World Bank, 1998, Vol.1, p. 22)

Industrial Restructuring

Although the economic frontier is constantly moving towards information-handling, traditional manufacturing industry and industrial change still dominate many medium-sized towns which have always been manufacturing-based. In developing cities, the industrial sector is moving from light manufacturing to more capital- and knowledge-intensive production of more durable goods. Intra-industry turnover is high and cities experience permanent industrial evolution. All industries have a high turnover of jobs, and high closure and start-up rates. Exit and entry seem to be relatively high in developing cities, considering that large parts of production occur in informal or quasi-informal companies. Overall net growth is slow, but industries are more precarious in developing cities. Firms are forced to function in a fluctuating and unstable environment, affecting monetary policy, transportation, demand, wages and regulation. Support for start-ups and assistance for their survival is therefore an important function of economic development policies, especially in developing cities.

Technology transfers are often generated by plants owned by multinationals. Besides generating productive research and development, multinationals also siphon off highly qualified labour from domestic plants. In both developed and developing cities, industrial restructuring and modernization of industry have not provided enough new jobs to employ new migrants, especially young people and an increasing number of working women.

In any city, poorly qualified workers have less opportunity to regain employment after losing a job in the formal sector or to enter the formal labour market for the first time. Under-education and under-qualification are the most urgent and resource-hungry investment gaps. Yet rarely are either central or local government strategies successful in combating structural unemployment which arises from the decline of basic economic sectors.

Economic decline is generally fought with political instruments. Subsidies in particular are attractive tools for politicians to palliate employers and workers who are joining forces in demanding social protection. However, economic forces tend to be stronger than public budgets, as cities like Liverpool or Duisburg have found to their cost. Cities such as Taipei or

Munich have been more successful in promoting new industries which need highly educated labour, cooperation between university research and high-tech companies, high-quality new locations, and connections to new networks of suppliers. Specialization was the basis of these cities' success. However, there is a long lead time before the effects of such policies plus locational advantages are reflected in job creation.

The 'new economic geography', which is associated with the work of Paul Krugman, has again drawn attention to the localized clustering of the fastest growing industries. The first and most important step is the arrival of one or a few companies that emerge as major players in an industry. Once these are established on the industrial landscape, the area becomes associated with a kind of activity. This pulls in other firms that broaden and deepen the subsectoral base, in the process inducing agglomeration economies that draws (sic) the industry into a virtuous spiral. The most desirable outcome is a dynamic, internationally competitive industry with a worldwide reputation. Agglomeration economies come in two forms: localization economies or urbanization economies (Jacobs externalities). The first refers to the accumulation of knowledge in a closely connected set of specialized firms, who fully exploit scale economies. By congregating together in a compact area, the firms minimize transport costs and can depend on Just-in Time delivery (JIT). Clustering encourages information exchange on high-tech activities and has the added advantage of lessening urban congestion as well as land rental costs . . . Urbanization economies are the product of the cultural variety and social interaction at many levels that can be found in a large and diverse metropolitan region. The possibility of realising Jacobs externalities attracts high fashion apparel, up-scale publishing, advertising and media services.

(World Bank, 1998, Vol. 2, annexes, chapter 1, pp. 18-19)

Information, Services and Cities

Many old industrial centres are declining. Where decline started early the process has bottomed out, as in Glasgow, Cleveland and Dortmund. Here, services – especially producer services – have replaced the old smokestack industries, becoming progressively more complex and differentiated as they have grown. Traditional services like banking have split into a whole range of functions as financial instruments have become more sophisticated. The same holds true for software and services for information handling, which were practically non-existent in most cities twenty years ago. Other high-growth sectors include legal services, management consultancy, accountancy, the media, advertising and marketing. Very often, high-tech production combined with research forms a parallel globalized complex with its own networks, its own demands on labour markets and yet the same demand for high-quality services and high-quality housing. These services are characterized by highly-qualified personnel, a rapidly-changing knowledge base and a distinct type of product. Such modern service complexes typically become part of specialized international networks, only loosely attached to their immediate regional environment.

Thus the specialized global service sectors define the character of a city. But they are seldom the leading provider of jobs. Employment still tends to be dominated by local non-tradable goods: retailing, local banking, construction, transportation, building management, security, education and health care. Because it is difficult to achieve gains in productivity in these sectors, they will still provide the bulk of employment. But their growth depends largely on the economic success of the globalized service sector and its profitability.

Thus there is a complex interrelationship between the local sectors and the international and interregional service sectors. In traditional slow-growth or declining cities, which remain more dependent on traditional industry, local services tend to be more old-fashioned, more dominated by traditional suppliers, less vibrant and less responsive to modern trends; even the local media reflect this fact.

The more complex the demand from the leading multinational firms, especially through their headquarters offices, the more attractive become the major service cities which alone can provide services of the requisite volume and sophistication and complexity. Specialization in differentiated networks becomes the important ingredient for success.

The concentration of human talents, of headquarters, capital, economic power, modern cultural infrastructure, and high-class consumer services creates a premier league of cities, which in turn become magnets for talented people, resulting in brain drains from all over the world. This creates a climate of intense competition as the pool of ambitious talented young people in the modern globalized cities breeds new ideas in the cultural or economic arena. The good news is that brain drains can reverse – as the explosion of entrepreneurship in Taipei and Bangalore amply demonstrates. In effect high-tech and 'high touch' and high creativity services exist in a symbiotic relationship. The strong competitive world generates resources and income which is necessary to feed the cultural or media markets. In turn, cultural and creative industries become an important source of economic growth, as shown by many examples of old industrial cities which have successfully reconstructed their economies, like Bilbao and Glasgow.

The political world of the global networked cities still functions within traditional borders and even traditional rules of policy-making. Local political services are still provided locally. Political and administrative innovations are still specific local events. But international contacts and cooperation constantly intensify. In the long run innovation in the public sector, especially within the global cities, will become more international, more driven by direct competition between cities through processes of imitation and adaptation. The modernization gap between the private and public sectors could thus become smaller and the innovation lag shorter.

Competition and Non-Competition among Cities

In a globalized world, cities cannot stand still. Urban economies are constantly affected by the migration of manufacturing and goods-handling activities to lower-cost locations in the developing world, as well as service industries which are beginning to relocate to the same areas. More developed cities discover that they have to 'run to keep still' by developing new areas of economic activity, particularly in advanced services. Less developed cities are the beneficiaries of this process, but they may find it difficult to establish themselves on the development ladder and to maintain themselves there, since the logic of capital is constantly to move to ever lower-cost locations. Cities depending on inward investment can soon find that they are affected by outward investment as a result of the globalizing economy.

For this reason, development economists argue that endogenous growth is a better solution. But this is not easy: there are too few Silicon Valleys, and all too many unsuccessful attempts at innovation.

In the twenty-first century, a flexible and skilled workforce will be the most important factor to attract inward investment and encourage locally-based innovation. Only the learning city, capable of harnessing latest knowledge and developing at the sharp end of progress, will be competitive and capable of generating income revenue based on participation and empowerment. The ability to create a favourable environment for research and innovation and risk-carrying investment in new technologies lies at the core of any urban development strategy aiming at high productivity.

Not all cities can be in the front line of technical progress and innovation. Many will lag behind the pioneers. They will concentrate on imitation, simple production and simple services. Even in the highly globalized economies of New York, London or Los Angeles, the great majority of employees in most firms are catering for purely local needs. In the growing cities of Latin America and Sub-Saharan Africa, large numbers of people have little contact with the outside world. They participate in informal economies which are essentially local systems of exchange, akin to a village at an enormous scale.

Urban Business Cycles: Boom and Bust

Cities do not tend to develop smoothly along a long-term stable path. At times cities can make progress almost without effort, such as Glasgow at the turn of the century or Rio de Janeiro during the 1960s. Subsequently, they may be hit by the decline of a leading industry, shifts in transportation or communication patterns, or political turmoil. Very often, real estate markets also play a destabilizing role.

Competition is thus not only a positive driving force. It can destabilize individual cities, if competitors – other cities or regions – are more innovative, productive or capable of delivering cheaper services. Learning how to adjust under competitive stress is a fundamental task of all cities, at all stages of development.

The last two decades have generated two examples of major disruption in economic development. The 'lost 1980s' in Latin America were followed by the 'shock struck 1990s' in many Asian cities. After the rapid growth of debt in South America, increased interest rates and parallel recessions in the leading world economies provoked a slowdown in the developing world which was intensified by declining terms of trade. The end of net lending had a crippling effect on debtor countries. Nevertheless, the economic crisis triggered democratic reforms and political restructuring which can constitute the basis of new prosperity.

The lost years of the 1980s in Latin America were partly the result of ill-conceived policies. Inequality and extreme poverty defied rational economic approaches. Conversely, in Asia it was possible to maintain investment and reduce consumption because of greater income equality. However, in the mid and late 1990s institutional deficits in Asia created a special crisis which was not triggered by external shocks. Internal over-investment in real estate was one reason for the crisis.

Across Southeast Asia, cities are reeling from the impact of the financial collapse that struck much of the region last year. Half-finished buildings dot the landscapes, and closed businesses line many streets. Residents who had enjoyed prosperous times only a few month ago now face a much darker future. Many have seen their savings disappear and their carefully built financial portfolios turn to dust. Some have lost their jobs – even their homes – and are scrambling to build new lives.

(Chatterjee, 1998, p. 5)

Surely, now the question is: What can cities do to avoid yet another lost decade?

Urban Contrasts: Winners and Losers

The world is projecting a vision of shared prosperity. In reality, differences in wealth between cities are greater than ever before in history. Sub-Saharan cities are not only thousands of kilometres away from Canadian cities, but also remote by thousands of dollars per capita. Their relative isolation increases, as contacts and exchanges multiply and deepen between

West Coast Canadian cities and Asian, especially Chinese, cities. Presently, there are no mechanisms in sight capable of reducing the gap between the richest and the poorest urban areas, largely located in Africa.

Cities may well voice demands directed at governments, or at supranational institutions which control the international monetary system and influence the global financial markets, but they cannot change the course of economic evolution. Developing cities which have managed to establish themselves as modern international centres very quickly can become the object of speculative real estate waves or inflated real estate prices. Radically fluctuating commodity prices tend to erode trust in local government as well. Cities may find it attractive to sail through boom periods, but unfortunately they tend to be short lived. Great hardship may ensue during a prolonged bust period while cities attempt to mend damages inflicted on the local economy. Large public debt, loss of private equity and forced reduction of private and public spending tend to affect the poorer part of the population disproportionately. Such financial crises are fuelled by global capital markets which weaken national supervisory powers and generate excess short-term debt. Most importantly, economic crisis creates idle factories. They remain technically as competitive and efficient as before, without being able though to produce at full capacity because they, or their country, are crippled by bad debts, lack of working capital, and waning demand.

At their earliest stages of development, cities are less integrated into the international division of labour and tend not to be overly affected by global crises. Many cities, especially low-middle-income cities in Asia, have greatly benefited from inward investment in manufacturing and goods-handling through technology transfer and international exchange. These forms of transformation do not tackle the issue of permanence and stability, though. Short-term business cycles and medium-term structural change may trigger further relocation of firms and factories.

Cities are unable to solve these types of crises themselves. Their task is to provide the technical preconditions for production and growth. Experience shows that national policies have to create environments of financial stability, even fiscal prudence, at the local level, as competition between cities and financial institutions tends to push risks too far. Over-investment in real estate or in excess production capacity of export goods cannot be avoided locally. Comparisons of the build-up of production and investment in cities – even of the developed world – show remarkable differences in the effects of boom and bust periods on local economies. They stem mainly from national valuation practices, bank regulation, or the control of local public sector borrowing, especially in the property sector. The differences in the real estate cycles between London, Paris, Frankfurt and Milan in the 1990s can be explained, to a great extent, by variations in national regulations; little can be attributed to differences in local planning decisions. Cities are thus shackled and limited in their financial capacity as they depend on national solutions.

Twin Problems of a Restructuring World: 'Underuse' of People, 'Overuse' of Resources

Urban economies seem to have created a series of miracles. A continuous stream of migrants is still arriving in developed and developing cities, as well as in the cities of transition countries, from foreign countries or the rural hinterland. They are seeking employment or other chances to earn a living. They compete with a huge pool of labour, predominantly young, stemming from high natural population increase. Despite such obstacles, most of them find jobs which are clearly more attractive than the rural employment they have left behind, or jobs which were available to earlier generations. Efforts to industrialize villages, from Hungary to China, have never proved very successful. Infrastructure and transportation were often prohibitively expensive. In contrast, urban regions create enormous advantages for industrialization and later the division of labour between different services.

But demands for jobs are growing and cannot be fulfilled adequately. At a UNDP colloquium in 1997 on Governance for Sustainable Growth and Equity, attended by 151 mayors, unemployment was declared the top urban concern (UNDP, 1998, p.198). In many cities of the developed and developing world, the private sector fails to generate a sufficient number of jobs, thus contributing to the growth of both inequality and the informal sector. Even many advanced-economy cities contain a growing informal developing-world sector. At the start of the new century, unemployment and underemployment are still a worldwide problem. They are the uncured disease of urban development, which – apart from rare examples – differs only in intensity from city to city.

This economic paradox can be attributed to lack of investment capital and knowledge, inequality in education, and high population growth caused by in-migration; but also, increasingly, to high natural population increase within the city.

In developed cities, unemployment does not result from lack of capital or investment potential, but from a failure of the management of cities and their economies. Problems are largely due to:

- Lack of education and training;

- Incorrect incentives or distorted labour markets where, for example, insiders have better chances than newcomers who have difficulties in getting access to jobs, or where marginal tax rates are too high, reducing incentives and growth;

- High tax burdens which reduce growth potential of the service sector, as services carrying high social overhead costs have to be paid out of highly taxed incomes;

- Inflexible markets, partly due to overregulation, which, *inter alia*, reduce the number of start-up companies;

- Highly controlled rationing and regulation through planning.

Developed cities can reduce unemployment to tolerable levels, as examples from Dublin to Auckland, Portland (Oregon) to Boston demonstrate. It is easy to point out best-practice examples, but it is difficult to organize the necessary changes even in developed cities. Each regulation or planning restriction, subsidy or public expenditure programme is introduced for a good reason and with important goals. The biggest obstacles to full employment in developed cities are vested interests, conflicting political goals and misunderstanding of essential tasks.

In the hypergrowth developing cities, the sheer numbers of inhabitants seeking to survive are overwhelming. They do not result in unemployment, since this concept is almost meaningless in a world without social security systems. They form part of a particular type of underemployment, in a system of informalized urbanization. Registered unemployment rates are low. Where work is the only basis for survival, it becomes a necessity. One consequence is unproductive, unstable, insecure, low-paid work. Social protection is a luxury good of developed cities, allowing people the opportunity to look for better-quality, better-paid work. Such a luxury is not available in most cities of the developing world. Economically, at the present stage of their development, these cities cannot accumulate sufficient capital and lack savings capacity to provide formal sector jobs for all. A solution can only be found in reducing population growth and increasing savings potential, as a country like Singapore achieved at the start of its growth path in the 1960s; for many cities, this is bound to take time.

At the beginning of the new century, most cities of the world still have a long way to go to achieve full employment. In this process, each type of city will need to resort to a different strategy. Problems are greater in developing cities, but the task in developed cities is not much easier, as wealth, high incomes and a complex landscape of vested interests make it difficult to bring about change. The competitive energy, set free by the developing cities as they have to change in order to survive, may force developed cities to adjust in order to protect their level of income and wealth. As throughout history, competition between cities, together with public investment and urban policies, could be the driving force of more employment and eventually full employment in cities. Thus, globalization and freer movement of capital play a paradoxical role: they destroy jobs, but can create others in their place.

Box II.2. Growth of urban labour force.

In the coming decade, growth of labour will continue. In the Asian Pacific countries the labour force will grow by nearly 330 million which will concentrate in cities. Estimates for the Asia-Pacific countries indicate that between 1980 and 1990, 40% of total labour force growth took place in urban areas. For 1990-2000, the corresponding proportion is expected to be 61%. The urban labour force of these countries will grow by 328 million in the 20 years between 1990 and 2010.

(ILO, 1998, p. 11)

Policies often provide the wrong incentives. National and local governments promote technical progress, which usually is labour-saving, to increase competitiveness. They tax labour, capital, or production and consumption processes, to generate revenue and, in particular, the use of land, energy and other resources. In developed cities, income taxes and social security contributions tend to be high, while land or the use of space and energy and other resources is taxed very little. Petrol is cheap, and this leaves the economic costs of traffic congestion unresolved. Such taxation structures are clearly perverse. It is nonsensical, both economically and socially, to increase labour costs through additional burdens in a world of unemployment. Ecologically, it equally does not make sense to promote the illusion that energy and other non-renewable resources are plentiful and can be used up cheaply. In a world of growing environmental problems and limited natural resources, high unemployment and urgent needs for work, the right economic policy would be for governments to ensure that labour is available at the wage that will employ it, while making the use of land and other resources, especially energy, as expensive as socially acceptable, thus creating the right incentives to achieve global and local sustainable development.

Distorted incentives through government intervention are only one reason for unemployment and overuse of resources. In developing cities, shortage of capital and under-education are equally relevant. The roots of urban problems in developed cities are more complex and controversial. One school of thought sees a general deficit of work places, as high growth in productivity leads into jobless growth, whereby less people produce more goods and services for a stable number of clients. Unemployment seems to justify this argument. Seen from a different standpoint, the appetite for goods and services is almost insatiable, even in wealthy cities. Wants and needs are not limiting factors for work as such, but organizing work to fulfil these needs in modern cities has become more difficult. There is no magic recipe for full employment.

Full employment cities must be flexible. They must facilitate entry into the labour markets. Insiders should not have unfair advantages. Education has to be accessible for all, and not just during childhood; it needs to become part of a lifelong process. Learning has to become a habit and to be integrated into the workplace. New start-ups should be made possible at low cost, with little waiting time for permits and access to loans. Wages should mirror the productivity of the workers. Distortions through public taxes or social insurance contributions should be minimal.

Such a list of abstract requirements can be extended indefinitely. Indicating the direction towards possible solutions and some factors involved is easier than climbing the difficult path to full employment in reality. There are many good examples of successful cities with high employment. They are difficult to imitate, though. Cambridge, Dublin, Munich or Taipei, Singapore, San Francisco and Santiago were more successful than many other cities. Each followed the general rules mentioned above but used their own specific components towards their local solution. Often, success has only been achieved after many failed excursions and even disasters. The way back to full employment requires strong efforts and innovative strategies based on the specific resources of each city.

The Informal Sector

The Informal Economy: Its Key Characteristics

The informal sector has been the subject of analysis since the early 1970s. It is characterized by ease of entry, reliance on indigenous resources, family ownership of enterprises, small scale operations, labour intensive technologies, and skills acquired outside the formal educational or training system, together with unregulated and competitive markets. In the last two decades, various definitions have been formulated. They are summarized in table II.3.

The formal economy requires high investment in human and physical capital, including education, infrastructure, housing, factories or offices. These investments are based on 'hardware' of capital accumulated in the past, and on inherited knowledge-intensive 'software' – about production, commercial law, organizations, public sector management, sales and marketing – which make up a growing percentage of total value added. The informal economy, too, could become a 'free rider' on some of this accumulated capital investment. Regrettably, many developing cities simply do not have any, or very little of it.

The informal sector will consist of economic activities related to local resources, family property and small-scale operations; it will be labour-intensive, with adaptive technology, skills obtained outside the formal education system, and deregulated and competitive markets. The formal sector will consist of economic activities with foreign capital, that are capital-intensive and large scale, with corporate property, protected markets, imported technology and employees specialized in the formal educational sectors.

(Taschner, 1992, p. 147)

Table II.3. Characteristics of the informal sector.

	Kenya Report, ILO Bromley (1979)	Vanderschueren (1995)	Schneider-Barthold (1995)	Bittner (1997)
Labour	Family ownership Skills acquired outside the formal school system	Low qualification Low productivity		Lack of legal protection No minimum wages
Production and products	Indigenous resources Small scale of operations Labour-intensive technology	Low capital expenditure	Small scale of operations	Low standards of security and hygiene No consumer protection
Relation to government	Rarely supported Often ignored or discouraged by government		Distance from government	No quality and environmental control

Source: MacDonald and Ziss (1999), p. 83.

Urban development is a process in which both elements – the 'hardware' and the 'software' city – grow and become more sophisticated. This capital-intensive growth is limited by high population growth as there is simply insufficient savings potential, and therefore not enough human, physical and knowledge capital for a large number of young people. It is obvious that in cities where the typical number of children per family exceeds two or three, it will be nearly impossible to fulfil the savings requirements of a formal economy. Growing population and high numbers of children per family reduce the potential to build up human capital, provide adequate infrastructure, housing and capital-intensive jobs, and invest in complex public and private institutions to organize markets and public management. Poverty, together with high population growth, thus necessitates a large informal-sector economy which is labour – not capital and knowledge – intensive, and which can survive with simple and direct forms of organization.

Box II.3. Economics of population growth.

It is simply impossible for any country to become rich in the context of a rapidly-rising population . . . To change new human beings into modern productive workers takes a lot of investment. If there are going to be very many of these new human beings, existing human beings have to be willing to severely restrict their own personal consumption in order to make the investments needed by those new human beings . . .

A few American numbers illustrate the problem. If a new American is to have the average amount of space, a $20,000 investment has to be made in his or her housing. Until that new American is old enough to begin work, he or she will require feeding – another $20,000. To get to the average American educational level, he or she will require $100,000 in public and private expenditures. For that individual to attain the average American productivity at work, another $80,000 investment will have to be made in plant and equipment. Yet another $20,000 will be necessary to build the public infrastructure (roads, sewers, water mains, airports) needed to support that individual. Basically, each new American will require an investment of $240,000 before he or she is capable of fitting into the American economy as a self-sufficient, average citizen-worker-consumer . . .

Simple multiplication reveals that if the United States were to have a 4 percent population growth rate, more than 40 percent of its entire GNP would have to be devoted to providing for these new Americans. Existing Americans would have to take a sharp cut in their present standard of living if new Americans were to have a chance to become average Americans. It does not take a deep understanding of human nature to know that existing Americans would not be willing to make the necessary sacrifices. They say so every day by having small families . . .

The absolute investments necessary to give new citizens the existing standard of living differ from country to country, but the fractions of the GNP that must be devoted to this effort do not. In the Third World the funds to support such an effort simply aren't there, regardless of willingness. A 40 percent reduction in current consumption leaves both new and old citizens near starvation, with no resources left over to devote to improving their collective future.

(Thurow, 1992, pp. 205, 206)

The informal sector includes a heterogeneous range of activities, such as petty trade, shoe-shining, gambling and street entertainment, domestic services, small-scale manufacturing and repair shops, transport and security services, as well as the provision of loans outside the formal banking system, uncontrolled land transactions, unregulated construction, locally organized supply of water, educational and medical services (MacDonald and Ziss, 1999). The precise types of employment vary considerably: from family workers' dependent and disguised wage-work to relatively stable and autonomous self-employment, with substantial differences in income. According to studies in African countries, most workers in the informal sector earn less than the national minimum wage, while some dynamic micro-entrepreneurs have incomes which are as high as, or even higher than, those of formal business men and women (Reichert and Boschmann, 1995).

The informal sector is only loosely tied to the outside world. In a world of globalization, informality still means almost total localization in a collective subsistence economy. It is however quite intensely related to the formal sector, providing low-skilled and low-paid services, or learning by doing work to serve the formal sector. At the same time, there is an internal division of labour within the informal sector, whereby food and clothes, housing and transportation, health care and retailing are organized in a highly complex division of labour to manage a local, large-scale, collective subsistence economy with low or no growth per head.

From the perspective of the formal sector, informality is always seen as slightly illegal, or at least not respectable, as compared to the well-understood, regulated and functioning formal system. The informal sector is seen as a 'free rider', paying no taxes, without formal contracts, and avoiding all kinds of regulations, from health to security. For that reason, many middle-income countries seek to limit it. Any assessment should recognize the strength of the informal sector, as formal institutions are substituted by less-costly informal contracts and organizations. Thus the boundary of an individual site is accepted as common knowledge in a neighbourhood, debts are paid back without written contracts, and everybody is part of a network of assistance. There is a strong incentive, therefore, to obey informal rules, because being cut off from the support system of informal networks means being without social security and assistance during periods of poor health or underemployment. The informal sectors have their own low-cost expertise, their own informal rules, and their own systems of controls and sanctions.

An Informal – Formal Continuum of Economic Activities

Of course, informal sectors are never totally informal. Activities which start informally may become formal over time. Indeed, this is the almost universal process, and it is quite fundamental to the development process in virtually every city. Instead of assigning activities to either the informal or formal sector, it is more appropriate to think of a continuum between the two extremes, and to see development as a process of slowly growing formal procedures and relationships (table II.4).

In some African countries, street vendors are required to pay a tax to public tax-collectors. Hawkers in Cali in Colombia do not have to pay taxes for exercising their street trade, but are expected to possess identity cards, municipal trading licences and health permits. Conversely, many workers in the lower segment of the formal sector have as little job security as informal sector workers and receive even smaller wages. People move gradually from the informal to the formal sector; it is very important that this process is handled delicately in policy terms, lest it stifles entrepreneurship and deprives the very poor of their very basis of existence. Rather, the aim should be to employ the poor in a wider range of informal communal activities, which help them to help themselves – in particular, by providing basic services. We return to this key point in Chapter IV.

Table II.4. Informal-formal continuum of economic activities.

	Completely informal	More informal than formal	More formal than informal	Completely formal
Clients	Only informal clients	More informal than formal clients	More formal than informal clients	Only formal clients
Links to other enterprises	Links only to other informal enterprises	Using machines and production inputs from formal industry	Subcontracting Sweatshops	Links only to other formal enterprises
Relation to government	Hiding from state control Non-existence of state control Tax evasion	Trading licences Bribes to officers	Small amount of taxes	Acceptance of state control Fulfilment of regulations
Employment	No legal protection No social security	Little social and legal protection Relatively stable	Partial social and legal protection Relatively stable	Full social and legal protection Trade unions

Source: MacDonald and Ziss (1999).

The Size of the Informal Sector

In many urban areas, the proportion of people working or living informally has exploded over the last twenty years. Towards the middle of the 1990s, approximately 40 per cent of the economically active urban population of the developing world – in Africa, Asia and Latin America, numbering 230 million persons – worked in the informal sector. If in addition, China and workers in Latin American micro-enterprises are considered, 430 million persons (53 per cent of the economically active population) were informally employed (table II.5). Real informal employment was still higher, as the figures understate female informal work and do not include child labour, nor informal supplementary work to formal occupations in the formal sector.

   Thus, in many developing urban agglomerations, more than half of the economically active population is both employed in the informal sector and lives in informal settlements. Both are expressions of urban poverty, but also in part of mismanagement or political distortions. But informal solutions also represent survival strategies and creative responses to urban crisis. They may often be sustainable and appropriate from the viewpoint of comprehensive urban management. So the point is not to condemn them; it is to understand how, over time, to help transform them.

Table II.5. Urban informal economically active population, 1995.

	Estimated urban EAP		Estimated urban informal EAP	
	(million)	(%)[1]	(million)	(%)[2]
Africa	92,569	79	41,602	44.9
East Africa	13,579	49	6,769	49.9
Middle Africa	6,113	22	2,140	35.0
Northern Africa	25,785	83	9,302	36.1
Southern Africa	11,820	94	1,175	9.9
Western Africa	35,272	89	22,216	63.0
Asia (incl. China)	593,184	54	316,692	53.4
Eastern Asia (incl. China)	293,396	96	194,068	66.1
East Asia (without China)	90,877	71	21,297	24.1
South Central Asia	186,647	92	80,422	43.1
South East Asia	81,243	80	35,170	43.3
Western Asia	31,898	46	7,033	22.0
Latin America & Caribbean[3]	124,679	92	45,435	36.4
Caribbean	10,848	17	7,187	66.2
Central America	29,222	17	10,805	37.0
South America	84,608	17	27,462	32.5
Latin America & Caribbean[4]	124,679	92	70,750	56.7
Caribbean	10,848	17	7,187	66.2
Central America	29,222	17	16,645	57.0
South America	84,608	17	46,918	55.5

EAP: Economically active population
1. Share of urban EAP in total EAP, according to World Bank
2. Share of informal EAP in urban EAP
3. non-wage employment only
4. Including micro-enterprise employment.
Source: ILO employment statistics for fifty-four developing countries.

Box II.4. A shanty town in Mexico City.

Migration, integration and employment
More than half of the settlers of rural origin were functionally illiterate at the time they reached Mexico-City. They had neither savings nor skills of any value in the urban labour market. Among those born in Mexico-City, the illiteracy rate was significantly lower. Only 17 per cent had never been to school, and nearly half of those had taught themselves the rudiments of reading and writing. When migrants reach the city, they normally move in with relatives. There is no escaping the economic imperative of living near some set of relatives. The place of initial residence is determined by the residence of pre-extant cores of relatives in the city. Few settlers have more than a very superficial acquaintance with other parts of the city, including the downtown area. Few of the men venture farther into the city than their jobs require. Women and children barely know anything of the city beyond a church, a market, or the home of some relative. When job opportunities seem sufficiently bright for a nuclear family to move into a new area, they soon bring in other relatives from nearby areas or directly from the countryside. Each migrant helps several new migrants to settle in the city, or to move from another part of the city to this shanty-town. This they do by providing temporary or permanent lodging, food, information, assistance in job-hunting, moral support, and the basis for a more permanent form of exchange . . .

Everybody maintains a closely knit community within the shanty-town. Social contact among the families is intense, and there is a great deal of mutual assistance among them.

The general economic setting is one of extreme poverty. A typical dwelling consists of a single room measuring 10 by 12 ft., containing one or two beds shared by members of the family. There may also be a table, a chair, a gas or petroleum stove, and sometimes a television set – 33 per cent of all households own one. There are three public water faucets in the shanty-town, which are used by most of the population . . . There is little public sanitation and drainage; more than four-fifths of the population use the bottom of the gully for a latrine . . .

Unskilled labourers or apprentices include hod-carriers and other construction workers (foremen excepted), house painters, sand-pit workers, brickmakers, bankers' helpers, tuckers' helpers, carpet-layers, electricians, gardeners, and other unskilled labourers paid by the day who earn the minimum legal wage or less. Semi-skilled or skilled journeymen or craftsmen include independent or freelance workers such as bakers, carpet-layer foremen, construction foremen, electrician foremen, truck-drivers, tombstone-polishers, carpenters, cobblers, blacksmiths, potters, and so on. These workers may earn higher wages, but their job security is usually as low as that of the unskilled workers. Some of them have developed a steady clientele and work with their

Box II.4. cont.

own assistants, usually relatives. Industrial workers are those who work in an industrial plant, usually with the lowest wages and qualifications: watchmen, car-washers, janitors, and unskilled labourers. The service workers include waiters, water-carriers, watchmen, icemen, and domestic servants. Traders include all kinds of street-vendors. None of these has a steady income or social security. The employees are unskilled workers who earn fixed salaries: municipal workers (street-sweepers, garbage collectors), and a few are similarly employed with private corporations. These workers have relatively high job security and other benefits. Finally, there are six households of ten whose income is mainly derived from rentals of property in the shanty-town . . .

More than 60 per cent of those who said they were working consider intermittent joblessness for variable periods of time to be normal. Thus, the majority of the working population in the shanty-town are underemployed and have no job security, no social security, and no fixed income . . .

Social organization
Most nuclear families initially lodge with kin, either in the same residential unit (47 per cent), or in a compound arrangement (27 per cent). Compounds are groups of neighbouring residential units which share a common outdoor area for washing, cooking, playing of children, and so on. Each nuclear family in such a cluster forms a separate economic unit. Any room or group of rooms having a single private entrance is defined as a residential unit: this excludes tenements of the *vecindad* type, consisting of a series of rooms opening on an alley with a public entrance gate, which may contain several independent family groups.

(Lomnitz, 1997, pp. 205, 207-208, 209)

Table II.6. Informality in selected cities, 1990.

City/Country	Informal employment (%)
Bamako (Mali)	83. 4
Lagos (Nigeria)	69.0
Ankara (Turkey)	5.5
Indian cities	65.0
Lima (Peru)	48.0
La Paz (Bolivia)	57.1
Bogotà (Colombia)	50.0
Santiago (Chile)	22.0

Source: MacDonald and Ziss (1999)

Box II.5. The female workforce in India.

In urban areas in India, almost 40% of the employed women are working in the service sector, 30% in the commercial sector, 15% in manufacturing industries, 8% in construction activities and 5% in raw material production. More than 60% of the women are self-employed and engaged in petty commerce: dairy-farming, pottery, manufacture and sale of dolls and statuettes, goldsmith work, food sale, fruit and vegetables, laundry, manufacture and sale of leaf, reed and bamboo products, manufacture and sale of fire wood and cow dung. The majority (57%) of the women work outside their houses, 43% inside. Only 8% of the women working outside enjoy safe working conditions, while the majority of them (more than 60%) have mobile working places or are working on the street sidewalks. The level of fixed capital in these mostly one-person enterprises is extremely low. Generally, urbanization and industrialization in India did not lead to professional diversification or professional upward mobility for women. Their share in management and decision making is still very low; rather their subordinated position has been maintained.

(MacDonald and Ziss, 1999)

The informal sector even flourishes in many advanced economies, in two distinct divisions: one an internal one, where distinct groups (like immigrant communities) produce goods and services for each other; the other catering for the formal sector, through such practices as subcontracting, work in sweatshops, homework and low-wage services to high-income private households. From London to Los Angeles, it is possible to observe this kind of dual economy, that formerly was associated only with the cities of the developing world. The significance is that one part, the first part, is quite closed and local; the other part, the second part, is directly or indirectly articulated into the globalized market economy.

The Dynamics and Limits of the Informal Sector

Depending on the dynamics of urbanization and economic development, very different groups – migrants coming from rural areas, urban workers or employees who have lost their formal jobs, or young people who are newcomers to the labour market – may be forced to look for informal employment. Under severe conditions of poverty, as in some African cities, even urban informal agriculture is growing. As a result of low-cost production or low capital intensity, the informal sector – in contrast to formal markets – can react immediately to growing supplies of labour. Self-help labour markets, with high percentages of self-employed people, create their own employment opportunities, very often supported by NGOs able to adjust to the economic style, the contract types or the capital or support requirements of the informal sector.

Box II.6. Food production – urban agriculture.

Especially in Africa one finds a highly productive informal sector in food production. Informal gardens can use submarginal land along railroads, between buildings along sewer systems This food is not only produced for personal consumption. It is sold on informal street markets and provides a substantial part of consumption. Of course, the relevance of informal urban agriculture is often the result of incomplete urban development, where vast tracts of land between buildings remain empty. This urban agriculture very often has been ignored by planners. Urban agriculture and street food belong together. Mostly women are the producers and vendors.

Informal agriculture is but one example of working from home for the industrial sector, and providing services for higher income people.

(Tinker, 1998)

As a rule the banking system – in general the most formal of all economic sectors – fails to provide sufficient credit and savings opportunities for the thousands of mini-entrepreneurs who need small, indeed tiny, funds to buy material or equipment, thus creating insurmountable barriers for them. Other basic problems are related to the complicated, time-consuming and costly formal procedures, which the informal entrepreneurs seek to evade, due to their restricted access to educational institutions and professional skills and to their lack of negotiation power.

A New Type of Growing Informality

Traditional activities provided by families are not traditionally considered part of the informal sector. But, as an increasing number of family services, such as health care, are transformed into market services, those social services still provided by family members have to be seen in a new light. The border between informal and formal services becomes blurred. Future changes, such as increased female employment, the declining number of children, and the growing percentage of elderly people in developing cities, will push the family towards new informal services in order to decrease the growing gap between gross income and net income after taxes.

Informal Work and Urban Sustainability

The informal sector has proved to be both remarkably resistant in times of economic crisis or slow economic development and highly flexible in times of increasing population growth. It is more flexible than the formal sector in providing at least a minimum opportunity for migrants or young people, entering the labour market, to earn a minimum of income, or in providing shelter for new households. Where formal markets acted as closed shop

77

systems with few openings for newcomers, the informal sector presents lower entry barriers. This is increasingly important, as the barriers to entry into formal labour markets tend to increase over time. Of course, even informal systems provide a premium for members with better contacts and wider networks which often need time to build up, but they do allow easier access. Once this is secured, participants can develop their own abilities and can widen their contact networks. Thus, the informal sector is not static. It is open and flexible, in a way that the formal sector has too often lost.

Box II.7. Self-Employed Women's Association (SEWA) Bank, India.

In a survey conducted by the women's wing of the Textile Labour Association (TLA), Ahmedabad, in 1970, it was found that self-employed women not only have insecure employment and earn much less than workers in the organized sector, but also have no support for their work or for themselves in times of difficulties. The survey also revealed instances of exploitation of women workers and the large number of issues untouched by unionization, government legislation and policies.

The Self-Employed Women's Association (SEWA) was born in December 1971, and after a long-drawn official battle SEWA was registered as a trade union in April 1972. Thereafter, SEWA started functioning as a confluence of three movements, namely, the labour movement, the cooperative movement and the women's movement. SEWA was born in the labour movement with the idea that the self-employed, like salaried employees, have a right to their wages, decent working conditions and protective labour laws.

The SEWA Bank was established in 1974 as a separate bank of the poor, self-employed women workers at the initiative of 4,000 self-employed women workers. These self-employed women workers included hawkers, vendors and home-based workers – like weavers, potters, beedi-, agarbatti-, pappad-rollers, manual laborers and service providers. One of the main demands of these workers was for credit at reasonable rates which they were unable to obtain from normal banks. The SEWA Bank was started with the specific objective of providing credit to the self-employed women with a view to empower them and also to minimize the uncertainty of availability of credit through money sharks at exorbitant interest rates. At present the Bank lends to its members in three major areas: (a) for working capital; (b) for work tools; and (c) for housing.

A silent revolution is the method by which the Bank acts as an instrument to transfer assets to the names of women. The ILO statistics show that only 1 percent of the world's assets are in the name of women. SEWA Bank insists that since its loans for housing are in the name of a woman member, the house itself should also be in her name. SEWA also recovers mortgaged agricultural land of the family and puts it in the women's name as part of its asset-building program. In this way, houses have been transferred in women's names.

Box II.7. cont.

By establishing a relationship of trust and getting involved with the whole life of the borrowers, high recovery rates have been established. This has not only enabled the members to come out of the clutches of private moneylenders, but has also enabled them to develop the skills of dealing with formal organizations. In the process, their self-confidence has been enhanced. The vicious circle of indebtedness and dependence on middlemen and traders has been broken. This has changed the bargaining position of these women. They can now organize themselves, bargain for higher wages and, in case of a need, form their own economic units like cooperatives. Most importantly, the Bank provides its members with monetary security (as the members have savings accounts in the Bank) and gives them a the control over their own incomes. It has also provided the badly needed banking infrastructure that serves the self-employed and small businesses.

The SEWA Bank has thus contributed directly in achieving, to some extent, the larger SEWA goals of organizing and creating visibility for self-employed women, enabling them to get a higher income and to have control over their own income. A large number of members now have their own hand-carts, sewing machines, looms and tools of carpentry and blacksmithy to work with. Many of them have upgraded their skills and developed more business. The SEWA Bank has targeted its efforts not just towards the 'symptoms' of homelessness or poverty and their alleviation, but on the structural causes, including long-term capacity-building of the poor women and their institutions.

(UN Best Practices Database)

Compared to the formal sector, informal sector production needs less resources and energy per head, but this is mostly the consequence of low productivity, low capital intensity and lack of potential to consume and employ available natural resources. It does not arise from sustainable technologies, thus it does not offer a solution in the longer run. More sustainable lifestyles or more sustainable technologies will still need to be developed.

The cities in the developing world have a dual economy side by side: wealthy formal-sector cities and their sister cities with informal neighbourhoods. There is a symbiotic relationship between the two, and over recent decades it has often been stable amidst rapid growth. Of course, income and quality of life have improved in many informal settlements, but the wealth of formal cities has risen even faster, at least in absolute terms. There is an undeniable danger that the social and economic distance between these twin cities of the developing world, with their two divergent socio-political organizations, may further increase over time, as long as population growth is not reduced. A higher quality of life under informal conditions does not necessarily demand a transition to formal ways of working and living. It does, however, demand a more stable population, which will allow the population to concentrate on the improvement and upgrading of the informal city, rather than on the accommodation of further and disruptive growth.

Economic Chances – Economic Risks

History shows that growth, above all growth per head, is the key indicator of economic progress. But for the future, we will have to assume that – at least in the developed world and in the low-income world with high rates of population growth – income per head will grow slowly. In the cities of the developed world, which experience large and growing income inequalities, slow growth could make the problem even harder to resolve – particularly because, after fifty years of growth, the poor have developed the same high expectations as everyone else.

Worse: these inequalities could even widen, because incomes will more and more depend on knowledge, that is on long education and specialized training. But there is one realistic hope: that modern technology can bring an educational revolution in learning, through distance learning via the internet. Very soon, it is virtually certain that the computer will become the basic tool of learning, of communication and participation. Computer literacy will become the minimum condition for a job, and for effective participation in society or democratic life. The point is that it can be achieved at sharply falling cost: education will be the great growth industry of the twenty-first century, as the automobile industry was in the twentieth, and it will prove possible to bring it to the masses as Ford did with the Model T, through technology and mass production. Thus high-quality education can be made be readily available, even to the urban poor.

This is a huge opportunity, but also a huge challenge. It means that personal motivation and energy, not income, will become the key factor to successful learning and a successful life. Cheap access to universal internet education will become a liberating force for millions of highly-motivated parents and their children in low- and middle-income cities. But it could still exclude those groups living in declining or segregated neighbourhoods or other demotivating environments.

Social Change and Urban Development

The Engines of Social Change

Trying to put social change into a framework of sociological or statistical analysis is like biological analysis, in which people are dissected and described in terms of bones or skin or organs without regard for the fact that they are living human beings. The key, in all analysis of social change, must be first to bring out the general trends and forces, but then to demonstrate their effects in individual cities with their own history, economy, cultures and traditions.

Thus, in any city, we find that personal preferences, individual lifestyles, local patterns of activity and inherited values all influence social behaviour and the social fabric. Three key features, which interact, are the role of the family, the involvement of women in the labour force, and the movement from the informal to the formal economy. Strong family structures in Asian or Latin American cities, with family members working together in home-based informal economic activities, generate life patterns that are quite different from the more individualistic lifestyles of developed cities and dynamic middle-income cities, characterized by a breakdown of traditional extended families and even of nuclear families: here, the increasingly typical norm is the one-person household, where working men and women live alone in a separate apartment or small house, possibly with a long-term relationship with another person in a far-distant city. In consequence, the market comes to perform many of the functions previously performed by the family: in rich high-density service cities, more time is spent in restaurants, bars or other commercially managed meeting places, reducing the significance of the private home. In this individualized urban world, the most evident trend is the declining number of children, which in the long run will change the kind and degree of support children can give to their parents in old age.

Beyond this, a whole host of institutions and organizations may impact on the people of the city. Strong religious and social organizations can create core political or neighbourhood movements; while neighbourhood activists can organize whole quarters against eviction and redevelopment.

As already discussed, at the millennium poverty is becoming more urban and less rural. Therefore a central concern must be with poverty and its effects. Over the last century, the sad and surprising fact is that in spite of unexpected and even unimaginable economic growth, poverty has remained a fact of urban life in most parts of the world. The optimistic high-growth period after World War II saw poverty in retreat; even experts could not imagine that inequality would increase again – yet in many countries and cities, it has.

Of course, economic growth matters: one percentage point in real growth reduces poverty by measurable dimensions. But population growth has continued to work in the opposite direction, pulling back cities and nations, absorbing resources and income, space and infrastructure capacity. Therefore in many cities we still stand where we were in 1980 or 1990: slow economic progress, coupled with high population growth through migration and lower birth rates and even faster growing life expectancy, has limited the economic potential of many individuals.

This is not true merely of developing cities like Rio de Janeiro and Buenos Aires, but also of a transition-economy city like Moscow and even of advanced global cities like London, New York and Los Angeles. Everywhere, inequality has remained stubbornly high or has actually grown. One basic reason is that urban economies have evolved and changed much more rapidly than the skills and education levels of urban people – even though those, too, have seen staggering changes. Human capital has been in short supply, and the rent paid to education and skill has risen, while wages for unskilled workers have relatively fallen.

Economic Change and Social Evolution

The Role of Technology

The strongest factor in social change, in most countries and most time periods, is economic change. It influences different sectors of the urban economy, with major effects on the occupational structure. In turn, occupation and level of earnings are highly correlated. Earnings define which goods and services can be purchased. Income differences remain the most important indicator of inequality. Side by side we find regions with high income growth next to regions in decline, where people have increasingly retreated into the informal sector in order to survive.

Technology has produced breathtakingly profound economic transformations. In the cities of the developed world, hard physical labour, which once dominated people's lives, has mostly vanished. In the industrial cities of the nineteenth century, workers were traditionally worn out by the age of 40, their short life expectancy marked by poverty and sickness. Most people in cities now do jobs that did not exist in 1900, working with technology that came into being in the last forty years: personal computers, e-mail, copying machines. Life expectancy has risen to nearly 80 years and will grow further, which will increase demand for personal services. In 1900, the car was a rarity; now, in developed cities, car ownership is the norm. The changes in technology and communication which dominate our lives are so extreme that as the beginning of the twenty-first century many ask: have they been too great, too rapid?

At this point, for the first time in history, the young know systematically much more in certain important areas than the old. It is difficult to imagine how the scale of this change can be absorbed, comprehended and managed. But change only occurs as people change, as people are able to cope with it, are even drawn to it and as – at least in part – people are excited by the new potential. Of course there is another side of the coin. The young grow into new systems of thinking and perceive new problems, and new technologies have become second nature to them. But many older professionals become the new illiterates, unable or unwilling to learn as the demand for their services disappears and their knowledge depreciates. Unemployment among people over 50 has become a difficult problem, partly in consequence of the speed of change. Thus, the transformation of the labour markets through technology and income growth has both positive and negative aspects. In spite of unemployment and growing inequality, we find more people

- Using new technologies they find more interesting and acceptable than the old;

- Learning new professions which their parents do not understand, feeling comfortable about them as they demand more intellectual challenge and openness;

- With increasing mobility, using cars, planes and trains in a new freedom, which did not exist two generations ago;

- Discovering new lifestyles and a new feeling of freedom which give them more variety, from food to media to travel.

Rapid Growth and Rapid Decline

Economic growth is still an important indicator for change in an urban society and for the tensions created in the course of development. Periods of rapid growth, especially rapid growth per capita, are periods of reduced political and social tension and of changing lifestyles and values. So-called post-materialistic values as a mass phenomenon can only be observed in cities with high average income. Historically, the 1950s to the 1970s remain the best examples. Since the 1980s growth per head in Western cities has slowed, reducing the growth of labour demand and resulting in higher unemployment. Connected with the decline was the financial crisis of Latin American cities. Here the political changes demonstrate that periods of decline can also be periods of positive change in spite of the standard experience that times of declining income are times of social unrest and tension, as can be observed in Asian cities nowadays.

In many newly industrialized countries, rapid growth has resulted in a sharp rise in overall living standards and in the creation of a new middle class which brings with it more home ownership and more distribution of wealth in real estate. The financial and foreign exchange crisis in Asian cities will postpone further growth of income, but in the long run, as many examples in the history of European and American urban development have demonstrated, the consequences of even enormous speculative bubbles will be overcome. Consider the collapse of the capital markets as a consequence of property and railway speculation in New York City in 1873, which set off a chain reaction leading to unemployment and the banking crash; or the crisis of the early 1930s, when the newly-completed Empire State Building came to be known as the 'Empty State', or the property collapses in London in the early 1970s and early 1990s.

Economic growth does not automatically trickle down to the least fortunate. Urban development can exclude large numbers of undereducated, unintegrated, unconnected people. Economically, a prolonged period of fully elastic supply of low-skilled labour hinders the growth of income, in spite of general economic growth, because of the enormous inequalities that result. It becomes a question of political power, or of the fairness and effectiveness of the political system to mobilize more resources for education or investment in infrastructure or for more capital for new companies.

Earnings and Income Inequality

The critical – and discouraging – result of economic change is a growing inequality, found in nearly every type of city. During the 1980s and 1990s income inequality has increased in the majority of OECD countries: the income of the lowest deciles as a proportion of median income has fallen, while the income of the highest deciles as a proportion of the median has risen. Only a few countries – Belgium, the Netherlands, Italy and Canada – have showed a contrary trend of declining income inequality. Deindustrialization has been accompanied by growing unemployment, especially among young men. The high-tech knowledge city delivers a skill premium for the highly educated. The young undereducated unemployed male has become a new negative role model at the beginning of the twenty-first century. It seems that the service city is becoming more female. So far one can only speculate whether the income differences between female and male earnings will shrink or even disappear. In part, this is already happening.

The reasons for the present tendencies for higher inequality (which is closely connected with high unemployment) in many developed cities are still not fully understood. Rigidities in the transformation of the urban economy and society are an abstract explanation, but some more specific trends appear to explain most of these changes:

- Developed cities experience intense pressure on old industries and all types of low-skilled production which either substitute capital and highly-skilled labour for unskilled and semi-skilled labour, or move away to lower-cost production areas, making industrial workers redundant;

- This is exacerbated by low education levels in relation to the needs of a sophisticated advanced economy, which demand aggressive measures to improve human capital; cities in developed countries have not risen to this challenge, though it has long been evident;

- At the same time, the rapid growth in the number of dual career professional households, often without children, where both partners earn substantial incomes, has increased the number of high-income households;

- There is a parallel increase in low-paid casual employment in services, but these cater mainly for younger people and offer few lifetime career prospects;

- In developing cities, the declining growth rates of industrial employment, accompanied by slow growth of formal sector jobs, has created a growing informal sector, further augmented by migration and population growth;

- In both developed and developing cities, both underemployment and (especially in developed cities) open unemployment create inequalities. This results not only in inequality of income but also in social exclusion and lack of contact with stable and growing labour markets. It is a sign of a growing skill gap, as formal sector employment under conditions of abundant labour supply demands high-level qualifications or specialized skills as a pre-condition;

- In recent periods, the radical fluctuations of the global economy have led to fluctuations in international trade. Real estate boom and bust phenomena, devaluation and high levels of accumulation of bad debt have racked many cities, where entire areas are lined with half-finished high-rise buildings in which empty condominiums are waiting for buyers. As a result, many urban dwellers are forced suddenly to reorient their lives, finding a new basis for living which may mean a return to the ancestral village or a descent into the informal subsistence economy.

Occupational Change

In developed cities there is a constant upward occupational shift in the economically-active work force. A new post-industrial class structure is evolving. The number of semi-skilled and unskilled manual workers is declining, while the number of professional managerial and technical employees is growing. But the professionalization of the economically-active labour force is paralleled by a growing number of economically inactive and unemployed workers. Polarization has arrived back on the urban scene since the 1980s, after being half-forgotten in the 1960s and early 1970s. The changing occupational structure has resulted in incomes rising faster at the top than at the bottom of the income distribution. In many cities the proportion of individuals with below half average income has risen substantially.

In most developing cities the growth of the professional, technical and managerial classes is slower than in the developed world. Many of these developing cities are characterized more by an alarming process: the

Box II.8. Migration: South Africa as a test bed.

In most African urban communities, there is a persistent dissociation between paid productive activities 'elsewhere' and 'at home', in which local organizations – ethnic, religious, neighbourhood – play an important role instructing the complex relationships between multiple communities. Many come to South Africa because it allows Africans to 'go West without going overseas'. This migration has been aided by the expansion of unconventional and nonregistered cross-border trade circuits, facilitated by the proliferation of air links and well-organised long-distance taxi services from places as far away as Dar es Salaam, Nairobi and Kampala. They come from almost every country. Mozambicans and Angolans have increasingly gravitated to remote peri-urban areas, most living in extreme destitution, while southern Africans have largely penetrated the established black townships, working as artisans, hawkers and clerks. The inner-city areas contain large numbers of Mozambicans, Zimbabweans, Ghanaians, Nigerians, Zairois and other Francophones. Already sectors of the central city are close to having a foreign majority African population.

(Simone and Hecht, 1994)

In South Africa, apartheid brought a specific form of local organization, the civic society. There was a massive growth in informal settlements due to conversion of agricultural land into townships, residential migration from formal townships because of overcrowding, and migration from rural areas.

Simone's study of Phola Park, one such community that developed in 1985-86 outside Johannesburg, shows that the internal economy depended greatly on nominal ANC members engaged in various theft rings with hostel neighbourhoods farther afield. The majority however were long-term urban residents who had previously lived in backyard shacks in next-door Thokoza; they were active in urban political struggles and sought to make a stable and serviced neighbourhood. Residents became involved in complex patterns of association to protect their property. Many of them had formal sector jobs and were active in local SANC politics or civic affairs, but others acted as 'advisors' to gangs, providing transportation, refuge and theft opportunities in return for payoffs. Additionally, white gangs and drug-trafficking rackets based in a number of military battalions recruited people; these gangs were opposed by groups of returning MK guerrilla fighters, who used their connections in Angola and Zambia to engage in smuggling activities. The paradox was that the local residents' association opposed the proliferation of weapons and criminality, while the community benefited from the gang networks. Because of battles with Thokoza Park over service charges, the community leaders found it hard to maintain their credibility, and they were compelled to make further deals with the murky and diffuse associations and gangs, perhaps to enrich themselves and consolidate their power; this weakened the Association's power. In 1992 the Association was overthrown in a coup staged by interests linked to the informal structures, who have since maintained it as inactive

(Simone, 1997)

growth of the informal economy, which provides a bare subsistence income for people newly arriving in the city and for many who have lost better-paid jobs in the formal production economy. This picture is however not uniform. Informalization has been less evident in some Southeast Asian newly industrializing countries (NICs) (Singapore, Hong Kong, Taiwan, Korea) which successfully eliminated all or most of the informal economy during the 1960s and 1970s; in some of the rapidly-developing cities of Latin America, a rapidly-growing professional and managerial new middle-class can be found juxtaposed with a large informal sector. But in Sub-Saharan African cities, the growth of the informal sector has been an all-pervasive feature since the early 1970s, associated with an alarming collapse of urban living standards.

There is a debate about the impact of economic restructuring and urbanization on income distribution and on the scale and magnitude of poverty in the developing world. The ILO (1998) found that 'Urbanization has brought an alarming rise in the incidence of urban poverty', and UNDP estimates discussed in Chapter I indicate that more than half the poor are now concentrated in urban areas. The picture in Africa is particularly bleak. Many of the African urban poor are now in a worse position then the rural poor and rural-to-urban migration has slowed down considerably, and even reversed in some cases. Informal agriculture in many urban Sub-Saharan areas is a sign of a growing subsistence economy where the participants are only loosely connected to formal markets or to sectors which produce tradable goods for interregional exchange.

Present Public Policies and Social Change

Public policies usually try to reduce inequality and promote social integration. Education, unemployment insurance, health care systems or public pensions have had major impacts which become especially clear if one compares the results of different cities with different systems.

The Western welfare state has solved many basic social problems which plagued previous generations of city dwellers. Elaborate pension systems have reduced or even almost eliminated poverty in old age. The welfare state guarantees income during times of sickness and unemployment. But as an unwelcome side effect, it has created what has been called a culture of dependency, which to a certain extent, in major cities today, has deteriorated into what may even be called a culture of paralysis and stigmatization. The welfare state attempted to reduce risks and to integrate minorities. But, as is now apparent, in certain areas it has driven people, housed in peripheral estates, into segregation and social exclusion. The European welfare system will suffer increasing strains through a combination of ageing and low productivity growth: there will be a rapid growth in the numbers of old people without children, needing specialized and labour-intensive professional care. This will put a growing burden on a working population which will be shrinking in size. The overall economic effects are as yet unknown; they are likely to be very problematic.

The employment problems facing cities in the developed world in the past twenty years have proved highly intractable. The continued decline of manufacturing industry and its (partial) replacement by the service sector has led to rising unemployment, especially among males, and to a growing polarization of earnings and income as between the more highly skilled, who work in professional and managerial jobs, and the less skilled, who are either unemployed or are working in low-paid service sector jobs. Public assistance programmes have reduced social tensions and made the prolonged employment crisis more tolerable. But it is most likely that social security systems have prolonged unemployment or reduced incentives for work. The poverty trap is a well known phenomenon in most European cities.

Many difficulties arise in European cities with high immigration. Here, the highly regulated economies and highly regulated labour markets have created an insider society which is closed to newcomers, especially to migrants from other countries. This phenomenon is very nearly a cultural contradiction. The welfare state and the highly regulated economic and social system, which are supposed to reduce risk and uncertainty, have instead created hierarchies of permits, fixed requirements for formal training, highly specialized tests for individual professions or complex licensing systems to start up new enterprises. This highly regulated system functions as a closed shop against newcomers. A more informal economy, more open to newcomers, would aid the reduction of unemployment. However strategies in this direction often come into conflict with traditional labour unions, positions, professional pressure groups, or powerful bureaucracies which prefer controlled markets. This has resulted in the growth of an informal 'black' market sector. Cities thus need more informal legal sectors, open to people with energy and skills, thus increasing opportunities for learning by doing and reducing formal requirements to entering the labour market or into self-employed activities.

The Persistence of Urban Poverty

Even though most of the world's poor are still rural, a disturbing fact, already touched on, is that during the last twenty-five years poverty has become more and more urban. Nearly a third of the world's urban population lives in poverty, and the absolute numbers were expected to grow from 400 million to 1 billion during the 1990s. According to World Bank estimates, based on an international poverty indicator of a daily per capita income of US$1, approximately 30 per cent of the population in developing countries are poor (quoted in MacDonald and Ziss, 1999, p. 88).

The hope of overcoming urban poverty through growth is still realistic; but population growth, economic crisis, unequal development or political unrest always seem to lead inevitably to a permanent postponement of final goals. The descriptions of poverty over more than a hundred years and more are very similar, demonstrating just how slow progress has been.

Of the 1.3 billion people living in poverty, 70 per cent are women. Although life expectancy and literacy rates are increasing, economic opportunities for women remain limited. In most cities of the world it is still more difficult for women to get access to work, resources and services. Within low-income households, women have primarily the responsibility for childcare and household management. The lives of women are usually more centred around the home, which may explain why they are often intensely engaged in community organizations fighting against the lack of infrastructure and services. These activities are little appreciated and often limit women's opportunities to earn an income. The situation is even more difficult for female-headed households, which, in many low-income settlements, account for more than 30 per cent. Men are either temporarily absent or have left their families because of separation. Services that would help to combine family and employment – like crèches and child-care centres – are often deficient (UNCHS, 1996b, p. 121).

Discrimination against women often starts during childhood. Child mortality rates are higher for female than for male children, and boys attend school longer than girls. In some African countries 90 per cent of the female population over 25 never went to school. Women make up 65 per cent of the world's illiterate people. Policy successes to end discrimination depend very much on successful education, the strongest force against deep seated habits.

This has many causes: migration into the cities of very poor people who cannot make a living on the farm; wars and natural disasters; economic crises; subsequent structural adjustment programmes; and sheer inability to control urban growth. As indicated in table II.7, the absolute number of the poor increased more in urban than in rural areas between 1970 and 1985: out of a total of 212 million additional poor, 129 million lived in urban areas. But, because total urban population has risen so rapidly, the proportion of the urban population in poverty fell from 35 per cent to 32 per cent, a lesser decrease than in rural areas; it still remained true that in 1985, nearly three-quarters of poor people in the developing world were rural. Life in the informal economy on the streets of the city, it seems, is still marginally preferable to life on the farm.

Asia has succeeded in effecting a significant reduction of poverty in both urban and rural areas. However, it continues to be the region with the largest number of urban poor and with the largest increase in absolute numbers (60 million between 1970 and 1985). In Africa, the percentage of the urban poor decreased, but the absolute figures almost doubled. Latin

Box II.9. Poverty in the course of the century.

London, 1891

There is struggling poverty, there is destitution, there is hunger, drunkenness, brutality, and crime; no one doubts that it is so. My object has been to attempt to show the numerical relation which poverty, misery, and depravity bear to regular earnings and comparative comfort, and to describe the general conditions under which each class lives . . . The special difficulty of making an accurate picture of so shifting a scene as the low-class streets in East London present is very evident, and may easily be exaggerated. As in photographing a crowd, the details of the picture change continually, but the general effect is much the same, whatever moment is chosen. I have attempted to produce an instantaneous picture, fixing the facts on my negative as they appear at a given moment, and the imagination of my readers must add the movement, the constant changes, the whirl and turmoil of life. . .

The lowest class consists of some occasional labourers, street sellers, loafers, criminals and semi-criminals, I put at . . . 1.25% of the population . . . With these ought to be counted the homeless outcasts who on any given night take shelter where they can, and so may be supposed to be in part outside of any census. Those I have attempted to count consist mostly of casual labourers of low character, and their families, together with those in a similar way of life who pick up a living without labour of any kind. Their life is the life of savages, with vicissitudes of extreme hardship and occasional excess. Their food is of the coarsest description, and their only luxury is drink. It is not easy to say how they live; the living is picked up, and what is got is frequently shared; when they cannot find 3d. for their night's lodging, unless favourably known to the deputy, they are turned out at night into the street, to return to the common kitchen in the morning. From these come the battered figures who slouch through the streets, and play the beggar or the bully, or help to foul the record of the unemployed; these are the worst class of corner men who spring forward on any chance to earn a copper, the ready materials for disorder when occasion serves. They render no useful service, they create no wealth: more often they destroy it . . .

The 'very poor' with casual earnings add up almost exactly to 11.25% of the whole population . . . They do not, on the average, get as much as three days' work a week, but it is doubtful if many of them could or would work full time for long together if they had the opportunity . . . There is drunkenness amongst them, especially amongst the women; but drink is not their special luxury, as with the lowest class, nor is it their passion, as with a portion of those with higher wages and irregular but severe work. The earnings of the men vary with the state of trade, and drop to a few shillings a week or nothing at all in bad times; they are never high, nor does this class make the hauls which come at times in the more hazardous lives of the class below them; when, for instance, a sensational newspaper sells by thousands in the streets for 2d to 6d a copy.

(Booth, 1891, pp. 289, 290, 291-292, 293)

Box II.9. cont.

New York 1966

Once the culture of poverty has come into existence it tends to perpetuate itself. By the time slum children are 6 or 7 they have usually absorbed the basic attitudes and values of their subculture. Thereafter they are psychologically unready to take full advantage of changing conditions or improving opportunities that may develop in their lifetime . . . People in a culture of poverty produce little wealth and receive little in return. Chronic unemployment and underemployment, low wages, lack of property, lack of savings, absence of food reserves in the home and chronic shortage of cash imprison the family and the individual in a vicious circle. Thus for lack of cash the slum householder makes frequent purchases of small quantities of food at higher prices. The slum economy turns inward; it shows a high incidence of pawning of personal goods, borrowing at usurious rates of interest, informal credit arrangements among neighbors, use of secondhand clothing and furniture.

(Lewis, 1966, p. 220)

Los Angeles 1995

. . . Comprising the homeless (as many as 80,000 people are homeless on any given night in the Los Angeles region), the new orphans (children as well as the elderly), the new slaves (illegally imported house servants kept privately by their 'owners'), the unemployed and welfare dependant, the products of what is called the feminization and latinization of poverty, and more generally the composite group that has received the greatest attention from contemporary urban sociologists, the permanent urban underclass.

(Soja, 1995, p. 133)

Thailand 1986

Slum and squatter settlement surveys in Thailand in 1986 found that the urban poor have larger households (5.6 persons) and fewer income earners per household than the non-poor. They have older, less educated household heads and are less mobile than the non-poor. Those in larger cities were employed primarily as general labourers, production workers and street vendors. Those in smaller towns tended to be marginal farm operators. Though the urban poor derive a greater portion of their earnings from non-cash sources than the non-poor, this portion of income is still much less than that received through salary and wages. In order to make the most of their income, there is a strong reliance on self-produced food, clothing and household goods. Life patterns and livelihoods are spatially restricted to relatively small areas in the city, each of which has its own set of conditions and constraints. The poor, being less mobile than higher income groups, are more dependent on their immediate employment and living environment for their well-being. As a result, programs to aid the poor need to respond to the specific local circumstances of the poor.

(ILO, 1998, p.15)

Table II.7. Urban and rural poverty by developing regions, 1970 and 1985.*

		Percentage poor		Population (million)		Share of total (%)	
		1970	1985	1970	1985	1970	1985
Asia	Urban	42	34	110	170	11.7	14.7
	Rural	61	47	552	567	58.5	49.0
Latin America	Urban	25	32	41	89	4.3	7.7
	Rural	62	45	75	57	7.9	4.9
Africa	Urban	32	29	26	47	2.8	4.1
	Rural	50	58	140	226	14.8	19.6
All developing regions	Urban	35	32	177	306	18.8	26.5
	Rural	59	49	767	850	81.3	73.5
	Total	**52**	**44**	**944**	**1,156**	**100.0**	**100.0**

* excluding China.

Source: MacDonald and Ziss (1999).

America is a relevant example of the changing spatial patterns of poverty: while in 1970 only 37 per cent of its total poor lived in urban areas, by 1994 this proportion had grown to 65 per cent. Here, the urbanization of poverty occurred mainly during the 1980s, paralleled by a strong expansion of the informal urban sector. According to ECLAC, urban poverty affected 135.4 million Latin Americans in 1994, three times as many as in 1970.

In Sub-Saharan Africa the average annual growth of GDP dropped from 1.7 per cent between 1980 and 1990 to 1.4 per cent between 1990 and 1995 (World Bank, 1997). The increase of poverty took place in a context of explosive urbanization, high population growth and decline of economic growth, related to low productivity of agriculture, stagnation of manufacturing and services, and limited access to productive resources. In the 1990s, African formal labour markets have been absorbing less than 25 per cent of the newcomers. The logical consequence is an increase in people formally unemployed or, as they cannot afford unemployment, of informal employment at a survival level.

When economic conditions are unstable, the old observation: 'The poor pay more' holds true – because of their immobility and lack of access to good shopping opportunities, they pay more than richer people for the same goods. In developing cities this is especially so for such basic needs as drinking water and building materials. But the poor have to pay more in an economic crisis, because they carry higher adjustment costs. Families without savings are hit hard when incomes decline and food prices rise. Exchange rate crises very often hit people who never deal in foreign exchange or are not connected to the international economy. But they depend on markets which are tied to international movements of interest or exchange rates. Instability is a brutal force of social change with very unequal distribution effects.

Poverty and Crime

The overwhelming majority of poor people the world over are law-abiding members of civil society. But it is an empirical observation that poverty, whether it results from long-term unemployment or social disruption, tends to be associated with higher than average rates of crime, and that where poor people are segregated from mainstream societies these crime rates may locally become very high. The poor and especially the very poor are therefore ironically the main victims of crime, and they suffer above all from the constant fear of crime. This is partly because some poor people are prone to alcohol and drug abuse, which leads to crimes such as criminal damage and violence against the person, and also because for some – especially the young – illegal drug dealing becomes an irresistible source of easy money. In addition, poverty is associated with the breakup of partnerships, which in some cases may be associated with domestic violence.

There are of course measurable economic costs:

- Police and prison costs are the most direct.

- Private insurance and security costs including lawyers' costs in many cities are growing but hard to measure as they are paid in shopping malls, banks or private homes.

- Welfare costs, including unemployment pay, assistance to lone parents and housing benefit, which may place many in a 'poverty trap' making them reluctant ever to take work again.

In developing cities, the formal costs are generally lower but the logic is the same. In all cities, low-income households carry a disproportionally high burden. Crime concentrates on areas of notorious poverty and hits poor people harder than wealthy citizens. Anti-poverty policies promoting social integration can thus bring double benefits.

Social Change and Spatial Patterns

The dominant experience in developed Western cities – cities of mass affluence – has been a growth in mass consumerism. Usually a majority of households own a whole set of durable consumer goods as well as a single-family house or a flat in a condominium building. Affluence, in a highly mobile car-owning urban society, has provided the economic and technical basis for a widespread suburbanization. In many countries the suburban way of life has become the dominant lifestyle, with low- density living in

Box II.10. Urban population and crime.

At least once every five years, more than half of the world's population living in cities with 100,000 or more inhabitants are victims of a crime of some kind . . . World wide, urban violence is estimated to have grown by between 3 and 5 per cent a year over the last two decades, although there are large variations between nations and between different cities within nations in the scale of urban violence and in the extent of its growth. Violent crime has increased in most cities in recent years – and generally as a proportion of all crimes. It includes murder (or homicide), infanticide, assault, rape and sexual abuse and domestic violence and it now makes up between 25 and 30 per cent of urban crimes in many countries . . . High levels of urban crime and perhaps especially of violent crime are bringing major changes in the spatial form of many cities and of their built up areas and public spaces. Violent crimes are more visible in cities, and they help create a sense of insecurity that generates distrust, intolerance, the withdrawal of individuals from community life, and in some instances violent reactions. Increasingly, higher-income groups are living, working, shopping and taking their leisure in what are essentially fortified enclaves and are no longer making use of streets or public spaces which are abandoned to the homeless and the street children.

Table 1: Per cent of the Population who are victims of crime in urban areas with more than 100,000 inhabitants over a 5-year period

	Theft and damage of vehicles	Burglary	Other theft	Assault and other crimes of personal contact*	All crimes
West Europe	34%	16%	27%	15%	60%
North America	43%	24%	25%	20%	65%
South America	25%	20%	33%	31%	68%
East Europe	27%	18%	28%	17%	56%
Asia	12%	13%	25%	11%	44%
Africa	24%	38%	42%	33%	76%
Total	29%	20%	29%	19%	61%

* Includes mugging, aggravated theft, grievous bodily harm, sexual assault.

(UNCHS, 1996*b*, p. 123)

stable neighbourhoods, integrated into systems of networks, clubs and informal relationships. The same process is under way in many developing cities with a growing wealthy or middle-class population.

In the core cities, the growth of professional and managerial occupations and the rise of young, university-educated inhabitants with a strong cultural orientation towards the facilities of the inner city has led to the spread of gentrification accompanied by high quality services and differentiated cultural activities, while former working-class areas either became gentrified or, very often, were given over to a new influx of foreign immigrants. The upgrading was accompanied by new neighbourhood-oriented lifestyles; traffic calming in many areas gave the streets back to the inhabitants. In spite of the growth of out-of-town shopping centres small inner-city shops still flourish with a more personal range of goods and services. Former factories are transformed into art centres or host leisure activities, demonstrating how in an age of transient experience, enduring old structures can become the basis of new life, giving cities depth and a sense of memory, retaining the past in the present, allowing people to show their sense of belonging to their city and their affection for it.

In contrast to the wealthy suburbanites and the central city gentrifiers, many social or public housing estates built in the 1960s or 1970s are increasingly inhabited by members of minority groups. Here, unemployment tends to be high. Broken families and young mothers with children living on welfare are signs of a segregated society: the socially and economically integrated parts of society experience less and less spatial contact with the low-income, poorly-integrated households, who are locked into areas of reduced economic activity, suffering basic difficulties in getting access to the labour market, and are thus locked out, bystanders in an otherwise lively and active urban scene.

These differences are exacerbated by differential migration. In developed countries, poor immigrants – including increased numbers of refugees from political conflict or persecution – usually try to find their first homes in the cities, often in the most decayed public housing where no one else is prepared to live. They may share these with excluded sections of the indigenous population, the long-term structural unemployed, those suffering chronic problems of physical or mental health, and those in dysfunctional household units: 'the mad, the bad and the sad'. Conditions on these estates are often depressing, with decaying physical structures, high crime rates and a pervasive fear of crime, and a prevalence of anti-social behaviour accompanied by a breakdown of social relationships and civic standards.

Those able to do so leave for better conditions elsewhere in the cities or in the suburbs. Concerns about crime and poor school standards tend to drive white-collar families with children to the suburbs. The city may increasingly become the residence of choice only of single people and childless couples, who prefer to live close to their jobs, and whose lifestyle depends on the availability of public space in the form of shops, restaurants, bars and meeting places.

In developing cities differences are even more radical. On the one side, there is American-style suburbanization of the wealthy; on the other side, informal low-rise high-density shanty towns, with their separated local economy, their own networks and self-help organizations, their family traditions and their highly differentiated self-organized economy. Here also are found the urban social movements which organize land occupations, and which sometimes provide a rare but much-needed element of social order. Such cities, well illustrated by examples in Latin America, are the extremes of the segregated city with different lifestyles based on differences in income. The same is true of Africa, save here the privileged are far fewer in number. Here the explosive urban growth has transformed the inherited concentric spatial form of the traditional colonial city by multi-nuclear urban spaces, each of which maintains a substantial degree of independence. A deconcentration of production and service activities within a diversity of neighbourhoods is under way. Differences of quality and stages of urbanization co-exist.

The concentration of poor people or of illegal immigrants in specific areas of cities has far-reaching consequences. There is widespread concern in many developing cities, but also in cities in advanced countries, about unequal access to education and about uneven performance standards. Many schools in poverty and minority areas record below-average performance. Many children of disadvantaged parents, living in spatially concentrated poverty areas, will find that their initial disadvantages of birth will be progressively deepened and exaggerated, leading to the threat that their disadvantage may replicate itself in the next generation.

Undereducation is thus probably the most serious disadvantage; others, like overcrowding or daily stress, are aggravated by violence and even high crime rates.

U.S., U.K. and West German cities are undergoing functional transformations from being centers of goods processing to centers of information processing. The data for the U.S. show that the education levels associated with urban jobs have risen faster than that of the labour pool – particularly the minority labour pool – to be found in those cities . . . These minority populations in the U.S. and Europe were attracted by the economic opportunities cities had to offer. A dynamic of family reunification and chain migration was set in motion that resulted in increasing minority populations even after the opportunities had dwindled. The result has been high unemployment and social distress in our urban centers.

(Kasarda, 1997, pp. 308-309)

Families with Children: The New Urban Minority

Changing lifestyles reflect reactions to different phenomena. Mass affluence is obviously very important. Of relevance are also: declining household size; changing values; different structure of professions; higher education; higher mobility; declining density of urban development; higher wealth; increased flows of information and information overload – combined with a few dominant trends like growing suburban lifestyles or the increasing relevance of singles. Immigration and other factors such as discriminating housing markets have resulted in growing ethnic or income segregation.

Around these dominant trends one can observe a multitude of individualistic differentiations based on social milieu and specific values (alternative green lifestyles, traditional religious values with the consequence of family oriented lifestyles, health and sports oriented lifestyles, and all kinds of freaky minorities centred around special cults and habits from eating to cultural activities). High income and individualism are the breeding ground of a multitude of lifestyles in wealthy cities, which make political integration and a reliable solidarity less likely and more difficult to establish and protect.

The most relevant indicator is the declining household size observable in most cities. In developing cities the number of children is declining, while in developed cities the number of childless couples and the number of singles is growing rapidly.

Box II.11. Nairobi: A city without citizens.

In 1945, Nairobi was a city with more than 100,000 inhabitants (61,000 black, 10,000 white, 35,000 Indian inhabitants). In 1965, the population reached a quarter of a million, the number of white people had grown to 25,000, the number of Indian people to 95,000. Since then, the white and Indian population has declined while the total population has reached more than two million (approximate estimates). These inhabitants, whose parents invariably lived elsewhere, lack the 'Nairobian' background of parents and grandparents who lived there, very often in the same neighbourhood, who grew up in a stable culture with stable habits and a stable political local system. Civic society is weak, it is difficult to be proud to be a 'Nairobian'. One assumes that cities are melting pots, but melting needs time. The influx of people coming from different regions, with different tribal or national roots, into a weak economic system, where large parts of the population struggle to survive, is too rapid to permit easy integration. Even the normal communal bond, the common language is missing . . .

Comparing Nairobi with cities that have a strong city society and social capital which has been built up over centuries, we find explosive population growth, varied sources of migration, lack of common national tradition, a weak political and administrative system and a weak formal sector which . . . results in a fragmented unstable complex which is not urban in the true sense. It is in an early state of integration and it will take time before the social change forms a new urban society. The contrast – between a population still not rooted in a city where many come merely to try to find work, leaving their families in the villages and cities where shops have been owned generations by the same family, where property owners have inherited from their parents – could not be more extreme. It shows that in a world of rapid social change, the label 'urban' has different meanings, the consequences of which are often underestimated.

(Krabbe, 1994)

Childless living is one factor which explains the growth of leisure activities, the growing habit of eating out, of short vacations or long weekends. The declining number of families is mostly seen as a deficit or even a crisis of urban living. As most young people in cities do not plan a childless life, the growth of childless living seems to be an adjustment to outside pressures which is more a defeat than a free decision based on preferred lifestyles. Family values are strong but not strong enough to overcome scarcity of time, career stress or scarcity of neighbourhoods which are family oriented.

The long term costs of cities which are not geared to the needs of families and children are probably high. A restructuring of cities for families and children would be an act of self-interest. But the self-interest does not seem strong enough to change the tide.

Lifestyles cannot be separated from the built environment they are connected to or from the economic base which carries them. Values and lifestyles in urban development create change, orchestrated by the economic constellations which dominate people's lives. The more people escape from poverty or unemployment, the higher are their chances for self-expression and the better are their opportunities to participate in an urban life which gives a sense of belonging and connectedness. But far too many are left behind, with no choice at all: 'lifestyle', for many of the world's urban population, depends on a level of income to which they can never aspire.

Social Change and the Built Environment

People express themselves in the buildings they live in and the neighbourhoods they frequent. The high-rise tower next to the park is a demonstration of a privileged private life. The semi-detached single or two-family house in its typical price range expresses a desire to belong to a group of similar people. Buildings in cities are always public because they create the communal environment; they are part of neighbourhoods and the physical basis for social networks. The 'hardware city' of infrastructure and buildings is interrelated with the 'software city' of habits, traditions, networks, markets and social relationships. Social change therefore cannot but demonstrate itself in a change of the built city.

The rapid growth of developing cities, the extreme inequality, the duality between the different stages of the informal sector and the formal sector, the luxury and poverty side by side in the same urban fabric, create a very fragmented, incoherent, disrupted city which does not grow or change smoothly. Rapid growth and extreme inequality lead to radical measures of urban surgery, like highway construction which bulldozes informal settlements, or urban renewal schemes which clear poor people's informal houses to accommodate new central area functions like offices or retailing.

In typical developing cities, 40-60 per cent of the population live in an underserviced, neglected informal sector. The only choice they seem to have is between gentrification or ghettoization. The intermediate group daily becomes smaller, as the remaining middle classes leave for the suburbs.

At the other end of the scale are medium-sized service cities with high-income, stable populations, like Basle, Zürich, Freiburg or Karlsruhe. They develop smoothly; old buildings can be protected as opportunity costs are low, suburbs can be developed in small piecemeal attachments to existing settlements, the attractive open landscapes make it easy to develop a political consensus against American-type sprawl. High-density living and high-density development form part of a widely-shared system of community values, which includes a welfare base with links into all

Box II.12. Social transformation in Johannesburg.

The inner city of Johannesburg is undergoing radical social transformation. Previously off-limits to blacks, it has been racially, economically and demographically restructured as over 250,000 blacks have taken up residence there during the past eleven years. The overwhelming majority of these are migrants and, given the absence of stable black institutions, the inner city is also becoming an increasingly desperate place, living on an edge without a strong core of cohesiveness . . . Despite increased tensions and white flight, the inner city retains a strong multiracial character . . . The accelerated turnover of the population of the central city, which has changed from being 80% white ten years ago to 70% black today, has provided a cover for the sizeable immigration of foreign Africans to Johannesburg and a socio-cultural transformation of inner city life and commerce. The various migrant groups have found 'niches' in Johannesburg's urban space and economy. For example, Mozambicans and Angolans have increasingly gravitated to remote peripheral urban areas, where most live in conditions of extreme destitution. Southern Africans work as artisans, hawkers and clerks in the established black townships. The inner city neighbourhoods contain large numbers of Mozambicans and Zimbabweans, but also significant numbers of Zairois and others from francophone countries. The national groupings themselves present a heterogeneity of disparate interests, allegiances and social classes. Despite the significance of this phenomenon for urban planning and policy, there has not yet been an adequate assessment of the demographic composition of the central city. Transient populations and rapid turnover rates, in both occupancy and ownership of inner city dwellings, make conventional social surveying difficult . . . The absence of durable community institutions and particularly schools in the central city means there are few countervailing forces acting against the territorialization of residential space according to nation. Foreign Africans increasingly dominate the informal trading sector in the central city.

(Simone, 1997)

neighbourhoods. Cities like Freiburg have an easy task: political differences are small, inequality is tolerable and stable. They are not comparable to the big mega-cities of North America which have developed in a different tradition, with different planning concepts and different value systems. The Los Angeles experience shows the enormous gap between such a western North American car-oriented city, and a medium-sized middle-income European-style public transport-oriented city. Such a comparison also shows how far we have to go if we are to reduce tensions arising from social change, and to create the basis for greater economic and social equality which will find expression in the physical fabric of a city. Cities mirror societies, cities mirror social change. Good urban design is not possible in a fragmented and unequal urban society.

As long as migrants pour into cities in large numbers, accepting overcrowded tenements and high-density shantytowns, rapid turnover and shifting of ethnic groups and social classes will be the rule in certain parts of certain cities. In the 1990s, Johannesburg, a target for huge numbers of illegal foreign immigrants, has become a new African melting pot.

Trends in Civil Society

Applications of main technological innovations, such as information and communication technology and biotechnology, are increasingly affecting the urban future. Meanwhile, the change of work and free time remain on the urban scenario agenda, together with the need for changing attitudes and values, engaging in life long learning and endorsing empowerment and self-reliance to achieve alternative lifestyles. Positive scenarios include: sharing work, civic duties and economic resources among the entire population throughout the whole life cycle, autonomous and self-sufficient actions by individuals and local collectives, as well as new forms of participatory local organization. Subsidiary, local autonomy and self-reliance are bound to increase with greater involvement of consumers as entrepreneurs. Their actions include skill bartering, local currency and neighbourhood support networks, practised extensively in the informal urban economy of developing cities. Local economic entrepreneurs will show greater territorial loyalty as their flexible work practices will be bound into local economic and social networks and supply local markets.

Social relations will continue to change within the family, with further fragmentation and continued high rates of divorce or separation. But they will be treated less as individual failures and more as consequence of highly mobile and individualistic modern lifestyles. In particular, young single mothers will receive more assistance. On the one hand, young persons will leave their family unit earlier, and older persons will live alone; on the other, closer knit neighbourhood communities, tenant associations, credit unions, mutual assistance bodies, peer group space sharing and travel, and many other local networks are forming and will continue to form. Such interest groupings, including religious, ethnic, cultural, leisure, as well as occupational ones, substitute more and more for blood relations and obligations. Together with the voluntary sector, they will drive urban development just as much as the curtailed public sector.

Connections between Micro and Macro Worlds

These changes in socio-economic and cultural relations at the local level will interact with macro-economic changes resulting from globalization. Monopolistic concentration through mergers and acquisitions is seen to weaken competitive powers in the longer term and to offer new opportunities for small and medium size enterprises, woven into the local economy and urban culture.

Signs of changing values are also becoming apparent in local governance. Involvement of all stakeholders in local affairs, not just the accredited traditional electorate, is becoming increasingly widespread. Urban development agencies and neighbourhood pressure groups are new forces displacing traditional public management, at least in part.

Similarly, those living in 'informal' housing are creating neighbourhood organizations which manage their local environment and urban needs. Demands for decentralization down to small urban entities may well be a reaction to the growing number of supra- and international organizations and their concentration of powers. They are putting pressure on local democracy, as urban dwellers cannot and do not wish to identify with far distant levels of government, and feel that powers at local level are being eroded. Greater involvement of the private sector in urban services through privatization, contracting out, concessions and downsizing is compounding the frailties of local democracy. An example of how trust in local public institutions and politicians is waning is the weakening of public sector intervention, planning and development control in cities. Local fiscal policies are also curtailed by international agreements and geo-political dimensions of planning (such as international airline requirements, superhighway networks, etc.).

Akin to developments in the private sector, public top-down hierarchical and autocratic institutions may well have to give way to accountable flat management structures with continuous public participation and stronger checks and balances than the traditional voting system. However, real devolution of power, with related fiscal and material resources, to the local level of cities and neighbourhoods still encounters resistance. Remaining a fundamental force of future cities, the form of local governance has not evolved to reach the expectations of the most demanding reformers. The flows of people, goods, capital and information (Castells' 'space of flows') are creating a global network of nodes where urban powers will

101

concentrate (Castells, 1996, p. 348). Nevertheless, while urban communities may attenuate territorial identity and break up localism (Castells' 'space of place'), they will also have to invent new forms of local decision making and controls from the bottom up to sustain their quality of urban life.

It could be argued that local governments are losing their *raison d'être*; add to that the theoretical possibility of electronic decision making by the local population (though rejected by political bodies), and city government as we know it might become redundant. Genuine devolution of powers instead of 'empowerment' or 'enablement' (arguably top down notions) may be the answer to the stubborn residue of urban problems, in particular the provision of sufficient and adequate housing and work, especially in the developing world. There is no reason why liberal principles which are granted to markets should not apply to the individual.

Numerous examples (for instance, the informal economy in Latin America) show that the poorest pay many times more for their basic needs compared to the better off. Why should the inhabitants of these often 'informal' areas not be free to supply their own basic utilities on a more level playing field? Their informal local economy of essentially non-tradable goods and services is already making up the bulk of large cities in the developing world. They have produced their own housing, often successfully in very adverse conditions (no tenure, threat of eviction, no infrastructure, remote location from work opportunities, worst physical and topographical conditions, etc.). The proof of their success is the gradual absorption of their housing into the formal sector. Their way of mobilizing their own resources and organizing their own development collectively according to their own values and wishes could perhaps become a model for future more accountable and accepted local governance.

More assertive protest movements, more self-help and direct action, more self-assured entrepreneurship by more assertive consumers – all these reflect a change in the behaviour of citizens who are dissatisfied with low service delivery and want a greater say in the way (urban) administration is affecting their lives. Without necessarily changing existing urban institutions, attitudes and values towards local governance need changing to achieve greater people empowerment. Local administrations need to come to terms with community action and respond positively to collective and individual lifestyles based on changing values and behaviour. Urban lifestyles and aspirations will influence the local economy, the real estate market and more generally urban ways of life, just as much as information technology or globalization, and shape the future of cities. Unless they take into account the local context and stage of urban development and unless they obtain the support of the local population, urban policies devised by politicians are difficult to achieve and unlikely to become reality.

The standard of living of the developed cities in the developed world will depend very much on the way they solve the growing problems of inequality, especially inequality in education. Cities which are going to be competitive and human in the future have to be cities of learning and equal access to learning, and cities of order shared by individuals who tolerate each other.

Put bluntly, if countries wish to carry on becoming richer, their people have to learn to behave better.

(McRae, 1994)

Social tension, crime and inequality in a world of ever increasing mobility of capital and talents will become self-defeating in economic terms. This is the central social challenge that cities face in preparing for the twenty-first century.

Environment

What is ecology? A taxi painted green? In Mexico City, taxis painted green are called 'ecological taxis' and a few sickly-colored trees that survive the stampede of cars are called 'ecological parks'. . . The Metropolitan Commission for the Prevention and Control of Environmental Pollution recommends, and I quote, that on very polluted days (and nearly all are) the residents of this city 'should go out of doors as little as possible, keep doors, windows and vents closed, and not exercise between 10 a.m. and 4 p.m.' . . . To travel by bicycle on the streets of any large Latin American city, which have no bike lanes, is a most practical way of committing suicide . . . Cars don't vote, but politicians are terrified of causing them the slightest displeasure.

(Eduardo Galeano, 1995)

Problems created by man can be solved by man.

(John F. Kennedy)

Nature as Resource, Space and Environment

The Concept – A Triple Role

Cities are concentrations of buildings, production, consumption and transportation. They need labour, capital, technology, natural resources and space as inputs for working and living. Any listing of the different factors in urban development makes it manifestly clear how important but how difficult is the balance that must be struck in order to achieve sustainable urban development. For instance: increasing welfare through rising income and production will – other things being equal – mean more jobs, more cars and more housing, which in turn will need more space and more natural resources. Thus, increased welfare through rising income will reduce the quality of the natural environment, which in turn – since human beings are part of nature, and need contact with it, just as they need food and shelter – will reduce welfare.

Seen more closely, nature plays a complex triple role in urban development:

- As a resource input;

- As a location space; and

- As a shell for our emotional and physical existence; that is, as a consumer good.

This triple role propels all nature-related policies and behaviour into a central position in urban development, creating a demand for innovative solutions which can reduce the trade-offs, sometimes painful, between different needs and priorities, many of them urgent but also conflicting. And these conflicts are most pressing in developing cities, because there:

- Technology and capital are scarce, so that use of resources is often very wasteful;

- Poverty and the struggle for daily survival allow little concern for the needs of future generations. Technology can overcome some of the constraints nature places on us, but it is often expensive, and the poor often cannot afford to wait; because they cannot afford the bulldozers to carve terraces in the hills, they build their homes on unhealthy and hazardous floodplains.

Cities and Nature

This triple relationship between nature and cities has shaped cities in the past and will shape cities in the future.

Cities are man-made physical structures, placed in natural settings. Well-planned, well-built cities – Paris, Prague, Washington DC, Canberra, New Delhi – exist in aesthetic harmony with nature. But during the entire twentieth century, the relationship between urban form (or the built environment) and nature has generated an unending source of tensions, and controversies in urban design. Thus, the traditional high-density city dominated by the geometrically-repeated building block – Berlin, New York City – offered easy access to open landscape but internally not much space for nature; a city like London, with its unusually low density and numerous neighbourhood parks, was a rare exception.

The garden city solution, proposed by Ebenezer Howard at the very end of the nineteenth century, was one answer to the problem of the over-compact, over-dense nineteenth-century city; the Corbusian city of towers, set in an open parkland landscape, was another. The first sought to return human beings to nature, by creating a new settlement form, 'Town-

Country'; the second sought to compensate them for their loss of daily contact with nature by producing private or semiprivate space, in balconies above ground, in parklands around the apartment towers. In the best examples – in British new towns like Harlow or Milton Keynes, or the Barra da Tijuca in Rio with its clusters of big towers or the Hansa-Quarter in Berlin built in 1952 as part of a building exhibition – these built forms realize the potential of their original visionary precursors. But too often, replicated without imagination and with too little funding, both can produce substandard environments. Neither under-serviced suburbs of tract housing lacking public open space, sprawling low-density areas nor high-rise towers set in a no-man's land lacking any real natural quality, offered an adequate resolution of the constant tension between nature and urbanity. In the 1960s, Jane Jacobs called for a return to traditional urban patterns, with high-density housing set in traditional streets; and the 'new urbanism' of the 1990s clearly reflects her influence. But it can all too easily result in a return to the nineteenth-century city where all sense of nature is lost. So far, no enduring solution has been found. The nineteenth-century consensus has disappeared. Nature and city provide one of the unsolved questions for the agenda of twenty-first-century urban planning.

Cities and the Environment

Further, though they are remarkably economical users of land, cities constantly need more resources and are constantly growing, from the urban core into suburbs and from suburbs into exurbs, separating people more and more distantly from natural landscape. Thus planning has to work with real estate markets, to reconcile need for urban building space and open landscape. The tension between spatial urban growth, the need to respect ecosystems and the growing scarcity of resources pose one of the deepest contradictions for mankind.

Paradoxically, they are the consequence of both poverty and wealth. Thus, though all cities share in some global environmental challenges, such as global warming and limits of spatial growth, the nature of the environmental problem is different, even contrary, in poor and rich cities. Poverty forces people to live in a day-to-day struggle for survival, ignoring longer-term consequences; it compels the inefficient use of natural resources to produce basic goods, from housing to food; it enforces 'overuse' and neglect of the natural environment. Thus, in a typical low-income country, people depend for fuels very much on biomass in the form of wood, dung, wheat, straw, coconut shell, cotton sticks, rice hull, corn husk, bagasse, tobacco husk and similar materials. But they generally pay more for energy, and are unlikely to be able to make the investments that are necessary to make use of higher-quality foods; so they actually increase their poverty. Not only this: the use of biomass has a negative impact on

105

health, especially when burned indoors, and so may promote higher medical expenses and diminish the ability of poor people to work productively. Finally, insofar as the use of biomass in urban areas promotes deforestation, its costs may increase in future, further diminishing the living standards of the poor. Similarly, the poor cannot afford piped water and have to pay more to obtain water from carriers or from polluted wells; they cannot afford proper sewerage systems, and so may suffer from public health problems.

Rich cities have to cope with vested interests, including enormous fixed investment in the past. Together with lack of awareness and the lack of clean technologies, they create growing risks for the environment, in particular through their large and growing 'ecological footprint' on the resource base. The only good news is that sustainable development can overcome the challenge of poverty alleviation and environmental degradation, and that richer cities generate new forces, new coalitions, in support of environmentally-sustainable policies:

- As the need to balance ecological factors and human settlement requirements becomes more urgent;

- As the direct need for nature becomes stronger;

- As improved technology makes it easier to pollute less, to save energy and resources;

- As long-term concerns become better recognized.

Environmental imperatives force urban decision-makers into a race for sustainable development – thus shaping the city, the transportation system, or the mode of production so that they become progressively more environmentally sustainable.

Challenges to the Urban Environment

Cities as Risk and as Chance

No city is well prepared for a sustainable future. All cities cause climate change, emitting toxic chemicals; all participate in the extinction of species or are active in deforestation through growing the consumption of goods. As many cities are located next to oceans, a high percentage of marine degradation is a consequence of urban waste. Only a few cities record a diminution in environmental problems. Urban environmental problems – air pollution, overuse of water resources, climate change, resource degradation – cross all city borders, threatening health, prosperity and jobs. Urban systems are interrelated through global markets and global environmental problems. They share problems and responsibilities.

Box II.13. Industrialization in the nineteenth century.

Manchester 1835

Thirty or forty factories rise on the tops of the hills . . . Their six stories tower up; their huge enclosures give notice from afar of the centralization of industry. The wretched dwellings of the poor are scattered haphazard around them. Round them stretches land uncultivated but without the charm of rustic nature, and still without the amenities of a town. The soil has been taken away, scratched and torn up in a thousand places, but it is not yet covered with the habitations of men. The land is given over to industry's use . . .

Look up and all around this place and you will see the huge palaces of industry. You will hear the noise of furnaces, the whistle of steam. These vast structures keep air and light out of the human habitations which they dominate; they envelope them in perpetual fog; here is the slave, there the master; there is the wealth of some, here the poverty of most; there the society has not yet learnt to give. Here the weakness of the individual seems more feeble and helpless even than in the middle of a wilderness. A sort of black smoke covers the city. The sun seen through it is a disc without rays. Under this half-daylight 300,000 human beings are ceaselessly at work. A thousand noises disturb this dark, damp labyrinth, but they are not at all the ordinary sounds one hears in great cities. . .

The footsteps of a busy crowd, the crunching wheels of machinery, the shriek of steam from boilers, the regular beat of the looms, the heavy rumble of carts, those are the noises from which you can never escape in the sombre half-light of these streets. You will never hear the clatter of hoof as the rich man drives back home or out on expeditions of pleasure. Never the gay shouts of people amusing themselves, or music heralding a holiday. You will never see smart folk strolling at leisure in the streets, or going out on innocent pleasure parties in the surrounding country. Crowds are ever hurrying this way and that in the Manchester streets, but their footsteps are brisk, their looks preoccupied, and their appearance sombre and harsh . . .

(de Tocqueville, 1835, pp. 117,118)

Coketown 1854

Seen from distance in such weather, Coketown lay shrouded in a haze of its own, which appeared impervious to the sun's rays. You only knew the town was there, because you knew there could have been no such sulky blotch upon the prospect without a town. A blur of soot and smoke, now confusedly tending this way, now that way, now aspiring to the vault of Heaven, now murkily creeping along the earth, as the wind rose and fell, or changed its quarter: a dense formless jumble, with sheets of cross light in it, that showed nothing but masses of darkness: – Coketown in the distance suggestive of itself, though not a brick of it could be seen.

(Dickens, 1854, p. 125)

In environmental terms, cities are both a problem and an opportunity. They are a problem because the high concentration of people, production, consumption of energy, water, goods and services puts enormous stress on the local and global environment. Cities play a central role in degrading the environment. Since the very beginning of industrialization, high concentrations of exploitative production have turned natural areas into scenes of devastation. Industrialization has made very attractive buildings and cities possible, but at the same time in other places has butchered nature and devastated the landscape, as many observers have described in shock and fascination.

Modern cities have developed new types of degraded landscapes. Vast highway systems connect shopping centres, factory areas, suburban housing, leisure centres, sports facilities, warehouses and office parks, interrupted by railroad lines and other networks which create residual pieces of land, unusable for any purposes. Year by year, urban sprawl invades fragile ecosystems or so far undisturbed nature. Cities are nodes of consumption of energy and water and areas of highly concentrated pollution. Growing water needs result in ever growing distances to obtain water, with the consequence that farming or the ecosystem will be affected. Cities as agglomerations of buildings – often high-rise buildings – cut into the soil, seal large areas or cover them with waste and toxic materials. Recycling is usually technically possible but often too costly and difficult. Parts of cities become uninhabitable or unhealthy. Not infrequently, after periods of urban use large areas have to be sealed off as health hazards. In other cases landslides or flooding are a consequence of urban development which neglects nature and its needs, or of development in dangerous locations. Planning has often proved too slow, too reluctant to intervene, or based on unrealistically high standards which were ignored, with the consequence that poor people were forced to live on land that presented serious hazards.

In spite of this urban environmental degradation, cities are also potential solutions – or at least provide advantages: dense concentrations of people, production and buildings present the opportunity to economize on scarce environmental goods. In cities a large percentage of all energy is used for heating and cooling, production and mobility. Saving energy is a general economic and political objective, but cities can be especially successful in achieving it, as energy-saving technologies can be diffused faster than in dispersed areas. Heat from energy production can be used for heating buildings and does not have to be lost to water or air. High-density living increases the return on energy-saving measures and makes them economically more viable compared to areas of urban sprawl.

Many cities have been very successful in developing creative policies to promote their own sustainability. They have maintained medium to high densities which support good public transport services. Thus they have shifted the modal split away from car use and into environmentally advantageous mass transit systems. They have developed co-generation of heat and power, introduced two-part tariffs to reduce the use of energy, encouraged the insulation of buildings, and developed more sustainable planning concepts. Some European cities – Zürich, Freiburg, Basle, Karlsruhe, Copenhagen, Bologna – have provided the models which many other cities have emulated.

Box II.14. Copenhagen, strengthening the city centre.

Changes in mobility patterns are seen to be most difficult as car ownership and use is also related to other socially motivating factors such as status preservation and recognition. The example of Copenhagen in Denmark, however, shows with regard to transport policies that a change in behavioural patterns can be achieved with an integrative approach, a combination of municipal instruments, and within an appropriate but mid- to long-term time frame. Conventional wisdom was said to be 'Denmark has never had a strong urban culture', 'Danes will never get out of their cars, and 'Danes do not promenade like Italians'. Within twenty years, starting with an transit-oriented urban form and faced with problems that would arise from the growing use of private cars, traffic was reduced considerably and the public realm was made more attractive. Social and recreational activities in the streets tripled making the city area more vital. Another result was that the market for semi-detached houses on the urban periphery was declining because it was seen to be 'too far away' from the attractive centre. Measures introduced and continuously maintained for years were a combination of city housing projects, reduction in the space for parking, pedestrianization of streets, measures to make streets more attractive to pedestrians and to street life in general.

(UNCHS, 1996*b*, p. 318)

Environmental Knowledge – A Precondition for Action

Urban dwellers, for the most part, live separated from the production processes of the goods they use. They have only limited knowledge of the ecological consequences. The ecological footprint, as a measure to fill an ecological information gap, can substitute for this lack of personal experience. It is a method for estimating the area of productive land required to produce the necessary energy and materials for production and to get rid of the waste generated through present-day lifestyles of urban dwellers. The footprint index is a simple measure to demonstrate the enormous ecological space that even high-density cities need for their day-to-day existence. It shows how far away most cities still are from sustainable development and how far distant the idea of sustainability still is from our everyday urban culture and from our current urban political debates.

Box II.15. A new philosophy of a sustainable industrial enterprise.

An example of an enterprise that seems to have succeeded in changing its philosophy is Interface Inc in the USA, a worldwide enterprise in commercial and institutional interiors. Its vision is to become the first sustainable industrial enterprise in the world, constantly striving to reduce its footprint and taking nothing from the Earth that is not renewable. To do so requires that the company examines every facet of its operations, from the shop floor to the boardroom; reinventing commerce in the process, completely changing relationships with employees, customers and suppliers. In 1995, the Chairman articulated the new philosophy after running the company for more than twenty-three years with no thought to the environment beyond regulatory compliance. Sustainability is now perceived as a strategic commitment positioning Interface to compete in a global marketplace; an arena where companies will be forced to rely less on finite natural resources. His 'awakening' is said to have become his life's mission and he put his personal reputation and company's credibility on the line when he publicly committed to this ambitious course.

Issues to be addressed are:

- energy efficiency,
- producer responsibility,
- production/consumption cycles,
- resource conservation,
- waste reuse and recycling,
- water use and consumption.

(UN Best Practices Database)

Sustainable urban development as a concept is well understood, but this does not mean that it has become the leading principle of everyday life. An American citizen imposes twenty times the environmental burden of a Bangladeshi resident, and – as already noted in Chapter I – an earth three times the present size would be needed to sustain 6 billion people whose consumption patterns were those of today's average Canadian. Measured in terms of sustainability requirements, the 'North' is either totally overpopulated or hopelessly resource-profligate.

An Unsustainable Present

No city today is environmentally sustainable. Only the types of unsustainable development vary. In rich cities people own more CO_2-emitting cars and use more energy. In poor cities they lack sewer systems or clean water, and their old, poorly maintained cars pour out pollution, thus exposing their citizens to unacceptably high health hazards.

Box II.16. People – the source of pollution and degradation.

In addition, people are the ultimate source of environmental pollution and degradation. As the number of people grows, the quality of the earth's environment can only fall. Environmental projects are merely holding actions that slow the rate of decline. Over the course of its lifetime an American baby born in 1990 produced 1 million kilograms of atmospheric waste, 10 million kilograms of liquid waste, and 1 million kilograms of solid waste. To have the average American standard of living, he or she needed to consume 700,000 kilograms of minerals, 24 billion BTUs of energy (4,000 barrels of oil), 25,000 kilograms of plant foods, and 28,000 kilograms of animal products (the slaughter of 2,000 animals).

(Thurow, 1996)

Local governments in developed and developing cities are confronted with too many demands and too limited fiscal capacity to fulfil all urgent needs. In developing cities, lack of resources is the overriding bottleneck. In developed cities, vested interests and sunken capital which does not allow rapid responses form an obstacle. And in all types of cities, ignorance and neglect make it difficult to set the right priorities necessary to promote sustainable environmental urban development.

Income growth both poses dangers and improves the opportunities for solutions. It poses dangers because growing income means more and bigger cars, more housing, more travel, more use of sports facilities or other leisure activities. Rich people are environmentally more dangerous or risky than poor people, because poor people do not have the means to pollute in the same way. But poor people suffer more severely from environmental deficits, as lack of clean drinking water or adequate sewer systems creates serious health hazards. The risks for rich people are more indirect, and this may explain their low willingness to pay for more investment in the environment.

Environment and Urban Development

Urban environmental problems thus depend on stages of development. Poverty in basic consumer goods in developing cities creates a parallel poverty in environmental goods and thus becomes the enemy of the environment. However, poverty is foremost the enemy of people. Poverty, dirty technologies and unhealthy living go together.

The immediate crisis and the global concerns cannot be isolated. They are intertwined and distinct. Resources used to combat global warming cannot be used against polluted water, or to reduce child mortality. The trade-offs between different goals enforce difficult choices on urban and national governments and on individual people. These trade-offs can sometimes dramatically be reduced. Innovations can reduce poverty of income and environmental poverty at the same time. But as long as scarcities reign over our lives, they will never disappear. In the short run all cities have to make difficult choices. In a long- and medium-term perspective technical or organizational progress can reduce trade-offs and conflicts, as it should be possible to increase labour productivity and save energy in production at the same time. It is possible to reduce the trade-off between more private market goods and more environmental goods. This needs investment and research, adjustment of behaviour and better public management techniques. At the heart of all problems and their solutions we find the need for

- A permanent search for improvements to create the necessary technical progress;

- Willingness by individuals to adjust behaviour and by politics to generate the right incentives and the right regulatory framework.

Development changes the structure of the local economy and therefore the nature of environmental problems. As economic activities in cities become less and less extractive or energy-intensive in nature, economic development tends to reduce pollution or energy consumption. This means that local environmental problems can be solved. However urban plus economic development results in higher income, thus generating more and more traffic, more and more space demands, and increases in heating or cooling energy; as a result, there is an increase in global problems like changing climate. There is no linear progress in overcoming environmental poverty: rich cities can be environmentally poor, since pollution does not disappear automatically; rich cities create enormous risks as CO_2 emissions threaten the climate and the basis of urban prosperity.

Growing income, in many cities in an early state of demographic evolution, can increase pollution, as higher income generates more resource-intensive consumption patterns, and as cleaner technologies are not used. In later phases, improved information and preferences for a green environment, clean air and healthy living strengthen political support for environmental strategies.

Of course there are quite radical differences as a consequence of different political traditions, values and power structures. Figure II.4 symbolizes the different choices. Poor cities have a limited ability to invest in environmental and public goods as basic needs (food, clothing, housing use up most of their income). Wealthy cities have more freedom of choice, as the different shapes of the stars demonstrate. They can put priority on private consumption (US-type development) or give more weight to environmental and public goods, symbolized by the example of Sweden.

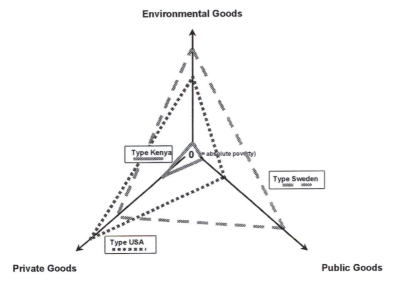

Figure II.4. Choices of investment.

Cities at the same income level may thus undertake very different efforts to achieve sustainable development. The range of choices is enormous. Gasoline consumption per inhabitant varies greatly as between high-density cities with highly-developed mass transit systems and fuel-intensive urban sprawl type cities. Density reduces pollution; thus urban density poses probably the most important environmental choice cities can make.

This is especially relevant, because growing income allows more and more people to live in low-density areas, which increases pollution and energy consumption as long as we are constrained by the present technologies in transportation or building. In the future, when the fuel-cell based on renewable energies or new building technologies (smart buildings) will be available, a huge increase in our freedom of choice among a much wider variety of transport technologies and urban forms could be possible.

Urban Growth and Change

Cities in Competition

At the turn of the century, *globalization* and technological change have increasingly brought cities into worldwide economic competition. No place can be sure of retaining its traditional place in the urban hierarchy, its traditional role, for long. In the developed world, within a few years, cities have lost their manufacturing base to newly industrializing countries and cities in distant parts of the developing world. They have lost ports and port-related industries to estuarine locations that can take the big container ships. But they have enhanced their roles as financial nodes, as command and control centres of the new global economy, as preferred locations for the media and creative activities, and for conspicuous consumption and tourism. In the developing world, within less than half a century, cities have boomed as low-cost manufacturing locations, have traded up the learning curve to become high-technology locations, and have shed large parts of their manufacturing base to become command and control centres for vast new low-cost manufacturing regions that have mushroomed around them. The speed of change is breathtaking, and it will not slow down.

To understand what has been happening and will continue to happen in the early twenty-first century, we need a new concept of location and a new taxonomy of cities, both at a global scale. These need to encompass both changing relations *between* cities, and changes *within* city regions. The key is that despite the centrifugal impact of technological change, leading to constant decentralization and deconcentration at both scales – down the urban hierarchy from larger to smaller cities, outward from cores to suburbs and exurbs – there are still profoundly important centripetal forces or agglomeration effects, causing important areas of activity to cluster in the centres of the most important cities. This is particularly important for two kinds of service activities: high-technology producer services, such as banking and finance, command and control activities and media services, which require access to large amounts of information both electronically and face-to-face, and the lower-technology personal services (restaurants, bars, fast food outlets, hotels, clothes shops, haircutting salons, gymnasia, sports stadia, entertainment of all kinds) that cluster around them. The cores of the great global cities – London, New York, Tokyo – illustrate this symbiotic juxtaposition most perfectly; but it can be found in dozens of other cities which compete for global status, at least through niches in particular regions (San Francisco, Sydney, Buenos Aires) or in particular services (Paris, Zürich, Milan).

Other kinds of service activities do not need such high degrees of face-to-face information exchange, but are concerned with more routine information processing. These decentralize to concentrations of offices either at accessible points in the suburbs, or in the cores of smaller towns within the metropolitan orbit, which are effectively networked into the urban system of activity. Stamford and Greenwich in Connecticut, Croydon in London and Reading west of London, and Omiya in Saitama prefecture north-west of Tokyo are quintessential examples. What is most notable about them is that though decentralized, they are effectively reconcentrated, and are similarly served by a wide range of associated personal service functions, albeit less specialized than in the metropolitan cores.

Equally important, other kinds of specialized activity also exhibit the need to cluster in order to enjoy face-to-face contact. This is particularly true of so-called 'innovative milieux' housing high-technology industries, of which the classic cases include Silicon Valley, Highway 128 around Boston, Kanagawa Prefecture outside Tokyo, or the Western Crescent around London's Heathrow Airport. Generally these are dispersed at a metropolitan scale but are reconcentrated in science parks, often near motorway interchanges. Recently, in a significant development, these activities have begun to fuse with the traditional media activities of television and film-making, clustering both on the low-rent fringes of traditional downtown cores (New York's Silicon Alley, San Francisco's South of Market area, London's Soho) or in traditional high-technology areas (Silicon Valley, Los Angeles' Aerospace Alley). It also appears that some emerging high-technology production, and associated specialized start-up service activities, may be growing in highly accessible rural areas within two hours' travel from major downtowns and international airports (the Cambridge region and the Cotswolds in England, northern Marin County in California). These may represent the beginnings of a process of extended metropolitan diffusion, in which highly complex urban networks extend over far distances into the surrounding countryside.

The resulting taxonomy of cities is complex. Cities cannot be classified on one dimension alone. Size does matter, and places like Mexico City and São Paulo are important because they are among the world's largest urban areas. But function is also important, and neither of these places stands in the top rank when it comes to the specialization and global significance of their activities. Here, a few key indices – international air traffic, telephone and e-mail traffic and courier package traffic, hotel beds – are far more significant. Kinshasa is far larger than Frankfurt or Zürich, but Frankfurt and Zürich are far more significant as global centres.

In fact, a large part of the world's urban population is almost totally unrelated to the global economy; it makes few telephone calls, still fewer international ones, and its daily dealings are almost entirely conducted within the local neighbourhood. Even where it is connected, as with the workers of the Pearl River Delta who make electrical goods for export, the connection is a very indirect one: like their equivalents in nineteenth-century Lancashire, who made cotton textiles for the world, these people have no connection to the global economy save through the goods they manufacture.

Even in the most globalized cities, in fact, people live localized lives most of the time. Tycoons who fly the world business class come home to their families and spend their evenings and weekends in their local neighbourhoods. They shop locally, they go to local cinemas, they see local friends, they cultivate their gardens. Their children, who do not have driving licences, lead almost entirely local lives.

115

Thus, most people have contradictory demands and motives. They want space, in order to accommodate a growing variety of goods and activities: bulky consumer durables, especially cars, special study rooms for each of the children, home offices. But they also want access: to shops, schools, leisure, transport. And these are extremely difficult to reconcile. As these people grow older, as so many will in the developed cities, they may well care more about close access, and that may limit the spread of the city. Increasingly, we may see cities segregated by age and lifestyle: gregarious, vibrant, dense inner-city loft districts for the students and young professionals, suburbs and exurbs for child-bearing and child-rearing, and a return either to the city or to health resorts for the empty-nesters and the pensioners. But that will depend on income, and even in affluent cities not everyone will have the means to afford their preferred choice.

Global Winners and Losers

In the competition among these cities, international real estate investment plays a critical role. It produces a limited number of global champions: London, New York and Tokyo are preferential locations. But new contenders like Shanghai, Bangkok or Moscow arise within a very few years, becoming members of a premier league of locations.

This extreme concentration of international investment demonstrates at the same time that most of the other cities are still dominated by local investors and local finance. Even in highly developed economies like Germany, only a few cities – Frankfurt, Berlin, Munich and Hamburg – become truly international centres. That is true elsewhere: London dominates the UK, Paris dominates France. But the climate is changing: international real estate companies provide comparable standardized information and improve transparency. Banks accumulate knowledge and experience; international clients demand the quality and type of space they are used to in their home markets. The Euro will speed up cross-border investment in all of Europe.

Thus, more and more cities find their real estate markets on the international map. Cities which so far have not been part of the international competition need to be prepared to profit from international capital flows when the time comes.

Lessons from the Developed World:
Urbanization, Deurbanization and Reurbanization

The early twenty-first century city will see an intensification of the trends of the late twentieth century. Technology, economic requirements and social preferences will operate through real estate markets to produce a set of progressive changes in the patterns of urban activities and land uses. But

Box II.17. The Thai real estate boom.

The decade 1986-1996 has seen the rapid emergence of a large modern real estate industry in Thailand. This is a development that reflects the rapid growth of the economy as well as Bangkok's ambition to be a leading economic center for the region. Unfortunately, the amplitude of the Thai real estate boom that was originally built on sound fundamentals has been magnified and distorted by outdated banking practices and weak credit risk management in a financial sector that was itself experiencing an extremely rapid growth. Currently, structural flaws in both sectors have been starkly revealed, and both sectors are under stress. The real estate boom that peaked sometime in early 1995 is now followed by oversupply and a very severe asset deflation which parallels the deflation of financial assets on the stock market.

This paper has aimed to show the short-term importance of reviving liquidity and trading in the sector in order to permit businesses as well as households to restructure their balance-sheets as promptly as possible. A point of central concern is that losses on bad assets are accumulating rapidly in the short-run. While they may not always be readily measured, high carrying costs have a large opportunity cost in terms of missed business opportunities and jobs lost. Therefore public policies that can facilitate loss recognition in the sector and the stabilization of prices to a new level should be encouraged. The paper has suggested areas where such policies are likely to be of value in specific segments of the real estate sector.

Looking beyond the crisis, several reforms can enhance and strengthen the real estate sector and reduce its volatility. International experience has identified structural and regulatory improvements that can shorten the recovery period and prevent the recurrence of the extremely sharp real estate cycle that Thailand has just experienced. Provided that the Thailand economy resumes its growth soon and reforms are implemented, strong growth will be one factor that is likely to mitigate the impact of the very high vacancy rates in the Bangkok Metropolitan Region compared to mature markets like Houston. Its real estate sector is increasingly professional but it remains immature. Thailand can expect significant further urban growth and this will give the BMR the capacity to absorb the effects of this very costly first major cycle.

(Renaud *et al.*, 1998, pp. 41-42)

these changes will be far from simple or uni-dimensional. In fact, they may well appear contradictory. As throughout the last century of urban history, there will be powerful forces of decentralization, pushing and pulling people and activities out of city centres, and out of cities altogether, to suburbs and smaller towns. But there will be contrary forces of centralization, causing some activities to pack together as tightly as ever. And there will be forces of recentralization, causing some of the decentralized activities to reconcentrate in new downtowns or 'edge cities'.

Table II.8. Value of the real estate stock in the Bangkok Metropolitan Region at the end of 1997.

Sector	Space/Unit	Estimated Value (billion Baht)
Commercial Real Estate Properties		**563**
Office	6.2m m²	220
Retail	3.3m m²	270
Industrial*	16,127 rai††	73
Residential Real Estate Properties†	**1,291,407 units**	**1,608**
Luxury condominium	29,212 units	123
Low-income condominium	278,126 units	278
Detached house	407,384 units	839
Townhouse	476,265 units	316
Luxury apartment	7,711 units	31
Low-income apartment	92,709 units	22
Total Estimated Value		**2,171**
Estimated value compared to GDP of Thailand		45%
Estimated value compared to GDP of Bangkok‡		118%

* Industrial real estate refers only to serviced land.
† Residential properties include housing built after 1988.
†† 1 rai = 1600 m².
‡ Bangkok 1997 GDP is extrapolated from 1996 data.
Source: Renaud *et al.* (1998).

These trends are strikingly evident in the cities of the developed world. They are echoed in the cities of the developing world, albeit often on a much larger spatial scale. The booms of the mid-1980s and mid-1990s, coupled with the increasing tendencies to globalization and tertiarization of economies, brought intense city centre office development to all cities that could claim global status and above all to the indisputable market leaders, London, New York and Tokyo; but many of the sub-global cities have grown similarly and have similar problems of congestion and deconcentration, with the largest reaching the 3-5 million size (and Osaka even bigger) combined with downtown employment concentrations of between half and one million. This however depends in part on their age and hence their tendency to deconcentration; some of the newest, in the American West and in Australasia, are characterized by the transport planner Michael Thomson as highly deconcentrated, 'full motorization' cities (Thomson, 1977, pp. 98-129).

The difference usually consists in the scale over which development impacts extend: whereas in the global cities they may extend anything up to

100 miles (160 km) distant, here the effective radius would seldom be more than 30-40 miles (50-65 km) and generally a good deal less. A few of them, in the highly decentralized American West (Los Angeles, San Francisco) however have development impacts which stretch fully as far as those of the global centres; and the same applies, of course, to the mega-cities of Latin America, Mexico City and São Paulo.

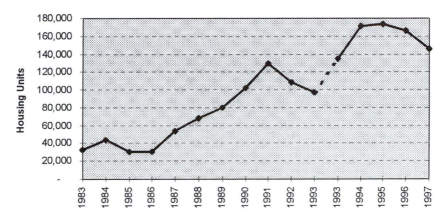

Note: From 1993 onward, the data include five provinces instead of three.

Figure 11.5. Annual housing completion in Bangkok Metropolitan Region. (*Source*: Renaud, *et al.* 1998)

Deconcentration . . .[1]

The early phase of urban deconcentration, which can be traced in many of the world's largest cities from the late nineteenth century, predominantly involved a shift of residence from central cities to their suburbs, dependent on public transport technologies and in particular on electric commuter railways and metro systems from the end of the nineteenth century on (Clark, 1951). A distinctly new phase, beginning after World War II, involved decentralization outside the traditional limits of effective public transport, and thus dependent on the use of the private car for most trips including the journey to work. This pattern of decentralization was observable in the United States from the 1950s onward (and indeed perhaps from the 1930s, though interrupted by the war); in Europe it spread progressively from Britain and the Benelux countries to involve all the countries of the European Community by the early 1980s (Hall and Hay, 1980; Cheshire and Hay, 1989).

However, at first it remained predominantly a residential movement, with some relocation of residentiary services. Employment, in contrast, remained concentrated in central complexes in the downtown metropolitan cores: the City, Whitehall and West End in London, Downtown and

119

Midtown Manhattan in New York, Kasumigaseki and Marunouchi and Otemachi in Tokyo. Within these were specialist sub-agglomerations: finance, government, and business services, attesting to the strength of traditional agglomeration forces. But, beginning in the United States during the post-war boom of the late 1950s and 1960s, and then progressively gaining pace, a parallel decentralization of employment began to be observable.

Three kinds of activities showed themselves particularly prone to relocation. First, manufacturing and associated warehousing, which was drawn to suburban locations because of access to large areas of land suitable for efficient single-floor flow production next to the new national motorway systems, under construction everywhere during the 1960s, and also because the skilled blue-collar workforce was also moving to the suburbs. Second, research and development (R&D) and associated high-technology manufacturing, which was attracted to high-amenity areas near the rural fringe, such as Santa Clara and Orange Counties in California, parts of Connecticut and New Jersey around New York, Berkshire in England, the Munich region of Germany, and southern Kanagawa prefecture in Japan. Third, large offices engaged in electronic processing of standardized information, such as insurance or credit card operations, tended to disperse to major suburban nodes with easy access, lower office rents and supplies of suitable clerical labour: Reading west of London, Stamford in Connecticut, or Omiya and Kawasaki near Tokyo.

One key question is where this process might end. Where central rents are particularly high, it may extend widely: around London, back offices have now diffused very widely across South East England and even outside that region altogether; BT have dispersed their London information service to remote regions; in the United States Omaha (Nebraska) has managed to create a specialized service niche, telemarketing, around top-quality telecommunications networks and a supply of the right kind of labour (Brooks, 1991; Feder, 1991), and Salt Lake City has attracted American Express's telephone-based traveller's cheque operation, on the somewhat extraordinary ground that its ex-Mormon missionaries are highly motivated and proficient in languages (Sellers, 1990; Donnelly, 1991; Johnson, 1991). These instances, admittedly anecdotal, may presage a future trend for such functions to disperse to relatively remote places with low rents, low wages and/or a high-quality workforce; but up to now the process seems constrained by the need for quick face-to-face communication between main office and back office. There is similar anecdotal evidence that some cities may be losing their attraction even for top-level headquarters functions: in California, some major banks and utility companies (Chevron; Pacific Bell; Bank of America) are decentralizing from downtown San Francisco to suburban locations in the wider San Francisco Bay Area.

. . . and Reconcentration

But these are far from conclusive examples. The evidence so far is that this pattern of deconcentration naturally tends to extend only into the surrounding metropolitan sphere of influence – effectively, to the outer limits of the commuter field. Here, it reconcentrates around existing medium-sized urban centres (population range, 50-200,000), typically county market towns serving as administrative and service centres for surrounding regions (counties, départements, Kreise, shi) within a radius of about 15-20 miles (25-35 km); these are distributed in a more or less regular Christaller-like fashion (modified, perhaps, by the Lösch transport-rich principle) within the metropolitan sphere of influence (Christaller, 1966; Lösch, 1954), . We might distinguish this as a third level in the urban hierarchy, after the global and sub-global cities. Perhaps the most spectacular example is London, where between 20 and 30 such centres can be identified in the so-called Outer Metropolitan Area, between 15 and 50 miles (20-80 km) from Central London, especially along the major road and rail corridors, about a dozen in number, which radiate from the city; the region around Tokyo presents a similar picture, while in the New York case the development is more highly clustered along the historic routeways which parallel the coast.

Interesting exceptions to this rule are Paris, where the corresponding pattern of outward diffusion is historically much weaker, and Berlin, where an earlier diffusion trend was completely halted during forty years of communist control; a fascinating question for students of urbanism is the rapidly-evolving pattern of development, since the end of West Berlin's isolation in 1990, in the artificially sterilized strip on either side of the ring motorway – itself an historic anomaly from the 1930s, built (for reasons of military aggression and national prestige) decades before its equivalents in the world's other great cities.

Apart from these exceptions, the medium-sized cities have thus proved very dynamic economically wherever they have been favourably located to receive the outward flows of people and jobs from neighbouring mega-city regions (South East England, the lower Rhine, New Jersey, the I-680 corridor in California) (Stanback, 1985; Cheshire, and Hay, 1989). Even in declining older industrial regions, many have been successful in preserving and enhancing their reputations by removing the scars of industrialization; Durham and Preston (England), Lille (Belgium), Essen (Germany) and Lowell (Massachusetts) provide examples.

A particularly interesting sub-group has prospered through specialization in service functions that have shown exceptionally rapid growth: local government, educational services, health services, defence contracting (Noyelle and Stanback, 1984). Examples include Reading, Oxford and Cambridge; Rennes and Aix-en-Provence; Marburg and Heidelberg; Lund and Uppsala; Padua and Bologna; Columbus, Austin, Salt Lake City and Sacramento; Kyoto and Nara. The success of these places has little to do either with metropolitan location; but if well-located in that regard also, they may exhibit exceptional dynamism, to the degree indeed that they may exhibit symptoms of overgrowth (Reading, Heidelberg, Kyoto).

Old and New Downtowns

However, downtown cores remained highly attractive to a wide range of informational services which required central agglomeration economies, as witnessed by the office construction boom that took place in all major metropolitan cores worldwide during the 1980s. Peter Daniels points out that in London this exceeded any previous such construction boom, and emphasizes that – despite the obvious importance of modern offices well-equipped for information technology – traditional location considerations, including prestige, remained important (Daniels, 1991, pp. 225-226). Similarly, in American cities, despite increasing competition from suburban sub-centres, the downtown cores retained their attraction for key high-level services. As a result, by the 1980s, metropolitan dynamics entered a new phase: the pressures on downtown space for traditionally agglomerative activities, both in the global and the largest sub-global cities, were so intense that they led developers and planners to explore new, non-central locations for major activity concentrations within the metropolitan envelope. At least four types can be distinguished:

- *New commercial sub-centres*, sometimes constituting downtown extensions, on reclaimed or redeveloped dock or freight-handling areas (London, Amsterdam, New York, Toronto, Hong Kong, Tokyo, Osaka-Kobe);

- *Metropolitan sub-centres* dependent on major inner- or middle-suburb public transport interchanges, sometimes serving as 'new downtowns' (Croydon, La Défense, Lyon-Part Dieu, Lille-Euralille, Newark Waterfront, Rosslyn, Ballston, Shinjuku, Shin-Osaka, Paulista);

- *'Edge cities'*, speculatively developed around highway access and lacking public transport access (the New Jersey Zip Strip, Tysons Corner, Aurora between Denver and Fort Worth, Mesa outside Phoenix, San Ramon-Dublin-Pleasanton in the San Francisco Bay Area) (Dillon *et al.*, 1989; Garreau, 1991);

- A special case, *'edge cities' developed around public transport interchanges:* generally in redeveloped older cores of formerly free-standing cities (the county town case, considered above), in course of incorporation into the wider metropolitan sphere of influence (Reading, Berkshire; Stamford, Connecticut; Omiya, Saitama Prefecture;

Kawasaki, Kanagawa Prefecture); occasionally on new sites, either as planned new community centres (Cergy-Pontoise, St Quentin-en-Yvelines, Massy, Lille Val d'Ascq, Ebbsfleet) or as spontaneous developments (Walnut Creek, Shin-Yokohama). Even 'full motorization' cities have begun to try to build urban rail systems and to densify areas or corridors around the new stations (Los Angeles).

The forms are very varied, and not easy to bring into a single schema because of the great variation in form from one metropolitan area to another; the Paulista in São Paulo falls into the first two categories, and could even be called a downtown 'edge city'. But overall, the clear tendency is for all very large metropolitan areas to become fairly steadily more polycentric in form. Even where this has been most carefully planned and coordinated with new public transport provision (as in the classic cases, the Stockholm region and the Région Ile-de-France), the clear tendency has been for this trend to be associated with a steady shift away from use of public transport and toward reliance on the private automobile: in the Paris region as in the San Francisco Bay Area, suburb-to-suburb trips are made overwhelmingly by car, though Paris does manage to handle a respectable minority by RER and métro. Thus Cervero's 'suburban gridlock' tends to present a problem just as much for Europe's metropolitan centres as for their American equivalents (Cervero, 1985).

The process of deconcentration has also been fundamentally affected by the fact that most of these metropolitan areas had made some serious attempt, by the early 1990s, to limit and guide their growth into planned channels, through a variety of devices such as green belts, green wedges, buffer zones, green hearts (in the special case of the Dutch Randstad), regional park systems and preferential development axes. These devices could profoundly affect the outward appearance of the metropolitan region, as can be well seen by comparing London (where they were used successfully) and Tokyo (where they were not). Given the basic dynamism of these regions, however, and coupled with general growth control and growth management policies even outside the defined green zones, the general effect of these controls was to channel growth pressures to even more distant locations, often further exacerbating the problems of automobile suburb-to-suburb commuting, as illustrated by the pressures on London's M25 orbital or California's I-580 connecting the new growth areas in the Central Valley with the Bay Area employment cores.

One critical question, in this complex process, was whether the decentralization process would lead to some kind of re-equilibration, whereby employment would progressively move outward to the distant zones from which the commuters originated and, by reconcentrating there, lead to some relief. There was fairly clear evidence that this was happening in the outer London region in the 1980s, as the smaller centres in the outer ring became steadily more important not merely as local service centres but also for some manufacturing (high-technology industry along the M4 corridor and more generally in the entire 'Western Crescent' around London) and decentralized offices (of which Reading was only the most spectacular example) (Buck *et al.*, 1986). It was not yet evident in the San Francisco Bay Area; there, it appeared that despite considerable 'edge city' deconcentration of employment, the frontier of new residential development was steadily moving even further out. Here however difficult terrain, which created natural barriers, may have exacerbated the phenomenon.

Generally, the pattern in all these mega-city-regions is one of increasing deconcentration of both residences and jobs, but with a strong degree of reconcentration into smaller centres, some existing town centres, some 'edge cities'. The striking feature is the increasing economic interdependence and networking, expressed partly in flows of people both to-work and in-work, but also in immaterial electronic flows. This is the pattern evident in South East England, Randstad Holland, the Upper Rhine Valley, New York-Northeastern New Jersey, and Southern California. The evident problem is that most of the resultant journeys are by car, and that the urban pattern is increasingly ill-suited to supporting a viable system of public transport.

Contrasted Outcomes in the Developing World: Mega-Cities and Informalized Urbanization

The countries of the developing world differ not only in their urban systems, but also in their urban economic performance. Between 1989 and 1992, 72 per cent of Foreign Direct Investment (FDI) to developing countries went to just ten countries, while the forty-eight 'least developed' countries got just 2 per cent. Asia got half the total during 1983-91, two-thirds in the late 1980s. But parts of Asia and Latin America, and much of Sub-Saharan Africa, had very little, and saw their share of world trade decline; Sub-Saharan Africa's share of global exports has steadily declined from 2.4 per cent in 1980 to 1.1 per cent in 1989, and its share of manufacturing trade fell even more sharply, from 1.2 to 0.4 per cent. Even within the select countries that are the main FDI recipients, large regions remain relatively untouched (Shatkin, 1998, p. 379).

Explosive Growth in Eastern Asia[2]

At one extreme is Eastern Asia, the industrializing powerhouse of the world until crisis brought its growth to a halt – at least for the time being. Here, industry at first concentrated in the main cities, but has increasingly diffused out of them into smaller cities within two or three hours travel time, which are networked into mega-city regions, what Terrence McGee calls 'extended urban regions', where many choose to stay in rural areas at the periphery, engaged in a mixture of on-farm and off-farm activity (McGee, 1991; Drakakis-Smith, 1995). Essentially, these are Asian versions of the kind of complex deconcentration-reconcentration that has occurred around London or New York City or San Francisco, but they have occurred on a much larger scale and over a much shorter time; typically they have developed since the 1970s and embrace anything between 10 and 30 million people living in a series of large and medium-sized cities, closely networked.

They have certain defining features:

Exo-Urbanization: These complexes depend essentially on exogenously impelled growth through Foreign Direct Investment. In the Pearl River Delta, the share of Foreign Direct Investment in production rose from 7 per cent in 1979-80 to 35.5 per cent 1990-93 (Sit and Yang, 1997, p. 648).

Internal Division of Labour harnessing different factor endowments, such as Hong Kong-Southern China and Singapore-Johore-Riau Islands. Within them, a global or sub-global city increasingly exports capital and expertise (Yeung, 1996, pp. 26-27). Essentially, this form promotes the growth of hundreds of small towns and villages, whose economies are increasingly integrated into the global economic system through Hong Kong, which acts as regional co-ordinating centre (Sit and Yang, 1997).

Desakota: McGee argues that the Asian mega-city is a basically new urban form, quite different from anything that occurred earlier in developed Western countries. In the land stretching along the linear corridors between large city cores, there is an intense mixture of agricultural and non-agricultural activities, for which McGee coins an Indonesian term *desakota*, from *desa*, village and *kota*, town. They are linked by cheap transport, especially two-stroke motorbikes, buses and trucks, which make it easy to move people and goods. McGee comments that 'The challenge to urban planners is how to take advantage of the positive aspects of these new sorts of urban rings, while controlling their negative ones' (McGee, 1991, p. 9).

Urban Mega-Projects: There are mega-projects in other parts of the world: La Défense, London Docklands, New York's World Finance Centre. But in the 1980s, they have emerged as a key feature of the new Eastern Asian urban form. Kris Olds defines them as: 'large-scale (re-)development projects composed of a mix of commercial, residential, retail, industrial, leisure, and infrastructure uses . . . developed primarily in the inner city, on large tracts of former port, railway, industrial, military, or racetrack lands, or on 'under-utilized' suburban, agricultural, swamp, or island land within the extended metropolitan region'. They include major development of seaports and airports; high-technology office districts including teleports, often acting as functional nodes in far-stretching development corridors which facilitate the movement of goods, people and information; and linked luxury residential districts for the capitalist elite. They are particularly associated with the globalization of property markets and the rise of transnational firms including professional organizations like chartered surveyors and architects. Olds lists one in Singapore, two in Malaysia (Johor Baru and Kuala Lumpur), one in the Philippines (Manila), one in Thailand (Bangkok), one in China (Lujiazui), and five in Japan (Tokyo, Yokohama and three in Osaka), as well as four in Australia (one in Sydney, two in Melbourne, one in Adelaide); oddly, she excludes the Chinese Special Economic Zones (Olds, 1995, pp. 1713, 1717, 1720-1721).

Box II.18. Exo-Urbanization in the Pearl River Delta: A new form of development.

> In this most 'open' area of China a new pattern of exo(genous)-urbanization has emerged, as distinct from the endo(genous)-urbanization (or urbanization driven entirely by intra-national or regional forces) which existed in the pre-1978 period in the PRC and which is still prevalent in most parts of the country. This foreign-investment-induced exo(genous)-urbanization is characterized by labour-intensive and assembly manufacturing types of export-oriented industrialization based on the low-cost input of large quantities of labour and land.
>
> (Sit and Yang, 1997, p. 649)

In such complexes, the central city plays a command and control function; thus, within a few decades cities like Singapore, Hong Kong, Shanghai and Taipei have transformed themselves from manufacturing into informational cities.

The most extraordinary example is the Pearl River Delta embracing Hong Kong, Guangzhou, seven medium-sized cities and thirteen *xians* or counties, plus two out of four of China's special zones, Shenzhen and Zhuhai. In 1993 its total population was 22.1 million Between 1980 and 1991 its GDP multiplied more than seven times. With lower than average GNP per capita in 1980, by 1991 it was 64 per cent above it; by the 1990s it was top in foreign capital utilization, exports, investment in fixed social assets and agricultural production. It makes cameras, cassette recorders and electric fans, refrigerators, washing machines and colour TV sets (Lin and Ma, 1994, p. 82; Maruya, 1994, p. 65; Sit and Yang, 1997, p. 651; Yeung, 1994, p. 7).

The key was foreign investment, above all from Hong Kong, to some extent from Taiwan. By the end of the 1980s, the Pearl River Delta had become a major production base for Hong Kong manufacturing enterprises, employing 3 million, five times the number in Hong Kong itself, and all in labour-intensive, light manufacturing branches in which Hong Kong had originally specialized. There is thus an internal division of labour, in which Guangdong specializes in heavy industry and R&D, Hong Kong-Shenzhen acts as a 'window' to the outside world for the latest developments in technology, design and world market trends, Hong Kong is the hub for finance, insurance and shipping, and the intervening areas become a manufacturing base. The model is 'front shop, back factory' (Guldin, 1995, pp. 113-114; Sit and Yang, 1997, pp. 651-656). By the mid-1990s no less than 5 million people in the Pearl River Delta were employed in factories controlled by Hong Kong interests; manufacturing accounted for only 18 per cent of the Hong Kong workforce, services accounted for 60 per cent (So and Kwok, 1995b, p. 259). As So and Kwok put it:

The colony has upgraded itself to be the financier, investor, supplier, designer, promoter, exporter, middleman and technical consultant of the Pearl River Delta economy.

(So and Kwok, 1995a, p. 2)

Likewise, Shanghai is changing its economic base very rapidly: industries are relocating not only to suburban Shanghai but also beyond the city boundaries, to the wider Yangtze delta region. About half the delta's industrial output is now created outside the city, mainly in smaller townships and village enterprises; and an industrial corridor is emerging, almost 200 kilometres long, from Shanghai to Suizhou, Wuxi and Changzhou, in an area of villages and hamlets with little or no land use controls or supporting municipal infrastructure. Migration could take the population of the delta to 22 million by 2005. Unplanned development threatens not only to deplete cultivated land, but to affect air and water quality in Shanghai (Leman, 1995, p. 10).

The Contradictions of Latin America

Latin America in the 1980s and 1990s has shown a series of urban contradictions. With rare exceptions, its economies have grown more slowly than in the boom years of the 1960s, though hyper-inflation has been largely brought under some degree of control. The main problem remains that of highly unequal distribution of urban income, resulting in a dual urban economy and a highly segregated urban social structure: luxury apartments and elegant high-rise office and hotel towers in the city centres, huge shanty-towns on the outskirts. Since the continent returned universally to democracy in the 1980s, popular social movements have been much in evidence, and have achieved some results in slum improvement programmes. Car ownership is relatively high, partly because of low petrol taxes and generous highway-building. Since this region has a number of the world's largest metropolitan areas, the resulting patterns are highly unsustainable.

The Dilemma of Sub-Saharan Africa

In the period 1965 to 1990, Sub-Saharan Africa showed negligible average annual economic growth, completely out of line with other world regions (Hoogvelt, 1997, p. 202). In many parts of Africa, imposition of neo-liberal orthodoxy has actually contributed to the descent into anarchy and civil war (Hoogvelt, 1997, pp. 175-176). Thus, since 1980, Sub-Saharan Africa 'has effectively become sunk in a pervasive crisis of stagnation and decline' (Jamal and Weeks, 1993, p. 18).

Yet migration to the cities in absolute terms increased, even though in some cases the rate declined (Jamal and Weeks, 1993, p. 20). Official figures suggest that in the 1980s Africa had the lowest rates of urbanization but the highest urban growth rates (Potts, 1995, p. 245). However, Potts' work suggests that these figures are wrong: in Ghana and Zambia, and to a lesser extent in Tanzania, urban growth slackened (Potts, 1995, p. 252). 'A form of counter-urbanization, which in this African context refers to a situation where the number of urban residents opting to leave the city and move to rural areas has exceeded the number of rural-urban migrants, has definitely occurred in some countries, although the incidence of this has been quite variable for the different centres in this urban system' (Potts, 1995, p. 259).

Even so, it was a mark of the economic crisis that migration continued into the cities. Redundant wage earners from the collapsing formal sector joined impoverished rural migrants to flood into the cities, where they entered the informal sector, struggling at the very margin of existence (Jamal and Weeks, 1993, p. 131). The extraordinary fact was that in many countries, urban populations suffered savage declines in living standards: in Uganda, the real wage fell 90 per cent between 1972 and 1990, and a rough calculation suggests that the 1990 wage would buy only one quarter of a family's food needs; similar declines occurred in Tanzania, Kenya and Ghana (Jamal and Weeks, 1993, p. 43).

During this time the crisis was exacerbated by IMF policies to reduce urban economic growth, based on the remarkable notion that urban incomes were too high in relation to rural ones, and also by war in Angola, Mozambique, Sudan and Liberia which caused migration into the cities (though in Rwanda and Somalia war has had the reverse effect), by prolonged drought in Sahelian countries such as Mauritania, and by the end of apartheid in South Africa which was followed by a flood of in-migration from all over Africa (Potts, 1995, pp. 246-247). Jamal and

Weeks calculate that during the 1970s and 1980s, the urban/rural gap either vanished or reversed (Potts, 1995, p. 248).

The evidence is thus overwhelming – it is not only that urban poor have become much poorer in many countries, but that their lives have become an almost incredible struggle. The huge gap between wages and minimum necessary expenditure has been termed the 'wages puzzle' by Jamal and Weeks (1993): how are people surviving?

(Potts, 1995, p. 250)

They are surviving through a great increase in informal sector activity, with previously non-earning household members entering the petty commodity sector, and wage-earners taking on supplementary activities; and the development of food-growing on any available patch of ground. Remarkably, there seems to have been no notable increase in malnutrition, because family members went into food production. 'One witnesses in Uganda a regression to a primordial state of society in which the division of labour begins to break down. Along with that regression disappeared notions of class and explanations of income distribution based on distinct classes' (Jamal and Weeks, 1993, p. 42). This throws extra burdens on women (Potts, 1995, p. 250). In the 1990s, since the end of apartheid, there has been a remarkable growth of long-distance migration from many parts of eastern and central Africa into Johannesburg; most of these migrants are engaged in petty trading activities, which provide almost the sole economic opportunity for many of them.

We can call such a form of urban growth informalized urbanization: a form whereby cities grow without a formal economic base. According to the United Nations Population Fund, many big cities in the developing world are experiencing a rising proportion of poor and unemployed people. In some countries, migration and immigration have resulted in high unemployment among urban youth. This is related to rising rates of crime and violence. In urban areas experiencing high population growth, infrastructure and services may have reached capacity limits. There are increased needs for housing, sanitation, water supply, waste treatment facilities, and transportation. Stress is placed on public facilities, such as sanitation and sewage treatment that can lead to environmental problems.

A very similar phenomenon seems to be occurring in some cities of the developed world, which in effect are invaded by the developing world. In Los Angeles, a city which has seen massive immigration – both legal and illegal – from Latin America and Pacific Asia, Ed Soja refers to a 'carceral' city: one that has become ungovernable, with walled-in estates and protected shopping centres, gangs protecting their turf, and high-technology police (Soja, 1995, pp. 133-134). He describes 'the new topography of race, class, gender, age, income, and ethnicity has produced an incendiary urban geography in Los Angeles, a landscape filled with

129

violent edges, colliding turfs, unstable boundaries, peculiarly juxtaposed lifespaces, and enclaves of outrageous wealth and despair' (Soja, 1995, p. 134). There may be an element of exaggeration here; but also an element of truth.

The Smaller Cities: A Neglected Problem

Cities range in size all the way from mega-cities with 20 or 30 million people, down to small provincial places acting as central places for agrarian hinterlands. In spite of their differences, they share common economic functions, and common problems of housing markets or infrastructure. And, though the big cities steal the limelight, most city dwellers actually live in these smaller places. (In Vietnam, though two big cities have 30 per cent of the population, nineteen other cities have between 100,000 and 500,000, and there are 450 cities in all.) Small cities, acting as service centres where people earn their living by retailing, trading, or transporting goods and people, can act as administrative centres or as local growth poles, thus attracting part of the rural-to-urban migration and reducing the pressure on the big cities. Like the big cities, these small places are experiencing high population growth through high birth rates plus migration. Indeed, there is clear evidence that in Latin America, for instance, they are growing far faster than the very large cities, where growth has slowed down. Like them, they grow through industrial and agricultural processing activities; they have increasing numbers of cars, with accompanying pollution and congestion, and intensive building activities which tend to threaten their attractive appearance.

Usually, they suffer even more than big cities from the lack of financial autonomy. Professional and technical manpower is very often non-existent, partly as a consequence of a weak financial resource base, but partly also because labour markets operate to attract high-quality professionals to the large employment magnets of the better known prestige cities. Their political influence on the central government is small, for they lack the power of big numbers or national prestige. Thus deficits in infrastructure and lack of services in informal housing areas may be even more intense than in big cities. Capacity bottlenecks in the municipal administration can result in mounting problems for the public sector, which is preoccupied with firefighting and has too little time or energy to promote democratic decision making. This means that the challenge to develop more decentralized responsibilities and stronger local democracy may be even more acute in these small secondary cities.

Urban Form and Urban Transport

Dispersion of homes and jobs in the largest cities, more rapid growth in the smaller cities, have a similar effect: they work to increase reliance on the private car, which is one of the main challenges to urban policy in the developing world. Developing cities, with GNP per capita of less than US$ 5,000, show the fastest rate of car ownership growth (Kidokoro, 1992, p. 74). At present, about 70 per cent of all vehicles are in OECD countries, but over the next twenty-five years, from 1995 to 2020, the distribution will change: in the developing countries, the number of vehicles will increase by a further 75 per cent, and by 2020 43 per cent of the world's vehicle fleet will be in the developing countries (table II.9). In the year 2005, the global numbers of vehicles will exceed 1000 million for the first time, and before 2030 the number of vehicles in non-OECD countries will exceed that of the OECD countries. Cars account for about 60 per cent of all vehicles in both 1995 and 2020, but they are more important in the OECD countries; in the developing countries, light trucks (15 per cent) and motorcycles (32 per cent) form important elements in the vehicle fleet. The scale of the problem is vast and increasing.

Table II.9. Expected growth in worldwide vehicle ownership.

		1995 (in thousands)		2020 (in thousands)	
		Cars	All Vehicles	Cars	All Vehicles
OECD	North America	170,460	231,557	247,328	335, 056
	Europe	160,215	203,429	244,720	300,054
	Pacific	52,654	101,188	82,193	147,251
Total OECD		**383,329**	**536,174**	**574,421**	**782,361**
Rest of the World		**111,255**	**240,357**	**283,349**	**580,288**
Global Totals		**494,584**	**776,531**	**856,590**	**1,362,649**

Notes: All Vehicles includes cars, light trucks, motorcycles and heavy trucks.
OECD North America – USA, Canada.
OECD Europe – Austria, Belgium, Denmark, France, Germany, Greece, Iceland, Ireland, Italy, Luxembourg, The Netherlands, Norway, Portugal, Spain, Sweden, Switzerland, Turkey, UK, Finland.
OECD Pacific – Japan, Australia, New Zealand.
Mexico is a member of OECD (since 1994) but is excluded from these OECD figures.
Source: OECD/ECMT (1995).

As seen in Chapter I, these cities have already seen dramatic traffic growth in a short time. Developing cities are thus coping with an extraordinary combination of rapid motorization (10-15 per cent per annum) and an urban population that is growing by 6 per cent per annum (World Bank, 1996). This is further compounded by the fact that at comparable levels of income, car ownership rates in developing countries are much higher.

But in virtually all these cities, in addition, there is less road space available. In European cities 20-25 per cent and in Manhattan over 30 per cent of urban space is devoted to transport activities, but in Bangkok and Calcutta only 7-11 per cent (World Bank, 1996). Large Asian cities have to cope with much higher volumes of traffic per unit of road space, exacerbated by their incomplete networks, vehicle mixture, the use of street space for trading functions (an historic legacy, which brings benefits to those who must shop locally), poor traffic management and – most critically – the absence or inadequacy of a segregated mass transit system. This is exacerbated further by the concentration of functions in the CBD and the development of residential districts at ever-greater distances from the centre (Kidokoro 1992, pp. 75-76).

This means that even at lower levels of car ownership, city roads in developing countries are more congested. In Mexico City peak speeds are 16 km/hour; in Metro Manila, less than 15 km/hour on the most congested one quarter of the network and 10 km/hour in the CBD; in Bangkok, probably the world's worst, an average of 13 km/hour (Brennan, 1994, p. 246). Most of these cities have recently experienced extraordinarily rapid growth in vehicle numbers – Cairo 17 per cent per annum, for instance – and this is typical. Fuel is cheap and often subsidized, and there are few attempts to limit the growth of traffic.

And the environmental effects are proportionately much worse: slow-moving traffic and ill-maintained vehicles cause greater levels of pollution than those emanating from more efficient modern vehicles operating in less congested conditions. Land costs and high housing rents in central areas contribute towards huge, sprawling, land-consuming cities with increasingly long and slow journeys to and from work, which in extreme cases may take over five hours a day or even more. This is the classic 'Bangkok Effect', where congestion and pollution are so bad that it is quicker to walk, and vehicles are 'abandoned' on roads. In Bangkok, businesses are already decentralizing out of the most congested zone: from 1978 to 1987 twelve companies, or 21 per cent, shifted their offices out of the CBD to fringe areas; seven of ten new offices located outside, between 5 and 10 km distant (Kidokoro, 1992, p. 80); in 1978 seven out of ten shopping centres were in the CBD, but two-thirds of new shopping centres built subsequently were outside it (Kidokoro, 1992, p. 84). But this will almost certainly cause the congestion to spread over an even wider area. Because of this, there is an urgent need to develop forms of urban growth that will support adequate public transport.

Micro-Patterns of Urban Growth: The Problem of Mega-Scale Development

Both in the developed and the developing world, it is evident that two important processes are occurring in parallel at two quite different spatial scales: deconcentration and reconcentration at the macro-scale are accompanied by a huge increase in scale and separation at the micro-scale. This is evident both in large-scale commercial developments in Western cities like Canary Wharf or La Défense, in new edge city shopping centres like Bluewater in England, or in the equivalent mega-developments in Malaysia, China or Japan. No better illustrative contrast can be found than that between the retail pattern of the Asian city, dominated by small shophouses along main streets, and the huge scale of new developments in Yokohama, Kuala Lumpur or Shanghai. These latter are characterized both by their vast size and complexity, and their tendency to segregate monofunctional land uses. The irony is that such scale and segregation are completely contradictory to the principle of sustainable development, which demands the very reverse: small scale and mixed use.

Conclusion: Markets and Planning

The above account might suggest that processes of urban growth and change are and will be in some sense natural and universal, following general technology-driven and market-driven forces. To some extent, of course, this is true: urban mass transit, and then the diffusion of car ownership, have massively diffused metropolitan areas, but also – at least initially – have helped to concentrate activities in their downtown cores. But beginning in Los Angeles in the mid-1920s, and spreading almost throughout the developed world, the private car has also helped powerfully to spread employment, creating polycentric urban areas with criss-cross commuting patterns. This is a universal pattern in both developed and developing city regions, as true of London as of Los Angeles, of Sydney as of Buenos Aires, of Tokyo as of New York.

However, planning processes powerfully work to affect the outcome. It is simply untrue, at least in the year 2000, to say that all major metropolitan areas in developed countries, still less developing countries, exhibit identical trends and features. The contrast between the spread-out polycentric London region, and the relatively compact Ile-de-France region, will make that point. Even more striking is the difference between almost any large European city and its North American equivalent. Broadly, European cities are very much denser and more compact, and for that reason they support a much higher level of public transport than their North American equivalents; though even there, Canadian cities are denser than American ones. And Asian cities tend to be denser still, as the splendid public transport systems of Tokyo and Osaka, Hong Kong and Singapore, will testify (Newman and Kenworthy, 1989).

Planning, and in particular its main tool, zoning, have thus had a profound effect on cities. But they work best if they bend and shape market trends, not if they work against them. Rigid zoning codes give landowners huge powers, and in growing cities these powers represent huge potential profits, yet the city has little ability either to change established zoning or to profit from the system it has itself created. At the same time, in many middle-income cities, such rigid zoning merely results in the multiplication of informal housing, outside any system of control whatsoever.

This illustrates a central point: planning is only one of the public actions that shapes growth and change in cities; taxation is another, equally important. Yet taxation and land use planning are almost everywhere developed separately, by different bureaucracies, with different goals. Some few cities have sought to effect a reconciliation, developing a land-use planning system that bends and shapes the market, and using taxation in parallel. But they are a small and fortunate minority. The others have found it all too difficult, buffeted as they are by rapid growth and fast-changing macro-economic constraints.

Urban form and urban density are profoundly influenced by the costs of mobility. It is important to realize that at present, all types of mobility are subsidized, or at least do not cover their full economic and ecological costs. Mobility systems based on full economic and ecological cost recovery would reduce the spatial division of labour, increase residential densities and create more incentives for mixed-use development. Planners would experience less resistance if they developed guidelines enforcing higher densities, faster recycling or less functional specialization of land uses.

In other words, the account ignores the complex relationships between market forces, intellectual concepts and ideologies, and regional/local policies. In many parts of Europe and some parts of North America, a well-organized and militant movement campaigns for sustainable urban solutions; it just so happens that these concur with NIMBY movements in these areas, and with the slogans that are used whenever such a proposal for development is rejected. The central problem, in all such cases, is to distinguish self-interested rhetoric, from sound arguments about real sustainability issues. The striking fact is that in the 1990s, governments across the world have begun to make major shifts in national policy in accordance with the agreements of the Rio (1992) and Kyoto (1997) summits; sustainability is on the agenda in a serious way, and this represents a major shift.

In particular, it represents a recognition of the economic externalities of transport. The movement of people and goods is an essential basis for economic life. But it uses natural resources which, given present technology, are non-renewable, it creates pollution, and it contributes to global environmental impacts such as global warming. At present, these are not properly represented in systems of national accounting or in decision making; in effect, all national governments have subsidized mobility in ways that fail to take regard of externalities. There is a consensus in nearly every country that locational decisions, whether about new commercial developments or new residential developments, should embody these considerations; but agreement as to how this should be done is developing only slowly. The need is to develop a new framework, a new set of policy parameters, that would make it easier to do so.

In doing this, we need to be constantly aware that cities are different, in at least two ways. First, mayors and councils in poorer cities will inevitably have different priorities and constraints as compared with middle-income cities, and they in turn will have different priorities and constraints as compared with very rich cities. It is inappropriate, and certainly unhelpful, to apply lessons from one to another, without considering whether they are appropriate. It is not, however, inappropriate or unhelpful to ask how richer cities went about tackling their problems thirty or more years ago, when they were as poor as the poor cities are now. But here enters a second kind of difference: even at any given level of development, there are huge social and cultural contrasts. The high-density East Asian city cannot simply be exported as a solution to the sprawling low-density metropolitan areas of Latin America, though it is almost certainly a more sustainable kind of city environmentally.

Nonetheless, there are surely some absolute qualities that ought to provide a basis for planning. A city where densities are too low to support an adequate bus system, even for the poor inhabitants who depend on it, is clearly not working for its citizens. Yet this kind of development is occurring around many cities of the developed world, and – even more alarmingly – around middle-income cities too; people are thus forced on to substitute systems that are less sustainable, or into running cheap cars that are less sustainable still. There is an absolute need to say that everyone, rich and poor, young and old, has a right to mobility.

Common Problems: Different Stages

There is one key concluding question: to what extent will the urban world of 2025 display common problems and, conversely, to what extent are the developed and the developing worlds following different, even contradictory, paths? We have argued that the same forces will operate worldwide, and that they interrelate. High population growth reduces the possibility of growth of income per head; conversely, rising per capita income is in general associated with falling fertility rates and so with lower rates of population growth. In contrast, mature cities, with an ageing (and, in the long run, declining) population, may display relatively high rates of household formation, with consequent effects on demand for housing and consumer durables: population growth becomes decoupled from spatial needs, which will lead to increasing dispersal from cities into surrounding suburban rings and at low densities, which will make services more expensive.

135

Box II.19. A note on transition cities.

The cities of transition countries in Eastern and Central Europe have common problems, which are different from cities in the Western World and in developing cities.

The population in transition cities is stable or declining; birth rates are low. Migration from rural areas in many cases is higher than in Western Cities. The resulting demographic structure is more homogeneous than in Western cities and not comparable to a developing-world city where the population is young and the number of children who have to be fed and educated is very high. In transition cities life expectation is lower than in the West (as an example: life expectancy in Romania and the Russian Federation is still under 70 years) and there is a smaller percentage of old people than in developed cities while the percentage of people of working age is very high. In St. Petersburg, the percentage of people of employment age is 59%; this proportion is going to increase due to a significant reduction in the population below working age.

Income per family or per inhabitant is lower than in the West, with extremely wide gaps between income groups. Growth in Moscow has resulted in income levels for the economically active population which are extremely high compared to the rest of the country, but there is also a wide income gap within Moscow's population. In 1995, the incomes of Moscow's upper 10% were 47 times higher than those of the lowest 10% of the city's inhabitants. One in three persons lives from welfare payments. Other cities like Sofia or Bucharest still have lower per capita income. But low income is a consequence of the transition. The level of education in transition cities is high (in St. Petersburg, 32.6% of the economically active population are higher education graduates), and technological knowledge is highly developed creating basic preconditions for high productivity growth. As demonstrated in Western Europe through the integrative process of the Common Market, more intense integration into an international division of labour should lead to a relatively rapid economic development process.

Unemployment rates of the early transition period were high as export industries lost markets. New imports substituted for local production. So far, subsidized industries which did not produce cost-effectively have declined. The transition from a central planning system where marketing and distribution of products did not exist as a special business function has created enormous difficulties. New accounting methods and reduction of overhead costs and bureaucracy reduced employment. Increased productivity is based on growing production with smaller numbers of workers.

Car ownership has increased rapidly. Even if it is still only one-quarter to one-half that of Western Europe, there are already 2.5 million cars in Moscow. This number is expected to rise to 4 million in 2010. In Vilnius, the number of cars has increased by 7-8% annually between 1991 and 1996, and by 16% between 1996 and 1997. The transition cities were traditionally geared to public transport and a low percentage of car ownership, and enormous bottlenecks exist in infrastructure. Cities like

Box II.19. cont.

Warsaw, Prague and Moscow are plagued with severe traffic jams, similar to cities in the developing world. However, infrastructure investment is growing.

Economic restructuring and the growing number of cars, together with new housing preferences for lower densities in smaller buildings, trigger the well-known process of decentralization and declining density. But the overall structure of the cities is still influenced by the history of planning and investment. Many attractive, often quite central, areas are still dominated by old industrial complexes whose use has disappeared. Vast areas are ready for regeneration. New office complexes and shopping centres are being built. In fringe areas high-rise housing estates were produced with only small service centres, especially for shopping. This transformation will take time as enormous up-front investments are necessary to demolish old structures and prepare clean sites for development. The provision of new infrastructure, necessary for the reuse of the land, will also demand up-front planning time and investment.

Housing and physical infrastructure, an inheritance of the past, are of low quality. Unfulfilled demand is enormous. The early years of the transition process saw a reduction of housing starts as traditional financial systems broke down. Inflationary processes did not allow stable long-term loans. A new legal basis for mortgage systems and mortgage banks had to be created. In the meantime, most countries have established new systems of real estate finance. The traditional highly centralized construction companies have changed their organization and produce new types of housing, together with new, sometimes foreign companies. Traditional prefabricated industrial housing is being displaced by the growing production of single-family houses and smaller buildings. There are also strategies for the refurbishment of old prefabricated housing estates. In Moscow, several high-rise luxury apartment complexes were built by private investors in recent years. The price per square metre in Kountsevo, a new neighbourhood with its own schools, shopping and leisure facilities in South West Moscow, is US$1750.

Commercial real estate, from shopping centres to office complexes, is being principally developed by foreign developers and financed by foreign banks. Rents for office space with European standards are between 500 and 900 US$/ m^2.

Many cities experienced extreme fiscal crises as the traditional sources of revenue from central governments disappeared. New sources of tax revenue were weak. As a consequence, traditional subsidies – especially for housing – had to be phased out, and rents increased. But market rents, apart from informal markets, are still the exception. Very often, maintenance had to be reduced, at least for a transition period. In most countries, the public housing stock was privatized and mostly handed over to sitting tenants at low prices. In the meantime, in most countries the market for owner-occupied housing has increased. Small suppliers typically sublet units.

Box II.19. cont.

As an overall result, the economic structure, the transportation systems, and planning and provision of infrastructure today are more decentralized. City governments are more independent and have more authority to handle their own affairs. The single-family house and the car – both posing problems – are the symbols of the new urban age. Democratic governments and the growing relevance of markets will shape the future.

(Based on surveys in Urussowa, 1998*a,b* with additional data from OECD/ECMT, 1995 and UN, Economic Commission for Europe, 1997

Thus there are a number of similar tasks worldwide. We can identify five common global tasks:

- Reduce population growth;

- Increase productivity of labour;

- Reduce environmental pollution that crosses national and urban borders, especially through eco-saving technologies;

- Manage the transition to renewable energy and a recycling economy; in this context, reinvent urban transportation, especially the car;

- Establish a system of more rapid diffusion of best practice in a dense, common international urban network.

And there are five communal local tasks:

- Establish good governance; further decentralize, democratize and strengthen local government;

- Promote human and economic development, especially through better education;

- Avoid local environmental degradation, in part through better provision of infrastructure;

- Promote social integration;

- Build attractive, functional and liveable cities within networks of cities.

These common and communal tasks unite cities in different countries and continents, as day by day they demonstrate their fundamental similarities. At the same time everyday experience demonstrates that cities vary, and will continue to vary, to a huge degree. The temptation is to say that every city is unique. But there are typical constellations which can be observed again and again, and on this basis (without covering all observable typical variations) we can make a basic distinction: between three kinds of city, representing three typical constellations of demographic-socio-economic evolution.

The City Coping with Informal Hypergrowth. This is represented by many cities in Sub-Saharan Africa and in the Indian subcontinent, by the Muslim Middle East, and by some of the poorer cities of Latin America. It is characterized by rapid population growth, both through migration and natural increase; an economy heavily dependent on the informal sector; very widespread poverty, with widespread informal housing areas; basic problems of the environment and of public health; and difficult issues of governance.

The City Coping with Dynamic Growth. This is the characteristic city of the middle-income rapidly-developing world, represented by much of Eastern Asia, Latin America and the Middle East. Population growth is reducing, and some of these cities face the prospect of an ageing population. Economic growth continues rapidly, but with new challenges from other countries. Prosperity brings environmental problems.

The Weakening Mature City Coping with Ageing. This is the characteristic city of the advanced world of North America, Europe, Japan and Eastern Asia, and Australasia. It is characterized by stable or declining population, the challenge of ageing and of household fissioning, slow economic growth and adaptation, and social polarization. But it does have resources to tackle environmental problems, if it chooses. Its cities are characterized by very widespread dispersion and by reconconcentration, leading to the growth of smaller cities and a challenge to the viability of the older central cities.

All three types of city will be shaped by the same basic driving forces that we have outlined in this chapter. In the short and medium term, at least, urban policy-makers must accept these forces of change and these constraints as given; but they can bend and shape them, to serve their objectives. Here the magic of compound interest will help, as small changes will accumulate into major differences. In the longer run, after adjustment periods of between 10 and 25 years – in particular, through slower population growth – we can potentially shape the driving forces themselves. The political process, itself one of the drivers, can transform the way the economy and society and technology and culture develop. It should do this, through twin concepts: *sustainable human development*, delivered through *good urban governance*.

We have posed the resulting dilemmas here, without seeking to address the answers. We return to them in discussing policy questions in Chapters IV and V. Before that, however, we must ask where these trends are likely to take us in the absence of any positive policy intervention to bend or shape them. We do this through a 'business as usual' scenario. We then contrast this with a scenario based on the idea that intervention is both possible and desirable: that the trends can indeed be bent.

Notes

1. The following sections (pp. 119-124) are taken from Hall (1995).
2. The following sections (pp. 125-127) are taken from Hall (1999).

CHAPTER III

Two Scenarios:
The Urban World in 2025

III. Two Scenarios: The Urban World in 2025

The driving forces are taking the world's cities in certain directions – and taking them there very rapidly. Here, we start by forecasting where they will take our three types of city – cities coping with informal hypergrowth, cities coping with dynamism, and weakening mature cities, coping with ageing – by the year 2025. This 'Trend' or 'Business as Usual' Scenario assumes that there is no major intervention by government, either at national or city level, to change the underlying trends. Then, we pose the critical question: suppose governments act, positively but sensitively, to influence the driving forces and thus to deflect the trends? This 'Bending the Trend' Scenario represents the outcome of positive policies. In Chapter IV, which follows, we spell out what those policies would need to be.

The City Coping with Informal Hypergrowth

'Trend Scenario'

Basic Trends

Deficiencies in knowledge, savings/ investment, and production, and the needs of hypergrowth cities dominate all political activities.

Demography

Large numbers of young families: a

The City Coping with Informal Hypergrowth

'Bending the Trend'

Basic Policy Shift

Economizing scarce resources, using them most effectively for priority needs, plus reduced population growth provide the key to a more socially- and environmentally-balanced scenario.

Demography

More radical education policies,

demographic bomb. Though better social security can reduce the need to have large families for protection against poverty in old age, high birth rates continue because of sexual ignorance, superstition, poorly educated women. Reducing urban population growth particularly difficult in India, which overtakes China to become the world's most populous country.

As AIDS spreads, the race intensifies for an effective low-cost treatment for the developing world.

Continued migration to cities. Tripling of urban populations by 2025.

For most Sub-Saharan Africa: rapid spread of AIDS among young adult males and females; big loss of young working population and growth of a dependent orphan population.

and more aggressive policies to reduce birth rates, reduce the population pressure. Most effective: female education, with postponement of childbearing. Governments and international agencies agree with drug companies to support a major programme for an effective low-cost AIDS treatment, providing a model for a more general attack on health problems.

Economy

Immigration of low-skilled labour, plus high birth rates, produce long-term surplus of unskilled labour, which reduces income growth and creates huge inequalities. The informal sector remains much too self-sufficient and separate, as access to loans or input markets is weak. Division of labour makes only slow progress. Hard to increase infrastructure per head or provide adequate jobs or homes or school places (thus a human capital problem); survival problems of the young generation overpower all other considerations.

Poor people double in number; women form the majority of the

Economy

Intensified international cooperation, plus adjustment to the needs of the modern industrial sector, allow faster growth and more foreign direct investment. In some cities, productivity growth in advanced manufacturing brings a sharp increase in average income, but further threatens the livelihoods of those in the informal economy. Continued growth of the informal sector becomes a major issue. Complex strategies – decentralized urban management, training, better cooperation between formal and informal sector – improve growth expectations outside the formal sector. Cities develop effective poorest. Life expectancy and literacy rates increase, but economic opportunities for women remain limited, especially for female-headed households (more than 30 per cent of low-income population).

Struggle for survival in informal economies, local systems of exchange, with little or no outside contact.

The formal sector, still relatively unproductive, struggles to compete on external markets. Under-education, bottlenecks in infra-structure, unstable input and credit markets result in higher risks, quality and delivery problems. Integration into global markets remains weak.

policies to help formalize the informal economy: strengthening relationships to the mainstream city on input and output markets (microcredit, building materials, food, water, transportation). Communal self-help neighbourhood projects, backed by informal levies to pay for materials, help to overcome bottlenecks in infra-structure.

Microcredit networks play a key role in developing the informal sector. These networks increase rapidly. Poor women benefit most of all.

In some cities, schemes (supported by international agencies) expand mass education, especially for teachers, through cheap information technology. Schools in poor areas are comprehensively networked; teacher-tutors manage the work programme and supervise progress. This brings dramatic im-provement: reductions in illiteracy, plus increased numbers obtaining secondary educational qualifica-tions and continuing to further or higher education.

Thus, cities attract foreign direct investment, offering a well-educated labour force at competitive wages. Employment in the formal in-dustrial sector increases sharply; the low-paid informal economy shrinks and increasingly diversifies into an intermediate sector, with some characteristics of both the formal and informal economies. This becomes increasingly integrated with the formal public sector and the globalized trading sector - either directly (for instance by subcontracting) or indirectly (for instance by performing services for workers in the modern traded sector).

Society

Informalized urbanization: cities grow without a formal economic base; rising rates of crime and violence.

Most people live in the informal society. Informal sprawl is the dominant solution for neighbourhoods. As the formal city grows too, cities become even more fragmented and incoherent: informal housing areas explode out of control, next to formal or even luxury housing.

Society

Most cities formulate and execute more effective policies to improve informal housing, developing informal cooperative assistance policies. International agencies play a role at the start, but cities become more self-reliant. Basic assumption: informal populations are creative, energetic and enthusiastic to improve their housing environment. Key: simple, low-cost planning of upgradable development concepts, through help to local leaders to organize neighbourhood cooperative movements.

Housing/Infrastructure

Infrastructure and services reach capacity, with increasing needs for housing, sanitation, water supply, waste treatment facilities, and transportation. The poor pay more. But even under conditions of extreme poverty, the value of housing and infrastructure in the older more stable informal settlements grows slowly. Most cities accept the need to stabilize the legal position of informal owners. Techniques of cooperation and organized self-help slowly improve through learning by doing.

Housing/Infrastructure

Private provision of water and sanitation becomes a growth sector, promoted by international institutions and wide spread imitation of best practice. Key: private provision of infrastructure in the formal city, market solutions for trunk sewers, water mains, main high-tension lines, plus detailed solutions for self-help cooperation in informal neighbourhoods.

Time lags for public sector innovations shorten, through intensive efforts to spread information and experience. The information age becomes an age of faster diffusion of successful or best practice.

Environment

Struggle for survival forces ineffi-

Environment

Better education produces changed

cient use of natural resources to produce basic goods, from housing to food; overuse and neglect of the natural environment. Little concern for future generations. In stabilized areas, slow improvement of water or even waste treatment. But later generations of new informal settlements start in substandard conditions, with little or no outside help.

priorities: environmental goods and health become higher priorities. Progress in combating air pollution through availability of low-emission vehicles, better emission control of old cars and better waste treatment. Key: improvements through tight cooperation between city-wide task forces and neighbourhood groups, assisting these to become more effective. High growth, a negative factor earlier, now becomes a key driving force for more sustainable development and an opportunity, as growing pollution, traffic congestion, urban sprawl and health risks mobilize popular energies to reduce risks and to improve living conditions. Policies to reduce pollution and improve waste water treatment gain from scale economies across an entire urban area.

Transport

Poor city dwellers remain dependent on walking; as cities grow, this drastically reduces their capacity to participate in urban labour markets and to access services, and they remain effectively trapped inside their own informal neighbourhoods.

Transport

National policies encourage bicycles as a major means of mobility and access for the urban poor. Cities contract with private contractors to develop low-cost bus services on major urban corridors, with informal para-transit services filling the gaps.

Urban Form

A chaotic series of informal settlements, at the margin of survival both economically and environmentally. Permanent threat of catastrophe. Fragmented appearance and fragmented growth creates an image of chaos and disorder, which is only slowly attenuated.

Urban Form

The formal city develops rapidly, but informal areas still dominate many areas. Cities remain fragmented and incoherent, but begin to grow together through upgrading and better integration between sectors.

147

The City Coping with Dynamism

'Trend Scenario'

Basic Trends

Rising productivity produces rising standards and widening possibilities of coping with problems, but also introduces new challenges of sustainability.

Demography

Despite large numbers of young people, birth rates fall sharply through urbanization. Contraceptive knowledge spreads and the economic value of children declines, as costs of education and living increase faster than income. More intensive child care and education increase the quality of human capital.

A workforce bulge: the ratio of working-age to non-working people rises, contributing to economic growth. But later, as large groups born in the 1950s and 1960s retire, they place a burden on smaller numbers of working-age people. However, the proportions of old people remain relatively low in most cities.

Economy

A dual economy: wealthy formal-sector cities and informal neighbourhoods. Problem of the modern sector: threat of deindustrialization, as capital moves to lower-income

The City Coping with Dynamism

'Bending the Trend'

Basic Policy Shift

These are true learning cities, extremely successful in using international experience and knowledge, and increasingly moving themselves to the forefront of sustainable development.

Demography

Policies to encourage lower birth rates, especially through education for women, have run their course. But an emerging concern about the implications of ageing in 20-30 years' time.

But problems are much smaller than in mature ageing cities – especially as expansion of elaborate pension systems is mostly avoided: individual savings form the basis of most pension systems, thus savings rates are higher than in most high-income ageing cities. Private pension systems create incentives for later retirement. Together with more efficient education, this increases the working life, thus reducing the burden of ageing.

Economy

Nearly all middle-income cities, particularly in Eastern Asia, resume growth, though not at same speed. Many more join Singapore and Hong Kong as fully-developed cities. Progressive formalization of the informal sector.

economies; others – particularly in Chinese coastal provinces – join the middle-income category.

Manufacturing moves into more capital- and knowledge-intensive production. Major cities turn increasingly to advanced services.

Flexible, skilled workforces attract inward investment and encourage locally-based innovation. Cheaper access to education becomes highly relevant, building on students' and parents' motivation, and helps reduce inequality – especially in Latin American and Caribbean cities. Some possible negative impact on declining or segregated neighbourhoods – but even here, information technology can bring an educational revolution.

Society

Larger cities continue to attract migrants, and decentralize through peripheral growth, often far from the centre, through both formal housing for higher-income groups and informal occupation by the poor. Rapid growth of a new education-oriented middle class. More mixture of formal and informal settlements, sometimes with resulting social tensions. Growth of polycentric mega-city regions, with up to 20-30 million people, and a networked division of labour: advanced services in the central city, more routine services and manufacturing, in the periphery.

In some cities (especially Latin America) social movements organize land occupations, and

Society

Economic transformation improves the position of many workers, who begin to receive regular earnings and to care about their children's education. Promotion of small businesses and a better business environment strengthen middle-class values; the middle class expands and formalizes informal neighbourhoods.

149

sometimes provide social order. Danger of polarization between the formal and informal city.

Housing/Infrastructure

Numbers and sometimes proportions in informal housing developments continue to rise, often in risky and unsustainable sites, far from employment or services, and having no or minimal infrastructure, therefore presenting health and environmental hazards.

Housing/Infrastructure

With fragmented local administration, pressure comes from the neighbourhoods, for more effective local self-help, and from the region, for more integrated metropolitan government and revenue-sharing. (Some resistance from entrenched central powers, gradually overcome). Result: a two-level solution, with metropolitan government for infrastructure provision and basic service delivery, and neighbourhood councils to mobilize local human resources, making best use of limited funds. People in informal neighbourhoods create local organizations to manage their local environment and urban needs. Model schemes for upgrading of informal housing, based on local self-management, and local taxes spent according to local political decisions, spread rapidly through emulation. These areas progressively become middle-class suburbs.

Environment

Urban plus economic development results in higher income, generating more traffic, more and more space demands, increases in heating or cooling energy, and increased pollution. In poorer areas, industrial plants continue to produce toxic emissions and wastes in the early phases; little or no attempt to control emissions. Later, political support for environmental strategies.

Environment

New challenges produce new policies: some cities develop imaginative solutions to their problems, with programmes for recycling, good quality public transport, and encouragement of sustainable urban development. They emerge as Best Practice cities with a worldwide reputation for urban innovation. Combined heat and power supply through

Dispersion of homes and jobs in the largest cities brings growth of low-density areas, increasing pollution and energy consumption through reliance on the private car: very rapid growth of car ownership and use. World oil production peaks around 2010, as consumption begins to rise more rapidly because of growth in car ownership and use, leading to a sudden and dramatic increase in world oil prices – a third global energy crisis, recalling those of the 1970s. Increasing evidence of global warming, with major floods in low-lying areas, especially in Asia, impinging on informal urban settlements.

cogeneration, reduced private traffic through efficient and comfortable public transport, efficient supply of food and consumer goods, better environmental education, all set in a paradigm of the 'learning city', serve as an example for others to follow.

Transportation

Rapid income growth feeds rapid growth of demand for cars in most cities. High-density inner city areas limit street widening or new construction, even for cities growing in wealth and tax revenue. Thus, a transportation crisis: public transportation is only a partial solution, as the exodus of jobs and people into low-density areas makes increasing numbers of households car-dependent. Prime illustration of the sustainable development paradox: unless economic growth all too easily produces negative outcomes, such as pollution.

Infrastructure investment falls behind: particularly, rail and subway systems are poor. High dependence on bus service, often poor-quality. Thus, high car dependence (much higher in relation to income than in mature

Transportation

Cities develop a sophisticated urban competence to solve ever-growing transportation problems and related tasks of managing urban growth, as international contacts grow and best-practice knowledge spreads rapidly. Solutions from Singapore, Hong Kong and Curitiba are quickly exported. Best Practice cities package their sophisticated solutions (price rationing of access to cars, electronic pricing, incentives to share cars, electronic hitch-hiking) for export to other cities, producing a worldwide export service which revolutionizes urban traffic. But a continuing problem in car-dependent peripheral areas, only resolvable by development of the supercar based on fuel-cell technology, plus a superbus version offering rail-quality service at low cost.

cities), with crisis as fuel prices escalate. Deconcentration of people and jobs exacerbates this process. Serious traffic congestion, traffic-based pollution, very long journeys to work.

Urban Form – Two Alternative Forms

Explosive Growth in Eastern Asia: growth diffuses from larger into smaller cities nearby, networked into *mega-city regions* or extended urban regions, with 10-30 million people.

The Contradictions of Latin America and the Caribbean: Highly unequal distribution of income results in a dual urban economy and a highly segregated urban social structure: luxury apartments and elegant high-rise office and hotel towers in the city centres, huge shanty-towns on the outskirts. Very rapid increase in car ownership and use, bolstered by low car-driving costs, which aids urban dispersal. Little possibility of compensating by new metro construction. Often, extreme negative consequences of scale and rate of growth: serious traffic congestion, traffic-based pollution and very long journeys to work, erratic and unequal distribution of basic services.

The high-density East Asian city appears more sustainable, but cannot simply be exported as a solution to the sprawling low-density metropolitan areas of Latin America and the Caribbean.

Medium-sized cities, with up to

Urban Form

These cities vary: some have high densities and highly-developed mass transit, some are fuel-intensive, more polluting, urban-sprawl type cities. But a general trend towards higher densities and to support public transport, especially for those lacking access to cars (the poor, the young, the handicapped). This does not usually mean metro construction, which is expensive and limited in impact; efficient bus systems and segregated bicycle lanes prove more cost-effective in many cases.

one million people, show extremely high and accelerating growth rates. They relieve pressure on the larger cities. But they too may suffer poor environment, particularly as some fail to develop administrative capacity or fiscal autonomy to handle the consequences of rapid growth.

The Weakening Mature City Coping with Ageing

'Trend Scenario'

Basic Trends

Wealthy cities: most people highly-educated, though poverty has not been overcome; almost all are mature democracies, with good administration and a strong tax base. Problem of layers of vested interests. Therefore, politically slow-motion cities with difficulties in adjusting to the needs of an ageing population.

The Weakening Mature City, Coping with Ageing

'Bending the Trend'

Basic Policy Shift

Enlightened Self-Interest as Driving Force: Ageing is a slow process, so easy to forecast and thus to influence. Some cities manage to escape from over-protective, over-consensus-oriented politics and to grasp necessary radical cures, by:

- Reform of the taxation and pension system, to reduce the burden of income taxes and social security taxes;

- Deregulated markets, intensifying competition and reforming the public sector combine to increase efficiency;

- Reducing collectively-funded pension entitlements, thus increasing private savings;

- More funded pensions to increase lifetime savings and lifetime work through later retirement – which also increases incentives for life-long learning;

- High costs of unemployed immi-

153

grants, plus the need for highly-skilled workers, lead to increased efforts for better integration of immigrants;

- Promotion of informal self-help among the old, to reduce dependency on formal service organizations.

Demography

Central problem of declining city populations, with birth rates as low as 13 or 14 per thousand in European cities. American variant with higher birth rates and immigration rates.

Declining populations bring lower education costs, but increasing social security obligations because of rising numbers of old people (including very old people). Shortages of capital, because savings ratios of older people are low. Increases in capital intensity will slow, making it more difficult to increase labour productivity. Human capital will age. Without radical changes in behaviour, growing productivity risks.

Mature cities tend to be unfriendly environments for young families. Therefore low numbers of children and high numbers of working women. Reduced capacity of the family to provide services for the elderly. Need for expensive professional services grows rapidly if no new informal solutions arise.

Growing costs of the welfare state. Political tension between the younger population and the older longer-settled populations.

Demography

Birth rates can be increased, as Swedish or Finnish cities have demonstrated. But a more family-friendly environment will produce results only after 25 years - too late to influence this scenario.

Cities seek to rejuvenate themselves through immigration of well-qualified young people, especially those with key skills (e.g. health personnel). But, given high unemployment rates among foreigners, to be effective the shift must be radical. Restrictions on double passports or naturalization disappear. Schools take on new responsibilities. Labour markets become more accessible. Universities attract more foreigners in order to integrate them and forestall the formation of a ghetto underclass. Skill structures are improved; multi-ethnic and multi-cultural cities become more common.

Mature countries modify their retirement policies. At first this has little effect. But around 2025, new cohorts of retirees arrive who are not so generously funded, and have to rely much more on individual savings. These help overcome the capital shortage and also increase the incentive to work longer and to learn longer. Taxes on income will be lower and less progressive.

Experiments with cooperative living schemes where the young old begin to care for the old old are gradually transformed into a mass movement.

Economy

The shift to service industries, especially human services, continues in localizing labour markets, but is limited by price increases. Good quality services become a luxury.

An ageing workforce proves advantageous in complex work such as that of lawyers, bankers or high-level consultants, but lags behind in many other fields – especially high technology – where technical knowledge or analytical methods are based on new knowledge.

Mature cities rely on long-accumulated depreciating investment in the built environment. With declining population and employment, it proves difficult to maintain extended capital-intensive and maintenance-intensive infrastructure (subways, sewer systems). Immobile ageing people consume more space per head; population densities decline. Economic contraction reduces demand for office space and even more so for factory space, creating problems for real estate markets. Thus, refurbishment instead of new construction, and fewer spectacular architectural projects.

Economy

Interrelated strategies to overcome the burden of ageing will have drastic consequences for labour markets:

- Through higher incentives to work, producing a smaller gap between gross and net income;

- Through larger labour supplies because of a longer working life;

- Through lifelong learning and integration of learning into the work process;

- Through reduced prices of services as a consequence of lower taxes on income.

Better-functioning labour markets make cities more attractive for outside and local investors. Investment is higher, capital intensity increases, bringing higher productivity, higher income and a broader tax base – positive shock waves through the economic system.

The changes profit the city budget. Social spending on the unemployed and the elderly becomes much lower; the total budget is higher. So spending on infrastructure, promotion of economic development, training or housing can increase.

Society

Unemployment does not automatically disappear as labour supply declines, because of the continuing mismatch between demand for high-skilled workers and supply of under-educated workers. Unemployment concentrates in low-quality inner-city areas, increasingly isolated from mainstream society. The affluent move out to safer, more attractive areas, where social disruption risk is lower. Growing geographical and social division, with a semi-permanent educational underclass: widening gap between educational standards in affluent areas and in deprived areas where truancy and exclusion are common. Unemployed and low-income groups are increasingly aware of their plight, and vent their frustration against the affluent. More deprived young adults take to hard drugs, becoming permanently detached from regular employment and social aspirations.

High crime levels, with major increases in burglary, car theft, assault and drug-related crimes; streets in deprived areas become no-go areas. Urban riots and disturbances become regular occurrences.

Increasingly, old age again means poverty for those unable to save. Old people will again become dependent on their families, who may be reluctant to shoulder the burden.

Society

Traditionally, an ageing population tended to generate greater inequality, structural unemployment and low growth. But now, more intense international competitiveness produces new, more flexible economic behaviour, higher productivity growth and improved competitiveness. Key instruments: education and learning together with incentives to higher savings, longer working life, and more intensive integrative measures for immigrants, combined in a complex strategy. More people participate in public-private partnership projects and cooperative efforts in supportive neighbourhoods. Targeting of funds on schools in poor areas greatly reduces educational disparities, so inner-urban areas begin to lose their stigma, and a new generation of middle-class professionals seizes the opportunity to buy subsidized housing at very advantageous prices. The shortage of young people increases the willingness to invest in each individual, to develop human capital to protect and develop high standards of living, especially for growing numbers of ageing people.

Radically new habits evolve, as the family cannot fulfil its traditional function of providing informal services, especially health care services. New informal relations among neighbours and networks of self-help groups slowly provide a substitute, overcoming traditional attitudes and behaviour patterns.

Environment

Mature cities have the highest consumption of energy, water, space per head, and materials, and thus need to be at the forefront - first in energy savings, later as the prime movers in the transition into a new energy age. But political inertia intervenes. The ecological footprint continues to increase until 2015, continuing to override technological advances which secure reductions in resource use.

Environment

Cities aiming to become more healthy and more attractive will become active pressure groups for emission-free cars, since they will suffer most from smog and air pollution. In a decentralized world of powerful cities, transformation of urban transportation is quite quickly achieved. New large-scale traffic management systems – incorporating road pricing, new logistical systems with strong incentives for high-occupancy cars, more efficient delivery to businesses – increase street capacity and traffic speeds, simply through more efficient use of each vehicle. Mature cities catch up with the advanced traffic management systems of pioneers like Singapore and Hong Kong.

Increasing budgets allow cities to improve infrastructure and provide more attractive environments for (new) companies and inhabitants.

Prices are used to economize the use of water, electricity and heating and cooling energy. Cities cooperate with industrial companies to launch large-scale recycling efforts for industrial waste and household waste.

High prices for fossil fuels and atomic power help generate an energy revolution - the transition to the solar energy/hydrogen age - which allows more decentralized independent energy production. Buildings are transformed by a new wave of energy modernization, including a transition to smart buildings where sensors and

157

computers will control optimum use and production of energy, allowing a more efficient and comfortable use.

Urban Form

Despite low population growth, the growth of smaller households, coupled with rising living standards for some, and the inertia of old people who remain in their housing, produces further pressures for deconcentration of people and activities. These meet NIMBY policies in neighbouring rural authorities, which paradoxically divert pressures farther out. But ageing may reduce Nimbyism: demands from the aged will bring an influx of younger people, especially families, who need cheap land and housing. As young people become scarcer, their needs become a priority for many cities and suburbs, and among these will be a greater supply of land for housing.

The growth in numbers of retirees, and their relative wealth, helps produce growth of smaller towns in rural and coastal resort areas, sometimes far from the retirees' former homes (e.g. southern France, southern Spain, Florida, southern California). An ageing city needs more space per head than the city of today with a younger population.

Mature cities are not and will not be homogeneous. They can be subdivided into:

- A European-type high-density city, with well-functioning sys-

Urban Form

Spatial growth is higher than in the 'Business as Usual' scenario, as people are wealthier and able to afford more housing. There are more jobs, so demand for office space grows. More flexible markets aid adjustment of housing consumption to meet changing needs. Cities and neighbourhoods work together to develop ways of adapting homogeneous housing stocks, designed for families, to the needs of an ageing population. Mobility within neighbourhoods is encouraged, allowing older people to move into more convenient smaller houses or apartments; empty sites are used for infill housing. Thus, different generations can live together in the same neighbourhoods: the precondition for mutual aid among generations, which is the essential basis for reduced dependency on market services or communal services for old people. These flexible three-generation neighbourhoods will use less capital and less space than segregated housing areas. Reinventing the car and reinventing energy will give households greater freedom to select locations according to individual preferences.

Cities use their planning powers to combat market trends towards lower densities and more car-oriented living, especially shopping;

tems of planning controls enforcing minimum densities which
control the tendencies of markets
to overuse space in low-density
developments and by green belts
and other areas prohibited from
building.

- An American-type sprawling
  city, with densities so low that in
  part public transport disappears.
  This may experience extreme
  difficulty as more very old people
  demand personal services which
  cannot be provided efficiently
  under conditions of low-density
  sprawl and decreasing numbers
  of people per individual family
  home.

Many European-style mature
cities are physically well-main-
tained, but some lose population
from older inner areas, compensated by partial regeneration close
to the centre. In problematic cases,
this results in widespread abandonment. But smaller cities and towns
continue to grow rapidly, fuelled by
their roles as local service centres
(health, education), and as incuba-
tors of innovative small firms.

cities retain their traditional
medium-density urban form. Protection of urban heritage becomes a
priority: irreplaceable buildings,
squares or ensembles of buildings
are seen as having great value.
Dynamic but historic cities, driven
by enlightened self-interest and by
emotional ties to their own past,
compete to demonstrate the successful incorporation of their
heritage into their present-day
structures.

CHAPTER IV

Rising to the Urban Challenge: Governance and Policy

IV. Rising to the Urban Challenge: Governance and Policy

Guiding Principles for Urban Governance

Fundamental Goals and Requirements

We must now move from prediction to prescription. The central task is to confront the trend-based scenario of Chapter III with a set of policies, derived from the fundamental principles from Chapter I, that will 'bend the trends', steering the urban world in different and more sustainable directions.

Successful urban strategies will be possible only if national and local governments work in close cooperation, if central governments define more clearly the most efficient distribution of functions between the different levels of government (state, provinces, regions, cities, counties, suburbs), and if political activities follow a common framework.

Sustainability: from Concept to Implementation

Everyone has the right . . . to have the environment protected for the benefit of present and future generations, through reasonable legislative and other measures that . . . secure ecologically sustainable development and use of natural resources, while promoting justifiable economic and social development.

Section 24, South African Bill of Rights

At the end of the twentieth century, accumulated knowledge and experience – some of it still painful, as at Chernobyl and Bhopal – has brought a consensus, stated in Chapter I: *sustainable (urban) development should be the guiding principle for urban policy and governance*. This means searching for a policy that will successfully achieve rapid economic growth and also redistribute incomes; a struggle to reduce social inequalities, to promote social and political integration, and achieve the protection of the environment. This is easy to state in general terms, much harder to achieve in everyday decisions. Building a basic consensus around the general principle was an important step, achieved slowly over the past decade. Better implementation and promotion must be the central task of the years to come.

The task is compounded by the fact that there are interrelationships between different strategies. A strategy may promote multiple goals. Thus the problem is to try to reconcile the objectives. Economic and social goals used often to be seen as quite separate, but can be reconciled through the pursuit of more efficient production coupled with targeted initiatives to alleviate poverty. Environmental tasks used to be seen as a burden on development, but since the early 1980s we have accepted the accumulated evidence that environmental degradation is itself a major barrier to development. Thus, in recent years it has become possible to see economic development, equity and environmental protection as aspects of the same task.

Strategies can serve multiple ends: a better-quality physical and social environment can help a city generate new economic growth. For this and other reasons, we need to integrate environmental concerns into our economic decision-making: using new technology to reduce resource use, incorporating environmental concerns into our economic accounting, and increasing incentives to secure more efficient resource use in both production and consumption. That way, we can improve our consumption standards and our environmental standards all at once. But it will not always be easy: the most severe trade-offs arise between social and ecological objectives, where helping poor people may compromise the environment.

Thus there has emerged a new and broader understanding of the central task – to achieve multi-dimensional sustainable development – and also of some ways to achieve it. Good governance, seen as an integrated effort on the part of local government, civil society and the private sector, will set sustainable development as its central objective. The effort should involve people, groups, individual companies, and a multitude of public state and local agencies. Figure IV.1 demonstrates how the different agents cooperate.

Good governance will act as the motor and political driving force, keeping the different elements of sustainable development in balance, integrating them in policies, and ensuring that all the different agencies in the city share the responsibilities and the benefits. Sustainability as the principle, good governance as the practice, thus become the twin aspects of good urban development.

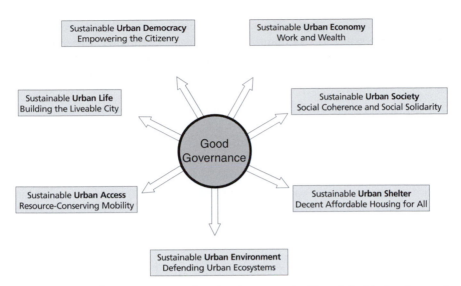

Figure IV.1. Good governance, an all-embracing concept with sustainable development as its central objective.

Box IV.1. Definitions of sustainable development.

> Humanity has the ability to make development sustainable – to ensure that it meets the needs of the present without compromising the ability of future generations to meet their own needs.
>
> (WCED, 1987, p. 8)
>
> Sustainable development means improving the quality of human life while living within the carrying capacity of supporting ecosystems.
>
> (IUCN, UNEP, 1991, p. 221)
>
> Sustainable development is development that delivers basic environmental, social and economic services to all residents of a community without threatening the viability of natural, built and social systems upon which the delivery of those systems depends.
>
> (ICLEI, 1996, p. 4)

Rules for Good Governance

Subsidiarity and Solidarity

Subsidiarity means that decision-making should be made at the lowest possible level, and that services should be provided at the lowest level which is technically able to provide specific cost effective services without creating too many overspill effects. The segregation of rich and poor people into different political communities can increase inequality: differences in private income and wealth are extended into the public sector – and, in the worst case, into the quality of schools and education or health care.

Solidarity is important because without it, local autonomy can all too easily lead to intolerable inequality, especially where education depends on local revenue. The key instrument to combat inequality between different municipalities consists of equalization grants from central government, which should guarantee a minimum level of resources to enable fiscally-poor local governments to fulfil their most basic functions. Citizens' basic urban rights should depend as little as possible on the fiscal capacity of individual local authorities.

Varieties of Capitalism: Working with Markets

Since the collapse of the communist system at the end of the 1980s, the market economy has literally spanned the globe. It has shown its superiority to any other model for generating capital accumulation and increasing the world's wealth. But it has also become very evident that there is more than one way of managing such a market system; there are different forms of contemporary capitalism, and they result from deep cultural differences that may originate far back in history. An Anglo-American form of capitalism, emphasizing entrepreneurial innovation, free competition and deregulated labour markets, exists next to a mainland European model ('Rhineland capitalism'), characterized by stronger frameworks of regulation, managed labour markets, employee protection, co-determination in management, and generous social benefits (Albert, 1993). And there is a third model – the Japanese or Pacific Asian model – characterized by low public spending as a percentage of GDP, relatively weak social benefits and emphasis on self or family provision, consensus in decision-making in both the economic and political spheres, and cooperative management to improve quality in the workplace.

These differences have deep historic roots: 'Rhineland capitalism' can be traced back at least to Bismarck's welfare reforms of the 1890s, and even to Stein's educational reforms, which established the Prussian state as a strong generator of scientific and technological progress The Japanese state became similarly involved in generating technological advance soon after the Meiji revolution in 1868, while the tradition of consensus seems to lie much further back in Sino-Japanese culture.

In Asia, Singapore and Korea have developed quite distinct forms of economic management, in contrast to Indonesia or the Philippines. Both have kept a balance between private investment and infrastructure. Housing has had a high priority in their development strategy. While other countries accepted big differences in housing quality, with a high percentage of informal housing without adequate infrastructure, they have large housing estates with high-rise buildings: a visible sign of a different development concept, in which the state accepts greater responsibility for urban and economic development.

Three important conclusions emerge:

- There is no one single best way of running a capitalist economy or a city. What works for one country may not work for another. What works for one period may not work for another;

- Differences stem from cultural origins that may go a long way back into history;

- All economies at all times operate within rules or parameters set by policies. Even Victorian Britain at the height of *laissez-faire* had such a system, visible in a very distinct style of building and urban design. No government is willing to give over the operation of the system entirely to the market: the risk of market failures, ranging from waste of natural and human resources to the risk of gross inequities, is only too evident.

But urban policies do best when they work with market forces, not against them. That does not mean that policy just has to accept market forces as given: the essence is to understand how far they can be bent and influenced to achieve defined policy ends. Regional policy provides an apt illustration: after World War II, many countries sought to divert industrial growth from more highly-industrialized, congested regions into less developed areas, but such policies often resulted in 'cathedrals in the desert' which were not economically viable; while countries as diverse as the UK and France or Egypt also sought to decentralize people and economic activity from their capital cities to new towns on the metropolitan periphery, and this policy was successful where it anticipated market forces: both manufacturing industries and routine services were actively interested to decentralize to nearby locations where they could enjoy lower-cost operations, while still sharing in the agglomeration economies of the metropolitan region.

Another example: Singapore in the 1960s deliberately sought to achieve rapid economic development by climbing the learning curve, starting by specializing in low-value labour-intensive goods that could compete on low price, moving then into progressively higher-technology production and finally into becoming the service centre for a much wider economic region; it anticipated the process whereby manufacturing employment would decentralize into lower-cost offshore locations, and made sure that it was correctly positioned for a new economic role. Intelligent anticipation of market forces and trends, and deliberate generation of policies to take advantage of them, rather than being overwhelmed by them, are the essence of successful economic policy – including urban economic policy.

Government and Civil Society: New Forms of Partnership

There is an inherent tendency for governments, which are under constant pressure from companies and citizens to pursue policies in their favour, to try to achieve too much and to take on responsibilities they cannot shoulder. Good governance demands that government limits itself to the most urgent and most productive tasks, and that outside energies and resources be mobilized. This means close cooperation with civil society in all shapes and forms: with neighbourhood groups, with NGOs, with religious groups, with self-help activities, and also with individuals willing to improve the supply of collective goods, or to build up networks among people needing help and other people willing to provide assistance.

Integrated Action of the Various Levels of Government

Governments have to fulfil various economic functions which are necessarily shared between different levels of government and often between different institutions. In abstract terms, three tasks have to be resolved:

- Stabilization,

- Distribution, and

- Allocation.

Best practice normally reserves the stabilization and distribution functions to the central/federal level of government, while allocation dominates the local level. Fundamental equity issues must be handled essentially at the central government level. In particular, central governments can use demand side instruments such as negative income tax, income tax credits, vouchers or allowance payments. At the local level the basic principle should be that people pay for publicly-provided local services according to cost.

Of course, there are also typical central allocative government functions; thus, national highways as parts of national networks are obvious central government responsibilities. Local governments should be responsible for local services and infrastructure: schools, sewer systems, parks and streets, administrative buildings with regional or urban catchment areas. Taxes and other sources of revenue can only be defined adequately if we simultaneously define responsibilities. Fiscal needs arise out of responsibilities; sources of revenue should correspond to responsibilities.

One could argue that in developing countries – especially countries with low income and high population growth – more of the allocative functions should be performed above the local level because (1) absolute poverty requires immediate allocational remedies, and (2) higher-level governments are better equipped to provide what is needed, and cities often do not have the capacity or the technical knowledge to perform certain functions. But on average central governments cannot be richer than cities. Centralizing functions in most cases does not reduce costs through economies of scale. They can only take away resources which should have gone to cities in the first place. Only in cases of absolute scarcity of management capacities is it rational that central governments should concentrate specialized capacities as a precondition of delivery. In this case development should bring decentralization.

The Need to Prioritize

This principle is one of the fundamentals of economics, and indeed of a rational life: it is impossible to do everything we want at once. In the cities of the developing world, above all, there are so many urgent necessities, and that means some very hard, even ruthless, decisions about what must be done first. One top priority must be to respect human life. That means, first, priority for health, above all for mothers and their children in the months of pregnancy and in the first year of life.

The second priority should go to education, as economic progress depends on human capital. But it is also a matter of the critical early education that parents give their children in the first years of life. And here, women's education is crucial. There is a close link to the health priority: the evidence is clear that the fastest and most effective way to reduce excess births is through educating the mothers. Stating general priorities, again, does not help in deciding individual cases; there is always the question 'how much', since other less urgent demands cannot simply be reduced to zero. General priority rules are no substitute for careful assessment of the individual case or situation, comparing the priority to be given to shelter, work, or mobility as against health or education.

Delivering Local Services Locally: Decentralization

People want control of their own affairs, and should have that control. Autonomy demands decentralization. As constant feedback between delivery organizations and clients is a necessity, flat hierarchies are desirable – sometimes even in cases where scale economies would suggest larger capacities and more centralized delivery systems.

Decentralization must not be seen as the result of a generous central government giving away powers it owns. Decentralization is an

169

optimization of power and responsibility which belong to the people; the people have to decide how best it suits them to express and organize their political will.

Optimization demands that we look at technology, at communication, at the size of minimum capacity to deliver goods and services, at the size and integration of cities or fiscal capacity. Technical progress in the last decades has very often worked in favour of smaller, more decentralized service providers. Electricity can be produced in decentralized small plants; computers are ubiquitous and allow direct access to central information; there are all kinds of innovative precedents for decentralization.

But decentralization can slow down diffusion of knowledge and best practice. Therefore all decentralized systems have to give priority to communication, exchange of experiences or imitation of best practice.

Separating Policy from Delivery

The basic general principles are fiscal autonomy, internal checks and balances, and a public sector which provides basic goods for the development of the city. This does not demand public production, though tradition and political interests would often suggest that it does. To the voters, all that matters is the results. Therefore, in developed and developing countries alike, local governments should opt for the most efficient solution, which often means trying to shrink their production activities, transferring or transforming them to competitive market producers. This can of course include subsidization of unprofitable activities and regulation on the consumption side, to ensure that private producers supply goods and services in harmony with the political goal of sustainable development.

Good Governance in Practice

The Central Concept: Governance Equals Cooperation

Good governance is much more than simply a rule book for regulating the behaviour of government. It is a cooperative effort for sustainable development, undertaken in concert by local government, civil society groups and the private business sector. It is entrepreneurship to achieve public goals. It is a creative answer to local needs, using local resources, creating organizations and institutions which coordinate a multitude of efforts integrating community organizations, private companies and governmental actors.

Good governance will not be possible if public administration is corrupt or inefficient. It will not be possible if neighbourhood groups act in isolation without assistance from NGOs or public agencies. It will not be possible if the private sector acts as an isolated profit maximizer, neglecting the burden imposed on private households who have to live with the pollution or squalor created by unfettered production activities. Good governance needs a climate of tolerance and cooperation. It needs integrative institutions and decentralized participation. It has to survive with a permanent tension that will always occur between stable organizations and spontaneous activities which arise as answers to urgent needs or to urban crises.

Governance in Search of Better Results

(Urban) Government Matters

The enormous differences between the performance of cities and states which act in the same global world economy can be explained, at least partially, by differences in governance which, in turn, are connected to basic values and behaviour of the people. Governance does matter. In its 1997 development report the World Bank demonstrated the relevance of governments in promoting development.

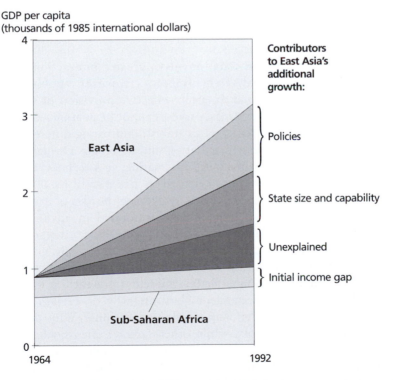

Figure IV.2. Good government: A help to understand the income gap between East Asia and Africa. (*Source:* World Bank, 1997)

171

As figure IV.2 shows, GDP per capita in East Asia in the 1960s was about the same as in Africa. By the 1990s, it was five times higher. Government consumption in Africa had expanded one and a half times as much as in East Asia. It is widely believed that the superior performance of the State in East Asia – the limits it set on its own growth, the soundness of the policies it adopted, and the effectiveness with which it delivered services – has made a powerful contribution to the growing gap in the quality of life experienced by the average citizen between the two parts of the world (World Bank, 1997). However, the relationship between governance and economic performance is not a solution in itself. It does not answer the question of how to create conditions for better government; how to organize effective government; how to fight corruption; or how to motivate voters to vote for effective politicians with sound development concepts and not for populist bosses who promise instant gratification without a sound economic basis; or to participate in political movements which will promote effective development strategies.

The relationship between good governance and development is more complex than assumed in the 1960s, when five-year central government plans were common practice, and politicians in North and South acted on the assumption that economic development could be influenced directly or even controlled by a few economic instruments. Development as a task limited to a few governmental agencies and instruments has failed, or at best has had only limited success.

The development process today involves greater interaction between government agencies and civil society. However, public sector administration is still required to ensure effective provision of needs and use of resources. But in many areas, success cannot be guaranteed by direct control. The central role – to act as a catalyst, motivating different groups to come together in cooperative activities, and involving a wider range of people – has made governance more fascinating, less technocratic, more political, more human behaviour-oriented. It has moved away from the gear shifts of departments and cabinets, away from the idea of driving cities and countries according to fixed plans formulated in advance. Good governance means openness, listening, motivating, integrating or convincing people to participate according to their own goals: goals which are part of a wider democratic will, self-formulating and self-regulating. This is the vision, however imperfectly achieved at present.

Of course there is the permanent question: why do certain solutions work and others fail, under very similar conditions? Why do certain programmes mobilize people, while others attract clients who hope to become free riders? There are many good examples and a growing knowledge about good governance. One has to look at the details of successful cases – the incentives provided for different actors, the distribution of responsibilities which avoided gridlock, the relationship between available resources and the size of the tasks – to see that too often, trying too much with too few resources has been the precondition for failure. Yet more than knowledge and information is required. One ingredient of success: cities need creative and innovative learning, so as to use the best practice of other cities for their own purposes and possibilities.

A Decentralizing World

A Changing Power Structure

The 1960s and 1970s: An Age of Centralization. In the past, most countries have been considerably centralized. Exceptions, such as Switzerland and the United States, were due to specific political traditions and foundations of the state. Traditionally, in most countries, city governments have been weak. In cities of hypergrowth, their powers were mostly limited to local services like refuse collection or street cleaning, while important functions or powers – e.g. police, education, housing, health care or even urban planning – were in the hands of central or provincial governments or state agencies which, moreover, controlled municipal finance through grants. Local taxes were the exception. Local tax collection was weak. As a general rule, local public sector spending by developing cities was as little as 15 per cent of total public spending in the 1970s, in contrast to some European countries (Denmark, Sweden, Finland) where local spending (including regional spending) reached 40-50 per cent of total government spending.

Such centralization brought many negative consequences:

- Mayors were often appointed by central governments, which meant low accountability;

- Local politics tended to be weak as voter turnout at local elections was low, because people were well aware of the insignificance of their vote;

- Plans took longer to prepare and even longer to implement;

- Local preferences had only a limited influence on public spending, which was determined by central administrations according to their own, often uniform, interpretation of local needs.

The 1980s and 1990s: An Age of Decentralization. The late 1980s laid the foundations of a totally new approach across Africa, Asia and Latin America, by focusing on three themes: *Accountability, Markets and Democratization.* In a globalizing world the nation state was in retreat ideologically and seemed less relevant than twenty years before. Supranational organizations like the European Union and other intra-continental groupings became more relevant. In several countries regions gained more internal autonomy. A new regionalism found a stronger base among voters and acceptance at the central level in such different countries as the UK, Brazil or Australia. Decentralization is not always a harmonious change, though. Regional movements can get into conflict with the central state, as in Spain or the Philippines; and sometimes, the difference between separatist movements and decentralization is difficult to tell.

The dominant trends were:

- Keynesian macro management of the economy and strong centralism reinforced each other;

- For an increasing number of people, both in the developed and the developing worlds, the concept of the powerful central state, using its taxing and distributional power to control and promote economic development, was losing at least some of the attraction it once had.

The passive state has given way to the active; or at least the ultimately responsible, historically exceptional era of unfettered market relations is over.
(Crosland, 1956)

Structural changes, such as long-term unemployment and the growth of social inequality, were also seen as a result of powerful but misguided central state policies, which were too often incapable of managing highly differentiated local and urban problems.

The failure of the centralized socialist planning model in Russia and Eastern Europe, the growing relevance of decentralized market mechanisms, and the beginnings of the dismantling of central planning in China had similar effects. In each decade, the development task progressively became more complex. Intellectually it changed from a simple matter of forced industrialization to the new emphasis on sustainability as a complex issue of governance. Policy-makers began to see intractable problems with the old development model, such as:

- Ambitious programmes with little or no administrative capacity to realize them;

- Inability to guarantee quality of services at the local level;

- High administrative costs in over-centralized organizations remote from the point of delivery;

- Difficulties in coordinating different ministries which were jointly responsible for a single set of programmes.

Empowerment of local government now appeared as a stronger, more reliable basis for democracy. After a period of capacity building and transfer of resources, empowerment had become a better solution for many development tasks which involved urban needs and participation of the urban population. Extensive worldwide experience brought about a new consensus in favour of more flexible, independent, responsible and efficient local authorities. Good governance, based on local democratic control, became a significant driving force. The process was also driven by regional traditions, tribal wishes for autonomy, demands for ethnic self-control, the growing self-confidence of local voters, and increasing differentiation of public goods and collective needs which demanded local solutions. Of the seventy-five developing and transitional countries with more than five million population, all but twelve claim to be engaged in some form of transfer of political power to local units of government and in undertaking decentralization efforts in different fields from health care delivery to infrastructure (Dillinger, 1994, p. 1).

Box IV.2. Effects of decentralization.

By the end of the 1990s decentralization was widely perceived as an instrument for promoting democratization, market development, and administrative and fiscal efficiency, although often little attention was paid to the capacities of local administrative units or local governments to take on new responsibilities. Advocates argued that when applied appropriately decentralization can help break through the bottlenecks of decision making which are often caused by central government planning and control. Decentralization can be a means of cutting through complex central bureaucratic procedures in getting revisions made and implemented. It can also increase government officials' sensitivity to local conditions and needs. Moreover, decentralization can help national government ministries reach larger numbers of local areas with services and allow change over time. Clearly defined and relatively uncomplicated planning and management procedures for eliciting participation of local leaders and citizens and for obtaining the cooperation or consent of beneficiaries are also needed.

(Rondinelli, 1998, pp. 8,9)

Because local governments are better than national governments at recognizing the needs and preferences of local residents, and because local governments are at least as efficient as national governments at delivering public goods that benefit only local residents, it will be more efficient to have local governments provide the optimal level of public goods in each local jurisdiction. Local governments can be expected to be more efficient than national governments because local residents may find it easier to hold accountable local, as opposed to national, officials. Moreover, decentralization can increase efficiency by forcing local governments to 'compete' for residents, because whenever residents have to pay fees for public services, they are free to change jurisdictions to find better and cheaper services.

(Burki and Perry, 1997, p. 81)

In Latin America, the debt crisis and structural adjustments coincided to produce a new relationship between state, local government, civil society and markets. The twin reforms of political and social democratization created a new flexibility and a wider involvement of different movements. More voluntary associations than ever before have become involved in solving poverty or environmental problems. The new democracy has resulted in less exclusive, more grassroots-oriented groups, based on neighbourhood or community movements, environmental lobbies, women's movements, human rights associations or ecclesiastical organizations. In Europe, a set of forces – new demands for direct governmental responses to local needs, inflexible reactions of central governments to growing unemployment, and increasing demand for more personal public goods, coupled with new regional movements in several countries – have made local government more popular and more powerful as central government was adjusting to new attitudes. In Asia, the growing complexity of urban management and the increasingly sophisticated demands of a growing middle class, politically competent as a result of rapid economic growth, enforced more direct government with more independent power.

Progress has also been made in some African states. In Uganda, the Local Government Act was revised in 1997 to achieve decentralization and devolution of functions, powers and services. It establishes the sources of revenue and financial accountability of the councils. Another sign of greater local responsibility is the introduction of block grants, started in 1993-94. In Mali, a decentralization initiative rooted in the new constitution began formally with the decree of January 1993 creating a mission for decentralization. In Asia, the Philippines 1991 Local Government Code is considered as one of the most revolutionary government reform laws. It transfers power to local government and routes more services through regional offices, and it provides for active participation of people in local governance (Tapales, 1996).

It would be wrong to see decentralization as a tidy or a logical process, still less as a smooth one. Many observers agree that decentralization is not a carefully designed sequence of reforms aimed at improving the efficiency of public services delivery. Rather, it often appears to be a reluctant and disorderly series of concessions by central governments attempting to maintain political stability. Very often it is a reaction to crisis in local government or frustration with the results of planning and implementation.

Yet, despite difficulties and partial and often substantial failures, reformers can still point to huge opportunities for administrative improvement, better accountability and more competent management. Clearly, there will be a long process of transition, in which local political leaders will become progressively more accountable in a fundamental democratic sense, and grow into their new responsibilities of managing

Box IV.3. Patterns of transition.

The mixture of forces and motives creates very different patterns of transition.

In Hungary, as in other transition states decentralization happened as an expression of fundamental political convictions, without detailed technical and financial preparation. The new, more responsible local authorities would have been without means of finance if they had not relied on their large property holdings, consequence of socialist economic order.

(Dillinger, 1994, p. 9)

In Brazil, decentralization was part of a general process of more democratic government and constitutional reform. Brazil's 1988 Constitution transferred significant autonomy and power to municipal governments . . . which are considered as a constitutive part of the Brazilian Federation, together with the states and the union. Brazilian municipalities are run by democratically elected mayors assisted by municipal councils. Urban policies are to be implemented at the municipal level, following the directives of Planos Diretores (Master Plans), rendered compulsory to cities with more than 20000 inhabitants pursuant to the Federal Constitution of 1988. Municipalities are exclusively responsible for providing local services such as urban public transport, water and sewage, local roads and for the planning and control of land use. General directives on urban development, housing, sanitation and urban transports at the national level are competence of the Federal Government. All levels of government are responsible for better conditions of housing and sanitation; environmental protection; historical and cultural heritage preservation and for the promotion of social integration, fighting against the causes of poverty and social exclusion.

(World Bank, 1998)

In Ghana, local political authorities were mostly created as a concession to demands for decentralization but the elected local councils do not have the power to appoint the municipal executive and the heads of municipal departments.

(Dillinger, 1994, p. 9)

It must be expected that political decentralization without empowerment will not be a viable solution. In the Philippines, a 'Local Government Code' has been enacted in 1991 which has transformed the former highly centralized politico-administrative government structure and devolves the responsibility of basic services (such as health, infrastructure, social welfare etc.) and some taxation powers to the local governments.

(Manasan, 1998)

Local Indonesian Governments provide the following services, either directly or through their enterprises: Water Supply, Sewerage, Solid Waste Management, Roads, Housing, Kampung Improvement,

Box IV.3. cont.

Education, Health, etc. But the centralized system of bureaucracy still exists and local government administrations are weak, dependent on central government grant funding. Regional governments only raise about 7% of total government revenues which finance only about one-third of their expenditures. The weak part in the decentralization process is still financial autonomy. While in some European countries local authorities control up to 50% of government spending Latin American or Asian figures still after a long process of growth stay around 10-20%.

(Ter-Minassian, 1997)

Box IV.4. Decentralization of governance in Latin America.

There has been a 'quiet revolution': a decentralization of government, involving three elements: discretion to local government [though often this led to 'finances chasing functions', with excess local funds, local governments generally behaved responsibly]; democratization, not only in central government but in more than 13,000 units of state [intermediate] and local levels; and a new model of governance involving more people seeking office, more professional staff, and a new 'willingness to pay' for improved services among electorates. Many mayors have stepped up participatory consultations, making it more difficult to ignore public views later.

(Campbell, 1996, pp. 2-3)

their own affairs. Efforts at reorganization are very often seriously damaged by economic cycles and crises or the development of the world economy, which affect every city and every neighbourhood, and cannot be modified or removed by local political agencies. However, there is a real chance that resources will be distributed more evenly and efficiently in future. Allocative progress today is a necessary basis for progress tomorrow. The sooner improvements start, the sooner they generate results, attacking the waste of centralized bureaucratic allocation.

One successful approach is to learn from the ineffectiveness of previous policies. For instance, the Urban Housing Sub-Programme of the Million Homes Programme in Sri Lanka discovered that, although the government had built 150,000 housing units, for every house the government had built, people had built six. Thus the government changed its approach to provide a supporting rather than a providing role to meet the growing needs of the low-income population (UNDP, 1995, p. 16).

Of course decentralization is not a worldwide simultaneous process. In many countries traditional governmental structures have remained unchanged and efforts to achieve more local democracy have achieved little success so far. The main reason has been the lack of resources at the local level. Nairobi represents this type of city.

Box IV.5. Crisis and opportunities: The case of Nairobi.

Nairobi's system of urban government is in a state of collapse due to a number of factors, including its historical origins and its inappropriateness for dealing with present day social and economic circumstances. The central government manipulated the Nairobi City Council through most of its history by suspension, legislative change, nomination of council members and other means. This was disruptive rather than aimed at policy reform or good governance. The city was starved of revenue and prevented from responding to citizens' demands for services.

This is not to say that Nairobi City Council itself has, or could have performed well as an urban government without extensive central government interference. Constrained at the start by conflicting pressures of population growth, unserviced neighbourhoods, high standards and expectations and reductions in revenue, the elected local government faced an almost impossible task. Yet it showed the capacity of delivering affordable housing and services until internal mismanagement and external interference intervened in the early eighties.

Nevertheless, even these services and houses satisfied only a small proportion of demand. A lack of vision and willingness to come to terms with reality led to a situation where more than half the city's residents (1.1 million people) live outside the frame of reference of urban government. Citizens are routinely harassed and evicted from their homes and work, apart from being denied services.

It is obvious that good governance in Nairobi depends on the creation of a genuine negotiation mechanism among the various stakeholders and the establishment of institutional structures to accommodate their different interests. New institutional initiatives (for example Nairobi's Informal Settlement and Coordination Committee (NISCC)) represent the main opportunity of forging a new system of governance, which would need to incorporate the interests of the majority of urban residents in formal government structures. The NCC lacks capacity to deliver services even if it had the political will to do so. Yet citizens, whether they are high or low income, wish to improve their surroundings. They require institutional mechanisms enabling them to agree on how to achieve this for their mutual benefit. This onerous task should be tackled through negotiation and power sharing rather than exclusion, political confrontation and physical conflict as at present. The environment of social and political reform of the late nineteen nineties presents an opportunity for stakeholder groups to associate more freely than they have done in the past and to begin to participate in urban governance.

(Lamba and Lee-Smith, 1998, pp. 16-17)

Decentralization by itself does not overcome the reality of the gap in resources. Cities – still experiencing extreme population growth, in many developing countries- are at present simply too poor to provide adequate solutions to their huge environmental, educational, or management problems. They are torn between the demands of an influential formal-sector population and the exploding needs of the non-integrated informal areas, where growth occurs without provision of urban infrastructure. This fundamental lack of resources dominates all their activities and policies. The question for the next decade is whether greater local responsibilities will mobilize more local resources and more local partnerships to promote more sustainable forms of development. Equally important are new policies related to the informal sector, which need to mobilize local resources of labour, by offering incentives and assistance for neighbourhood organizations to begin a slow but steady accumulation process in infrastructure and housing wealth, based on stable tenure rights and financial help which can function as seed money.

Decentralization: An Ongoing Political and Economic Process

The transition – from traditional, centralized, administration to good, responsive, flexible, decentralized governance – is not going to happen overnight. The titanic efforts of the last two decades, and the limited successes so far, show how wearisome and fragile the process will be. For a large part of the urban population measurable results are yet to come. National governments are still slow in adjusting. A kind of law of political gravity seems to be pulling resources into the political centre and keeping power over-centralized, still ignoring specific local needs and wishes, and thus failing to generate adequate local programmes of urban development. Central governments still do not transfer power gracefully or rationally. Too often, they have to be dragged into local autonomy.

Meanwhile, the need for independent local policies, tailored to the demands of the local situation and the local citizenry, continues to grow. It would be a misunderstanding to see decentralization as a zero sum game where central governments give away responsibilities to local governments to concentrate on their own tasks. Central governments have to change their attitudes and adjust their behaviour in the process of decentralization. In reality, even after administrative decentralization, a clear-cut division of functions will be the exception. Central governments will remain in charge of local affairs, at least through enabling municipalities to fulfil their role and transferring information and knowledge. Central governments will always carry responsibility for the political climate or pace of implementation. They deal with public sector unions or with pension systems. They influence the dedication, status and self-esteem of civil servants or public workers, as well as the prestige and emotions generated by successes in local affairs. Decentralization is therefore a very fundamental political development, requiring a learning process on both sides to achieve a new balance of governance.

As so often in the past, at the heart of central-local relations lies the question of financial and regulatory autonomy. Thus, in spite of decentralization, in most countries central or federal legislation still defines the tax base of municipalities and the arrangements which govern revenue sharing between state and municipalities, or between one municipality and another. It also imposes restrictions on the management powers of municipalities. Thus, in Brazil, detailed federal regulations still define local activities in many fields. For instance, the federal Constitution prohibits dismissals (except for cause, the definition of which has been expanded by a recent constitutional reform), and nominal reductions in salaries, and requires municipalities to provide generous retirement benefits. Central government also makes federal transfers to the municipalities, and regulates the contractual borrowing of cities.

In 1995, own tax revenues of the (Brazilian) subnational governments accounted for nearly 38 per cent of total tax revenues (including social security contributions) and were equivalent to 10.5 per cent of GDP. The share of tax revenues at the disposal of subnational governments (defined to include own plus shared revenues) represented nearly 50 per cent of total tax revenues. In the same year, state and local governments accounted for about 60 per cent of public consumption and for 63 per cent of public investments. By contrast, the federal government (mainly through the social security system) maintained a preponderant (over 80 per cent) share in social transfers.

(Ter-Minassian, 1997, p. 438)

The growth of revenues and responsibilities should increase in parallel. Growing local powers will generate a growing interest in local democracy, and growing local control will increase demand for efficient, customer-oriented provision of services. Efficiency means the application of modern technology, improved resource allocation, and faster reaction to demands of the local client-citizenry and needs of neighbourhoods or groups. Thus, by combining traditional 'allocative efficiency' with 'democratic efficiency', more democratic control will lead to a more equitable supply of services and infrastructure.

In many cases, decentralization has had only weak measurable results; and many cities are still run by small oligarchic groups, while the great majority either have no voting rights or do not vote because they think their representatives will do nothing for them. However, implementation of institutional changes imply important time lags. Despite risks, local autonomy based on local democracy will be the long-term solution. Fundamental democratic convictions and popular demand are the relevant criteria which will make decentralized solutions more acceptable and more sustainable. Decentralization should strengthen local democracy by:

- Overcoming government by small elites, party leaders or representatives of interest groups to achieve accountable local government;

- Integrating members of the population who live and work in the informal sector, who are still largely excluded; and

- Improving access to schools as the long-term basis for economic stability, sustainability and democracy.

Only an educated and motivated citizenry can seize the opportunities and effectively benefit from such decentralization strategies.

Successful examples of deconcentrated federal systems exist in Western Europe, the USA and Canada. Some European cities, in particular, combine high standards of public management and local participation. But they are based on quite wealthy local authorities which have the means to react to the demands of the population, and on long traditions of self-government. Their successes did not happen overnight; they have emerged out of a long-term relationship between local autonomy and active local political involvement.

Box IV.6. Tasks in India's municipalities.

There are different administrative traditions but from India to Switzerland certain similarities occur. After constitutional changes, local authorities in India are responsible for a typical set of tasks which seem to become a general standard:
1. Urban planning
2. Land-use regulations
3. Socio-economic planning
4. Roads and bridges
5. Water supply
6. Public health, sanctions, conservancy and solid waste management
7. Fire services
8. Urban forestry
9. Slum improvement and up-grading
10. Urban poverty alleviation
11. Parks, gardens, playgrounds
12. Public amenities-street lighting, parking etc.

(Sinha, undated, p. 3)

In the developing world, it is likely that the full consequences of decentralization will only be seen over several decades. Here, greater local responsibilities cannot immediately overcome typical weaknesses in tax base, administrative capacity and political participation. Local autonomy and development will go hand-in-hand, in a mutually-reinforcing process.

Powerful mayors, exercising strong local powers which attract entrepreneurial figures, can play a particularly important role. Such strong political figures tend to formulate ambitious goals and to be successful in achieving them. Already, in many developing countries, mayors have become leading innovators in the public realm, setting off a succession of developments which attract attention not merely in their cities, but even internationally. Their cities become celebrated examples of 'good urban practice'. However, local conditions influence the quality of local leadership and its effectiveness.

Political localization will have a strong economic basis:

- While capital markets and markets for industrial goods together with financial services will further globalize, labour markets will localize, as more and more people work in producing low-tech non-tradable local goods. Labour markets will continue to be local markets.

- Production for global markets happens in plants or service institutions that often have a strong local basis. Thus, the effectiveness and quality of production for global markets have local roots. The quality of local goods is relevant for a high quality of global market goods. Local politics matters, even for the most global companies

- More intense local political involvement in the local economy could become an effective force for mobilization. More local powers, more intensive cooperation between the private sector and municipal administration, and more active voters should make the local political role more visible. Despite the problems of a long transition period, local autonomy remains a central political theme for active and effective local anti-poverty strategies.

Promoting integrated urban development after decentralization will remain a central political and economic task. In the first decades of the new century, slower population growth and new technical and organizational solutions should foster a more effective struggle against poverty. Local autonomy cannot be seen as an instant remedy, but it is a long-term basis for more intense and direct personal effort. The result, two or three decades into the twenty-first century, should be a network of powerful cities, much more independent than in the recent past, appearing as new winners in an international urban championship conducted in a new age of more closely interrelated markets.

Decentralizing inside the City: Power to the Neighbourhoods

Democratic governance demands the representation of all relevant groups. Decentralizing power from the nation to the city cannot stop in city hall. Participation of neighbourhoods and different groups in the process of allocation of local municipal resources has to be the local equivalent. Differences of interest, conflicts between groups, and uneven representation

Box IV.7. Old assumptions versus new visions in urban policy-making.

Old Assumptions	New Visions
Cities are the problem.	Cities are the sources of innovation and economic growth.
The countryside subsidizes the city.	The city subsidizes the countryside.
Cities are becoming too large.	The larger the city, the greater the opportunities.
Public policies should be aimed at limiting city size.	Public policies should be aimed at making cities work better.
Migrants to the city are the 'dregs of the barrel': those who couldn't make it in the countryside.	The migrants are the 'cream of the crop': more highly skilled and motivated than those they left behind.
The squatters are a drain on the urban economy and urban services.	The squatters contribute more to the economy than they receive in return.
Squatter settlements are hotbeds of unrest, criminality, and drug-dealing.	The majority of families in squatter settlements have the political 'values of patriots and the perseverance of pioneers'.
Cities contribute disproportionately to the population explosion.	Birth rates drop significantly with urbanization.
Cities and the urban poor are the enemies of the fight against environmental degradation.	Transformed urban practices are essential to global ecological sustainability.
Solid waste and human waste are garbage that must be discarded 'elsewhere'.	If circular (not linear) systems are used, waste becomes a valuable resource.
The government, planners, and experts will provide solutions for urban problems.	The most creative solutions arise from the bottom up rather than the top down.
Government programmes provide most housing for the poor.	The informal sector is the primary generator of housing and jobs and income.
Stronger city government authority is needed to cope with urban management problems.	Decentralized management facilitates a more effective match between resources and needs; removing the obstacles to such activities is the key.

(UNDP, 1995, p. 8)

are a permanent feature of local politics. Securing balanced representation and participation is still a challenge, especially in cities experiencing hypergrowth, where the informal-sector population is not fully integrated into the economic system or the city as system of infrastructure.

In mature cities with a highly educated more homogeneous population, representation of all interests and values may not cause problems. But in many poorer cities, substantial groups remain effectively outside the political process. Here, the democracy of the ballot box may fail to represent many residents adequately, in particular members of the informal sector and immigrants without the right to vote. Even where cities are divided into wards or districts which are represented in city councils, whole areas and groups can be excluded from political participation, if the system of representation fails to articulate their needs.

A 'project democracy', which enables local groups to become involved in decisions of direct concern to them and in their implementation, could integrate them into the political process. They would thus be in a position to resolve their own affairs. Special issues of general interest would be decided in local ballots. Budgets or other relevant themes would be openly and thoroughly discussed with community leaders or even entire neighbourhoods to overcome the dominant influence of bureaucracies or powerful interests. Functionally specialized city administrations would be transformed into more locally responsible district or ward agencies, accountable to their own localities.

Box IV.8. The changing responsibilities of Johannesburg's new local government.

The new councillors and officials experience government differently from the old councillors and officials. If councillors of the old Johannesburg City Council were to confront problems with trash collection or illegal subdivision, they would phone the head of a well resourced department and expect it to respond with alacrity. The problems concerning the constituents of new councillors are diffuse and most often they cannot be directly resolved by councillors themselves. They concern jobs, housing, services, violence, foreign migrants seemingly taking the best informal trading opportunities in the city centre, taxi lawlessness, and so on; and the councillors are a link in an under-resourced network where sometimes they can make a difference and sometimes not.

(Tomlinson, 1998, p.16)

There remains a problem: strengthening neighbourhoods does not overcome the problem of selecting and controlling community leaders. Local democracy in informal neighbourhoods will often be in its infancy, as the everyday struggle for survival or lack of contact with local leaders

Box IV.9. Participatory city budget, Porto Alegre, Brazil.

Porto Alegre is the capital of the state of Rio Grande do Sul in Brazil and home to some 1.3 million inhabitants. In 1988, a coalition of left parties led by the Workers' Party, or Partido dos Trabalhadores (PT), gained control of the municipal government of Porto Alegre and won consecutive elections in 1992 and 1996. Their most substantial reform measure, called 'Participatory Budgeting', attempted to transform the vote-for-money budgeting reality into a fully accountable, bottom-up system driven by the needs of the city's residents. This multi-tiered interest administrative arrangement involves the sixteen administrative regions of the city. Within each region, a Regional Assembly meets twice per year to settle budgetary issues. City executives, administrators, representatives of communities such as neighbourhood associations, youth and health clubs, and other interested inhabitants of the city attend these assemblies. They are jointly coordinated by members of the municipal government and community delegates. These assemblies are charged with (i) reviewing and discussing the implementation of the previous year's budget, (ii) setting the region's spending priorities – among issues such as transportation, sewage, land regulation, and health care – for the coming year, and (iii) electing delegates and substitutes to represent them at a city-wide body called the Participatory Budgeting Council (COP). The priorities of these fairly large, infrequent regional assemblies are in turn set from below, by many less formal 'preparatory meetings' in which 'individual citizens, grassroots movements, and community institutions' organize themselves for discussion in the regional assemblies.

The COP, a higher level assembly of citizens and officials, aggregates the decisions of the lower assemblies into a city budget. The COP is composed of two elected delegates from each of the regions, two elected delegates from each of five 'thematic plenaries' representing the city as a whole, a delegate from the municipal workers' union, one from the union of neighbourhood associations, and two delegates from central municipal agencies. The group meets intensively, at least once per week from July to September, to discuss and establish a municipal budget which conforms to priorities established at the regional level while still coordinating the needs of the city as a whole. Since citizen representatives are in most cases non-professionals, city agencies offer courses and seminars on budgeting for COP delegates as well as for interested participants from the regional assemblies. On September 30 of each year, the Council submits a proposed budget to the Mayor, who can either accept the budget or through veto refer it back to the COP for revision. The COP responds by either amending the budget, or by over-riding the veto with a super-majority vote of 2/3. City officials estimate that some 100,000 people, or eight per cent of the adult population, participated in the 1996 round of Regional Assemblies and intermediate meetings.

(Fung and Wright, 1998, pp. 10-11)

Box IV.10. Social capital: A theoretical framework.

Voluntary cooperation is easier in a community that has inherited a substantial stock of social capital, in the form of norms of reciprocity and networks of civic engagement.

Social capital here refers to features of social organization, such as trust, norms, and networks, that can improve the efficiency of society by facilitating coordinated actions . . .

. . . Like conventional capital for conventional borrowers, social capital serves as a kind of collateral, but it is available to those who have no access to ordinary credit markets. Lacking physical assets to offer as surety, the participants in effect pledge their social connections. Thus social capital is leveraged to expand the credit facilities available in these communities and to improve the efficiency with which markets work there . . .

As with conventional capital, those who have social capital tend to accumulate more – 'them as has, gets' . . . Most forms of social capital, such as trust, are what Albert Hirschman has called 'moral resources' – that is, resources whose supply increases rather than decreases through use and which become depleted if *not* used. The more two people display trust towards one another, the greater their mutual confidence . . . Other forms of social capital, too, such as social norms and networks, increase with use and diminish with disuse. For all these reasons, we should expect the creation and destruction of social capital to be marked by virtuous and vicious circles.

One special feature of social capital, like trust, norms, and networks, is that it is ordinarily a public good, unlike conventional capital, which is ordinarily a private good . . .

Building social capital will not be easy, but it is the key to making democracy work.

(Putnam, 1993, pp. 167-70, 185)

erodes democratic local control and even interest in participation. Representation of local interests can pass to community leaders who have ready access to the power structure of the city. Conversely, community leaders can become agents or brokers for people who lack the basic resources or contacts to express their own interests.

Because they have status, contacts or influence, self-selected community leaders can easily use their role for personal advantage. Such a democratic deficit is not likely to last; development will speed up the intensity of democratic control and participation, and uncontrolled powers will wane. Issues which are relevant for a neighbourhood will be decided and managed in an open discussion or process of management. This is not a future aspiration; successful examples are multiplying across cities of the developing world as part of a local agenda movement.

A delicate issue is the direct involvement of pressure groups in local politics. In particular, construction activities and private development of urban real estate open up possibilities for nepotism, special favours or outright corruption, making local politicians wealthy. Local governments can be inefficient, wasteful and selective. They may provide high-quality services for rich neighbourhoods while neglecting the informal settlements of the poor. Such contrasts are common. They can be overcome only by more transparency, by delegating resource allocation to the real clients, or by the broader involvement of communities and social movements.

Political practitioners, without any need for a general problem-solving theory, have intuitively found successful solutions by drawing on civic traditions which survive in informal neighbourhoods, where markets are relatively weak but the existence of everyday informal networks gives useful lessons in building up social capital.

No family can provide everything that goes along with a house. As families manage household construction, neighbourhood groups form, reform, and affiliate with non-neighbourhood groups in order to reach out to the public sector for water, sewers, electricity, garbage removal, pavement, schools, teachers, health posts, mail service, phones, buses, parks, municipal markets, and police protection. In Mexico, this process not only encourages but demands organization. What is needed is a years-long effort in which individuals within constantly shifting alliances make contacts, learn the ropes, ask, barter, and demand services from various extensions of the public sector.

(Annis, 1988, p. 137)

Innovative local politics have used partnership models where voluntary groups and professionals work together, using public grants as seed money to strengthen self-help and develop low-cost informal solutions, without the need for expensive professional help they could not afford.

The list in Box IV.11 gives examples of urban partnership activities in the Indian city of Ahmedabad.

The Mega-City: A New Balance of Power

Even within the boundaries of a single city, the problems of good governance and decentralization can be highly complex. They are complicated further by the growth of agglomerations and mega-cities. Here, the complexity of different urban and suburban areas, often overlapping, and even neighbouring mega-city complexes, creates acute problems of coordinating activities and services.

Such large agglomerations consist necessarily of a multitude of local governments. Within such growing urban systems, conflicts of interest –

Box IV.11. Range of urban partnerships in Ahmedabad, India.

Slum Networking
Green Partnership
Clean Ahmedabad Campaign
Revitalization of Walled City
Solid Waste Management (Clean City Partnership)
Street Partnership
Municipal Bond
International Finance and Trade Centre
Swarna Jayanti Saheri Rojgar Yojana (SJSRY)
Health Partnership
Internationally Affiliated Municipal School
Programme Management Agency
River Front Development
Comparative Health Risk Assessment
Reducing Urban Risks in Ahmedabad
Report Card on Basic Urban Services
Gandhi Ashram Redevelopment
Child Friendly City

(Sinha, undated, p.12)

between core cities and suburban areas, and between cities of different size, income level and economic function – are endemic. As an increasing number of people no longer limit their daily activities to one town or city but live and work across local borders, democratic control and representation become more difficult. Labour and housing markets become regional, while political responsibilities remain either national or local. There is a general lack of regional political organizations.

This is the second great democratic deficit, which can be observed in rich and poor urban regions alike, and which has to be overcome through a reorganization of responsibilities. Small is only beautiful if the small organization has the required resources or can mobilize them, and if services are consumed within small communities. Small will not be beautiful if it blocks the view of the wider problems of a region, which can only be solved at the regional level. Some degree of integration and coordination of small local authorities with the larger fabric is essential in the interests of all. A typical solution is metropolitan development authorities, designed to overcome fragmented responsibilities in interrelated systems.

Decentralization can have an ugly side too: rich, independent, powerful suburbs or towns can become 'group capitalistic' entities, maximizing welfare for their local populations by shifting burdens to other communities, or avoiding obligations which others have to carry. Autonomous 'NIMBY' suburbs can seriously hamper and disrupt regional development, increase social segregation, and maintain suboptimal settlement patterns. Traditionally, richer people seek to separate themselves from lower-income groups and to live in comfortable enclaves. They may thus pass fiscal burdens to middle-income groups, forcing them to finance local infrastructure and services which are then used by poor people who cannot afford basic public goods. Well-organized egocentric interests may overrule fair and equitable solutions.

Solutions to this problem must be created by central legislation. They will need to find a balance between different interests, taking account of the facts of overspill and negative externalities. Formulating these tasks and rules may seem somewhat idealistic, with few real consequences for everyday political life. But history shows that – just as with the green movement or the anti-nuclear movements – regionalism, decentralization and local empowerment can become strong forces if they articulate strong existential needs and form alliances with people who want to control their environment, their neighbourhoods, their school systems or their local transportation system.

In designing such solutions, there are two inter-related key considerations:

- The need is to create regional bodies responsible for region-wide tasks (mass transit, waste disposal, structure planning). This will be especially difficult where the core cities are dominated by poor people and many suburban areas are wealthy. Opening up the suburbs goes against the immediate interests of the middle classes but is necessary to avoid disruptive inequalities or spatial segregation which can result in unemployment in core cities while expansion in suburbs is slowed by shortages of space and labour;

- Without a strong regional influence, 'Nimbyism' will become a constantly growing bottleneck to development. The suburb that maximizes welfare for its own population, while ignoring the reality of inequality and creating a homogeneous local society served by low-cost labour from other communities, will not easily give up its privileges. Each such enclave will seek to compete for rich inhabitants and to fence other people out, thus stabilizing inequality and denying the poor the chance to escape from the city.

Over the last thirty years, experiments in metropolitan governance have come and gone. Some cities like London have gone through entire cycles, scrapping metropolitan-wide strategic authorities and then planning their reintroduction. In general, spatial growth plus population growth together make regional coordination and mechanisms of burden sharing, from transportation to waste disposal, more urgent. The need for coordination in cities like London and Paris and New York may be great, but the need in the growing mega-cities in the developing world, from Manila to São Paulo, is even more urgent and the practical problems of implementation are even more intractable.

Solutions have to be based on governmental structures. Where strong provinces exist, the solution is usually self-evident. Metropolitan governments with a few key agents, as in Johannesburg (Greater Johannesburg Metropolitan Council (GJMC) with four racially mixed Metropolitan Local Councils (MLCs)), Jakarta or Bangkok, reduce problems of coordination and burden-sharing.

Box IV.12. Metropolitan governance.

In India, the Indian Constitutional Amendment now prescribes a metropolitan planning committee to be set up in each large city with a population of more than one million. At least two thirds of the members of these planning committees are elected representatives of the municipalities and rural local bodies, in proportion to their population . . .

The Metropolitan Manila Commission that came to conspicuous power under Imelda Marcos was abolished by the Aquinas Government. The current government appointed a metropolitan authority performing inter-municipal tasks.

(Sivaramakrishnan, 1994, p. 10, 11)

National or state legislatures are reluctant to reduce the autonomy of wealthy independent suburban communities which prefer a situation wherein they protect their very homogeneous population.

Long-Term Trends

Political movements and trends are even more difficult to foresee than economic and social trends. But it seems certain that the tendencies toward decentralization will not be reversed, for several reasons:

- Information will be available and more accessible for everybody. Information monopolies, which once strengthened central government, will disappear;

- People's needs will increasingly differentiate. They will express themselves more directly and more clearly, using new communication methods, to participate in decision-making and voting, which can be extended especially at the local level;

- More people will work in producing local non-tradable goods. Labour markets are localizing. People will depend even more than today on local services. Local government will therefore be more relevant to them;

- Regional government should become stronger, especially in its integrating role, because the risks of damage through uncoordinated and dispersed urban development will grow. Central governments have to be active and even enforce cooperation by creating integrative powerful supra-urban entities. If they fail, Nimbyism will exert a strong and growingly harmful influence. Small politically-independent communities will still be able to exert disproportionate political leverage, using central city services or creating overspill effects without paying commensurately. For many local governments, maximizing welfare for their local population will remain the overriding goal, in spite of the fact that everyday activities will become constantly more overlapping in character;

- Better information will be a countervailing force. It will be easier to measure individual use of public services, to measure benefits, to develop more adequate tax systems and better pricing systems. Information technology could thus become a strong countervailing power against Nimbyism.

Toward Better Urban Management

Striving for Better Urban Management: How to Do It

The most important trends in urban management during the last twenty years can be described in terms of a few key concepts:

- Privatization and competition;

- Participation and self-management;

- Transparency and accountability;

- Product and client orientation.

These precepts can be translated into practical rules. One is for cities to provide public services – which does not necessarily mean to produce them. Production can be separated from provision. Responsibility for provision of local goods should be defined, wherever possible, as a new constitutional rule for urban government. But provision can come from a variety of agencies, including private ones and self-help organizations or groups. Where cost recovery for public services is impossible, bidding procedures for subsidies are possible in order to find the most effective solution. Cities should concentrate on basic public functions until they really work. Market loans and market projects should not be substituted by public lending or by public agencies trying to take over tasks which private companies can do better. Standards may have to be reduced until even poor people can afford them, if insufficient resources are available to fulfil formal standards and costs. Affordable minimum standards for everybody are better than high standards which mean effectively no standards for the poorer part of the population. Services which can be provided on a pay-as-you-go basis should not be subsidized. If poor people need help for special services, they should receive direct subsidies.

Cities should mobilize resources in neighbourhoods, developing solutions with clients who know best what they need and how to save money to get better results. They should refrain from enforcing standards that people cannot afford. Instead, people should be given a chance to decide how to spend a given sum of money for their most urgent purposes, by using small funds as leverage to mobilize their own efforts and get better results.

Starting under very different conditions, such individual experiments have proved so valuable and convincing that they have initiated one of the few successful institutional movements which has produced a new insider language, best practice techniques and measurable results. These developments were responses to a number of negative outcomes: inefficient and non-responsive government; rapid economic, social and environmental changes and demands; growth of differentiated human needs which could no longer be met by traditional methods; and the restructuring of the world economy, partly as a reaction to globalization. They strive to improve the productivity and competitiveness of the local economy through better infrastructure, more responsive public management, better education, less bureaucratic procedures, and increasing self-confidence of the voters and entrepreneurs in the local economy. They are strengthening their collective identity so that it becomes recognizable to the outside. In turn, they develop trust in the city and its responses to demands of production companies. The twenty-first century is likely to see an entirely new type of city government.

New Methods of Expenditure Control

In February 1989, the Finance Branch of the Hong Kong Government published a report entitled *Public Sector Reform*, containing proposals which essentially sought a change of attitude and approach to spending public money. The aim was to improve efficiency and to give a better service to the public by adapting and developing existing structures and procedures. Since then, a series of changes based on new principles have been introduced.

Hong Kong's efforts are just one of many to improve the budgetary process and to end the old concept of just spending money wherever new problems had to be solved. Spending driven by good intentions can no longer be seen as a solution. Instead, efficient or effective programmes should become a growing concern. Seven basic principles of financial management reform are listed as the aims of the Hong Kong reform package (Cheung, 1992, p. 42):

1. The whole of public expenditure should be subjected to regular, systematic review;

2. A proper system of policy and resource management should be introduced in order to evaluate systematically the costs and achievements of all government activities;

3. The responsibility for policy, implementation and resources should be clearly defined and delegated;

4. Managers should be fully aware of, and be accountable for, all expenditure incurred in support of their policy objectives;

5. The government should provide services through an organization and a management framework that is appropriate to the nature of each service;

6. Those responsible for policy should ensure that effective relationships with executive agencies are established and made to work;

7. Every effort should be made to encourage civil servants to become better managers.

These principles demonstrate the beginning of a worldwide change of attitude among local politicians and administrators. The kind and degree of change differs widely between cities. Progress in some regions or cities is slow, but the momentum is there. A more accountable, effective and responsive municipal government will be a precondition for competitive and liveable cities. In the long run, all cities will have to participate in this process, as globalization and more information exchange, coupled with more transparency for voters and businessmen, will push and pull cities – including those lagging behind – in the same direction.

Privatization and Competition

There are many ways in which local government can enter contracts with the private sector to harness for-profit incentives. These methods can be classified in order of increasing private responsibility: service contracting, management contracting, leasing, concessions, and entrepreneurship. Service contracting assigns specified operations and maintenance tasks to the firm. The government sets performance standards for the tasks, supervises the contractors, and pays a set fee.

Management contracting extends the contractor's scope of responsibility. Although remuneration can take the form of a set fee, it often includes an amount related to performance. For example, water and sewerage contractors' revenues are sometimes related to reduction in leakage or number of connections.

In a leasing contract, the firm pays the government a rental or licence fee for exclusive rights to operate the government's existing facilities and collect the revenues for providing a specified quality of service. The government retains responsibility for fixed capital and debt service, while the firm is responsible for operating and maintenance costs. Lease contracting is often used in solid waste collection and disposal.

Concession contracting includes most of the provisions of leasing, and adds contractor responsibility for financing specified fixed investments. The concession can call for an extension to existing infrastructure or an entirely new plant. The new capital assets are operated by the firm but owned by the government. That type of concession contract is a BOT (build-operate-transfer) because user rights are transferred back to the government. This can be contrasted with a BOO (build-operate-own) contract under which the firm which constructs the infrastructure owns it outright.

All these contracts with the private sector will afford greater efficiency gains if they are awarded through a process of competitive tendering. The contracts should clearly specify the required quality of service, the obligation to maintain the facility, procedures for enforcement, penalties for non performance, and the method for resolving disputes.

Most local government services require that costs be incurred for the installation of heavy infrastructure. The total capital investment and the variable costs to provide services should cover the local expenditure. In practice, marginal cost pricing is not applicable in many cases. Cities very often calculate their prices on average costs. This principle is politically more acceptable to most voters. The most difficult practical problem is that marginal cost pricing creates deficits. It is possible though to charge a uniform amount equal to the historical costs per unit (average costs). Another approach is to charge tariffs comprising a combination of access or connection charges plus marginal cost prices. These tariffs would be charged exclusively to service users. Higher-income groups could in effect pay higher access charges.

In pricing, we have to avoid the outcome that low-income groups drop outside the service system altogether. Charging higher-income groups higher payments could be one method of correcting this. Many public services create external benefits. For example, sewerage and solid waste disposal confer such benefits so that the price per unit of use should be below marginal costs of use. Another example concerns telephone services. Here, the externality is more connection-related than use-related: the more participants there are, the higher the value of the whole system. In cases like this connection charges should be low.

In many cases, charging for services is expensive and therefore not worthwhile. An obvious case is the use of streets, which historically has been toll-free. In the twenty-first century, new technologies will increasingly facilitate charging users for their amount and time of use. There might be ideological barriers against new areas of pricing, but an effective system which creates new markets would be fairer, because indirect financing out of tax revenue creates all kinds of advantages for certain groups and tends to create overuse.

Box IV.13. Privatization efforts.

Buenos Aires: In 1989, the city of Buenos Aires introduced progressive privatization policies, for instance refuse collection services. During the last few years almost all other urban services have been privatized. Management of city revenues/refuse collection, real estate administration, operation of sport facilities and the zoo, advertising in public places, part of the metropolitan rail transit system, parking, road maintenance, street lighting, telephone service, electric power, and gas were privatized in the early 90s. Water supply and sewerage were privatized in 1993 and the subway in 1994.

(Pirez, 1994, p.7)

Other cities can point to a similar list of privatization. In New Delhi for instance street lighting, primary solid waste removal, secondary solid waste removal, cleaning of public latrines, has been privatized. The estimated cost savings range between 15 and 70% of the original costs.

(Mehta and Mehta, 1994, p.9)

The Tilburg Model: a management plan so successful that the city trademarked the name and sold its ingredients to the multinational accounting firm KPMG . . . When the textile industry on which it depended collapsed in the late 1970s, Tilburg declined in a manner familiar to many post industrial American cities . . . Tilburg saved itself from intervention. Streamlining was the first step; the number of bureaucratic departments was reduced from 16 to 6, each headed by a single director instead of four. And by offering early-retirement packages and semiprivatizing services such as gas and electricity, the city slashed its payroll by almost 1,000 – without a single compulsory redundancy. The remaining workers were instructed to think of citizens as 'customers' and of traditional city services – marriage licenses, public parking, even the local museum – as 'products'. Every year, each agency responsible for a product must submit a minutely detailed 'business plan' to the city . . . Annual customer surveys – in which an independent firm polls 1,000 residents – reveal that Tilburg's municipal workers, once notorious for bumbling, now deliver products with the utmost efficiency. Only one worker handles each request for a building permit, for example, and, aware that its work could be farmed out to private bidders, the city printing department comes through with competitive prices.

(Koerner, 1998, pp. 33-34)

For a long time, privatization was an unmentionable topic for local politicians. They feared a loss of power, or saw an independent public sector organization as the only guarantor of equal or high-quality delivery to all their clients. But in the 1980s, privatization and provision of local public goods through competition became the trend of the decade. Privatization has turned out to be more than a passing fashion. It has changed, and will fundamentally change, the role of local government. Competition, not committees, is seen as the right way to control spending and product quality.

In fact, it is technically quite possible to privatize a major part of local authority activities. This wave of privatization has changed and will change the role of local politicians. Traditionally, mayors spent most of their time being administrators. Under conditions of maximum privatization, the management role of politicians is reduced. They can spend more time and energy on innovative tasks, on finding compromises, mobilizing groups, or providing assistance and leadership to important political movements.

Unplanned privatization may happen sometimes, for example when city services like waste collection break down. In particular, wealthy neighbourhoods can hire private firms to collect waste on a fee basis. But this is relatively inefficient, and in any case unsustainable.

A Special Problem: The Resource-Poor City of Hypergrowth in the Developing World

In the developed world, the new governance trends have been partly a response to overstaffed yet inefficient municipal capacities, spending too much with meagre results; in other cases they were a response to fiscal crisis created by inflated obligations. In cities with low resources and hypergrowth, better governance has been propelled much more by social movements as a response to inadequate public sector provision of services to entire areas of the city, or as response against the absence of services.

The most difficult constellations exist where weak markets and a poorly-developed private business sector compel public management and public supply of services. At the same time, the lack of flexible and innovative capacities in the public sector forces governments to cling to existing solutions and become structurally conservative. Scarcity of creative personnel is a barrier to innovation; weak local markets are a barrier to privatization and competitive tendering.

In the worst cases hidebound administrations prove to be inadequate service providers, but cannot jettison present systems because new solutions within the public sector would need more resources, better personnel or even more democratic impetus or control, which are presently unavailable. In these circumstances, privatization could be simply self-defeating. In such a boxed-in situation, real innovations, possibly with international assistance, beyond pure market privatization will prove necessary. There is a need to find new cooperative solutions which do not require more capital or more public sector capacities, but mobilize client resources and self-management capacities, thus changing the role of the public administration.

In some cities with excessive growth of needs, low-income neighbourhoods lacking basic water, sewerage, solid waste disposal, street lighting, or even streets, may be willing to provide the infrastructure and services for themselves with a minimal burden on local government finance. The payments can be both equity and cash. There are four requirements for success. Firstly, the organization should begin with small groups of residents who should be involved in setting priorities and planning and be committed to implementing and financing the projects. Secondly, the technology should be simple (the simplest would be water standpipes and pit latrines), for this enables the residents themselves to construct and operate the infrastructure, keeping the costs in money and kind affordable. Thirdly, technical guidance should be available to plan the infrastructure system. Fourthly, if the cost is not affordable without residents taking out loans, opportunities to borrow should be provided.

Such innovative solutions, devised under extreme resource constraints, can only be developed case-by-case, by assessing individual drawbacks in a specific area and finding specific solutions. This will be time-consuming, for each solution is locally a new invention, based on a careful assessment of deficits perceived by the clients' ability to pay or willingness to get involved in providing the services, and of self-help capacities. Providing finance may prove insufficient. Helping active and able agents, or promoting organizations able to coordinate and motivate participants, is the more difficult task.

A Local-Global Link

While market competition forces companies, established in different regions of the world, to use the same technology and become equally efficient, incentives to 'export or import' innovation in governance are weak. Again and again, one finds isolated islands of urban innovation, while other cities survive in equal isolation, using traditional methods but facing no danger of being eliminated in the marketplace.

Progress in governance has to be developed locally. Local politicians, local neighbourhoods or local administrators have to invest time and money, as well as emotional and intellectual energy, into what can be a risky endeavour. Innovative local solutions (like intellectual property) cannot be protected and marketed in a global system to generate profits for the innovators who carry the costs and the risk of failure. Governance innovations are not traded like new technologies in markets driven by competition. This explains the many pathbreaking examples which have been flourishing for years in unknown provincial cities until they finally became common knowledge.

Even this does not necessarily mean that they spread easily to other parts of the world. The lack of driving forces for the diffusion of good practice, coupled with limited incentives to innovate in the public sector, will remain a powerful barrier against diffusion of innovation. Innovations in good governance usually involve people who are willing to change and to learn. They also mobilize new forms of cooperation and new systemic elements in local politics. Recognizing these differences, the slowness of diffusion can nevertheless be dispiriting.

There are remarkable differences between cities and regions. We have already noticed the new age of local empowerment which started during the 1980s in Latin America. In recent years, African cities have also been progressing. But progress alone is not enough, for targets are also moving because of growing population, diversified needs, increasing demands of the business sector, and changing technology. What was good yesterday will be outdated tomorrow. Good governance demands permanent evolution, akin to private production.

International organizations can fulfil an important function in the process of diffusion and local reinvention of best practice developed in other cities or other parts of the world. The tools are manyfold: conferences to mobilize and motivate or to present new knowledge, best-practice databases, partnerships between cities, promotion of information networks or innovation circles where cities cooperate to learn from each other.

In many fields basic data are scarce. The United Nations Centre for Human Settlements (Habitat) is the only international institution with a specific mandate to assemble information on urban areas. The UNCHS established the Urban Indicators Programme (UIP) with the goal of improving the base of urban knowledge by helping countries and cities design, collect, manage, analyse and apply policy-oriented indicators data. Global transparency and information on urban trends have significant importance for local, regional, national and international policy-making. The main objectives of the UIP are:

- To develop networks for information exchange and capacity building;

- To develop policy-oriented urban indicators and indices;

- To develop tools for collection and analysis of indicator data;

- To analyse and disseminate global indicators data.

The essence of all diffusion of innovation is information at different levels:

- Internal information in terms of basic municipal indicators or business and planning information;

Box IV.14. The Global Urban Indicators Database.

> The first Global Urban Indicators Database (GUIDB) contains results of 237 participating cities.
>
> Through the Habitat initiative, some countries such as India for example started to assemble new data sets. The India City Indicators Programme (SDS) has been a collaborative effort between the government of India, various state governments, Habitat and the United States Agency for International Development. 11 cities were selected to represent the variety of urban processes within India, and indicators had to be assembled and harmonized. In most cases, statistical information to measure the indicators did not exist. In these cases, the SDS used other data to estimate these indicators.
>
> (WRI, UNEP, UNDP, World Bank, 1996, p. 156)

Box IV.15. Environmental quality in Italian cities.

> In Italy, 'Legambiente', an environmental organization, and the Italian Institute of Environmental Research (Instituto di Ricerche Ambiente Italia) published in December 1998 the 5th report 'Ecosistema Urbano 1998'. The report contains a ranking of Italian cities concerning environmental quality. Three categories of parameters have been analysed:
>
> - indicators of environmental quality (smog, noise, water pollution and respiratory diseases)
>
> - indicators of environmental burden (risk locations, drinking water consumption, energy consumption, solid waste, population density, and car ownership rate)
>
> - indicators of good governance (pedestrian areas, public transport, separation of solid waste, green areas, air and noise monitoring, environmental information)
>
> The report mentions good and bad examples. The direct comparison between the cities encourages local authorities to develop policies in order to improve their own situation. In 1998, the first twenty positions were taken by cities from twelve different regions. In 1997 it was only five regions.
>
> (www.legambiente.it)

- International benchmarking. Cities should accept and promote international benchmarking which enables citizens and companies to assess individual performances;

- Exchange of modernization experience between cities with similar problems and attitudes;

- Quality networks (or quality circles) of cities which help each other in a variety of areas, ranging from tax collection to the management of bus systems. Innovating cities in one policy field supply expertise to others, receiving reciprocal assistance in other fields from other cities;

- Such cooperation needs strong motivation and dedication, combined with knowledge and experience. It also requires an emotional basis, because people get involved for emotional reasons. It needs public acceptance.

The most important worldwide innovations would be:

- Stronger incentives (or better cost-sharing mechanisms) for cities that produce innovations in governance, which at present have no way of receiving recognition for their efforts;

- Better mechanisms for imitation, which include the ability to mobilize local voters and participants, coupled with central and local civil servants.

This abstract concept of innovation needs instrumentation. The following preliminary suggestions need to be tested:

- An international gold medal for good governance combined with a generous grant, delivered by a group of developed countries to promote competition and create public involvement;

- An innovation fund whereby cities can apply for grants under the condition that successful innovations will be shared with other communities. Learning from successful learning experiences could breed success;

- Setting up innovation or quality networks among cities with similar problems, which are trying to solve communal problems in a cooperative effort.

The Environment

Meeting Basic Needs in the Ecopolis

The twentieth century was a century of labour-saving technologies. The twenty-first century will need to concentrate on a new dimension: it will become known as the eco-modernization century, a century of eco-saving innovations. But this will be a much more complex and difficult task than simply substituting machinery for hard manual work: environmental damage is often indirect and hard to measure, and it can only be mitigated by collective action. Years ago John Kenneth Galbraith coined his famous term: 'private affluence and public squalor'. It has taken many years to provide collective goods in adequate quantity and quality – and environmental goods, which are some of the most important of all, are too often still lacking. Yet cities cannot afford to take much time in launching effective eco-modernization strategies, because nature cannot wait. The last few years have brought a new awakening and a new – though still not widely-diffused – consciousness. But, so far, it is not paralleled by adequate action.

The struggle for sustainability does not follow the same path and pattern in all countries and cities. Economic conditions differ, and so do local preferences and sensitivities about environmental problems. German cities are capable of recycling more than one-third of their urban waste, but gasoline is relatively cheap for car-crazed Germans, and cars still can race without speed limits on many motorways. Americans are obsessed with the health risks created by smoking, and they use their cars on highways in a very disciplined way, reducing risks for everyone. But they are willing to accept enormous environmental risks and waste of time in order to enjoy a lifestyle based on extremely low-density suburbs, which forces all participants to use the car as dominant mode of transportation. The slogan 'My car is my freedom' dominates many of their decisions, but finally often achieves precisely the opposite result.

In the short run, a great deal of unsustainable environmental development has to be tolerated, given the limitations imposed by poverty or scarcities, capital buried in real estate, or unsustainable production facilities. Although these limitations are in the short run often insurmountable, there are always improvements which do not need additional resources: a speed limit on motorways, lower temperatures in offices, or greater use of bicycles. Action is always possible, and action will keep the subject alive.

The idea of mobilizing resources for local environmental purposes in cities with low productivity and high population growth, with their urgent health problems, will find relatively easy acceptance. But poverty and the struggle for daily survival are barriers which have to be overcome by successful economic development. Raising these difficulties does not imply that environmental concerns have to proceed according to the concept: 'get dirty, get rich, and clean up later'. Environmental action is possible and necessary at all levels of income, even under extreme poverty. But environmental policies can become more effective through economic development.

Of course, different cities will place different priorities on environmental goals. Quite independently of the present subjective feeling of urgency, environmental risks need to be more accurately calculated. An ecological indicator movement is developing; it can build up international standards and create benchmarks which facilitate comparisons. This may convince people that changes in behaviour and technology are urgently needed to avoid health, climatic or economic risks. Based on improved knowledge of the urgency of environmental degradation cities and urban strategies need to:

- Mobilize resources to fulfil basic environmental needs;

- Change people's behaviour;

- Increase efficiency in order to secure environmental progress at the lowest possible cost.

Cities thus have to prepare the ground for an ecological restructuring of the built environment, as well as of consumption and production. The big hope and promise is the potential for environmental technical progress which will reduce trade-off or, in many cases, even avoid it altogether.

Environmental Efficiency

Factor Four: It Can Be Done

Given present use of technologies, the environmental task seems to be almost hopeless. Every day, society consumes huge amounts of energy and other finite resources without replacing them. Every day, water and gasoline, metals and minerals are wasted. The present eco-emergency demands a radical reorientation. The answer is to stretch our consumption of limited resources by changing from growing resource use to negative growth rates of consumption. This would gain time to develop substitute technologies. Present sources of energy can be substituted by renewable energy.

This will demand strong incentives, and rigorous as well as soft regulation to use innovation for more wealth creation with less use of resources. This presupposes an understanding of present market results, not taking them for granted but viewing them as the result of often blind incentives which make waste profitable. A new eco-capitalism should emerge instead, based on new incentives directed to permanent eco-modernization.

The Factor Four formula expresses this economic logic succinctly. It underpins the revolutionary concept: the message that it is perfectly possible to produce twice as much as now with half the resource input. Factor Four points to changes already visible. In the long run, if we are to reach sustainable development by the end of the twenty-first century, we may need something more like a Factor Ten, providing a growing world population with an increasing standard of living.

This may seem completely utopian. But some aspects of this efficiency revolution are already profitably available, at negative cost; other aspects can also be made profitable. The revolution in information technology has enabled computers to become continuously cheaper and smaller, while their information-processing powers are exploding. In the developing world, fewer farmers are producing an increasing amount of food for a growing number of people.

Box IV.16. Economic profligacy – and the answer.

When people think of waste, they consider their household refuse, exhaust gases from their cars and the containers of rubbish outside businesses or construction sites. If people were asked how much material is wasted each year, most of them would guess that a certain percentage is wasted, but not a great deal. Actually, humans are more than ten times better at wasting resources than at using them. A study for the US National Academy of Engineering found that about 93 per cent of the materials bought and 'consumed' never end up in saleable products at all. Moreover, 80 per cent of products are discarded after a single use, and many of the rest are not as durable as they should be. Business reformer Paul Hawken estimates that 99 per cent of the original materials used in the production of, or contained within, the goods made in the US become waste within 6 weeks of sale.

Most of the energy, water and transportation services consumed are wasted too, often before they have reached their users. They pay for them, although they do not provide a useful service. The heat that leaks through the attics of poorly insulated homes; the energy from a nuclear or coal-fired power station, only 3 per cent of which is converted into light in an incandescent lamp (70 per cent of the original fuel energy is wasted before it gets to the lamp, which in turn converts only 10 per cent of the electricity into light); the 80-85 per cent of a car's petrol that is wasted in the engine and drive train before it gets to the wheels; the water that evaporates or dribbles away before it gets to the roots of a crop; the senseless movement of goods over huge distances for a result equally well achieved more locally – these are all costs without benefits.

This waste is unnecessarily expensive. The average American, for example, pays nearly US$2,000 a year for energy, either directly purchased for the household or embodied in businesses' goods and services. Add to that wasted metal, soil, water, wood, fibre and the cost of moving all these materials around, and the average American is wasting thousands of dollars every year. That waste, multiplied by 250 million people, yields at least a trillion dollars per year that is needlessly spent. Worldwide, it may even approach US$10 trillion, every year. Such waste impoverishes families (especially those with lower incomes), reduces competitiveness, imperils our resource base, poisons water, air, soil and people, and suppresses employment and economic vitality.

(von Weizsäcker *et al.*, 1998, pp. xx-xxi)

What has been achieved in many economic fields should be possible for environmental purposes. New incentives, new forms of social organization, are desperately needed to mobilize energy, talent and capital for the 'greening business' and for 'greener cities', just as technical and social innovation was mobilized to develop labour-saving technologies during the last two centuries. Eco-modernization will have to be at the centre of all modernization efforts and modernization movements. The result will have to be urban systems based on renewable energy and – compared to the twentieth-century economy – services that require little or no material inputs or outputs.

Perhaps the most remarkable feature of this message is its lessons for the developing world. Countries like China, India, Mexico or Egypt have a huge supply of cheap labour, but are short of energy. Given those facts, the worst thing they could try to do is to learn from the energy-profligate rich countries. They need to plan their own path of sustainable economic development (von Weizsäcker *et al.*, 1998).

Six Good Reasons for Ecological Efficiency

Increasing ecological efficiency offers compelling reasons why the world should take the following action to become more ecofriendly:

1. *Live better.* Resource efficiency improves the quality of life. It is possible to see better with resource efficient lighting systems, produce better goods in efficient factories, travel more safely and comfortably in efficient vehicles, and get better nutrition from efficiently grown crops;

2. *Pollute and deplete less.* Everything must go somewhere. Wasted resources pollute. Efficiency combats waste and thus reduces pollution. Resource efficiency can greatly contribute to solving such huge problems as acid rain and climatic change, deforestation, loss of soil fertility, and congested streets. By themselves, energy efficiency, plus productive and sustainable farming and forestry practices, could eliminate up to 90 per cent of today's environmental problems, at a profit, if the knowledge gap can be overcome. Efficiency can buy time in which people could learn to deal thoughtfully, sensibly and sequentially with the world's problems (von Weizsäcker *et al.*, 1998, p. xxii);

3. *Make money.* Resource efficiency is profitable, or could be made profitable, by government regulations which would internalize all costs, and above all the costs of cleaning up environmental pollution. This would give businesses a positive incentive not to pollute, as otherwise their costs and prices would be higher than those of their non-polluting competitors;

4. *Harness markets and enlist business.* Since resource efficiency can be made profitable, much of it can be implemented largely in the

marketplace, driven by individual choice and business competition, rather than requiring governments to tell everyone how to live. However, the task of reversing perverse incentive structures remains;

5. *Multiply use of scarce capital.* Resources freed by preventing waste can be used to solve other problems. With less capital buried in inefficient infrastructure, developing countries, in particular, would be in an excellent position to multiply the use of scarce capital. If a country buys equipment to make very energy-efficient lamps or windows, which are more expensive than conventional windows, it can then provide energy services with less investment than would be required to buy additional power stations;

6. *Be equitable and have more employment.* Wasting resources is the other face of a distorted economy which splits society increasingly into those who have work and those who do not. Either way, human energy and talent are being tragically misspent (von Weizsäcker *et al.*, 1998, p. xxiii).

Overcoming Difficulties on the Path to Ecological Efficiency

Overcoming ecological poverty, through constant increases in resource efficiency, will need carefully designed policies. In reality, a daunting array of practical obstacles is still actively preventing people and businesses from choosing the best buys first. These include:

- The conventional education of nearly everybody dealing with natural resources, and the often insurmountable costs of replacing conventional personnel with the rare individuals who know better. This 'human factor' may actually be the biggest obstacle in taking action to change the way things are;

- Massive interests some capital owners have in preserving existing structures – and even more, inertia on the part of customers, who may simply be ignorant about what levels of resource efficiency they could demand;

- Discriminatory financial criteria that often require efficiency to jump over a hurdle ten times higher than resource supply (for example, the very common insistence that an energy-saving measure should repay its investment in a year or two, while power plants are given a 10-20 years payback period);

- Split incentives between someone who might buy the efficiency and someone else who would reap its benefits (such as landlords and tenants, or home and equipment builders and their buyers);

- Prices that say little about – and may severely distort – actual costs to society, let alone costs to the environment and to future generations;

- The greater ease and convenience of organizing and financing one huge project in comparison with a million little ones;

- Obsolete regulations that specifically discourage or outlaw efficiency; these range from preventing taxi drivers who take a passenger into another territory from picking anyone up on the way back, to letting manufacturers' lorries carry only their own goods; restricting window areas in buildings, even when the windows are of a newer kind whose increased area always saves energy; and preferential haulage tariffs that give virgin materials a cost advantage over otherwise identical recycled materials;

- The almost universal practice of regulating electric, gas, water and other utilities so that increasing the use of resources is rewarded, and increasing the efficiency is sometimes even penalized, an unfortunate side-effect of the restructuring of the British electricity system (von Weizsäcker *et al.*, 1998, pp. xxvi-xxvii);

- Massive perverse subsidies for unsustainable forms of production and consumption;

- Vested interests and sunken capital which block many changes, as it is difficult to organize diffuse interests to undertake changes which will improve life often only in the distant future. The time lags between environmental investments and their results, especially those designed to prevent climate changes, are usually high, and – especially in cities where most people live in poverty – may be nearly prohibitive in the short run.

All these obstacles can only be overcome by persistent and detailed attention to the issues. The guiding principles are: rewards for saving resources, not for wasting them; procedures for choosing the best buys first, then for actually buying them; and competition in saving resources, not only in wasting them. None of these transformations will be quick or easy; but not making them would mean solving problems in the future that are far more difficult.

In summary, although advanced resource efficiency is not easy, it can theoretically be powerful, cost-effective and widely applicable, and is getting more so in practice. In the mid-1970s, for example, the American engineering economics debate centred on whether cost-effective energy savings could total around 10 per cent or 30 per cent of total usage. In the mid-1980s, the debate spanned a range from about 50 per cent to 80 per cent – a factor of two to five. In the mid-1990s, some of the best practitioners have been discussing whether, in principle, the potential is nearer 90 per cent or 99 per cent – a factor of 10 to 100 (von Weizsäcker *et al.*, 1998, p. xxvii).

Box IV.17. Examples of economic incentives.

In the American electricity generation industry companies were rewarded if they saved customers money. One of the largest, in California, cancelled its entire programme of power station construction. Then, the companies started to pay their customers to use less electricity: selling Negawatts. And following that, the idea developed that saved electricity could actually become a commodity that could be bought and sold.

Designers of buildings could be encouraged to come together from the beginning to design the most energy-efficient buildings – such as the ones, already in existence, which give excellent environmental conditions with one-tenth of conventional energy consumption.

Commuters could be charged for parking spaces but given an equivalent commuting allowance which could be spent on public transport or ride sharing or bicycling or telecommuting.

Those who build new buildings could be charged for their environmental impact, but given a 'Freebate' if the building is more efficient than normal; the fees would pay for the rebates.

(von Weizsäcker *et al.*, 1998, p. 192)

Ecological Incentive Systems

In decentralized market systems, the key word for all effective strategies is incentives. Individuals and companies can only act rationally if the prices or taxes they pay signal scarcities or opportunities to make profits through new ecofriendly products. It is perfectly possible to develop economic frameworks that encourage individuals and institutions to use less resources. The entire system of economic incentives and disincentives could be turned on its head. The selected examples can only show some main directions.

Before thinking about ecological tax reform, cities and national governments should abolish subsidies that create incentives for unsustainable ecological practices. As long as subsidies acting against the future of the environment remain in force, eco-modernization will lack momentum and power. Desubsidizing the economy is a first priority and will be the basis for any credible strategy of eco-modernization.

Ecological Tax Reform (ETR) would be based on internalizing all so-called negative externalities. It would be the least bureaucratic, least intrusive and arguably the most powerful instrument to preserve the environment. There are many alternative possibilities to change consumer behaviour. Prices – especially energy prices – could be adjusted at a higher rate than the growth rate of average net income. Thus producers and users would know that increases will happen year by year, similar to wage increases which enforce labour-saving technology. Similarly, strong ecological price signals would create incentives for ecological savings. Making the use of energy more expensive for tradable products will only be acceptable and successful if international competitors experience the same shifts in costs. Isolated changes in relative prices can have the result that production simply shifts to low-tax areas, without any ecological result. This strong argument will not apply to the use of energy for heating homes or for local transportation.

The US or Japan or France is theoretically rich enough just to buy and waste a lot of energy and materials. It is highly uneconomic but not a disaster. But for India, Egypt or Colombia, it's tragic. Capital is scarce, energy is scarce, labour is abundant. Why should these countries concentrate capital spending (even if it is soft-loan money from the World Bank) in aggressively expanding resource exploitation while ignoring the opportunities shown by the Factor Four revolution? Why should they emulate 20th century robotics and neglect the efficiency technologies that are likely to characterize 21st century technology markets and that are so much closer to the actual needs of their countries?

(von Weizsäcker *et al.*, 1998, p. 208)

In many cases it already helps when cities demand economic prices which cover the costs or represent scarcities for water, energy, streets, public transport or waste management. Subsidizing the use of scarce resources is very often popular, especially where – as with transportation – large numbers of voters are affected, but subsidizing will reduce incentives to economize on mobility, water or land. Of course, for people living at the borderline of minimum consumption, this argument may seem cynical – or at least blind to the reality of everyday life in poor neighbourhoods in low-productivity cities. Income-poor people logically tend to ignore their poverty in environmental goods, intense though this often is.

There is a nexus, though. Overcoming income poverty demands a parallel reduction of ecological poverty or poverty in public goods provided by the municipality. In the past, social policy has too often reduced income poverty by using cheap resources, ignoring economic and ecological considerations. In the twenty-first century we shall need a more enlightened policy which does not create the illusion of cheap energy or cheap transportation.

Environmental Education and Soft Regulation

Sustainable development is an intellectual concept in which changes in many aspects of today's world are bundled. It has become the core of a mass movement. It has created strong organizations for the management of environmental progress. But, given the dimensions of the task, the progress achieved remains too slow. The scope and range of local activities must grow. The preconditions for a different form of growth, based on environmental concern and environmental action, have improved – partly because of growing local influence, influence at the neighbourhood level, and of tighter networks among activists, interest groups and urban governments engaged in specific strategies.

But local authorities cannot compensate for national policies. Pollution control in factories or from vehicles follows largely national standards. An invigorating competition between local and central policies could strengthen motivation and provide political and administrative input. The instruments and administrative techniques are constantly improving. They range through:

- Different forms of eco-reporting or eco-auditing;

- Special local environmental councils, round tables or environmental forums;

- Detailed environmental impact studies in the preparation of large investment projects, with those neighbourhood groups concerned participating in local planning or investment decisions;

- Municipal purchasing codes demanding eco-audits from supplier companies;

- Voluntary agreements related to waste; local energy consumption emission standards – especially for emissions that impact on particular neighbourhoods;

- Eco-villages or car free zones to demonstrate ecological life styles;

- Courses in schools or school projects where children take over responsibilities for polluted creeks or neglected green spaces in neighbourhoods;

- Environmental education which makes clear that sustainable strategies to overcome poverty or to protect present standards of living demand acceptance of the true costs of land, energy or water;

- Better and more detailed information systems which undermine the neglect of scarce ecological species, areas, etc.;

- Environmental neighbourhood projects which involve local groups engaging in cleaning up, planting trees, repairing ailing infrastructure or collecting waste.

In a more transparent world, even Nimbyism can be transformed into an acceptance of burden sharing. Agenda 21[1] is a concept supported by an organizational framework (see Chapter V) which will bundle local activities for sustainable development. It will advocate local strategies and the transfer of knowledge and experience.

The common message of all these different activities and techniques is simple: environmental concerns need expression through action. Eco-living needs learning by doing. Sustainable development needs a context in which national and regional policies are interrelated and paralleled by local action. Environmental norms, incentives and local action must strengthen each other and create synergy effects.

Ecological Urban Management

Improving infrastructure as the basis for sustainable urban development is more than just a pricing problem. In most of the really urgent cases, the inhabitants will be poor, hence unable to finance conventional solutions. Therefore informal solutions have to be found, involving people and local organizations, which – based on technical assistance – can use their own funds and their own labour to provide sewerage lines, latrines or water pipes. Maintenance can then remain the responsibility of the users, so as to avoid the high costs imposed by formal organizations. Combining these efforts with other projects, especially those addressing employment problems, can help to build up stable networks (neighbourhood councils, community development teams) which can become multi-purpose organizations, combining different activities – from garbage collection, through assistance for self-help housing, to maintenance of infrastructure – using limited public funds and large amounts of local labour, to improve living conditions and to make progress for sustainable development.

In mature wealthy cities with their formal organizations, provision of adequate infrastructure and protection of the environment for sustainable development will depend more on open debate about priorities. Here the most important decisions are about land use and density.

In all cities, efforts to reduce material input, and to increase recycling efforts to avoid waste, are a precondition for more efficient use of resources. Cities can organize the collection of paper or other reusable materials. They can run systems of deposits for environmentally harmful goods, or organize cooperation between companies to increase recycling. In particular, the rich cities, with their extremely high use of resources per head, need to intensify efforts to recycle material from paper to industrial waste or car wrecks. Cities are important in all fields where cooperation between organizations and companies is based on spatial proximity.

Ecological sustainable strategies have to be applied in all relevant fields, from energy saving to better use of water. In each field, an array of policies has to be established to cover the whole range of activities. Saving water, for example, demands:

- Reduction of losses due to obsolete water mains or illegal connections;
- Reutilization of used water where potential pollutants are transformed into valuable fertilizer, as already occurs in several countries;

- Fair prices. At present, both developing and developed cities make too little use of tariffs as a means to encourage economy in resource use. After the socialist free water policy was abandoned in East Berlin, prices increased almost fourteen times and water consumption per person dropped by one-third;

Box IV.18. Solid waste collection in Cairo, Egypt.

Several projects reported for Brazil, Indonesia and India aim at a better organization of the waste pickers, guaranteeing them rights to collect, integrating them into the waste collection services and providing them with basic tools to ensure at least a minimum prevention from health threats. For example, in the city of Cairo, Egypt, the responsibilities for solid waste collection had for a long time been shared by the municipal sanitation service and an informal-sector group of refuse collectors (the *zabbaleen*) and local contractors (the *wahis*). In a concerted effort by four main actors from the private for-profit and private non-profit sectors, the informal-sector group was transformed into a private company, the Environmental Protection Company (EPC) having the contracts for waste collection for several parts of the city. The *wahis* administer the system, market the company's services, collect household charges, and supervise services. The *zabbaleen* collect and transport the waste. They supply their labour in exchange for the rights to recycle the waste. EPC operates much more efficiently than the informal-sector group and with increasing earnings. Therefore, it is planned to expand the EPC services to other quarters of Cairo. The initiative was set up when local government officials decided to evict and move these collectors and contractors. Apart from the EPC, a neighbourhood upgrading plan involving the planning of streets, construction of a school, outpatient clinic, park, children's club and credit programme was supported, and finally implemented. In addition, the refuse collection vehicles were upgraded from donkey-pulled carts to small pick-up trucks. Other activities involved the provision of credit for the development of small and micro-enterprises, literacy classes, infrastructure (water, sewage and power lines), painting facades of buildings, planting trees, etc.
    Achievements were that:

- 300 families were settled instead of evicted and were allowed to continue to collect refuse;
- 200 tons of household refuse were collected per day at no cost to the municipal budget;
- 90 per cent of these 200 tons were sorted and recovered for recycling and re-manufacturing on a daily basis;
- the health conditions were improved;
- the construction of a dispensary created additional job opportunities for 45 persons (equally for young girls and men).

(UN Best Practices Database)

- Disincentives to pollution and waste. This demands strictly enforced legislation to combat pollution;

- Reduction of excessive consumption of water for agriculture. Worldwide, agriculture consumes almost two-thirds of all water. The efficiency of irrigation systems throughout the world is less than 40 per cent. Reduction of water consumption is possible and could improve availability of water for cities;

- Purification of water. Here new technologies will possibly bring better results.

Economic Policy

The Relevance of Local Economic Policy

In the present climate, the overriding goal of local economic policy is the creation and promotion of employment. Stable employment in a growing economy is the precondition of maintaining income and reducing environmental poverty. Macroeconomic trends, monetary conditions, national tax systems and globalization have major impacts on employment. However, cities can also affect economic development. Even quite small short-term policy changes can lead to considerable long-term effects on economic performance. They provide an enabling context and important inputs for the private sector, such as land for building purposes, transportation, real estate markets, urban design, information technologies and information networks. As cities have only limited and often only indirect powers to influence local labour markets and industrial or service sector investment, they need to devise steady and long-term policies. While globalization is believed to reduce the influence of policy at both national and local level, it constitutes an uneven leverage in attracting capital or people to specific locations. In such a changing context, several local factors will become more relevant in the future:

- Education and training: they are the most important input of the knowledge economy and highly influenced by urban policies;

- Close cooperation between institutions of higher education and private companies;

- Effective public services;

- Good housing and infrastructure;

- Strongly networked local companies;

- Flexible labour markets;

- Flexible, reliable and efficient regulations favourable to companies;

213

- A good image of the city which, in turn, enhances the image of companies;

- An attractive cultural life and good urban design.

Box IV.19. Cleaner production: pilot project in China.

The results of a cleaner production pilot project in China implemented by Chinese and multilateral institutions in cooperation with more than twenty Chinese enterprises were remarkable so that it was decided to extend the project to 3,000 Chinese enterprises.

Environmental and Economic Benefits of No- and Low-Cost Options

	Environmental benefits (as audited)	Economic benefits
Beijing Brewery	Water consumption reduced by 4 t/t of beer beer loss reduced by 2%	US$ 200,000 a year
Beijing General Electroplating Factory	waste water volume reduced by 2679 t/year heavy metal emission reduced by 24.5 kg/year	US$ 2,500 compared to end of pipe US$ 10,000 a year in materials
Qufu Cement Plant	dust emissions reduced to national standard	US$ 196,000 a year
Shaoxing Cereal and Oil Factory	cooling water saving of 921.5 t/year COD discharge reduced by 14.9 t/year	US$ 9,000/year for US$ 500 invested Oil production increased by 635t/year

(Selection from UNEP, 1996, p. 7)

A large and often growing part of urban employment exists in the sectors of local non-tradable goods such as construction, housing, entertainment, retailing, local administration, education and health care. The quality of local goods defines to a large extent the attractiveness of a city and its capacity in the sector of tradable goods. Cities are responsible for their local goods. Caring successfully for their quality will improve quality of life for their inhabitants while improving competitiveness.

All cities have to be aware of these realities, as competition has become tougher and more international. Competition between cities will become an important element of economic progress and standing still will mean lagging behind. With increasing opportunities, cities will try to influence locational decisions by improving the image of the city or lowering production costs. More mobile international (capital) markets will increase the potential rewards of policies which succeed in enhancing the overall attractiveness of a city.

Developing cities can use their readiness to work hard, and their cheap labour and their growing markets as instruments to attract a greater share of international capital. Developed cities will be forced to overcome their rigid attitudes or vested interests stemming from decades of successful development. Feeding each others' growth processes through competition will be the best strategy in overcoming inertia or shortages of capital and know-how.

Urban Economic Policy for Greater Employment and Equality

The Cooperative City

Close cooperation between local and national or regional government is a precondition for success, especially in countries where decentralization is in a state of transition, as in many African, Latin American or Eastern European countries. The clients of cities range from the owner of a small local sweatshop to the board of directors of a major company. 'Enabling' – the trademark of today's local politics – demands intimate knowledge of clients of all kinds so as to tailor regulations and services and the use of resources in the most productive way. Cooperation can reduce conflicts between companies and neighbourhoods and build up consent to new investment in a specific location. Integrating neighbourhood groups, labour unions, non-governmental associations or religious groups into a process of public-private partnership for investment will not be easy and perhaps impossible at times. Conflicts of interest will be unavoidable. Mobilizing endogenous capacities involves acting as a catalyst in bringing together different actors. Building up social capital requires the integration of all participants concerned regardless of their different interests.

As they are the weaker partners, cities can only succeed if they can reduce direct government intervention from above. Cooperation between central government and cities could concentrate on the actions set out in table IV.1.

In many cities, business organizations and their representatives act within an established framework of cooperation and representation. In others, where no institutional arrangements exist, cities could promote business or retail clubs as permanent partners in the planning and provision of services or communal activities. Open cooperation based on democratic representation can reduce corruption, make consensus easier and thus lead to more effective and responsive solutions.

The Learning City

Human capital, production and use of knowledge will constitute the essence of urban development in the twenty-first century. Although training and school management are not always within the remit of cities, they should be actively involved, as the promotion of a highly qualified workforce is one of their main goals. A climate of learning in cooperation with local companies is the essence. Earning the title 'learning city' depends on the quality of education. Setting up a lifelong learning infrastructure and a knowledge base for public administration should lie at the core of all public efforts to improve the foundations of urban development.

215

Table IV.1. Policy actions for employment promotion at city and national levels.

Actions at City Level	Actions at National Level
• Reorientation of public expenditure	• Devolution of authority to city administrations
• Improvements in public service delivery	• Improved sharing of resources
• Removal of constraints in public administration, regulation and delivery which inhibit the operation of small enterprises	• Reduction of fiscal and other policy biases which favour large, modern sector enterprises
• Location of schools and health centres in areas of high social exclusion	• Forging greater linkages between large and small enterprises
• Promotion of efficient and fuller utilization of industrial and social service infrastructure	• Removal of urban or anti-urban bias in economic and social policies (e.g., price distortions, trade protection, location of industries)
• Improvements in land tenure	
• Rent control reforms	
• Control of land speculation and promotion of rational use of vacant urban land	
• Promotion of community organization and participation in self-help schemes	
• Cost recovery through user charges	

Source: ILO (1998), p. 34.

Cities are networks of knowledge and experience. Information and information systems are very often collective goods, at least in part, as the private sector is not in a position to sell all relevant information in the market place. Where private suppliers are unable or unwilling to improve required information flows, cities can act as providers themselves. Public information on relevant facts of urban development or the network structure of local firms can make a useful contribution towards an improved division of labour between different companies.

Every generation benefits from the previous one by building on patient learning and innovations of former generations. Cities like London or Stockholm have taken centuries to develop their institutions, together with their political and administrative knowledge of the industrial age; a latecomer city like Nairobi is merely at the beginning of this process.

Box IV.20. Local School Councils in Chicago.

Chicago, Illinois is the third largest city in the United States and home to some 2.5 million residents. In the late 1980s, the Chicago Public School system (CPS) suffered attacks from critics on all sides – parents, community members, and area businessmen, who claimed that the centralized school bureaucracy was failing to educate the city's children on a large scale. These individuals and groups formed a small but vocal social movement that managed to turn the top-heavy, hierarchical school system on its head. In 1988, the Illinois legislature passed a law which decentralized and opened up the governance of Chicago schools[1] according to good practice institutional design principles. They are now governed by high school LSCs consisting of eleven members and one non-voting student representative. The law shifts governance power from principals and central offices to these LSCs: they are empowered, and required by law, to hire and fire the principal, write principal performance contracts which they monitor and review every three years, develop annual School Improvement Plans (SIPs) which deal with staff, programmes and infrastructure issues. They monitor the implementation of those plans and approve school budgets. These bodies meet monthly during the school year, and less frequently in the summer.

. . . programme designers discovered that individuals serving on LSCs often lacked the skills required to discharge their responsibilities with competence. New legislation requires each LSC member to undergo some 20 hours of training, provided by the central school administration, on topics such as budgeting, school improvement planning, principal selection, group process, and LSC responsibilities.

This reform created by far the most formally directly democratic system of school governance in the United States. Every year, more than 5,000 parents, neighbourhood residents, and school teachers are elected to run their schools. By a wide margin, the majority of elected Illinois public officials who are minorities serve on LSCs

. . . LSCs embody the five principles of deliberative democratic design laid out above. They build new bridges between state and society at the operational level by empowering individuals who had previously lacked substantial power over 'neighbourhood' school decisions – parents, teachers, and community members – in diverse governance groups.

1. The law affects only schools in the city of Chicago, which is its own school district.

(Fung and Wright, 1998, p. 12)

Under pressure of globalization and extreme population growth in many cities, learning time has been dramatically shortened. Thus intensity and productivity of learning must be improved. Knowledge exchange should form the content of expanded cooperation systems. Cities can and should export their knowledge and experience to other cities. Many city information exchange networks are already in place. In the next century, improved communication systems will reduce the need for 'learning by doing' practised hitherto. Enhanced exchange systems will enable cities to engage in interactive public debates and to share benchmarking and best practice. They will thus more rapidly find solutions for more successful development.

The Infrastructure and Land-Rich City

Infrastructure is crucial for economic growth. Cities need to avoid bottlenecks in infrastructure and land for development purposes. In cities of population hypergrowth, this can only be a long-term goal, as in the short run too many needs are competing for investment at the same time. But cities can show the direction of development and use images of future development as a way to mobilize resources. They can help neighbourhoods to understand their role in such a development concept. The security that comes from being part of a long-term plan can help to build up confidence and stable organizations, thus improving investment perspectives.

In the dynamic cities of strong economic growth but lower population growth, cities have to overcome the hurdles of mobilizing finance for investment. Again, simple intelligible plans can help to convince taxpayers and users to contribute to the financing of large-scale investment.

Developing countries spend roughly 4 per cent of GDP on infrastructure, and cities provide a growing proportion of this total. Cities require adequate financial techniques based on sound fiscal policies to provide appropriate infrastructure. They will only gain access to capital markets if commercial banks consider them creditworthy. As shortage of capital will dominate investment decisions, especially in fast growing cities, it will be crucial to define the right priorities.

Providing infrastructure for the private business sector is often regarded as a sign of dependency on business lobbies. However, power and influence of strong pressure groups are a fact of political life in all cities, and there exist a host of methods to assess the relative advantages of public investments. Improving the analytical tools in cooperation with international partners could result in common standards for investment decisions and reduce *ad hoc* political influence. Continued efforts are necessary to reduce capital shortage and increase the labour content of public infrastructure investment, especially in cities suffering from high unemployment. Infrastructure investment might be used to integrate marginalized parts of the labour force by improving access to the labour market. Economic development and social and economic integration can thus become twin aspects of the same policy.

Infrastructure provision is closely linked to land development. Providing sufficient land for development keeps land prices low and allows for efficient low-cost production which widens markets and creates employment. Cities can save capital and promote low-cost, labour-intensive production of infrastructure and housing by several methods:

- Contractual arrangements with private developers are useful to overcome financial and capacity bottlenecks in the supply of land for building purposes. Developers can be forced to sell a certain percentage of their development land to avoid local monopolies;

- Private developers can provide sites for self-help housing through linkage contracts. Cities can regulate prices for complex development projects by enforcing cross-subsidies between high and low-income groups.

Small Business Cities

Small businesses dominate the local economy of most cities. They are especially important to the economies of developing cities, as they generate more additional jobs than large mature corporations. However, formal urban bureaucracies tend to have difficulties in assisting small informal producers or providers of services. Cities have to develop dual administration systems:

- Costs of formal procedures for small informal companies have to be reduced and procedures simplified;

- Licensing has to be rapid and must not try to enforce standards which are not affordable by the customers of small businesses;

- Administrative systems have to be transparent in order to be understandable and manageable for small businesses. Integrated one-stop programmes can alleviate many of these problems;

- Big cities have big bureaucracies used to handle very large projects, especially for infrastructure. Planning and implementation rely on formal bidding procedures and complex formalized preparation.

Thus, cities tend to use large companies. Small micro-entrepreneurs and city hall officials move in separate worlds. Cities need to make special efforts to overcome this cultural gap. They need to set up agencies which practice informal procedures geared to the abilities and requirements of small producers. The buying power of cities should be used to promote small suppliers. If the long-term objective of municipalities is to fully integrate the informal business sector in the urban economy, they need to generate policies to that end.

Box IV.21. The 'Urban Poor Development Programme' in Bangkok, Thailand.

In March 1992 the Thai Government approved a budget of US$50 million to initiate the 'The Urban Poor Development Programme'. This programme is a project under the National Housing Authority, but it has its own independently working project committee and administration system, the 'Urban Community Development Office'. The UCDO is governed by a Board with three members from government organizations (Bank of Thailand, Finance Ministry and National Economic and Social Development Board), three community leaders, two members from NGOs and one from the private sector under the principle of partnership.

The UCDO uses credit as a mechanism to strengthen the community's capabilities to deal with its own development issues. The community has to start savings activities and define management structure, operating mechanisms and beneficiaries at least three months before applying for a loan. A loan can be granted for up to a maximum of ten times the amount saved. This system allows the community organization to add a margin of 2-5% on top of the interest rate on the UCDO loan. The resulting interest rate will remain the same as, or slightly lower than the market rate for members. This enables the saving and credit organization to increase and strengthen its capacity by allowing it to have its own resources for its internal operations and those activities agreed on by the members. This scheme guarantees that the community acts as initiator, organizer, planner, manager and main actor.

The project is also the basis for an 'Integrated Credit System'. It addresses the integrated needs of the communities and avoids sectoral approaches. The community can develop an integrated community development plan and receive credits by the UCDO.

Between 1992 and 1997 loans have been granted to 61 projects covering 87 communities and 4,900 families in Bangkok. US$7.2 million has been disbursed and US$I million has been repaid. About two thirds of the total credits have gone to housing. About 150 savings groups are supported by the UCDO.

The 'Urban Poor Development Programme' is a new community-building and management process in which the urban poor develop and manage their own flexible poverty alleviation programmes. Because the savings are from the members themselves, careful management and accountability are developed by the community. Concerning the housing sector the experience has demonstrated clearly that housing projects developed through the loan scheme are much more effective and flexible than conventional state or private sector housing developments. The projects in general are more quickly realized, cheaper and have better records of repayment.

(Boonyabancha, 1997, pp. 222-223)

Municipalities can take a number of steps to improve access to, and increase supply of urban land:

- Developing low-cost schemes, such as covered public markets and workshops, to rent or for owner-occupation. This is best done in conjunction with the private sector;

- Ensuring that some of the development value generated by urban infrastructure improvement is benefiting the local community which may otherwise be marginalized by the process;

- Trying to decentralize and democratize land-use policy and infrastructure decisions. Neighbourhood groups of small business owners should be viewed as a critical resource in setting infrastructure priorities, since they have the best market information on the bottlenecks to further growth (ILO, 1998, p. 43).

New companies or firms need premises, labour, capital (loans) and, of course, a marketable product. Cities can improve markets for premises or rentals. In addition they should try to improve the markets for loans, in particular small loans for informal businesses.

In most cities, access to loans is a major hurdle for small entrepreneurs trying to start up a business. Large formal mainstream lenders are unable or unwilling to provide what they consider minuscule loans to small businesses. However, informal loans from banks specializing in small-scale lending to the informal sector are spreading. The most famous and successful among such lending institutions, the Grameen Bank, was set up by Muhammad Yunus in 1974[2] (see table IV.2).

Table IV.2. Loan disbursement of the Grameen Bank.

	1997	1996	1995	1994	1993	1992
Yearly Loan Disbursed	**Million US$**					
(a) General	370.14	238.37	343.80	352.12	260.24	142.17
(b) Housing	15.63	4.13	17.82	33.53	42.09	14.81
Total Disbursement for the Year	385.77	242.50	361.62	385.65	302.33	156.98
Cumulative Total Disbursement	2224.10	1838.33	1595.83	1234.21	848.56	546.23
Cumulative Amount Repaid	1868.65	1526.89	1293.31	941.18	618.84	423.95
Repayment Rate (%)	93.18	96.22	99.28	99.37	99.01	98.17
Balance of Group Fund Savings	90.91	81.48	75.19	60.81	40.83	24.37
Number of Houses built	402747	329040	331201	295702	258194	157334

Source: www.grameen.com.

The Grameen Bank uses very simple but effective techniques to screen clients and to keep loan failures low. Each potential client becomes a member of a small group of five to ten persons. They thus know both the client and the context of the business idea, discuss the purpose of the loan and test the loan application. Later, the group acts as controlling institution or advisor in case of difficulties.

This simple technique has proven very effective. It keeps costs of processing a loan low and reduces the risk for the bank. Even developed countries like Norway are trying to adopt this idea, as access to small loans for people with little or no collateral assets is a problem everywhere.

Women run a high percentage of small informal enterprises. 'Facing substantial social, cultural and legal obstacles to credit, poor women have relied heavily on informal sources of credit, such as from family and friends, traditional money lenders and pawn brokers. They are thus especially vulnerable to extortionate terms' (ILO, 1998, p. 44). Small enterprises in developed cities encounter similar problems.

Box IV.22. Encouraging the informal sector.

The home in developing countries is also a workplace, especially for women. A key lesson for planners from the massive literature on slums and squatter community life, is that housing in these areas is not for home life alone. A home is a production place, a market place, an entertainment centre, a financial institution and also a retreat. Therefore, it is necessary to ease some restrictions, e.g. on use of buildings, while ensuring that work conditions are safe and environmentally acceptable.

(ILO, 1998, p. 38)

The report argues that the informal sector must no longer be seen as marginal but must be moved into the mainstream. This should be done by encouraging the formation of informal sector organizations as lobbying groups, and providing equal access to land, basic services, markets, credit, know-how, information and infrastructure to micro-enterprises. This includes reforming discriminatory legislation, developing low-cost schemes for renting or owner-occupation, ensuring a share of infrastructure improvements, and decentralizing land-use policy and infrastructure decisions.

(ILO, 1998, pp. 40-43)

Manufacturing Does Still Matter

In a time of deindustrialization it may seem less important to promote industry. Yet, industry matters more than its share of employment might suggest (Cohen and Zysman, 1987). More than the service sector, industry is usually connected to the outside world. Moreover, industry needs services, from banking to construction, from advertising to research.

For that reason, most cities – especially those in the developing world which still have growing industrial employment – should have special industrial policies. Cities should get to know the strength of the local industrial sector and its components. They should know what barriers or bottlenecks they can influence through policy. The relevant components vary from city to city, but typical demands from industry are to:

- Reduce licensing costs and speed up licensing procedures, or even reduce the thresholds below which regulations are not justified, or where their results in terms of general well being do not justify their respective costs to companies;

- Simplify taxes, make taxation calculable and reduce taxes on businesses wherever possible to a level justified by the benefit principle;

- Deliver good quality inputs for the business sector. Cities are important suppliers (of, for example, railroad stations, airports, water and sewage systems, traffic regulations, land for building purposes). They should behave like a supplier in a competitive market, adjusting the input to the needs of the client and providing value for money. If city agencies are unable to deliver high value for money, public services should be privatized and open tendering should be used;

- Promote cooperation where synergies are possible, particularly cooperation in research;

- Provide information to increase transparency of urban markets;

- Put pressure on central government to enter into a cooperative partnership with the local business world.

This list is not exhaustive, but it indicates the gist of business demands. The relevance of these components will vary from city to city.

Cities and Global Markets

Labour markets in all cities are dominated by markets for local formal and informal goods. But the economies of all cities are part of an international or interregional division of labour. Cities are productive because they allow efficient production of local goods as demand is differentiated and spatially concentrated. Cities are productive because local companies are part of an international or interregional division of labour which allows mass production or extreme specialization, often the precondition for high efficiency. Cities cannot directly influence the productivity of individual companies, but they can create a productive environment in which companies find high-quality input of public services and individual goods. Good infrastructure, a high-quality workforce and an effective administration are the preconditions for competitive companies which can grow on interregional markets. A strong export basis matters for the well-being of the population, and cities matter for the competitiveness of local companies on outside markets.

International direct investment matters for all cities. Mature cities want to differentiate their economic base; dynamic growth cities want a widening export base, while hypergrowth cities, still suffering from low productivity, need integration into international markets. Statistics show an extreme concentration of international investment on a small number of cities. Only cities which successfully promote their 'home-grown companies' and are able to develop their own markets of non-tradable goods will be successful in attracting outside companies. Therefore, economic success begins at home with local measures directed to local companies which will create overspill effects and make a city more attractive for outside investors. Only in a later state will it pay off to operate with specialized agencies which try to attract outside investors.

Planning and the Transition from the Industrial to the Information Economy

Handling the economic transformation of old industrial cities, with their declining industries and redundant harbour or transportation infrastructure, demands complex planning, land banking, management and investment efforts. Handling this transition is one of the more demanding tasks for mature cities. Large tracts of brownfield land – abandoned by industrial or goods-handling activities – have to be recycled for new uses. Much land of this type could be redeveloped for housing, because it is conveniently located near downtown workplaces, often with good public transport connections. Conversely, it could be used to provide new jobs in the fast-growing business services sector, especially in information-based services such as banking, insurance and finance, the print and electronic media, and professional services such as law, accountancy, advertising, public relations and design.

Two problems, location and access, may inhibit such strategies. Although brownfield sites are often close or adjacent to traditional city centres, they may still suffer from a psychological barrier, particularly as regards activities such as banking which require face-to-face contact. A negative image of heavy, unpleasant manual work and polluting industry, stemming from the past, may compound such an effect. Major transport investment may solve access problems, as, for example, the Docklands Light Railway and Jubilee Line Extension in London Docklands. Similarly, the area may be 'put on the map' by a major, highly visible development such as the World Financial Center in New York or Canary Wharf in London Docklands. Such regeneration schemes can be used to attract a critical mass of key tenants, in the hope that others will follow later.

Implementation mechanisms raise related problems. The scale and scope of such operations, together with the need for clearance and decontamination of former uses, puts them beyond the capacity of even large private developers. During the 1980s, such urban mega-developments have required special mechanisms and large amounts of public money to secure leveraged investment by the private sector. The London Docklands Development Corporation (LDDC) is a typical example, using large sums of public money in a highly entrepreneurial way to attract private investment. A key mechanism was the Enterprise Zone status, which allowed the LDDC to offer incoming investors major tax concessions in the form of a ten-year holiday from property taxation, a reduction in the rate of corporation tax and write off facilities of construction costs. Out of the pioneering redevelopment projects of the 1980s and 1990s will grow a best practice that can be used by many cities which will have to solve similar problems in coming decades, as deindustrialization becomes a worldwide phenomenon affecting many different types of cities.

Experience suggests that such developments carry high risks because of their dependence on business cycles, which affect property development in particular. The Canary Wharf development collapsed for a year in the early 1990s after its developer, Olympia & York, had ceased trading. The reclamation and development of Tokyo Bay was stopped because of the collapse of the Japanese real estate boom. A number of mega-developments in Asian cities, financed by Japanese banks, succumbed to the recession of the late 1990s. Indeed, these developments may have constituted a significant part of the bad loans which have created problems for major Tokyo banks.

Cities, Economic Policy and Levels of Governance

On the whole, cities cannot function on their own. They could benefit from partnerships with central governments to promote macro-economic stability. This means keeping public debt low or in balance with the economic potential of a city, especially when tax revenues fluctuate and borrowing tends to follow suit. Traditionally, it is the role of central governments to control access to capital markets and to assess ability to carry debt services. Where political difficulties exist – especially in the case of very important cities – banks could take over the monitoring of urban budgets and the assessment of credit-worthiness. Rating of cities should become an important task. It has the advantage that cities carry the ultimate responsibility for their loans.

The distinction between tradable, non-tradable and merit goods persists, with macroeconomics focusing on tradable goods, central government dealing with merit goods (e.g. education and health), and local entities being more responsible for non-tradable goods. Akin to central-local relations, similar interdependences could be formalized between citywide government structures and localized entities, such as neighbourhoods, including those driven by informal mechanisms.

The informal local economy will continue to make up the bulk of urban activity in the cities of hypergrowth. Here, the informal sector generates and produces non-tradable goods and services which also supply mainstream parts of the city. In the mature cities self-employment – as opposed to formal employment – together with greater self-reliability may have led to similar structural changes in the urban economy. Informal practices are here to stay, although they are likely to change their relationship with the formal urban economy and the tradable sector over time. Cities have to accept these emerging economic realities and indeed to promote them, as people rely on functioning networks and supportive environments.

Just as with merit goods, the tradable sector has an impact and draws on the non-tradable sector. Globalization is considered to drive the tradable goods and service sector. It brings with it greater concentration, mergers and acquisition, asset stripping, out-sourcing, down-sizing, loss and casualization of employment, footloose production and services which exploit temporary transient tax conditions without territorial loyalty to specific cities. All these structural changes have a direct effect on the urban economy and demand permanent compensation urban strategies. They create new losers and winners among cities, but they also tend to displace local production, networks of local suppliers and purchasers within cities. They perturb the local labour market and indigenous support structures, raising both expectations and despair and increasing income disparity. The local economy provision is further undermined by boom-bust real estate cycles, accelerated by globalization of footloose and liquid capital and its effects on municipal income in most cities.

Following the erosion of the productive sector, a fundamental shakeout in the service sector is now also under way, partly through decentralization towards the developing world, partly through capitalization and application of information and communication technologies. These processes are most noticeable in cities, albeit not only in the developed world. So far, central governments have been expected to deal with their adverse effects on employment and income polarization by resorting to top-down redistribution and allocation procedures, while cities were supposed to provide infrastructure despite weakening powers and reduced resources.

When the deficiencies of the welfare state are eroding, the living standards of the urban population tend to decline, causing the worst afflicted groups either to withdraw into resignation, or to resort to direct action, boycotting banks, fighting developments imposed from outside (such as motorways, closure of public services, etc.), infringing social and environmental law, and refusing to follow official procedures. The black economy is increasingly making up for loss of jobs and earnings, together with greater reliance on family and friends, barter and social solidarity, active and productive leisure activities. The markets which satisfy local needs have an influx of home-made products, local currencies and secondhand trade.

At the level of the individual, the consumer tends to become an entrepreneur, taking an active part in the process of supply and demand. Among these local consumer entrepreneurs, common values may emerge despite the diversity of urban groups and their uneven chances of survival or betterment. Skill exchanges, credit unions and mutual assistance networks all enable people to trade tuition, cultural activities and support services. Local associations are turning into small businesses, often run by women outside the formal system of employment. Work in formal employment is diminishing and changing. Flexible working hours, measured by targets, early retirement, part-time work, contracts allowing for time off work, learning periods, a shift between salaried and self-employed work and greater geographic mobility, are changing the status and value of formal work.

Meanwhile, the formal sector of the urban economy is reacting to the values of the informal sector by producing more durable goods which consumers can maintain and repair. Products become less technically sophisticated and more user-friendly, and are more concerned with environment, leisure and culture, thus more sustainable. Information technology is in growing demand by 'smart' or networked communities to organize their protests, compile their knowledge banks, constitute their local webs. They account for a significant proportion of the buoyant information and communication technology market, and they affect product requirements.

All these trends indicate that the traditional tripartite power relations between government, industry and employee organizations at the central and local levels may require change. A new relationship between the state, the market and the citizens needs to be devised to achieve a viable synergy between the demands of globalization in cities and expectations from local economic development.

Managing Social Change

Fundamental Social Changes and Types of City

Reducing poverty and inequality remains the overriding task of social policy and urban development. Greater equality can be achieved through a number of linked strategies: better education, especially for children of poorer families, growth policies generating high demand for labour, more integrated urban planning, and provision of infrastructure.

In the European mature city, social security systems have reduced poverty among older people: one of the great accomplishments of the welfare state. They have improved the income position of families with children, but usually not enough to overcome the growing disadvantages of urban life for families with children (growing relative prices for services; high housing costs; progressively longer education, producing a longer period of life in which raising children must be balanced against the demands of professional life; a higher percentage of working women). In income-rich, time-poor, big, stressful cities, families have thus been outstandingly the losers.

Mature wealthy cities rarely provide an adequate environment for families. Overstretched mothers are no basis for a long-term balance between different age groups or a happy family life. Urban development policy must ensure that families can establish themselves in more supportive neighbourhoods, supportive workplaces or supportive regulatory frameworks. Scandinavian cities have demonstrated how this can be achieved. Urban environments should become family oriented, more supportive to mothers and fathers. Labour markets should not discriminate against parents. This is easy to say, but it necessitates many different policies forming an effective set of changes which make urban family life less stressful. The instruments range from low-priced kindergartens, flexible opening hours of public and private services, to special vacation days for mothers, and incentives for private companies to hire more mothers.

Social policy measures have also been less successful in reducing poverty for the young and unemployed. One of the great disappointments of the late twentieth century was the failure of the welfare state to reintegrate the long-term unemployed into society. The poverty trap, a new kind of barrier to re-entering the workforce, has become almost a symbol of the limits of traditional welfare policy.

High rates of immigration of low-skilled labour, in a situation where unemployment levels among (foreign) low-skilled workers are already high, will put additional stresses on the urban system and on the welfare state. The high percentage of school dropouts among young immigrants or the children of immigrants has significantly reduced their chances of pursuing successful careers in urban labour markets. This increased inequality and unemployment will prove expensive for the public sector in future. When immigration ends in unemployment and poverty, it seriously impedes the process of social integration and undermines the growth of social solidarity.

Further, the growing numbers of old people, without families and traditional support systems, will increase the demand for expensive professional health care. This explosion of entitlements will overburden the next generation in many countries. Informal, less expensive, solutions for the needs of the elderly will surely prove necessary.

In the cities of high population growth and low incomes, we see an opposite set of risks. High birth rates plus migration, large informal sectors and unstable employment have created high-risk low-income populations where sickness or old age very often lead to personal crisis. Here the family continues to function as the dominant protective institution. Family and neighbourhood create supportive quarters which are a source of security for millions. This is the particular strength of informal neighbourhoods, which has been lost in the socially more atomized cities of the developed world, dominated as they are by small households and a growing number of childless households. In those cities where population is still growing, in future the number of births per family will be lower, population change will be slower and less dramatic than before; here, the basic processes of accumulation will have to be better organized.

However, the recent dramatic drop in birth rates in many Asian cities with high economic growth, especially in China, but also in Singapore and in Japanese cities, will reduce or even erode the traditional protective role of the family. Rapid urban change, paralleled by changing birth rates and changing roles of the family, will create a long-term imbalance in personal support systems. Western-style welfare states are not in place to provide adequate personal services, especially for these large numbers of ageing people. This deficit is reduced by high savings rates which will result in accumulation of personal wealth. It seems likely that accumulation of high personal wealth, coupled with a longer working life than in Europe, could become the norm in Asian cities – a difference which could be advantageous for the development of cities as social systems. But the risk of poverty in old age is very evident.

At the beginning of the new century we foresee a fundamental conflict – at first mostly in the mature cities, but in the future more often in other kinds of cities – between families with children and the growing number of childless people, who will depend later in life on the productivity and altruism of a smaller next generation. It is not at all unlikely that, as societies in many parts of the world progressively age, old-age poverty will again appear on the agenda. Growing numbers of old people, especially those without family support, will demand new forms of assistance, since traditional systems of pensions will not solve the problem of personal care. Prices for market services, and costs of services provided by municipalities, will keep on rising. Formal state or market solutions will become extremely costly in big cities. Tax burdens, including social security payments, are already high.

The risk of decreasing quality can probably only be overcome by informal private solutions in supportive neighbourhoods, whereby retired people help young families or younger pensioners assist old people who need personal care. So far, examples are rare. Municipalities should act as catalysts and provide neighbourhood centres where people can meet, find or build up contacts. They could help groups and individuals who want to live in close contact with others to organize cooperative patterns of living after retirement. Many experiments will be needed to demonstrate best practice solutions, worthy of imitation, so that dependency on public institutions can be reduced. Solutions which make people more independent, and allow them to help others in a mutual effort to become less dependent on state solutions, should be promoted by cities.

The overriding social problem for hypergrowth cities is to provide adequate education for the still growing number of children, and health services, especially for poorer people in the informal sector. Contraception to reduce birth rates which prolong poverty is still a basic need and still the most urgent precondition for balanced development.

Managing the Reduction of Poverty

Faces of Poverty

The face of poverty in cities with high population growth and low level of productivity is radically different from the face of poverty in wealthy cities, where poverty is very often the result of low competence, lack of social or economic skills, lack of access to work and labour markets, and an incapacity to respond adequately to incentives.

Poverty in the hypergrowth cities tends to grow out of:

- Absolute scarcity of resources – mostly a consequence of high population growth;

- Too many children per family and overburdened parents who cannot afford adequate education and very often have to rely on child labour for a living;

- Weak urban and national government and lack of infrastructure;

- A low level of accumulation of private capital, especially housing.

Poverty in the mature cities is more a consequence of mismanagement of the economy, or integration problems in a complex world. It arises out of

- Under-education and low productive skills which are the result of lack of training;

- Unemployment or substitution of low-skilled workers by modern technology;

- Spatial segregation or inadequate transportation facilities and other infrastructure;

- Deskilling as a consequence of unemployment;

- Over-regulated markets which reduce chances for growth or for starting individual companies;

- High tax burdens which reduce incentives for work or increase prices for services and labour intensive products;

- Unstable families, high divorce rates, unstable professional careers or lack of social networks.

Poverty, unemployment and crime are closely connected. Lack of social cohesion or social capital increases crime rates, especially crimes against the person. In developing cities, lack of capital, resources and skills dominates all other causes. They are easy to understand, but hard to overcome.

Poverty, in developing and developed cities alike, still means unhealthy living. The poor pay more partly because they are less connected and have fewer chances as a consequence of network poverty. The standard of living is more unequal than the level of income. The poor work under less healthy conditions and suffer more from high crime rates. They die earlier. The many dimensions of deprivation and inequality lead to a growing complexity of lifestyles or patterns of living. This makes it more difficult to formulate and implement integrative strategies to affect the trends which result from a number of overlapping forces.

Strategies for Cities with High Population Growth and Low Productivity

The Critical Role of Education and Training

Several strategies to combat poverty and unemployment have not been very successful, as for instance policies to restrict industrial development in prosperous areas and redirect it to depressed areas. Policies to retain existing employers or attract new ones by virtue of tax breaks, low-cost land and building provision, reduction of planning and other regulatory measures, or tax incentives to invest in certain areas, all have demonstrated only partial success. Sustainable strategies need to be more enabling. Here the most persistent difficulties to reduce poverty arise out of the mismatch between the existing skills of the traditional labour force and the structure which is necessitated by the growth sectors of the economy. The quality and skills of the labour force represent one of the most important assets of any city. If new employment is to be attracted or generated, the workforce must possess appropriate education, skills and work ethic.

Combating poverty under conditions of high population growth. Sustainable strategies need to be enabling strategies, especially in cities with very limited resources. Such enabling strategies can be used in housing programmes: they may include provision of building materials, granting of

231

titles to building plots, and assistance in do-it-yourself production of water pipes. Such policies can also address another basic problem: the mismatch or gap between the needs of the growing formal economy, and the lack of skills of the workers, most of them young. If new employment is to be attracted or generated, the workforce must possess appropriate education, skills and work ethic. Self-help building programmes can help them achieve these qualities.

Education policies, especially in cities of high population growth and large informal settlements, must be targeted, with priority for those areas with the lowest levels of educational motivation and attainment. Schools in such areas must be encouraged to raise their aspirations and those of their pupils. Disinterest and lack of motivation in education starts early. Parental attitudes are part of the solution.

- Additional resources may need to be directed towards schools in such areas to recruit good teachers, to provide adequate materials and to encourage parents to become more involved with schools;

- School performance in improving pupil attainment needs to be benchmarked and regularly checked, taking into account the differences in social composition of the intake in different areas which will inevitably affect overall performance;

- It may be necessary to offer incentives for parents to send their children to school, since earning small sums of money can seem more important or even a necessity for poor parents than investment in education;

- Skill training and employment schemes need to be available to equip people with appropriate skills and attitudes to work. It is pointless to foster higher levels of educational attainment if jobs and training schemes are not available;

- Subsidies to local employers to employ school leavers or unemployed workers, whom they could otherwise not afford to hire, can be of considerable value;

- In areas which have suffered large manufacturing job losses, retraining centres should be established where workers can be equipped with a new range of skills. The creation of 'intermediate labour markets', which create waged work experience for people who have had long-term unemployment, can also prove valuable;

- In addition to improved schooling, retraining of long term unemployed would have similar results;

- Whether the problem is to deliver effective education to children or retrain adults, the solution will increasingly come through the information technology revolution. Personal computers linked to the internet can provide highly effective self-teaching programmes at ever-lower cost. This will transform the character of education at every level from nursery school to university, and from the least to the most developed city worldwide. But it will have its greatest potential effect in the poor areas of rapidly-growing cities.

Urban economies and urban systems in cities in more complex economies demand new skills. Even highly-educated people now find it difficult to start a successful career, to adjust to new conditions in the labour market, to keep learning new skills or to build up new networks as old networks dissolve. Young people in cities have to overcome high thresholds to participate successfully in continually-changing labour markets. All urban systems consist of production and service networks, which are constantly undergoing change and rearrangement. Urban systems demand that people know how to become insiders, to find the clients or partners necessary for their skills to become effective. This needs two kinds of ability: professional or technical knowledge and the knowledge or ability to function within different urban networks, and within both formal and informal information systems.

Cities can help to build supportive networks which help to prepare people for successful urban life. Creating systems which are open, competitive and transparent can make life easier for newcomers, especially migrants and young people. Over-regulated insider systems become defensive and exclusive, create rigid insider markets and reduce necessary flexibility. Public policy in all areas should become more enabling, more catalytic. The traditional protective welfare state solution, which reduces risks and provides minimum guarantees, will have to remain in part; many people will continue to need help and assistance. But it is vital that it be supplemented by the new innovative approach.

New Labour Market Problems in the Mature Cities

In mature cities, which are often over-regulated, it can be helpful to deregulate labour markets so as to increase opportunities for low-skilled workers lacking formal qualifications. But low-skilled workers often experience adverse labour market conditions in which wages are too low to earn a decent living. One reason is high taxes, especially social security taxes which drive a growing wedge between gross and net wages. In consequence wages are too low to finance a basic livelihood and savings for old age. Thus, there is a paradox of the welfare state: taxes to support the financing of public goods may exacerbate the very problems they try to solve.

Many cities experiment with welfare payments which are used to increase income of the working poor. In other countries social security

Box IV.23. The 'Bill Gates of the *favelas*': Bringing the internet to Rio's poor children.

Three pairs of eyes look up briefly as I enter the classroom, and then return to the computer monitors, fingers busy at keyboards or pointing out words and images on-screen. There are still 10 minutes of class time left, and the children want to use them.

I make a humble retreat and wait outside until the lesson is over.

It could be any information technology classroom in any western school or college, but the shabby furniture and cramped room lit by a single bare light bulb tell a different story. This IT school is in the heart of one of Rio de Janeiro's infamous favelas, or shanty towns, and its pupils – disenfranchised by poverty and cultural stigma – are learning to access more than just the internet.

Armed with their new digital knowledge, they are finding paths that lead them away from their communities' customary routes into the drug trade or soul-destroying hand-to-mouth labour. They have found an electronic bridge across the vast social divide between the third world of their hillside homes and the first world riches just a stone's throw below.

This was the dream – now a reality – of 30-year-old Rodrigo Baggio, a former systems analyst and high school teacher who set up the awkwardly named Committee to Democratise Information Technology (CDI) with five PCs donated by C&A, the retailer.

Almost five years on, Baggio has negotiated multi-million-pound software donations with Microsoft and is dubbed 'the Bill Gates of the favelas' by the Brazilian media for his astonishing success at opening the doors of the digital revolution to the country's poor.

CDI's idea is simple: it tells favela community leaders how to set up IT schools and trains people to teach in them. Students pay R$30 (£10) for a three-month course in Word, Windows and Excel, using the £300m worth of software donated by Microsoft, and learning through exercises addressing local social issues. Most of the PCs they use are 'worthless' throwaways, binned by upgrading companies.

The CDI, which is funded mainly by private business and philanthropic organizations including the international Osaka programme and Britain's 'Network for Social Change', does not take a cent.

From the five computers it started with in 1995, the CDI now has 110 schools throughout Brazil, providing direct work for 262 teachers, and about 25,000 students have graduated from their classrooms.

But what they are doing is undoubtedly working. The CDI is compiling a survey on how many students have found work through the course; it estimates that about 10 per cent of new graduates are employed immediately.

Just as important are the less tangible benefits – raising the self-esteem and social awareness of students, which helps them to help their communities.

Rita de Cassia revealed how one adult student, who makes a living cooking savouries for local shops, printed adverts at the school, boosted her trade, and used the extra money to buy her own PC.

Box IV.23. cont.

The CDI receives daily queries about setting up new schools – and not just in Brazil. One has already been established in Tokyo and communities in Chile, Ecuador, Colombia, Argentina and the US have shown interest in the project. Baggio now spends most of his time jetting from country to country trying to spread the CDI message beyond South America and attract new sponsors.

Poor communities are not the only targets – at one high-security prison in Rio, a CDI classroom set up this year has almost eliminated illiteracy. Some prisoners wear wry smiles as a result of an interesting role reversal – CDI graduates serving sentences for crimes such as kidnap, murder and robbery are now giving IT courses to their guards.

Rogerio Viana de Santos, 32 years old and sentenced to nine years for robbery, told me: 'There are people on the outside robbing and killing. I'd sooner be in here, deprived of my liberty but learning something, than be on the street with nothing.' He plans to set up a computer maintenance firm when he gets out in three years.

Baggio's new goal is to give all the CDI schools a link to the internet, creating an on-line exchange for communities alienated by distance and poverty.

And Rita de Cassia, giddy with pride and optimism, who already has one machine with web access, can barely keep from bursting into fits of laughter when she ponders the future: 'Now we've got the opportunity to participate in the new millennium,' she says. 'Finally we can communicate with the whole world.'

(Eveleigh, 2000)

taxes for low wage earners are paid out of the budget. Technically these payments could be organized in different ways; the easiest is probably a payment to firms hiring low-skilled workers unable to earn a living above a tolerable poverty line.

Combined educational and labour market strategies and instruments, which increase the urban population's skill and social integration, can only be successful if supplemented by flanking developmental strategies and programmes.

- Greater investment in public transport in urban areas should be encouraged to enable easier access to employment by those without private means of transport;

- The wider urban environment must be sufficiently attractive to both new and existing employers. For this reason there has been a growing emphasis on the necessity for the physical regeneration of decaying or derelict older urban industrial areas;

- Many older Western cities have seen extensive programmes of urban regeneration to improve their physical environment and equip them to retain and attract new forms of employment. City governments have realized that it is necessary to transform industrial land to post-industrial uses to create an attractive urban environment. This requires the establishment of a variety of urban development or regeneration agencies.

The risk involved in urban regeneration strategies is very high. Modern buildings or upgraded buildings improve the appearance of a neighbourhood. But such upgrading can easily mark the beginning of gentrification. The poor move on to other unattractive areas, forming new pockets of deprivation and poverty.

The renewal agencies should upgrade the tenants and not the buildings.

(A tenant living in an upgraded building in Freiburg, Germany)

Of course such 'human upgrading' is much more difficult than the upgrading of buildings. Therefore we observe a natural – but ultimately counterproductive – tendency to concentrate resources on the upgrading of buildings.

A more sophisticated strategy would avoid the bricks and mortar emphasis in favour of integrated social and physical strategies. Most would probably agree with this position, which is however easy to formulate but difficult to implement. In recent years, experiments have been started in several countries (France: *Quartiers en crise*; UK: Single Regeneration Budget; Germany: Social Urban Renewal). Common elements in these programmes are empowerment, self-help, integration of employment measures with physical upgrading, or a combination of retraining and social measures.

From the original slum clearance activities to complex urban regeneration is a big step. It should not end there. Complex regeneration schemes are compensatory strategies after immigration or non-functioning labour markets have led to concentrations of poverty and unemployment, of crime and decay. In a truly well-managed city, immigration would not lead to unemployment. School-leavers would be qualified to compete in labour markets. Sustainable urban development requires precautionary strategies in the social field, similar to those developed in environmental policy.

Cities in their traditional roles, with hierarchical management, high functional specialization, driven and limited by strict rules and legal requirements, will find it hard to adjust to the new urban environment. Too often, solutions become problems. The most obvious case is the outer housing estates, built with the best of intentions, which so often have become the most deprived areas. The welfare state, providing dysfunctional solutions, can actively stigmatize its clients. Cities must begin a continuing search for more integrative solutions which do not treat their clients as carriers of entitlements, but as human beings who need assistance to develop their own talents, to take control of their own lives, or to integrate into a socio-economic system which because of its very nature demands more educational qualifications, more special skills, more knowledge and more social talents to achieve success.

Anti-Poverty Strategies in Hypergrowth Cities

In cities with high population growth, skill-oriented policies and policies to improve the housing situation and infrastructure will improve the basis for economic development. Social development and economic development, especially in the informal sector, overlap to a considerable extent: lack of resources or of income is the dominant cause of social problems. This is quite contrary to the position in the mature cities with stable and ageing population, where the relevant causes are the complexities of the educational, the economic or the political process, and the inequality tolerated by the political system.

Special difficulties arise in cities where population is growing at rates of 4-5 per cent per annum or more, where yet more migrants will arrive if poverty is reduced because nearly limitless reservoirs of labour exist in the rural areas. Here, 'solving' the problems of the poor is no solution: it simply attracts more people, who bring with them new difficulties in the form of increased labour supply, with the result that wages cannot grow. This neo-Malthusian condition – large-scale migration of people looking for even a bare minimum urban income – exists in many African and some Asian cities. Cities like Johannesburg and Nairobi cannot solve this problem in isolation. They can try to promote rapid growth of the labour market, but its growth potential will always be lower than the migration potential.

Thus, only concerted efforts by all cities in a given region of the world can reach results in the war against poverty. Anti-poverty programmes in the form of transfer programmes will be no solution in cases of highly elastic migration. Poverty can only be overcome by winning the race between productivity growth, growth in the number of jobs and population growth. Solutions should aim to push productivity up as fast as possible and to reduce population growth. Again education has a key function, because it improves labour market participation and reduces the number of children. More investment in people with low incomes is probably the only true equalizing policy, because it does not reduce the chances for higher growth of productivity; in fact, it improves them.

Support from the National Level

Distributional policies should as far as possible be financed out of central resources. If they are financed locally, the result will be more inequality:

poor areas, threatened by weak industries which need restructuring, will have low revenues and high social demands, a financial burden which cannot be borne.

In consequence, most distributional problems should be solved at the national level. In most cases there is, however, an important exception: people without (adequate) sources of income need a minimum of welfare payments or services in kind, and cities are the most adequate providers of such a minimum standard of living. This apart, financing welfare payments out of local taxes places a high burden on local authorities and local taxpayers in regions experiencing economic crisis and high unemployment. Their ability to promote economic development will be severely hampered if local welfare payments have to be financed out of local taxes.

Housing Policy

Providing Decent Housing: An Enabling Strategy

Housing policies in the twenty-first century should concentrate on enabling strategies. Massive accumulated experience demonstrates the risks and costs of policies which try to substitute markets by public programmes. They are extremely costly and end too often stigmatizing their clients. Any successful enabling strategy has to develop functioning housing markets with flexible supply mechanisms – especially a flexible supply of land and a wide range of price quality levels in housing supply to suit people of different income and preferences. Creating strategies which enable markets to function adequately is often more important than fulfilling targets of subsidy programmes.

Enabling does not mean that governments abdicate. Enabling has to be seen as a special form of care which concentrates on the ability for self-help and not primarily on the need for subsidies. Needs are almost unlimited. Subsidies and assistance are scarce goods. Successful enabling strategies increase the leverage effects of public assistance and create more shelter. Enabling strategies represent an attitude which does not concentrate public sector resources on a few areas and groups, hoping that through imitation they will replicate and grow. Enabling concentrates its assistance on areas and groups which are active and are prepared to mobilize their own resources. Enabling does not make promises without demanding community cooperation and participation in building or provision of infrastructure.

As the history of housing programmes has demonstrated, any policy to provide formal supply for low-income households requires substantial resources, which most cities cannot afford. The successful examples (Hong Kong, Singapore) are rare. Housing requires 3-5 per cent of GDP. Cities as major investors have to channel a high percentage of their resources into housing if they want to provide housing, either directly or indirectly, for large parts of the poorer population. There is a structural gap: even under favourable conditions – a non-corrupt and efficient bureaucracy, community participation, the latest state of technology – programmes become expensive, because clients' incomes are too low to afford even low-cost formal-sector services. For those living in an extremely cash- and income-poor world, formal-sector planning, financing, or provision of infrastructure is a luxury. The core of any viable housing solution for the poor is to economize on formal services

Urban housing strategies should provide more than shelter. The housing type, the character of residential area, the land-use mix and the spatial distribution of housing influence:

- The quality of neighbourhoods and the way people live in a community;

- Energy consumption, production and distribution;

- Generation of traffic (volume and type);

- Segregation or integration of different social groups;

- Chances of participation in labour markets, political life; and

- Family life.

Local housing policy as a consequence is always a housing 'plus' policy which involves community development goals, environmental goals, urban transportation and other forms of infrastructure (schools, hospitals, child care, etc.).

Types of Intervention

Supply-Side Policy

Housing policy tries to overcome the relative inertia of supply in housing markets caused by high up-front investment requirements. Experience shows that housing supply tends to be inelastic. Low-income households with no access to formal new housing, for sale or rent on formal markets, have to rely on filtering and thus on the behaviour of high- and middle-income groups which have to finance more production to increase the rate of filtering. The alternative is cheap informal housing with a high self-help component, or individual subsidies which allow low-income households to acquire low-cost simple housing.

The most important precondition for an elastic supply is an elastic planning system combined with land banking to build up flexibility reserves. The most intense conflicts can be observed in cities with tight planning regulations and shortage of land for building purposes which increases costs and prices for new construction and intensifies shortages for low-income households or families with children and a weak market position. The distributional consequences of such tight rationing of land for building combined with private ownership of land, in terms of its effect on the distribution of property, are stronger than practically any other form of state intervention in market processes, for the simple reason that housing is the most important private asset.

Therefore, rationing strategies for ecological reasons can only be justified if public agencies or municipalities use the increments in land value which can be realized on open markets to finance infrastructure. 'NIMBY' policies which increase market values of existing buildings and increase bottlenecks on housing markets will have extremely adverse distributional effects. If environmental concerns in urban regions lead to a policy of high density and low supply of land for building purposes, the municipalities or their agents should use their planning power to enforce densities, so that high-income groups cannot buy low-density housing. Rationing of supply of land at the regional or urban level demands rationing of the size of building sites in all individual cases to avoid growing inequalities in housing and guarantee access to scarce land for all households in need.

If supply is inelastic, and individual income or buying power determines the amount of land households will use, any demand shock will lead to an immediate price increase, to overcrowding and to crowding out of weaker tenants or buyers. Planners should never forget the market reaction they will create. Environmentally motivated supply restrictions can only be accepted when they do not result in unsocial distributional consequences and when the scarcity which will be created is distributed in a fair and even way.

The case for a supply-side policy, able to generate spheres and zones of limited spatial competition and more flexible market reactions, is even stronger in the context of rapid urbanization. Traditionally supply-side policy has meant social or public housing with all its deficits (high costs, excluded neighbourhoods). To avoid these deficits:

- Methods of public assistance should become more flexible. Instead of constructing, owning and renting out the units, state and local governments should make soft loans to investors who offer low-income housing. Public agencies can alternatively offer contracts to private owners who will rent to target groups and receive a payment (leased housing instead of subsidized production);

- Rather than directly being involved in housing production, cities can concentrate on influencing the supply of key inputs, or take over responsibility for financing and production;

- Cities can provide affordable land and infrastructure and help lower income groups to improve access to loans – thus promoting well-functioning markets as a precondition of resource mobilization and demand oriented production.

Demand Side Policies/Direct Transfers to Households

Demand instruments can be directly orientated to the poor and their needs, so as to overcome their inability to finance housing. The trend towards more demand-oriented instruments should be strengthened. Rent allowances for low-income households living in private rental housing are well tested in many countries, replacing (at least partly) housing programmes in many European countries. After disappointing results with public housing, the US turned towards credit programmes to enable homeownership of low-income households.

Demand policy targeted to urban low-income households should be based on two concepts: the support of housing finance in order to help low-income households provide their own housing, and the support of low-income households by direct personal subsidies in rental markets.

Direct transfers to households are the least distorting subsidy instruments. They can be more easily targeted to income level and family size than tax instruments (which typically produce high levels of mistargeting). They are also economically less wasteful than soft loans (which generally imply subsidies over the entire duration of the loan and mix funding with social policy tasks). Subsidies tend to have a permanent tendency to move up the income scale. Low-income housing programmes, mostly through administrative sloppiness and a structural affinity between middle-income households and public administrators, tend to change into middle-income programmes. Standards of infrastructure tend to be so high that only middle-income families can afford to finance them. Programmes have to adjust to the households most in need, not to the prejudices of the programme managers. To avoid erosion of programmes, they should be open and transparent, involving community leaders of target areas. All programmes should be reviewed regularly. Community leaders should participate and have the right to demand reviews.

In relation to their advantages, direct transfers are difficult, and potentially expensive to administer and implement. The more detailed targeting needed in comparison to loan programmes or public housing requires a decentralized administrative subsidy delivery structure that is capable of addressing the individual household and managing public funds. Often, such administrative structures do not exist in developing countries, or are expensive to bring into existence. A housing transfer system, in particular if it concentrates on homeownership, can therefore not stand alone as a major social policy instrument. Where it has been implemented successfully, it complements other social policy instruments, such as family

Box IV.24. The Chilean model of housing assistance.

Chile's direct housing assistance system started in the 1980s. Its philosophy is to leave low-cost housing construction and ownership to the private sector, and at the same time to provide potential home-owners with subsidies under a transparent system of selecting potential beneficiaries under a rule of means testing. Housing finance provision, in turn, partly remains with the government. The system has given rise to reform in a number of other Latin-American countries. It has been commended[1] for its approach to incentive compatibility by requiring minimum savings amounts from borrowers and operating with leverage-neutral capital subsidies. Low-income housing programs run by the Ministry of Housing and Urban Development (MINVU) are subdivided by income strata into three brackets: downpayment requirements grow and the subsidy content reduces with income.

For the lowest brackets, the progressive housing program and the basic housing program, the government organizes housing production. It solicits bids from private developers towards construction of units for fixed prices. The government then markets the houses to beneficiaries, and thereby directly delivers the subsidy. Bearing most financial risks, government is de facto in the situation of a public housing investor; on the other hand it retains strict control over beneficiary selection.

Under the middle-income program, loans are supposed to be given mainly by the private sector. It has turned out, however, that private lenders are only ready to make loans at around US$ 30,000, near the upper-income margin of the program and well beyond the capacity of the typical household. As a result, most lending in the program comes from the State Bank, a housing bank, or the Ministry of Housing directly. Nearly two thirds of Chilean housing production, which is high at around 8 per 1,000 inhabitants, are thus directly financed by government, at high fiscal costs.

1. For example, World Bank (1997) p. 56.

(Kusnetzoff, 1997)

assistance, livelihood programmes, redistributive pension systems or general social assistance ('welfare').

Interestingly enough, a supply-side bias persists in many Asian cities, partly due to different initial conditions that were caused largely by the low inelasticity of housing supply arising from shortages of land. Public housing still plays a strong role in Hong Kong, Japan, and Korea, though Singapore has switched to promotion of owner-occupiership. Renaud (1989) has shown, however, that high land and housing prices in Korea's main metropolis, Seoul, were caused by over-restrictive planning. In the Philippines, the main objective of housing policy is still a quantitative housing production target. Scarcity of funding and deficiencies in public sector development have pre-empted massive public housing. Compared to European or North American cities, higher-income groups in Asian cities appear to be more willing to live in high-rise housing; thus these cities avoid the problem that can too easily arise in Western cities, where suburban high-rise developments may be socially stigmatized.

Housing Finance

At all stages of housing policy, provision of a stable flow of funds is the precondition for adequate production. In all systems certain fundamental tasks have to be solved:

- Potential investors who are able to service long-term loans should easily be able to find access to such loans;

- Low-cost, unbiased and neutral systems of processing loans should allow different types of investors easy access to loans;

- Selection criteria should not create high risks for the financial institution or the client. On the other hand, risk aversion should not be so high that potential clients do not get access to loans;

- If borrowers cannot fulfil their obligations, fair, fast and reliable procedures should be employed to aid the borrower. If borrowers are permanently unable to fulfil their obligations, the property should be sold to protect both borrower and lender;

- Small borrowers and savers need special low-cost intermediation geared to their mostly informal sector needs. Lending to groups or informal outlets in neighbourhoods can reduce disadvantages on formal markets.

Housing policy has to develop and maintain rules to promote a flexible fair and effective market for housing finance.

In the US, housing finance has survived today as the main vehicle of housing policy. Government has provided for improved loan funding liquidity for private lenders through the Federal Home Loan Bank system and the foundation of a federal national mortgage agency (Fannie Mae). Credit risk for lenders, a problem in a country with high job uncertainty and heterogeneous population, could be substantially reduced by the Federal Housing Association that provides insurance for loans given to low-income households. Low credit risk for the lender means also easier access for low-income households to credit. Urban poor households have repeatedly been addressed by special programmes within this framework, with mixed results.

Private mortgage lenders and special financial circuits for housing, typically based on the mutuality principle, already existed in many developed countries before World War II. Nevertheless, most European countries built up, in parallel, public housing banks and soft lending programmes for low-income households which continue today as main housing policy instruments. A major reason was that high inflation between the wars and after World War II had partially eliminated the market for private housing finance. In many countries, public housing banks or similar financial institutions were given a monopoly position. A prominent example is Japan where public housing banks still provide for nearly half of all mortgage lending outstanding, including the entirety of low-income housing loans. Before the liberalization wave of the 1980s and 1990s, public housing or mortgage banks existed in at least partial monopoly situations in as diverse countries as France, Korea, Mexico, Sweden, Italy and Spain. In others, such as Germany, public banks indirectly fund a large proportion of the mortgage markets. Until the change in the economic system, housing finance in socialist economies was dominated by state-directed lending. The purpose of these systems was similar to the US system: to serve a market for low-income households which would otherwise have to be housed by the state through costly public housing; however contrary to the US, where public banks prevailed, the public sector fully absorbed the risks of mortgage lending, often in an unsustainable fashion.

Most developing countries have followed the example of Europe and the US, and are developing their housing finance systems through public financial institutions. As in Europe and the US before World War II, private banks mainly provide housing loans for the upper tier of the population, since the credit risk and the costs of access even for the middle class are perceived as too high. Since, due to economic instability, the market risks of mortgage lending are high, banks shift these to borrowers, further reducing the circle of potential borrowers. Due to institutional and general economic factors, mortgage loans with fixed interest rates that are suitable for funding homeowners are rare outside Europe and the US.

A number of Latin American countries have thus created public housing banks or social security funds responsible for the funding of mortgage loans for low-income households and development loans for low-cost housing projects. Similar models exist in India, Indonesia, Thailand, the Philippines, South Africa as well as in some Sub-Saharan African countries. Only in very few of these cases, however, do public bank or social security loans reach the truly urban poor. Programmes are generally called successful if they reach beyond the richest 50 per cent of the population. In many cases also, public housing banks assumed too high risks, or were too inexperienced or inefficient to perform business effectively, and went into bankruptcy. Financing models for low-income household mortgage loans were generally most successful where private lenders could be convinced to cooperate with the public sector in giving subsidized loans.

In addition, the approach of easy access to low-income lending often had negative consequences for the financial system. By lowering the interest rate or enhancing credit, often in combination with tax policy instruments, policies resulted in house prices rising uncontrollably. In Sweden, house prices in the late 1980s soared due to a combination of soft loans and high tax allowances on mortgage interest rates for homeowners. A similar development took place in the Netherlands in the second half of the 1990s. Thus, excessive subsidies for housing finance bear the risk that they accrue only to the more affluent parts of the population, at the same time crowding out low-income households even more effectively from the market, through credit-related property price increases.

Similar adverse effects were often caused where cheap housing finance was offered through the social security system. In many countries without developed capital markets, social security funds are the only source of long-term fixed-rate funding that would be affordable to low-income borrowers. In many cases, funds have been forced to invest in low-interest assets, with the result that contributors are subsidizing loan borrowers. Often, the access to loans is not transparent, and credit risk is poorly monitored. Also, the contributors are in most circumstances poorer than the loan borrowers.

Private Rental Housing – Key Sector of Global Urban Housing Markets

One of the paradoxes of housing policies worldwide is that the private rental housing market has been widely underestimated as a key strategic sector for urban development. Functioning urban rental housing markets are the most efficient supply source for migrants and young families. Low-cost moderate quality rental markets are self-targeted towards low-income households. In spite of the particular function of rental markets, in many countries landlords have been stigmatized – even in countries with liberal economic traditions – as archetypal representatives of capitalist exploitation. After an era of regulation and discrimination, including rent controls, this sector has been nearly eliminated in many cities.

The history of the formal rental sector may be seen as a textbook example of the destruction of a market, with serious long-term consequences. It is only recently that countries which have massively lost rental housing stock have initiated reforms such as the easing of rent control, changes in rent legislation, gradual removal of distortions through subsidy and public loan programmes.

Since liberalization in the 1980s and 1990s, this sector has stabilized and become more dynamic. For instance, rent legislation has been substantially reformed in policy environments as diverse as Spain and the United Kingdom.

Creating a formal private rental housing sector in developing countries is a basic tool for the reduction of informal shelter and hence inequality in living conditions in urban areas. It often merely recognizes and formalizes existing informal rental relationships. But promoting private rental housing has not been very attractive for wealthy investors. A better environment for private rental housing could create a substitute for social housing. The preconditions are:

- Low inflation rates;
- No rent control;
- Favourable tax system;
- Easy access to land and planning permission;
- Simple regulations for construction;
- Time-limited rental contracts.

Specific Tasks for Hypergrowth Cities

Overcoming Specific Shortages

In developing cities, improving living conditions in the informal sector dominates all other concerns of housing policy. Informal housing is the result of necessity: poor households find it impossible to buy or rent in the formal housing sector, because the costs – in particular, up-front costs – are too high for them. The task of improving housing conditions in the informal city is fourfold:

- Lowering the barriers between informal and formal housing is the central task;
- Building upgradable informal housing can help to reduce deficits in the medium term;
- Upgrading and stabilizing existing informal areas can most effectively reach the most clients. But schemes to upgrade infrastructure can have a pernicious side effect: if they increase the demand for housing in the upgraded area, without increasing the supply, they will invite gentrification. The buildings will improve but many former inhabitants will be worse off, as they cannot afford the higher prices in markets with scarce supply;
- Slum clearance strategies should only be attempted when there are serious health hazards which cannot be abolished, or where shifts in location have increased the opportunity costs of reserving valuable land which is urgently needed for inner city jobs. In both cases, the poor who are threatened should be offered accessible and affordable substitutes.

From the perspective of formal planning, informal housing is very often seen as illegal, disorderly and consequently as a problem. Cooperation, assistance and promotion do not exist. Eviction and slum clearance, against the wishes and the interests of the inhabitants, have become the exception, but still many informal settlements are merely tolerated and not actively upgraded; the wishes of the inhabitants, who alone can decide which improvements are urgent and which they can afford, are ignored. In practically all informal settlements, one can observe a slow upgrading and accumulation process as a consequence of net savings – even out of very low income. All cities should promote and strengthen this accumulation – at least by upgrading public infrastructure. Successful strategies to improve housing conditions would need to accept informal housing as a productive and creative solution. Realistic assessments of the needs of the informal sector are thus the precondition of any rational strategy.

Lowering the Barriers for Informal Housing

Local governments do not have the power to change income distribution or the macroeconomic, financial and legal situation of the housing sector. Within their boundaries, the number of poor families as well as the number of migrants has to be taken as a fact of life. To improve the housing situation of the poor who construct their own units, the most efficient assistance and support for new dwellers by local governments is thus to:

- Provide urban land with a security of tenure at low cost;

- Simplify the planning processes and provide building permits also for low-cost units;

- Enable or provide a minimum of servicing (which may include a guarantee of the cost recovery of infrastructure).

Concentrating planning efforts on the provision of affordable land with security of tenure is the most effective way of reducing inequality and allowing access to sustainable housing. Experience in developing countries suggests that within this framework, up-front investments in servicing, or equivalently capital values implied in transferring urban land or land-use rights to dwellers, should be kept at a minimum. High implied subsidies per household, whether generated directly (e.g. by transfer of land) or indirectly (e.g. by servicing land and underpricing or not enforcing cost recovery) may create a bias in the provision of housing services *vis-à-vis* rural areas or other cities. The consequence has often been further migration, and a subsequent repeated deterioration of housing standards. As long as there is a likelihood of such inconsistent policies as between one city and another, urban policy-makers will do well to pursue a gradual strategy: they should progressively grant formal planning permissions to occupiers of informal housing, but with specific attached conditions – for instance, a commitment by the owner to make investments in infrastructure.

Only through long-term development processes can the organizational bottlenecks and capital shortages in developing cities be overcome, so that informal housing progressively be eliminated. In the meantime, informal housing as a feature of urban development must be made more liveable and more healthy. This demands particular forms of informal planning, a simple low-cost infrastructure with indigenous technologies, better access to more informal loans, and promotion of developers geared to the needs of the informal housing investor as well as well-functioning markets for building material.

Informal housing is no longer an exotic fringe activity in urban development. It has become a leading, sometimes dominant way of life for millions. Informal housing is no longer a chaotic collection of carton shacks or sheet metal boxes. Informal housing does not arise through altruistic NGOs who organize mutual self-help, in which neighbourhood teams build homes in close cooperation with each other, pooling their financial resources, and using their leisure time. Informal housing is a major planning and development task.

One answer is to choose labour-intensive alternatives and to give priority to secondary and tertiary infrastructure which is more labour-intensive by nature, with local participation. Such labour-intensive methods can be cost-effective and of good quality. Likewise, low-cost informal sector housing will be more labour-intensive and may be more effective as a means of delivering shelter to poor urban communities. So-called low-cost housing may often be occupied by higher-income people because it is not affordable, as occurred in Thailand where 70 per cent of the eligible people sold their rights to higher-income families. In Zambia, informal sector housing produces six times as many dwellings, albeit of lower standard, per unit of investment, than formal sector housing (ILO, 1998, pp. 35-37).

As the traditional public sector solution, based on hierarchical public agencies, very often does not reach informal neighbourhoods, the new solutions should be more decentralized and community oriented. Municipalities would still have to provide the city-wide 'trunk facilities' which usually represent public goods outside of the reach and responsibilities of the neighbourhoods. In the neighbourhoods they could take over the role of advisor or promoter, employing an enabling concept and attitude, and giving up the concept of public provision. The consequence would be more community control and community maintenance and management, and even ownership of the system.

Investors in the informal sector generally cannot afford one-time 100 per cent solutions where all the necessary facilities are financed and provided. Informal development happens in stages. Early on, homes are used half-finished; they will be extended and upgraded as savings capacity or income grows. Infrastructure, even more so, will be developed step by step, with the special difficulty that not all owners will be ready to invest at the same time.

Such policies, providing infrastructure in stages to upgrade existing informal settlements, have a number of big advantages. Provided they are combined with guaranteed title to the land and property, they invoke pride of ownership, thus avoiding the risk that poor people will migrate to new informal housing sites, and increasing the likelihood of building a stable community in a stable neighbourhood. Further, because everyone is learning by emulation, they increase the probability that further improvement will take place, in a kind of domino effect. They constitute a key element, a cornerstone, in housing policy for any developing city.

Informal Land and Construction

Informal housing is inherently a matter of legal and regulatory definition, the outcome of political decisions as to building codes and land development standards that distinguish what is formal from what is informal.

The costs of land development multipliers are extremely high in most developing countries. In countries where per capita income is lower than US$ 5,000, developed land that meets the standards for sanitation, water, roads, subdivision regulations etc. costs between twice and sixteen times as much as undeveloped land. The main reasons are that the shortfalls in supply of infrastructure and municipal services are monopolized or operated by the public sector, or that such land suffers from poor environmental conditions (high transport costs, high costs for imported parts and machinery because of exchange rate risks).

Rationing of land for informal housing will result in high prices, which will mean that poor investors will have to spend too great a proportion of their capital on land, resulting in minimum construction investments. Where cities are unable to provide infrastructure, they should at least guarantee minimum planning and legal land titles for informal sites. A simple site plan as a precondition for later adjustments, and efficient upgrading is better than the absence of rational spatial investment patterns which will require later demolition and partial slum clearance.

Subdivision and land banking could be organized by private developers, but again high prices have to be avoided. Planning should open up opportunities for demand-oriented subdivisions, to create a competitive framework where surplus profits disappear. As a rule it is better to provide more land at lower prices with low or no infrastructure than to offer too small quantities of serviced land; shortages will produce informal settlements without legal land titles and without any infrastructure.

Existing informal squatting areas, which very often have existed for a long time, require recognition. Prolonged occupation and stable investment should be sufficient reasons to legitimize such settlements. Upgrading strategies and step-by-step upgrading investment by the inhabitants need a legal basis and tenure rights.

One outcome of the policy debate has been to allow gradual release of land for development in order to support the urban poor, or migrants; i.e. to let the provision of infrastructure and services follow housing development, rather than preceding it. Another element of success is the development of less expensive methods of construction. Again solutions must be found locally, with local materials based on local building traditions. Technologies such as stabilized earth bricks, produced in manual brick-making presses, can be used nearly everywhere. They are inexpensive and can also increase the rate of construction. Non-Governmental Organizations and donor countries can play a useful role in helping to diffuse knowledge about such low-cost self-help policies, of which there are many existing examples.

National and local housing policies have tended to neglect well-known traditional technologies. Low-cost, self-help construction needs more support from governments, because it is the key to solving the problem of urban shelter.

Finance: Enabling the Transition from Informality to Formality

A more comprehensive approach to the removal of economic barriers between the formal and informal sectors consists of the provision of finance for low-income households and groups. Finance generally requires macroeconomic and legal stability. There are two main risks for financial non-sustainability: the risk of changes in market conditions, and the risk of poor recovery of the funds. If market conditions change rapidly, for instance due to inflation, financial contracts tend to shorten. The traditional answer for funding low-income formal housing has thus been the provision of soft loans by governments or through the social security system, or the creation of savings and investment groups, or the mobilization of family savings. Experience shows that the second option is only relevant for very stable groups which are able to retain the benefits from mutuality internally.

For the control of credit risk, it is necessary to improve the efficiency of the collection of mortgage debts or rental payments. A first approach is to create a meaningful mortgage concept, but this requires appropriate valuation methods and – a harsh necessity – an effective foreclosure system for defaulting loans. Alternatives that have been tried in developing countries include leasing, increasing the amount of collateral required, and using group guarantees – an idea initially developed for small loans, but highly dependent on the stability of groups; here NGOs play a crucial catalyst role.

Box IV.25. The community mortgage programme in the Philippines.

This is an example of the group guarantee approach. Groups of beneficiaries living in slums or blighted areas become eligible as borrowers for loans extended by public banks, provided that they organize themselves in community associations. Loan recovery ratios are reported to be lower than in the case of individual loan programmes, but sufficiently high to sustain the programme.

(UNCHS, 1996*b*, p. 373)

Investment in informal housing is unlikely to appeal to conventional sources of credit, if only because those who live in it suffer from unstable incomes. And this will be even more true where the banking system is weakly-developed and has limited capacities for processing loans. Here, banks are almost bound to concentrate on conventional credit-worthy middle-class clients seeking to live in conventionally-designed neighbourhoods.

Competition for sparsely-developed credit services makes it unlikely that small individual low-income clients will be able to secure loans. In these conditions, the answer may be to make loans to groups, or to use groups to screen their own members, as practised by the Grameen Bank. NGOs can take over an intermediary role in screening customers or simplifying procedures. Helping low-income groups to finance informal sector investment is unlikely to be very profitable, but it will prove very rewarding in terms of the long-term consequences for individual households, entire neighbourhoods and urban development generally. Given the obvious cultural differences between informal living and formal banking, bridging the gap would represent a major success in urban development.

Conclusions

Cities in the developing world should learn from the developed countries, where in the decades after World War II national and local governments spent enormous sums attempting to overcome housing shortages. Despite housing subsidies that often totalled more than 2 per cent of GNP, the results were often inadequate, because:

- Counter-productive measures such as rent control or over-regulated land and construction markets limited their effectiveness; or

- Deadweight losses and crowding out of private unsubsidized construction occurred.

Empirical evidence, in particular with programmes to assist home ownership that have often represented the largest single element of social transfer, contests the view that housing policy can play a significant role in reducing economic inequality. One reason is that housing policy is hardly ever coordinated with strategies to combat high unemployment and marginal wages, which since the 1970s have lowered the incomes of many formerly-affluent households. True, real income levels are generally much higher than in the 1960s and 1970s, yet typically up to 40 per cent of urban households cannot afford to buy or rent unsubsidized formal housing, and continue to rely on subsidy for shelter.

Good governance in housing entails much greater efforts to improve the operation of markets and to reduce expensive formal social housing programmes for low-income groups which have proved so ineffective – in some cases providing subsidized housing for the middle classes, in others unattractive segregated housing which stigmatizes the poor. Balanced social housing is a commodity extremely hard to produce. In its place, better-functioning markets will widen choice, increase opportunities and reduce costs and rent levels.

This is true for all kinds of cities. In developed cities, efficient markets for lower- income households will probably be more successful than social housing. In developing cities more efficient informal markets, properly assisted and combined with upgrading efforts, and mobilizing a maximum of self-help, will probably create the highest benefits for citizens with below-average incomes.

Infrastructure

The Importance of Physical Infrastructure

Physical infrastructure is the basic public sector input for all urban development, above all housing. Cities must provide secure power supplies, clean water, environmentally sound sanitation, safe streets, and reliable transport links to achieve the goals of sustainability and greater equality of living conditions. The appropriate level of infrastructure services varies according to the local context. It ranges from the provision of clean water at public standpipes, drainage ditches and communal latrines in informal housing settlements to the provision of telecommunication infrastructure and cultural amenities like museums and opera houses in high-income urban centres. Without proper planning, certain infrastructure investments can create urban sprawl, while lack of infrastructure investment can lead to unserviced informal housing settlements which are sources of high morbidity and mortality.

A UNDP-World Bank report identified three reasons why poor people do not have access to utilities such as water and sanitation. Firstly, utility networks do not reach homes of poor people because of insufficient infrastructure or because the poor live in peri-urban settlements outside the normal service area; secondly, the poor cannot pay the connection costs; and thirdly, the poor cannot afford to pay for services (Alfaro, 1996). To overcome these deficits, according to the World Bank, between 0.2 and 0.5 per cent of GDP would have to be spent. It is not possible to install a traditional, full-service urban infrastructure in every poor (or even prosperous) neighbourhood, because their inhabitants do not have the financial capacity to pay for it.

Insufficient institutional capacity (leadership, training, skills) at the community level and 'a reluctance of professionals and bureaucrats to develop and accept alternative local innovations' (Lee, 1995) are also hampering the provision of adequate infrastructure. Ismail Serageldin, World Bank Vice President for Environmentally Sustainable Development, has put it bluntly: 'In effect, government regulations that now impose stringent housing standards in areas such as land use, which as few as 10 per cent of residents of many developing world cities can afford to meet, make it illegal to be poor' (quoted in Ordway, 1998, p. 12).

Therefore, local governments should not enforce consumption and quality standards on poor people, especially in the informal sector. Affordability is a principle which has to be applied in financing and providing infrastructure. People must not be forced to adjust to technical standards they cannot afford. Provision of infrastructure also needs to be adjusted to the needs and organizational or managerial abilities, especially of poorer clients, by relaxing standards of quality, materials, type of organization, involvement of clients, etc. It is just not feasible to plan infrastructure for the informal sector on the basis of the capital requirements and management practices of the formal sector. Universally enforced standards may have a perverse push effect: people may simply move to areas free of such standards, so that a best-case solution becomes a worst-case solution.

The Habitat Agenda Section IV B (60) addresses this question: 'adequate basic infrastructure, such as water-supply, sanitation and waste-management facilities; suitable environmental quality and health-related factors; and adequate and accessible location with regard to work and basic facilities . . . should be available at an affordable cost' (UNCHS, 1996a). It affirms that governments should adopt and/or adapt existing codes and regulations, to facilitate access to land for poor people. It also urges that authorities 'actively promote the regularization and upgrading of informal settlements and urban slums as an expedient measure and pragmatic solution to the urban shelter deficit. It encourages the promotion of 'development in accordance with indigenous practices and . . . technologies appropriate to local conditions' (UNCHS, 1996a).

Local authorities need adequate sources of finance to provide infrastructure of the right quality and in the right quantity. Despite its importance, infrastructure provision has to struggle with a multitude of difficulties: fragmented institutional frameworks, cumbersome arrangements for coordination, overspill into other jurisdictions and thus weak incentives, low sources of revenue (property tax, user charges, automotive taxes), and overcentralized financing powers with inadequate funds from central government.

Infrastructure investments in the developing world, totalling US$ 200 billion a year and constituting 4 per cent of developing countries' output and 20 per cent of their total investment, are increasingly controlled by municipalities. Moreover, institutions like the World Bank tend to provide finance directly to them. Yet such investments are often misallocated and may provide the wrong level of services. Service supplies are often sub-optimal because of inadequate maintenance, while in other areas they are non-existent or inadequate. Even if a city appears adequately serviced overall, there may be huge differences in the level of service within that city. Those who do not have access to public services may pay a much higher price than those who do, while the latter may not be paying the recovery cost (ILO, 1998, p. 35).

In the absence of public provision, private vendors fill the gap, but their services are expensive. 'The poor pay more' syndrome invariably applies to private water delivery where piped systems do not exist. Thus organizational deficits are often more damaging than people's inability to pay. Expensive buildings in poorly serviced informal housing areas are a common occurrence in many developing cities. They point to political or administrative bottlenecks stemming from over-centralized administrations which require urgent attention.

Some of these difficulties can be overcome. Public authorities do not have to produce or organize specific infrastructure investments themselves. Development contracts or BOT (Build-Operate-Transfer) solutions with private investors are flexible instruments to provide infrastructure, without the need for detailed involvement of the public sector. They are discussed below.

The establishment of land title, arguably a special type of institutional infrastructure, is a major problem. However, there is some evidence that marketable legal title, of the kind expected in the formal sector, is not essential if informal indications of ownership can evolve to reduce the uncertainty associated with informal occupancy of land. Omar Razzaz gives examples of informal registries run by neighbourhood associations in Brazilian *favelas* which issue their own documents as proof of ownership. He suggests that the solution to land occupancy may lie in authorities recognizing the validity of property interests which may be based on ethnic, territorial and community networks and customs instead of relying exclusively on the formal property title system (Razzaz, 1997).

Financing Infrastructure: General Principles

Beneficiaries should pay for infrastructure through special financial instruments. One-off development charges are a suitable method of raising up-front money for infrastructure. Traditionally, developers pay for infrastructure on the development site while the public sector pays for off-site costs. Alternatively, all social costs of infrastructure attributable to a specific development could be paid by developers. They should pay for the infrastructure required to serve their new developments plus the cost of ensuring that the infrastructure available to the rest of the community has at least the same capacity as before. Under this rule, the developer would not only pay for local residential streets but also for a slip lane to an existing highway nearby if required to reduce congestion. The attribution criterion is a 'best practice rule', particularly in industrial countries where local government administrators have the necessary level of sophistication to implement it.

A distinction is needed between (*a*) wholly attributable and (*b*) partly attributable infrastructure components to implement the attribution criterion. Wholly attributable infrastructure, built exclusively to serve the development, should be paid for in total by the developer, whether on- or off-site. The costs of partly attributable components, which both serve a specific development and increase services for the rest of the community, should be shared between the developer, who should pay for the attributable portion, and government or other developers who would pay for the remainder.

Private Provision

Private sector solutions have a long history. In the nineteenth century, when new housing areas in London, Berlin, Paris or New York were usually developed by private companies, the responsibility to develop and service the land was often separated from the responsibility to finance and construct the buildings.

Public authorities have many options to involve the private sector on a contract basis. So-called BOT projects represent a very advantageous solution, whereby private investors provide infrastructure on a contract basis and manage it over a period laid down in a contract, after which control of the infrastructure is returned to the municipality. Such schemes reduce the involvement of cities without removing their ultimate responsibility.

BOT solutions concentrate on large investment projects able to carry the high planning and management costs (including political risks) which are necessary to organize consortia to plan, finance, build and manage such projects. They are very often triggered by banks with good relationships with private developers, who can provide collateral and fulfil lending standards more easily than many municipalities.

BOT techniques create an asset which generates revenue with a value capable of raising loans. Where revenues are insufficient to recover the loans and the operating costs, subsidies can be used to cover the gap. Public subsidies create leverage and allow more investment with a given amount of revenue. BOT projects have become popular and have proved efficient in many countries (e.g. Malaysia, Pakistan, Argentina, Philippines). They can and should be used in different ways for different purposes.

Box IV.26. SODECI private water supply concession (Ivory Coast).

In the Ivory Coast a privatized solution was used by giving a water delivery concession to a company. In addition to privatization, village committees were empowered and given responsibility for water pump operations. The World Bank reports that annual maintenance costs fell by more than 50 per cent and breakdowns were reduced from 50 to 11 per cent.

Urban Problem: People in Abidjan, Côte d'Ivoire had no adequate or cost effective access to a basic need — water. The World Bank observes that in many countries, poor households pay up to twenty times as much for water from private vendors as households served by subsidized piped systems.

Best Practice Solution: In 1973, The Ivory Coast government awarded a concession to SODECI, the Water Supply Company of Ivory Coast. The World Bank observes: 'SODECI now manages more than 300 piped water supply systems across the country. It has 300,000 individual connections, a number increasing by 5 to 6 per cent a year. The company already reaches some 70 per cent of the nation's 4.5 million urban residents — 2 million in Abidjan, and the rest in settlements ranging from 5,000 to 400,000 people' (World Bank, News Release No. 96/69S). To facilitate service to the poor, SODECI foregoes direct hook-up charges on three out of four of its domestic connections. Despite this policy SODECI makes a profit. The World Bank notes 'The cost of SODECI water to consumers is no higher than in neighbouring countries with similar economic conditions, where rates rarely cover costs and service lags far behind' (World Bank, News Release No. 96/69S). In 1996, the government implemented a new 15 year plan to comply with the resolution of Agenda 21. One of its primary goals is to equalize expenditure and income throughout the country. In its policy statement the government notes 'the average cost price of a cubic metre (m^3) of water sold in Abidjan, is twice cheaper than in other parts of the country, whereas the quantity of water produced for the Capital is twice higher than for the rest of the country'. Abidjan's cost advantages are directly related to the fact that this is SODECI's original service concession area.

(Ordway, 1998, pp. 12,13)

Box IV.27. Community Infrastructure (Upgrading) Programme (CIP), Tanzania.

The Community Infrastructure Programme (CIP) is being implemented by the city of Dar Es Salaam in Tanzania. CIP was established in 1995 to address infrastructure problems in deficient communities by working with them. The programme involves the government, parastatals, communities and other stakeholders in the development process by adopting a partnership and participatory approach.

Since independence, the central and local governments have been the single-handed 'providers' of all the different services including infrastructure in urban and rural areas with people as 'recipients'. The inability of the City Council to continue providing infrastructure single-handed to satisfy the ever increasing demands due to rapid urbanization, prompted it to initiate and establish the Community Infrastructure Programme.

The establishment of CIP was an effort to supplement those of the City Council in providing infrastructural services to the city neighbourhoods through contribution and participation. It also creates a sense of responsibility to the communities and at the same time building their capacities in the management of the constructed infrastructure.

Since the introduction of the initiative into the two pilot communities of Tabata and Kijitonyama there have been remarkable achievements:

Capacity building of the Communities:

- Revision of communities' constitutions to allow maximum community participation
- Selection and training of neighbourhood and area representatives
- Preparation of community profiles
- Preparation of community development plans
- Collection of information related to land ownership (plot consolidation)
- Formation of sub-committees at community levels to address different problems as prioritized in community profiles

Institutional Strengthening:

- Establishment of offices in each community
- Establishment of a Steering Committee comprising representatives from all the partners
- Establishment of formalized institutional links between the relevant partners and the communities through signing of Memoranda of Understanding

Neighbourhood Infrastructure Upgrading:

- Prepare Terms of Reference pertaining to works and services to be undertaken
- Preparation of detailed engineering designs for the intended infrastructure to be upgraded (i.e. roads, drainage systems, sewerage, etc.)
- Formed technical sub-committees for monitoring and supervising the works and services

Box IV.27. cont.

> - Establishment of community (locally managed) own water systems. The communities are running these water systems at cost i.e. the community members buy the water and the money is ploughed back to run the systems. In Tabata community, part of the realized money is now being used for solid waste collection. The water committee pays for the collection services and the community members are charged collection fees for the service. This ensures community responsibility and sustainability of the provided infrastructure.
>
> (UN Best Practices Database)

Informal Provision of Infrastructure and Self-Help Solutions

Highly sophisticated market solutions cannot be applied in low-income areas because they are simply too expensive. But missing or inadequate infrastructure can sometimes result in creative ideas of self-help or informal infrastructure solutions. It has been found that as communities have the best information about their needs, self-help in construction and maintenance of infrastructure often proves the cheaper, better and most effective solution. Community members are involved in the planning and construction of a project. And they contribute money; it has been a wrong assumption that low-income people were unable and unwilling to pay for infrastructure services. Communities in unserviced settlements often pay 10 to 100 times more for water supply than the inhabitants of formal districts.

Many case studies have demonstrated that low-income households can afford the full cost of installing basic infrastructure, if all households of a community work collectively and contribute a small amount of money. The estimated cost per household may be as low as one seventh of what the local authority would have charged. And the participating community members get a sense of ownership and feel responsible for maintenance. At the same time, the participating community members got a sense of ownership and feel responsible for maintenance (see boxes IV.27 and IV.28).

While infrastructure projects for the provision of water and sewerage demand at least some technical support, the collection of solid waste is a service that can easily be provided by the informal sector. In many countries, especially in Asia, a great part of the waste is already collected by networks of informal wastepickers. In Indonesian cities, scavengers reduce total urban waste by one-third, and in Bangalore, wastepickers collect thirteen times as much waste as the municipal waste collection. In some cities, efforts are made to integrate the informal waste collection into the formal urban economy. For example, in Belo Horizonte, Brazil, and

Box IV.28. Empowering poor communities in Tegucigalpa, Honduras: Water supply management.

Tegucigalpa's piped water supply and sewerage system does not reach the densely populated communities on the steep hillsides around the city. Sprawling across hills and mountainsides, the rapidly growing squatter population lives in communities above 1,150 metres in elevation, where it is not economical to extend the main city networks. Forty per cent of the population living in this peri-urban area has no access to piped water even public standpipes and depends mainly on buying water from private providers visiting the 'barrios' with water trucks. To 80 per cent of the families, the costs of water represent 11% to 20% of their monthly salary.

The National Water and Sewerage Service (SANAA) has implemented an innovative alternative to central water supply services; it helps low-income urban neighbourhoods set up their own water associations. These associations install independent water supply systems, which the residents pay for and own, and which provide a regular supply of water at a much lower cost per litre than water bought from vendors. The communities take part in the construction by contributing unskilled work and local materials and they also take part in investment costs and run the administration, operation and maintenance through local water boards. The investments are shared by UNICEF, UEBD/SANAA, the Swedish Government and the community.

In less than four years, 45,000 people in 25 low-income neighbourhoods have been provided with a regular supply of domestic water. However, although residents now pay less than they used to pay when having to buy water from private water-vendors, they still pay more than the richer neighbourhoods served by the highly subsidized public water network system. The project, can however be justified on the basis that now the barrios have reliable sources of water at a lower cost than before, and that by demonstrating that the poor are prepared to pay the full value of water, the UEBD is lowering the political justifications for subsidies, leading to possible policy changes.

Impact:
- Water supplied to 50,000 beneficiaries after 5 years of the beginning of the project
- 21 community water boards established
- Community revolving fund established and funds being invested in new water projects.
- Less stomach and skin diseases.

(UN Best Practices Database)

Bandung, Indonesia, scavengers are organized in cooperatives. This can give them a political voice.

This has environmental and economic benefits for the cities: through recycling, resources are saved, costs of waste disposal are reduced, cheaper goods can be produced from the recycled materials, and jobs are created.

Some industries – like steel, paper and glass production – depend a great deal on recycled material inputs.

Box IV.29. Recife, Brazil: Selective solid waste collection and recycling project.

Similar to most Brazilian cities, Recife has serious financial problems. The municipal institutions therefore turn to social structures and community approaches as alternatives to public services. An integrated basic sanitation programme encompassing drainage, removal of sewage, urban cleaning and health promotion is implemented by a decentralized administration. The city is divided in 6 administrative sectors and sub-divided in three micro-regions each. Communities are represented on regional delegations; Sector Planning Councils and the Urban Development Council function at the sector and Municipal levels.

Urban cleaning is a major problem and the Programme of Selective Collection and Recycling of Solid Waste, initiated in June 1993, is a basic instrument for city cleaning. The programme aims at behavioural change for reducing the production of solid waste, encourages and promotes the commercialization of recyclable material and stimulates the generation of income. While there are special containers for recyclables in high-income neighbourhoods, a 'Communal Selected Collection Project' is implemented in middle-low- and low-income areas. People can exchange the separated materials for food, meal tickets or construction materials for a group's building.

The Selective Waste Collection and Recycling Programme is incorporated in three broader development programmes of the Municipality of Recife. The Municipality in the Neighbourhoods Programme aims at the systematic decentralization of the municipal administration in all sectors. It focuses on planning, programming and evaluation of sector and neighbourhood activities and is one of the means of social control through participatory budgeting.

Impact:

- 73% increase in recycled materials in two years
- 62% annual increase in volume of material for recycling
- 482 ton/month reduction in solid waste
- 56.5% reduction of special operations for waste collection and 285 dumpsites reduced to 124 (43.5% reduction)
- 5,796 tons/month less garbage collected
- 5 to 20 years expansion of the life of the dump site. Upgrading of the dumping area and waste treatment
- Food supply for approximately 2,040 recycling families

(UN Best Practices Database)

Conclusion

Cities, and especially poor cities, can become and remain fiscally sustainable in several ways. In the long run, central and provincial governments should enable local governments to establish their own revenue sources to become fiscally autonomous. Under all revenue systems equalization grants are necessary.

Much of the construction and operation of infrastructure should be handed over to the private sector. Because firms survive only by making ends meet, and because they are subject to competition from other firms, they are more likely than government to minimize and cover their costs of production.

In developing cities, communities could organize their own delivery of lower costs by using 'sweat equity' and contributing capital in cash and kind, to build and operate infrastructure.

Local governments can continue to make progress towards social integration and to alleviate poverty by employing efficient and equitable practices in public finance. Firstly, they can resort to private companies or fiscally autonomous public bodies to organize the production of infrastructure and services and thus to minimize production costs. Secondly, both the private or public providers of services can be required to charge the lowest-income consumers below cost and higher-income consumers above cost.

While central governments were relinquishing allocative functions, city governments could enhance empowerment by assigning tasks to the smallest, fiscally independent agencies which, in turn, encourage neighbourhood initiatives. Such changes provide community stakeholders with greater opportunities for meaningful participation in government. By resorting to user charges (rather than taxes unrelated to benefits) local governments raise people's awareness of the link between benefits and costs and make them more economically responsible. By introducing greater transparency and accountability, local governments become more responsive to their constituents. There is cause for optimism, as democratic institutions have been spreading and governments have moved closer to the people. Adopting best practice principles for local public finance in the coming century will bring greater sustainability, economic welfare, and empowerment to cities worldwide.

Transportation

Transportation planning is an important part of overall city planning, which needs to be considered in the closest possible relationship to land-use planning. For experience shows, and recent work emphasizes, that – as Colin Clark wrote in 1957 – transport is indeed the maker and breaker of cities (Clark, 1957). It exists in an intimate symbiotic relationship with urban form: the development of the city affects the transportation choices that are available, but in turn the transportation system will affect the city's future development. And so, particular urban forms tend to be associated with particular transportation mixes: contrast the traditional, dense, centralized model of a Paris or a Berlin with the dispersed automobile-oriented patterns of Los Angeles or Phoenix.

The conventional wisdom of the 1990s is that the first is 'sustainable' and the second not. In fact, though this particular proposition is probably correct, the relationship is more complex than that: people are still leaving European cities for suburbs, while places like Los Angeles are making big steps toward becoming model environmentally-sensitive cities. But it will do as an approximation. What this means is that transport policies must be assessed in association with land-use policies. There is no point in adopting a transport policy that demands an unrealistic land-use policy; and vice-versa.

There are strong arguments for policy intervention, as we have already seen in Chapter II. In hardly any city in the world is the urban transportation system optimal; in most cities it performs very poorly. First and foremost, it results in enormous losses of valuable time, especially on the daily journey to and from work. Second, delays and unpredictability lead to considerable psychological stress, most dramatically illustrated in the phenomenon of road rage. Third, it massively wastes non-renewable natural resources, creates pollution and contributes significantly to global warming. And fourth, the solutions currently posed are too often highly capital-intensive and thus unrealistic, above all in the cities of the developing world.

Box IV.30. The costs of congestion.

In 1990, Japan's international cooperation agency calculated that Bangkok loses as much as one-third of its potential output because of congested roads. The EU's transport directorate, in 1995, put the cost of congestion in Europe at 2 per cent of GDP. But such calculations assume a base of uncongested roads. Dutch economists believe the true figure for their country is as low as 0.25 per cent of GDP.

(*The Economist*, 1998, pp. 5-6)

The environmental costs of air and water pollution in Bangkok exceed $2 billion a year. Each car in Bangkok is expected to spend an average equivalent of 44 days each year in traffic jams. Traffic-induced delays lose the city about one-third of its estimated gross city product, in one estimate equivalent to $4 million a day. Time savings from a 10 per cent reduction in peak hour journey times would save $400 million annually. Excessive lead levels, chiefly from vehicles, contribute to 200-400,000 cases of hypertension and some 400 deaths a year. Rough estimates suggest that excessive lead levels can cause children to lose four or more IQ points by the age of seven.

(Stickland, 1993)

Main Policy Solutions

Solution One: Traffic Restraint

Since the early 1990s, governments worldwide have been reacting to a perceived crisis in urban sustainability, particularly in the field of transport. This led them, at the Kyoto conference of 1997, to agree on ambitious targets for CO_2 reduction. Many are already pursuing policies to restrict the growth of car use, or even to reverse it. These policies include:

1. *Fiscal Policies.* Raising the real cost of driving, either overall (through rises in car licensing fees or in fuel duty) or at peak times (through road pricing). Flat-rate taxes – seen in extreme form in Singapore – can restrain car ownership, but they are highly regressive in making ownership impossible for low- or middle-income people, which may be tolerable if a top quality public transport service is universally available (as in Singapore) but not in countries where service levels differ from one place or one time to another. Further, as appears to be the case in Singapore, they may have the perverse effect of actually encouraging car use among those rich enough to operate a car, on the principle that having paid a great deal, they might as well get the best value for money out of the car.

For this reason, a differential kind of taxation, more closely related to car use, is preferable. Cars can be differentially taxed according to their fuel consumption or their level of emissions (which in practice will not always be the same); it is possible to devise a two-tier level of petrol pricing, with a small basic allowance at a low price and additional consumption at a much higher cost; car parking charges, both on-street and off-street, can be raised and also differentiated to discourage long-stay commuter parking; finally, systems of road pricing can be introduced, which recognize the negative externalities that drivers cause when they drive in congested conditions.

This last solution, embodied in Singapore's system of electronic road pricing, is the most sensitive of all; but it too may be regressive if it penalizes low-income drivers who have no alternative, or a greatly inferior one. That, it could be said, is something policy has to live with: it is impossible to subsidize everything, and mobility is not clearly and unambiguously a merit good. The merits of road pricing are considerable, and the regressive effects can be in large measure compensated: pricing encourages ride sharing, and this can be further promoted through publicity and computerized information (Dial-a-Ride) systems; it is also possible to give exemptions for public transport and for cars that are shared, which are considered below.

Another important question is the use of the revenue raised by these means. Some will go to national treasuries, some to local ones. In either case, there is an issue as to whether all or part of the revenue should be hypothecated to support transport-specific measures, such as subsidies to public transport. It may be argued that all forms of subsidy to any form of transport are misguided, since transport is not a 'merit good'. This is debated below. One argument for such a transfer is a psychological one: that it makes motoring taxes more politically acceptable and that it encourages appropriate behaviour, since motorists can understand the economic signals that are being given.

2.   *Physical Traffic Restraints.*   Physical restrictions on the amount of space made available for driving or parking, including pedestrianization of central business districts (now more or less commonplace in Europe), traffic calming of residential districts, restrictions on numbers of car parking places (generally coupled with high and differentiated charges); these measures are frequently combined with promotion of public transport, walking and cycling, which are given prominent priority in the new arrangements (for instance, tramcars on pedestrianized streets, or transfer of roadspace to provide special lanes for bicycles in traffic-calmed areas).

However experience shows that such measures may have very partial effects. In many European cities they have reduced traffic volumes in and around the central business district, while the private car still dominates in the suburbs and beyond. In order to extend the benefits further, it is found necessary to introduce appropriate land-use policies which encourage the use of walking, cycling and public transport, such as the well-known Copenhagen or Stockholm examples of half a century ago, or the more recent proposals for chains of garden cities. Such measures may be controversial and will in any case take many years to implement. In the meantime, some experts advocate deliberate densification of lower-density suburban areas, coupled with severe restrictions on new greenfield development. This may prove effective, in part through raising land and house prices to the point that only higher-density development becomes viable, but it greatly restricts freedom of choice and may prove politically unacceptable.

Over time, such policies may achieve their impact, though experience in developed countries that have already tried to implement them suggests that at best they can slow the rise in car ownership and use, but not reverse it. And if successful, they may well produce side-effects. One of the most important will be to encourage a trend that is in any case already occurring on a small scale: the use of information technology to substitute for travel to work.

Solution Two: Substitution through Telework

Telecommuting, much discussed, could replace a substantial part of peak-hour travel to work, source of some of the worst urban congestion. Some routine workers, especially part-time workers, might work entirely from home or neighbourhood workstations; others might practise flexitime, coming to centralized meeting places for some hours or days each week, reducing the overall volume of traffic, and also redistributing it away from the congested peaks. The US Department of Transportation predicts that by 2010 total telecommuters in the United States will reach 7.5 to 15.0 million, telecommuting on an average of 3-4 days a week, and representing 5-10 per cent of the labour force. If self-employed workers are included, this rises by 25-30 per cent or about one worker in every nine or ten (Levin, 1997, p. 2). Bill Gates reports a total of 7 million telecommuters in the United States in 1994, and predicts that millions more will join them at least part-time.

Many of these will be flexible professional workers, like college professors, but they will be joined by increasing numbers of back office staff – computer programmers, researchers, management analysts, financial staffers or marketing personnel – who will be transferring work from central offices. Already, the places with the highest percentages of telecommuters include cities such as Manhattan but also high-tech suburban areas like Bethesda (Maryland), Greenwich (Connecticut) and Berkeley (California) (Levin, 1997, p. 2).

According to William Mitchell of MIT, telecommuting represents a reversal of the great historic divorce between home and workplace, which Lewis Mumford located in the seventeenth century (Mitchell, 1995, p.98). Others are more cautious. Andrew Gillespie and his colleagues at the University of Newcastle upon Tyne, authors of a major study on the subject, are avowedly sceptical; they conclude that:

. . . ever since teleworking from home became a topic of interest in the mid-1970s, its advocates have always and repeatedly argued that it is on the point of a 'breakthrough' into rapid growth. Rather like the predictions of Armageddon by certain religious sects, however, the breakthrough point has repeatedly been postponed, but only until tomorrow.

(Gillespie *et al.*, 1995, p. 141)

In California, where a large experiment has been carried out with state employees, the evidence is that commuting trips reduce virtually to zero; overall travel is reduced, especially at peak hours; non-commute trips do not increase; indeed, they actually decrease, they are to destinations closer to home, and in some cases trips by other household members have also declined. However, there is evidence that some telecommuters move home to more distant locations, presumably to get more space and better amenity at lower cost; hence, there is the potential that telecommuting would bring further decentralization (Mokhtarian, 1990, 1991*a*, 1991*b*, 1992).

But many telecommuters, perhaps 85 per cent, may be part-time, including so-called 'hot deskers' who visit their office only for a short time, sharing space with other similar workers. Given the exponential spread of the Internet during the early 1990s – some projections indicate the entire population of the world will be connected early in the next decade, though this seems inherently improbable given that most of them do not yet have a telephone – this could be the beginning of a major revolution in living and working habits. Thus, telecommuting need not cut people off, since people will still spend one or two days at the office; the definition of a telecommuter is one who works outside head office one day or more a week (Levin, 1997, p. 4).

Indeed, the most striking application of telecommuting at the turn of the century is one that still involves commuting, albeit over short distances: the growth of remote call centres for airline and hotel reservations or banking or telephone inquiries. In the UK, telephone banking has concentrated in the city of Leeds, 350 kilometres north of London; British Airways directs telephone inquiries to Newcastle, Glasgow, New York, and even Bombay; the Best Western hotel chain answers inquiries from the Arizona Women's State Penitentiary. The only limits to this process of diffusion, it seems, are represented by cultural/linguistic barriers. But the English-speaking world is very wide, so service activities (like manufacturing) could diffuse virtually worldwide; and the process could be associated with teleworking, though this is more likely to be through neighbourhood call centres than through dispersal into electronic cottages.

Overall, it is clear that there is no such phenomenon as 'telecommuting'; rather, there is a series of different phenomena, including the pure version ('telecottages'), part-time telecommuting and 'hot-desking', and local 'call centres'. They differ in their effect on travel, though it appears that all may reduce the amount of travel compared with the conventional alternative. However, there is an odd potential conflict: the more transport policy is successful in reducing peak-hour congestion, the less may be the incentive to telecommute.

Solution Three: The Eco-Friendly Supercar

Traffic restraint policies would provide a fairly massive further incentive to develop more sustainable forms of personal transport, including high-speed trains (principally as a substitute for short-haul air transport, but also to replace existing commuter services), environmentally-friendly successors to today's car, the injection of information technology into traffic management generally, both on-board the vehicle and off-board, in the form of highway congestion information systems, and finally automated guided urban transportation.

The key would be the emerging insight that the present car – a late-nineteenth-century technology – has no future. This could be prompted by the realization that in the near future, millions of people in middle-income developing countries will almost certainly acquire the means to buy cars. This will mean that even radical changes in the design and use of the present-day car – such as a three- or fourfold increase in fuel economy, which seems highly unlikely – will not be sufficient. At present roughly 500 million cars are in use worldwide; in 20 to 25 years the number will grow to 1,000 million cars. Even if they become radically more fuel-efficient, the resulting pollution from their emissions would prove intolerable.

But there are some key advances in technology, which are interrelated, and which could radically alter the use of cars in cities.

1. *The Fuel Cell Car*. This provides an alternative power unit to the internal combustion engine: the energy produced by the chemical reaction between hydrogen and oxygen is converted into electric power to drive a motor and hence the car. Water, the product of the reaction, is expelled through the exhaust pipe. But, since hydrogen is highly volatile, the vehicle carries methanol or another light-weight hyrdocarbon in its tank and a small chemical 'reformer' strips the hydrogen from this hydrocarbon fuel. Overall, the system is so efficient that it produces very little carbon dioxide.

Until a few years ago, fuel cell engines were more than 100 times dearer than petrol engines; in late 1998 the ratio was ten to one, and falling (*The Economist*, 1998). Already, Ballard – a firm based in Burnaby outside Vancouver in Canada – has a fleet of prototype buses operating in Chicago; it now aims to turn itself into a production company, setting itself the task of cutting costs by the 90 per cent necessary to make its products fully competitive by the year 2003. It is working with Daimler-Benz and Ford, though it has competition from a number of other companies worldwide (*The Economist*, 1998).

2. *Electronic Traffic Management and Road Pricing* to overcome traffic jams and increase intensity of use. Relevant technologies include *on-board driver guidance systems*, which are widely available in major urban areas, and which combine information about the most efficient routing with information about the state of congestion, from a battery of roadside sensors; *off-board displays*, in the form of roadside electronic signs, which similarly take state-of-the-system information and advise on alternative routes; and full *electronic road pricing*, so far installed in Singapore but under consideration in the UK and elsewhere, which similarly uses information about the state of the system to charge motorists according to the state of congestion, thus serving as a rationing device.

It has to be admitted that there is a degree of contradiction between these systems: pricing will ration and reduce flows, information systems could help increase them. So there is a balance that must be struck through policy. The right balance is to use technology to improve flow and speed while maintaining traffic levels steady, or at most allowing a small annual increase, while employing the pricing system to reduce flows below those levels. Given the projected traffic increases forecast for virtually every city, already reviewed in Chapter II, this would be a useful way of buying time.

Together, these systems would have the effect of reducing and optimizing traffic flows, allowing somewhat fewer vehicles to move with far less congestion. Many drivers would divert their journeys spatially, some would divert in time (driving before or after peak hours), and some would not make the journey, perhaps transferring to public transport, perhaps deciding not to take the trip. However, for those willing and able to pay for the journey, the car could well be perceived as more attractive in relation to alternative modes.

3. *Physical Priority to Public Transport and High-Occupancy Vehicles.* For this reason, it is desirable to combine economic instruments with another, physical, device which further optimizes flow and gives a clear psychological message that higher-occupancy vehicles have priority. High-occupancy vehicle lanes, widely used in American cities over the past decade and now being introduced in European cities, Jakarta and some other places, are an extension of the well-known bus lane principle: they give priority to buses, taxis and vehicles with more than one (sometimes more than two) occupants. They may be combined with preferential access to motorway systems. On the San Francisco-Oakland Bay bridge, for instance, such a preferential system not only saves High-Occupancy Vehicles (HOVs) the bridge toll, but also cuts up to half an hour from the morning peak commute as HOVs bypass the congested toll plaza lanes. Logically, in the same way, HOVs may be excused electronic charging, or offered a lower preferential rate.

4. *Full Vehicle Automation.* Fully automated vehicles are now a common sight on guideway systems such as those found in airports or on some urban systems (the Docklands Light Railway in London, the Tokyo Harbour system and the VAL systems in use at Lille and other French cities). The major challenge is to try to adapt such systems for the private car. Work at the University of California, in conjunction with the California Department of Motor Vehicles, has now resulted in a full-scale trial of automated cars on a special freeway lane in San Diego. In this, cars maintain controlled lateral spacing, allowing them to operate at much closer headways than in conventional driving. Lateral control (weaving) is still a problem, however.

A fully-automated system, which is a strong probability in the next twenty years, would in effect represent an effective successor to today's car. It would paradoxically allow much greater flows of cars on highways, but this would not present an environmental problem if the power units were environmentally benign. There might still be logistical problems, perhaps acute, in delivering the cars out of automated mode and into normal driver control, though this would not necessarily be more difficult than emerging from automated car washes, or out of cruise control in highway driving, where today drivers execute similar manoeuvres. To deal with problems of congestion, cars might need to be delivered into high-density locations (such as downtown parking garages) in automated mode.

These four technological advances would together create a new form of transport: *an environmentally-benign 'Ecocar'* (or *'Supercar'*), which would represent the biggest change in urban transportation since the invention of the internal combustion engine, and the development of electrically-powered train and tram systems, in the 1880s. Its invention is long overdue. We believe that some parts of the technology will be in place by 2010, and effectively all parts by 2020. They will have absolutely fundamental effects on patterns of living and working, and on patterns of urban social life and recreation, transforming cities as fundamentally as the electric tramcar and then the automobile did in their time.

These effects will very much depend on the economics of the new technology. For instance, if full automation required very expensive infrastructure that could be justified only on selected arterial corridors and downtown streets, that would fortify the position of traditional central business districts (and a few subcentres), just as traditional infrastructure-intensive urban rail transport has done. If the infrastructure could be installed relatively cheaply – comparable for instance to the installation of cable television – the effects could be diffused far more widely, and the new technology would act as an agent of urban dispersal as the traditional automobile has done.

Similar considerations apply when we consider how widely the new technology could disperse. A high-cost system might be prohibitively expensive for lower-income developing cities, save perhaps on a few corridors which could be effectively managed while the bulk of the city continued to operate traditionally (i.e. inefficiently). This could be highly inequitable, since in such cities the automobile serves as personal transport for at most 20 per cent of the population. The key here would be to ensure that it was available to the bus (and para-transit) systems that – together with walking and cycling – are the dominant means of mobility, particularly longer-distance urban mobility, for lower-income citizens in lower-income cities. And this is important, because in many cities these lower-income citizens find themselves on the distant periphery, where their access to employment is minimal. It is unsurprising that often, the problem defeats them: Manila has 16 per cent unemployment, 45 per cent underemployment. By providing adequate highway infrastructure and providing good quality unsubsidized transit service at full cost, which can be paid for if one family member gets an additional part-time job, lower-income people can be given the possibility to move out of congested inner-city slums into better-quality accommodation farther away (Gakenheimer, 1994, p. 341).

Box IV.31. The Curitiba approach.

In Curitiba, a Brazilian city of 1.6 million, 75 per cent of commuters use public transport despite car ownership higher than São Paulo, and traffic has declined by 30 per cent since 1974 although the population has more than doubled. The system, the 'surface metro', cost only $200,000 per kilometre, one-thousandth cost of of the Los Angeles Metro.

(Koerner, 1998, p. 32)

Curitiba's philosophy has been to use what it had. It used buses because it had buses. It had old buses, so it used them as mobile schools. Each problem was solved as it comes, to make the system work better. Its remarkable system is not the one-shot result of a single master plan, but of incremental development and adaptation, sometimes on a trial and error basis, in association with private interests, over 25 years. Ten private firms run the buses; a city-owned corporation provides route planning, roads, terminals, scheduling, and enforcement of standards, as well as collecting fares and distributing revenues. The system allows transfers to secure direct routing without going through the centre. When this gave a problem in sharing revenues, it was solved by a single fare and dedicated transfer points. This in turn gave a problem of how to share revenues, which again was solved through successive innovations.

(Rabinovitch and Hoehn, 1995, pp. 2-3)

In Curitiba, transportation and land-use planning complement each other. Land-use controls limit high density growth within the city centre, which is pedestrianized. They push new growth into the transportation corridors, known in Curitiba as structural sectors, which are served by high capacity express and direct buses, using exclusive central lanes on arterial highways. Before developing these corridors, the city strategically acquired nearby land and built low-income housing which gives households good access to commerce, jobs and recreation. It relates land-use density controls to public transport: the highest densities, up to six times plot ratio, are along the structural routes. It also encouraged new industry to locate in an industrial park at the city's edge. And it developed parks throughout the city, linked to the bus system and 150 km of special bicycle and pedestrian paths.

(Rabinovitch and Hoehn, 1995, pp. 1, 8

The results are spectacular. Between 1974 and 1992 ridership increased by 53 per cent: from 677,000 to more than one million paying passengers per day, not counting transfers; about 75 per cent of the city's commuters. One recent survey suggests that 25 per cent of car commuters have switched to buses.

(Rabinovitch and Hoehn, 1995, pp. 11, 27, 35)

Box IV.31. cont.

Table: Evolution of Curitiba's Integrated Transit Network and Passenger Load

Year	Passengers Carried Per Day (thousands)			Extent of ITN by Route Type (kilometres)		
	Total	Conventional	ITN	Express	Feeder	Interdistrict
1974	677	623	54	19.9	45	0
1992	1,028	398	630	80.0	266	166

ITN: Integrated Transportation Network. This plus the remnants of the conventional route system constitute the MTS: Mass Transit System (Rabinovitch and Hoehn 1995, p. 17).

The ITN ridership and route statistics suggest that high-volume express and direct routes and the lower-volume feeder and interdistrict services are strongly complementary. The high-volume routes offer fast direct service to those living in the high-density neighbourhoods near the high-density routes, but they do not realize their full potential without the feeder and interdistrict lines which link the high-volume routes into low-density neighbourhoods and with each other.

(Rabinovitch and Hoehn, 1995, p. 27)

Other Brazilian cities have equally big bus systems: indeed Curitiba's is the smallest per capita of any of the major cities with available data (Curitiba, Belo Horizonte, Brasilia, Fortaleza, Porto Alegre, São Paulo, Santos). This reflects the fact that it provides maximum access and convenience for the smallest network, by avoiding duplication and spacing routes to meet real demands. This means that a given number of buses provides more frequent service, even if each bus travels fewer kilometres, meaning that less resources are used and there is less waste and pollution; Curitiba buses carry more riders per kilometre than other cities, giving better financial results. The MTS and ITN operate without direct financial subsidy, though the city provides infrastructure and overall management.

(Rabinovitch and Hoehn, 1995, pp. 22-33)

Solution Four: The Role of Mass Transit: The 'Superbus'

In such cities, experience shows that even without any technological revolution, main arteries, properly managed – not usually the case in such cities – can handle 30,000 passengers an hour by bus. Rail transit systems can carry up to 80,000, but they need capital investment that such cities can seldom afford; in addition, they usually require subsidy. The few exceptions, which are supported totally by the farebox, result from unusually high residential densities as well as workplace densities; Hong Kong is the most conspicuous example, but is almost unique (and, because of the system of public landownership, it can directly benefit from the creation of urban land values around train stations). Elsewhere, rail transit systems can be supported only on the basis of draconian restrictions on the purchase and use of private cars, as in Singapore. As Ralph Gakenheimer points out, 'Cities could build several busways in parallel corridors for the price of one metro' (Gakenheimer 1994, p. 341). Curitiba in Brazil is the most celebrated example of this approach.

Solution Five: The Vexed Question of Costs and Subsidies

Curitiba brings us back to the vexed question of subsidy. For it shows that it is possible for a developing city to operate a very high-quality mass transit system without subsidy, so long as it provides effectively for those who depend on the system and also attracts car owners out of their vehicles. And there is a strong general case that transit subsidies should be avoided, especially at earlier stages of development where scarce government resources are better spent on other programmes, such as education. (Hong Kong, which uses rising land values to finance major investments, is perhaps a special exception; for here, unusually, the state has always owned and leased all land.) If subsidies are employed at all, the important consideration is to target low-income users, especially to cut the time and money costs of their journeys to work. The most effective way, demonstrated in Curitiba, is almost certainly bus-based systems with provision for bus priority on the highways, and even special busways which may be shared by high-occupancy (shared) cars.

But the Curitiba model, albeit outstanding, is not the only one. Lagos in Nigeria suffers from gross inadequacies in public transport, overcrowded buses, poor road infrastructure, environmental pollution and absence of integrated traffic management measures to combat congestion. Yet the city has proved adaptive and innovative with a stream of old imported minibuses and old cars used for unconventional, deregulated and unregistered public services called *kabu-kabu* (Bolade, 1993, p. 7). Such a system is considerably more anarchic, and almost certainly less efficient in the strict sense than Curitiba's more highly-regulated system; yet it does a good job in serving the city's 7.7 million people, and it could do even better if it functioned on a Curitiba-style infrastructure.

However one must be careful. In Santiago de Chile, deregulation led to a doubling of the city's bus fleet from 5,200 to 10,500 between 1979 and 1989, and to a considerable ageing of the fleet. Congestion worsened, driving became worse and the condition of the bus fleet deteriorated. The government responded by prohibiting access to the used vehicle fleet, banning the import of used spare parts, and controlling emissions; it intends to introduce tolls for access to the most congested streets (Figueroa, 1993, p. 11).

This suggests that it is desirable to steer a careful course between top-down provision and deregulation. The traditional approach – direct provision of infrastructure, and regulation of services – has had three consequences: assets have not been maintained, infrastructure and vehicles having run down; service has not responded to needs, for instance on developing urban peripheries; and costs have been much higher than they need have been. In Argentina, privatization of the railways showed that labour costs were more than double those needed to maintain a financially viable system; in the UK average operating costs per vehicle-kilometre fell by 30-40 per cent after deregulation and privatization (World Bank, 1996, pp. 33-35).

But there are at least three cases where it may be desirable to retain some regulation: where duplication of supply would be wasteful or impractical, as with indivisible infrastructure; where lack of regulation could produce duplication, excess capacity or dangerous practices; and where there is a need for socially-necessary but unprofitable services. And within a competitive transport market, it is also critical that charges for the use of infrastructure be set correctly. Charges for the use of road infrastructure are the critical central element (World Bank, 1996, pp. 37, 49).

The optimal package, though it will differ from city to city according to the level of economic development and the previous pattern of physical development, will involve three key elements: first, fairly sensitive charging for the use of road space by private drivers, probably coupled with special priorities and dispensations for those prepared to share rides; second, reservation of dedicated routeways or corridors for the use of designated categories of vehicle, including light or heavy rail, buses, para-transit including taxis, high-occupancy vehicles, and bicycles (these last desirably segregated from the others); third, zoning for selective higher-density development along these corridors, especially interchange points, where subcentres of concentrated employment would be allowed and even encouraged to develop. These prescriptions appear equally valid for cities of every kind – hypergrowth, dynamic, mature -though their precise application will vary a great deal from one city to another and from one kind of city to another.

In this regard, Curitiba (see box IV.31) and Singapore (see box IV.32) make an interesting contrast. Both can be regarded as model best-practice cities, and have been widely noticed and admired throughout the world. Both share some similar features, including dense public transport corridors along which higher-density development is encouraged. But the two cities started differently and have remained different. Curitiba is a typical sprawling Latin American metropolis, even though its land-use policies have resulted in greater compaction; it has relied on high-quality bus transportation. Singapore is much more compact because of its island site and lack of land; it took a bold decision to build a high-capacity mass transit system and to encourage high-density development along it. Both models are worthy of imitation. Cities worldwide will need to decide which is more appropriate in their case – or whether some combination, or intermediate model, might work best for them.

Bundling the Solutions

So the rapid growth in demand for travel, the increase in car ownership and the high external costs of transport are very strong and fundamental worldwide trends. But they are leading us steadily away from sustainability: this is the fundamental policy dilemma. To resolve this dilemma, within the time frame of the next twenty-five years (to 2025), there are two clear parallel lines of action. They are easily seen as alternatives, even incompatible alternatives. We argue that on the contrary, they are complementary.

Box IV.32. The Singapore approach.

Singapore is a medium-sized city state measuring only 42 by 23 km, with a land area of 646 square kilometres and a 1995 population of 3.0 million.

Singapore has recorded one of the fastest sustained growth rates of any country since independence, averaging 6-8 per cent per year. But one result was rapid increase in numbers of cars: from 142,674 in 1974 to 217,119 in 1984 and 303,864 in 1993. In response, Singapore built new roads: total length increased from 1,761 km in 1965 to 2,173 km in 1975, 2,645 km in 1985 and 2,989 km in 1993, including nine high-capacity expressways which, when fully complete, will cover 141 kilometres. In addition, increasingly, Singapore introduced measures to manage traffic flow on the system: GLIDE, a central computer system that controls traffic signals by allocating 'green' time based on actual traffic demand, extended in 1999 island-wide to include 1,250 traffic signals, and TrafficScan, which uses satellite technology and taxis to collect and disseminate traffic speeds on arterial roads. These will be brought into an Integrated Transport Management System (ITMS), for full implementation in 2002, which will provide real-time traffic and public transport information to motorists, commuters, commercial vehicle operators and government agencies.

From 1975 onward, however, Singapore incrementally developed a remarkable battery of policies systematically designed to achieve three integrated objectives: to restrain car ownership and use, to encourage use of public transport, and to plan land-uses and activities around a high-quality public transport system.

Traffic Restraint
There are two main policies: restraint on ownership, and restraint on use.

Restraint on ownership is enforced through a quota scheme, introduced in 1990. People intending to buy a car have to obtain a

Box IV.32. cont.

certificate of entitlement (COE) through a bidding system. The price of cars has escalated rapidly: a new 1.3 Toyota Corolla jumped from S$28,500 in 1985 to S$80,600 in 1992. A car that would cost $11,000 in Britain would cost six times as much in Singapore. These have been combined with high vehicle registration fees, stringent driving licence requirements and high fuel costs. The growth in car ownership has slowed since the introduction of the COE system.

Restraint on use was introduced as early as June 1975 through the Area Licensing Scheme (ALS): a motorist needed to purchase and display a paper area licence, obtainable at many sales outlets on the approach roads, to enter a restricted zone (RZ) in the city. Entrances to the city were marked by overhead gantry signs. During the hours of operation – daytime hours on weekdays and half-days on Saturdays – these signs were lighted up at overhead gantries. The cost of licences was higher for the morning and evening rush hours (7.30am-9.30am and 4.30pm-7.00pm). Different categories of vehicles also paid different prices. A similar manual Road Pricing System (RPS) was implemented during morning rush hours at four points along three expressways in 1995 and 1997.

ALS and RPS were successful, but were cumbersome, labour-intensive and inflexible. Consequently, work on an Electronic Road Pricing (ERP) scheme started in 1989 and was implemented in 1998. It uses pairs of overhead gantries about 15 m apart above the road, communicating by radio with a smartcard on each vehicle, together with cameras to take photographs of rear licence plates of violating vehicles. On each vehicle, a unit about the size of a small pocket diary is powered by the vehicle battery and has a back-lit LCD display to show the cash balance in the smartcard when first inserted and when the vehicle passes a gantry point. This card is issued by a consortium of seven local banks and is available at banks, post offices and petrol stations; it can be topped up at many automatic teller machines, can also be used in supermarkets, petrol stations etc., and has a stored value varying from S$20 to S$500.

The point is to make motorists more aware of the true cost of driving. Charges are levied according to time and congestion levels. Motorists choose whether to drive, when to drive and where to drive. They may choose a different route, destination, time of travel, or not to travel at all, to car-pool or use public transport. Those who choose to pay get a smoother, faster ride. With more effective control of congestion, more COEs can be released.

Experience shows that conditions along priced roads have generally improved, though some traffic has diverted onto unpriced parallel routes. This is as predicted.

Development of Mass Rapid Transit (MRT)
In the mid-1980s, when it was realized that traffic restraint solutions might not be effective by themselves in curtailing traffic growth, it was decided to invest in the MRT . . . A north-south and an east-west line have been built, totalling 83 km and intersecting in the central business

Box IV.32. cont.

district, and radiating out to serve planned new towns. In 1996, the government announced construction of a 20-km North-East Line, running from the World Trade Centre in the south of the island, bypassing the Central Business District, to the new towns of Hougang, Sengkang and Punggol. The first stage should be complete by 2002; extensions will occur as surrounding developments generate enough passenger traffic to make them operationally viable.

Integrating Land-use and Transport Planning
The concentration of activities in the CBD contributes to congestion. Therefore, the Singapore government has encouraged planned decentralization of government offices and then private businesses to suburban sub-centres. This requires large-scale planning to achieve scale economies, and demands infrastructure investment.

The process began with the Long-Range Comprehensive Concept Plan of 1972, with a ring of new towns around the central area; massive land acquisition and resettlement of population took place in the 1970s, together with relocation of retail and manufacturing; offices however continued to cluster in the CBD, with a 50 per cent increase in floorspace between 1985 and 1993, accounting for 78 per cent of total office space by the latter date.

The Revised Concept Plan of 1991 is based on four major new regional centres, Tampines, Jurong East, Woodlands, and Beletar, served by MRT and a supplementary LRT. Thus transport and land use are totally integrated. The plan discourages dispersed low-density development in these centres in order to increase accessibility to public transport.

Comprehensive planning has been made possible by the fact that (in 1994) no less than 87 per cent of the population lived in public housing. This was the result of a vast construction programme that increased the number of residential units from 190,000 to 736,000 between 1970 and 1990, and then to 786,000 by 1994, including construction of no less than 20 new towns. Planning is based on what Singapore calls Asian adaptation of western principles, including repeatable quality standards for mass development and high-rise high-density housing where needed. From the start of urban renewal, the government accepted that land values had to be relatively low to uphold the authority of the master plan and environmental quality, while giving investors an adequate return.

(UN Best Practices Database)

The Longer-Run Solution: Technology to the Rescue

In the longer term, we can be certain that the ecocar will become a reality, primarily for use in urban areas. Although resources (mainly renewable and recyclable) will still be needed to construct the vehicle, it would be powered by hydrogen fuel cells. It will probably be available within ten years, but – given current turnover levels – it will not have had a major impact on the total stock of vehicles for a further ten to fifteen years. This means that the ecocar would only be in general use by the end of our time frame (2025) in mature cities and a little later (because older cars may remain longer) in dynamic and above all in hypergrowth cities. During this period, technologies to produce hydrogen with solar energy will need to be improved.

A first set of policy actions must be to facilitate the research and development of the ecocar and to give clear signals to the motor manufacturing industry to invest in the small city-based vehicle.

- To increase our research and development budgets on the ecocar and associated technologies;

- To develop the necessary supporting infrastructure so that it can be used when available;

- To provide tax incentives for companies to invest in the appropriate technology and to take it to the production stage;

- To provide tax disincentives for purchasing large inefficient vehicles for city use;

- To phase out all forms of subsidy to the private car (e.g. company cars);

- At a later stage to develop a scrappage programme to encourage people to purchase the ecocar.

The purpose of these actions will be to speed up the process of innovation, and to give clear signals to industry and people that the ecocar is the replacement technology for the current car stock. There is no real problem in promoting an efficient vehicle based on fuel cell technology as the industry would be the main promoter of change, and as incentives would be given to encourage replacement of inefficient vehicles. The main remaining issues are:

- The possible initial high cost of the ecocar, initially perhaps more than twice the cost of existing cars, until the substantial development costs have been recouped;

- The role that the ecocar should play in cities in developing countries where the fuel cell technology and the appropriate supporting technology may be less applicable to the great bulk of personal movements;

- The lifespan of the vehicle – whether it should be built to last much longer than current vehicles – this is a trade-off between costs, technology, taste and other factors;

- Development of the appropriate infrastructure for the ecocar (and other eco-vehicles) through intermediate technologies (e.g. electric, methane, LPG and natural gas vehicles);

- Development of an environmentally-neutral system or systems allowing the energy sources, and much of the associated technology (e.g. guidance systems and control systems) to be recycled;

- Resolving the interim problems of congestion and the allocation of scarce road space.

The Short-Run Interim Solution: Restraining the Growth of Demand

That last point needs emphasis: even if the 'technological solution' is promoted, there still remains the historic problem of transport growth (congestion) and the 'gap' between now and the time when the ecocar is in common use. To tackle the problems of congestion requires strong action now, so that the almost certain growth in demand can be accommodated in our cities through the most efficient use of the existing infrastructure. Most of the options are well known and have been outlined in detail elsewhere (Banister, 1999).

The key assumption is that sustainable living must be based on urban areas, as high levels of accessibility and proximity can only be maintained there. This means that people should be living in settlements that are of a sufficient size (some experts suggest 20,000, others over 50,000) so that the full range of facilities can be provided within walking, cycling or public transport distance (less than 5 kilometres). These settlements should be at a medium density (at least 40 persons per hectare), and should have mixed land uses and high levels of accessibility to the public transport network (for inter-urban travel). It also means that these areas have to provide a high-quality environment within which people wish to live. This includes access to open space, a safe and secure environment, peace and quiet, a wide range of social and recreational opportunities, as well as the other benefits of urban living. Most services and facilities can be provided locally, but the most difficult to provide is local employment. Even here, in the timescale given, services and technology-based employment can be dispersed to where people live.

These constraints concern the framework within which transport policy options can be placed. Most of them require a strong planning system at the city and regional levels that will direct development to achieve larger, higher-density, mixed-use and accessible cities. Although the planning system is not immediate in its effect, in the medium term it is one of the most important determinants of travel patterns. As a general rule, the shorter the journey, the greater the probability that it will be walk, cycle or public transport based. The planning system should be seeking to ensure proximity between where people live and the services, jobs and facilities to which they wish to gain access (see table IV.3).

A second constraint is the role that technology (in its widest sense) will have on travel demand. We have earlier reviewed the potential for substitution of travel through telecommuting. Likewise, huge impacts could come from the growth of teleconferencing, teleshopping, telebusiness and other forms of e-activities. There continues to be much debate about their effects (Salomon and Mokhtarian, 1997; NERA, 1997). It is clear that the scale and the nature of change induced by technology will be substantial and complex, with adaptations to existing patterns of activity. It will not affect all people in the same way, but will provide greater choice and flexibility to many 'computer literate' people.

Table IV.3. Context and constraints.

Context	
Transport Technology	• Ecocar in mass production by 2010 • Measures to promote rapid replacement of existing fleet • Research funding increased substantially from EU and other sources • Industrial support for new energy and environmentally efficient technology • Tax incentives to buy ecocars and scrap old vehicles
Transport Demand	• Traffic still increasing as car ownership rises • Capacity limited so congestion increases • Measures required for demand management • Allocation of road space to improve accessibility and proximity
Constraints	
Physical	• Size > 50,000 • Density > 40 persons/hectare • Mixed land use • Proximity to public transport interchanges and corridors
Quality	• Open space • Safe and secure environment • Peace and quiet • Social and recreational opportunities • Full range of services and facilities

Source: Banister (1999), p. 46.

Alternative Strategies: 'Radical' and 'Pragmatic'

Given these parameters, there remain broad policy long-term alternatives. The 'radical' alternative is to work progressively to reduce the growth of car use and finally to diminish car use. Even here, the intention is not to prohibit the use of the car; this would be both difficult to achieve and would be seen as being against notions of freedom and choice. The intention is to design cities of such quality and at a suitable scale that many people would not need to have a car and they would choose to live in a car-free location. This solution would entail maintaining the key features of the 'interim' solution – cities over 20,000 population (preferably over 50,000), with medium densities (over 40 persons per hectare), with mixed use developments, and with preference given to developments in public transport accessible corridors and near to highly public transport accessible interchanges – indefinitely, linking them together to form agglomerations of polycentric cities, with clear hierarchies that would allow a close proximity of everyday facilities and accessibility to higher-order activities.

Such an urban form could keep average trip lengths to below the thresholds required for maximum use of the walk and cycle modes. It would also permit high levels of para-transit and public transport priority so that the need to use the car would be minimized. Through the combination of clear planning strategies, cities would be designed at the personal scale to allow both high-quality accessibility and a high-quality environment. In transport terms, this is the vision of the sustainable city.

The logic of this argument is that the car would play only a limited role in the twenty-first-century city. This would demand either a major change in the value system of individuals and firms, or an ecological disaster directly related to the problem of the car – for instance, some kind of health epidemic of a sufficient scale to change values and priorities. But even if such an event occurred, it would also have to result in a fundamental reassessment of values.

The conclusion we draw is that this might happen in a demonstration or experimental city, which decided to become the world's first 'car free city'. But we doubt that it would be acceptable very generally. Realistically, it is hard to believe that the radical solution is achievable in the short term, particularly because current lifestyles are so transport-dependent. Enormous amounts of capital are tied up in cities, in local and national economies (especially in real estate), and in the motor industry (not to mention private cars). Apart from the direct impacts on vehicle manufacturers and their suppliers, the city would have to alter its structure so that efficient local movement could take place. Massive declines in real estate and other fixed assets dependent on the use of car would be inevitable. Given the enormous sunk investment in low-density suburban forms in much of the developed world, the bulk of it less than fifty years old, the costs of moving towards a new structure would be prohibitive save in the very long run. It might occur as and when there was a technology (the ecocar) that could be seen as an alternative way of pursuing current lifestyles rather than a total and radical replacement for them. But, short of this, the radical strategy carries very high risks, and may well be deemed politically unacceptable.

The alternative 'pragmatic' strategy is to recognize that the car will still form an essential element of the transport system, but to reduce or alter its impacts through new forms of pricing, restraint and regulation. The underlying argument is that we must look for ways to maintain economic growth with less transport (decoupling), and strong incentives (market and regulatory) should be given to promoting efficient and clean transport by all modes. This strategy will provide a pathway allowing us to move from the current situation to the sustainable city. It provides the means to reassess priorities, it begins to revalue space in cities, and it gives some indication of the sustainable city. As such, it will help to change value systems. In more detail, it combines top-down and bottom-up approaches, derived from actual successful experience in best-practice cities like Curitiba and Singapore.

Nationally. The taxation system should be changed so that taxes are based primarily on consumption, rather than production (labour). A carbon tax in the transport sector would allow the price of petrol and diesel to be substantially raised so that clear incentives would be given to users to drive economically, to purchase fuel efficient vehicles, to switch modes, and to consider whether a journey is essential or could be carried out locally or as part of a tour.

Clear direction would also be given to industry to produce more fuel-efficient vehicles. Tradable permits for zero emission vehicles could also be included in this package, whereby targets would be set for manufacturers to produce and sell a certain percentage of particular types of vehicles by certain dates (as in California). The ecocar would form part of this package, so that a phased programme could be introduced. Coupled to this would be increases in research and development programmes, and the means to accelerate the transfer from old technology to the new eco-technology.

Measures would be taken to ensure existing car fleets are operating efficiently, with testing, emissions regulations, the phasing out of old vehicles (scrappage programmes), the use of feebates to encourage change, efficiency targets for new vehicles, promotion of renewable energy sources and other forms of low-carbon fuels.

The intention of these macro-economic and regulatory policies would be to encourage change and a more rational use of energy in transport. The impact should be fiscally neutral, with investment taking place in public transport, the research and development costs of the ecocar, and the technological alternatives for traffic management and demand management measures.

Locally and Regionally. Priority would be given to the most efficient forms of travel – walking, cycling and public transport – with road space being reallocated to these modes, together with preference in demand management and traffic management.

- Road pricing would be introduced in cities to fully internalize all the social and environmental costs of using the car.

- The use of smartcard technology would allow the charges to relate to the traffic conditions prevailing (i.e. levels of congestion) and the characteristics of the car (e.g. its pollution profile, the number of passengers etc.). Higher vehicle occupancies would be promoted through pricing and preferential allocation of space (road space and parking space).

- Speed limits in cities would be lowered, parking would become taxable, clear zones would be established, and all forms of subsidy to the car would be eliminated.

- Subsidies to public transport should also be eliminated on sustainability grounds as all travellers should pay the full costs of travel. However, there may be grounds for subsidy to individual users of public transport for social reasons and for particular services.

- Public transport would be promoted through (public) investment, financed from the tolls raised from road pricing on the car in urban areas and the revenues from parking fees.

- Actions in the planning and development sectors would ensure new development is located where trip lengths can be reduced, and that existing development is refurbished for reuse along with vacant sites within cities – mixed use and high-density developments.

- The availability of parking in the city would be severely limited, and travellers from outside (and inside) would be encouraged to use park and ride (or bike and ride) facilities.

- All decision-makers in the city would be involved in discussing how traffic reduction and pollution targets could be reduced.

- All employers would have to devise commuter plans for their employees, and retailers and others (e.g. leisure centres) would also have to prepare and implement plans to reduce levels of car dependence for their customers.

- Similar strategies would cover schools, educational activities, hospitals and other public (and private) services.

- Sustainability forums would be established to discuss targets, programmes of action and best practice from elsewhere.

- In the information sector, actions would be taken so that the full advantage of the technologies can be realized. For example, information dissemination would cover targets for the city, whether they are being achieved and hot spots of pollution or congestion.

- Technology would form an essential part of the high quality public transport system with smartcard ticketing, so that all forms of public transport in the city could be used and information/choices on alternatives in real time could be presented to the user.

- Information would be given to the car driver about the possibility of car sharing, parking and routes to reduce fuel consumption.

- Experimental and high profile demonstration cities to test policy packages.

The motor industry has an instrumental role to play in changing attitudes of consumers and in promoting new environmental benign technology. Vehicle manufacturers are beginning to accept the environmental imperative and the more limited role that the car should play in cities. As part of the move towards sustainable development and new technologies, they should be given a clear set of responsibilities that permit innovation and technological development, so that they participate in the process as equal partners seeking the same goals of more efficient management and use of city road space. With the switch from current technology to the new technology and the replacement of polluting vehicles, there is a tremendous opportunity for the motor industry.

The Application to Developing Cities

Many of these measures would be equally appropriate in mature, dynamic and hypergrowth cities, but some of the more technologically sophisticated measures may be less suitable in hypergrowth cities. Here the focus would be on physical restraint and the reallocation of road space to public transport and the bicycle, together with high petrol prices, parking controls and new enforcement methods. In the dynamic and hypergrowth cities, there is already a rich choice of para-transit, and this could be enhanced with shared taxis and cars. Even in dynamic and hypergrowth cities, the road building option should be only considered as an extreme choice as many simple management options are available. Investment should take place in the public transport system (new efficient vehicles), in new flexible operating systems (more demand-responsive), in maintenance and upgrading of the existing network (including high-occupancy vehicle lanes), in providing space for pedestrians and cyclists (i.e. city-wide cycle routes), and in low cost information systems for transport users. It is likely that road space will always be scarce in developing cities, so public transport and para-transit must continue to play the major role in providing accessibility. Permanent differences will continue – there will be no convergence and cities will maintain their individuality.

A critical question here concerns the quality of urban governance. Mature cities have a tradition of strong local government, which is democratically accountable and has powers to raise local taxation. In promoting new forms of sustainable development, action needs to be consistently applied across all cities as there may be (perceived) first mover disadvantages: if one city takes a leading role, then other cities may benefit and travel may increase as demand switches to alternative (more distant) locations. Questions also have to be raised about the suitability of current sectoral structures within local authorities and whether these are the most appropriate for dealing with sustainability concerns. But in many dynamic and hypergrowth cities, there is much less of a tradition of democratic local government, so new decision structures need to be established that enjoy the powers, the responsibilities and above all the respect of all parties.

The Social Implications of Policies

In devising a strategy for transport and sustainable development there will inevitably be winners and losers. The new focus on policies, which shift the pendulum from the economic imperative towards the environmental imperative, should not ignore the social imperative. New roads through inner-city areas provide quicker travel for high-income car-owning suburban dwellers and a poorer environment (more noise, pollution and community severance) for lower-income, car-less inner-city residents. It is only with the acquisition of a car that new drivers join the polluting class and their travel patterns change dramatically. But with every new car, the environmental costs are increased, and the demand and quality of the alternative services are reduced. Even with car ownership at saturation levels, there will still be 25 per cent of the population without exclusive access to a car. Sustainable cities allow a real opportunity where lifestyles need not be car dependent and where community welfare can be matched with high levels of accessibility through non-car based transport.

The classic argument here is that at present road space is rationed by time; and this is seen as being socially just, since all road users have the same amount of time available. But rationing by time is inefficient and pricing is the best available means to allocate a scarce resource, such as space. Even if equity is a high priority, there are fiscal mechanisms (e.g. investment in public transport, reductions in social contributions) that would allow the reallocation of most of those revenues. When the environmental dimension is added to the economic and social dimensions, the arguments are even more emphatic. As noted above, it is the non-car-user and the urban resident who is exposed to many of these environmental costs. There is a strong case that any reallocation of revenues raised from pricing in transport should be targeted at improving the quality of life of those city dwellers without access to a car – this would include housing and investment in local services and facilities.

The arguments presented here are consistent with the priorities of the United Nations, as clear preference is given to poverty alleviation, environmental sustainability and good governance. Measures have been promoted that will allow the poor to make more efficient use of their time.

At present in the non-OECD countries, the rich travel more than the poor, but the poor often spend more time to travel less distance. The poor do not even use public transport, but walk almost everywhere. In some continents (e.g. Africa), cycle ownership is low (3.5 per cent), but elsewhere the levels are much higher (e.g. 40 per cent in Asia). It is important to improve the efficiency of travel, as this will allow more productive use of time for education and other wealth-creating activities. As stated above, it is important to invest in the public transport system (including para-transit) and non-motorized modes, so that the access for the poor can be significantly improved.

A high priority is to improve the quality of public transport within cities, particularly for low-income residents (often in informal housing) so that access at a reasonable cost (and time) to work is possible. High capacity dedicated bus (and para-transit) routes to city centres would be a cost-effective way to increase the capacity of the road system and reduce inequality.

The Benefits of Change

The main benefits of moving towards a sustainable transport system are that it is socially inclusive (all parties benefit) and the quality of life in the city improves. However, this conclusion has to be qualified, in at least two respects. Firstly, the revenues raised from the additional fuel costs, the parking charges and the road pricing systems must be retained in the city and used for investment in the transport system and other socially important priorities (e.g. public services and social housing). If the revenues are retained in large part by government, the benefits are substantially reduced and the city may become a less attractive rather than a more attractive place to live. Secondly, the policies being adopted in the city must have the support and confidence of the people living there and the other major interest groups in the city. This acceptance requires all parties to be involved and empowered by the process. The changes being proposed here will fundamentally change the way in which people get around the city, and such radical changes require political and public support. Otherwise, these changes would be political suicide.

A difficult question here concerns hypothecation and subsidization. If the proceeds of highway taxation are reserved and used for investment in public transport, it may be argued that this may represent an inefficient and inequitable use of resources. For instance, there is no obvious case for subsidizing commuter transport, especially when this encourages long-distance decentralization that leaves other household members dependent on cars. On the other hand, without this element of hypothecation political support may be lacking. It is a matter of balance: in general, hypothecated taxes should go to investments likely to aid the poorest members of society, such as bus priorities.

Complementary Paths

The conclusion is that cities everywhere should pursue two complementary paths:

- In the short term (until about 2020) they should seek to manage traffic growth through fiscal and physical restraint, using revenues from parking charges and road pricing to support good-quality public transport and para-transit, and using the land-use planning systems to support urban forms that permit and encourage maximum use of cycling and walking for shorter trips.

- In the longer run, beyond this date, they should provide for general phasing-in of the ecocar, while recognizing that this will be more rapid in the mature cities than elsewhere, and that in hypergrowth cities it may be necessary to plan on the basis that general access to the ecocar will still be far in the future.

The important point is that these different development paths can and should be complementary. At all stages of development, whatever the available technology, the optimal system may be one that manages scarce road space optimally, by a combination of regulation (e.g. bus lanes, bus priority, high-occupancy vehicle lanes, peak-hour loading bans) and fiscal measures (e.g. road charging and parking charges) to give priority and favoured fiscal treatment to those vehicles that use road space most effectively: buses, para-transit vehicles and high-occupancy vehicles. These corridors could be managed so as to embody technological developments, in particular vehicle automation, as they become available. But they need to be seen in an even wider context.

In the medium term (2020 and beyond), we can conceive of a realistic scenario, depending on technologies that are either available, or likely to become so: a system of high-speed inter-city ground transportation at speeds up to 300 or 400 kilometres an hour, linked to automated on-demand ecocar systems in the cities, and perhaps to informal means of short-distance personal transport such as collective bicycles and scooters. Such connections may in turn aid further concentration at high-order nodal points, as the experience of the Japanese Shinkansen system seems to show. And they would be used, through coordinated land-use planning, to encourage further concentrations of activity not merely in traditional downtown areas, but also in sub-centres distributed throughout the metropolitan area, including suburban sub-centres close to people's homes. These, importantly, should be reachable on foot, or bicycle or public transport.

Over the medium term, this is a highly plausible scenario: nations and cities will not simply adjust to the new environmental limits, but will opt for radical changes in transport technology to overcome these limits, so promoting further growth in eco-friendly personal transportation. But it will not happen effortlessly; it will require encouragement and guidance, both at national and international levels to set the frameworks that will speed the evolution and take-up of the technologies, and at regional and local levels to provide appropriate spatial frameworks within which they can be fitted.

Shaping Urban Space

Managing Urban Space: the Ultimate Scarce Resource

All cities are in constant flux; indeed, if they fail in dynamism they risk decay and death. They grow at the periphery and they change at the centre. And in fast-growing cities – places like Chicago and Berlin in the nineteenth century, Los Angeles in the early twentieth, or any city in the developing world today – this process can be frenetic: speculative development, driven by the perpetual optimism of the investor, leapfrogs far out into the open countryside; closer in, land that was peripheral a few decades ago is suddenly subsumed into the central business district; in the suburbs, new sub-centres mushroom almost out of nowhere.

In the twenty-first century, this will be truer than ever. Cities must increasingly compete for highly mobile professional workers and globally-oriented business firms. As a result of securitization, financial derivatives, and the deregulation of financial intermediaries such as pension funds, insurance companies, real estate investment trusts, and banks, much of the world's available supply of investment capital is no longer very restrained by national boundaries.

This is a fact of life, and is even to be celebrated: it is part of the mechanism that generates new wealth for the people who flock into the city. But at the same time, it may generate what the economist calls negative externalities, or the lawyer calls nuisances: incompatible land uses next door to each other, such as polluting factories next to residential areas; perpetual uncertainty as to the character of a neighbourhood and the value of land; traffic congestion and traffic pollution.

These factors are more important than ever before, because they may now threaten a city's very livelihood. To maintain their economies, cities of the twenty-first century must be liveable. Growth of some sectors of the service economy, such as tourism, is absolutely dependent on liveable and attractive cities. Tourism in most nations is dependent on foreign travellers. Currently, an estimated 300 million tourists take their holidays overseas, representing the largest earner of foreign currency for many countries. In Asia, environmental issues, traffic congestion and overcrowding have been identified as serious impediments to tourism; it would be equally true of cities anywhere. To keep or enhance their share of tourists, business firms and skilled professionals, cities must be liveable.

For this reason, almost all cities in the developed world, and most in the developing world, have tried to plan for their future development, and to control it: they have made plans for future development, and they have developed mechanisms for enforcing those plans through a system of zoning permits or land-use controls. Invariably, the plans have specified broad land uses, including especially changes of use, and some indication of the density of development, coupled with proposals for transportation and open space. These systems have come into being, and have been modified, over a long period, sometimes accompanied by fierce controversy. But they have become a fixed and accepted feature of urban life, with a considerable political constituency; for planning produces a degree of certainty, allowing private agents like commercial companies or individual households to make their own plans in the knowledge that their immediate environment – including their sunk investments in real estate – is secure.

But in every city there is a major complication. Urban space is quintessentially scarce, and so expensive. And, in rapidly-growing cities, it escalates in value: land, that a couple of decades earlier was suburban, becomes enveloped in the central business district; high-rise offices and hotels may be found interspersed with the informally-built shacks of the poor.

In the cities of the developed world, policy-makers have grappled for over a century with the resultant problems of land valuation and land taxation. Public policies, in the form of a new highway or a new transit line or a new zoning map, fundamentally change land values, and make fortunes for lucky landowners. In these circumstances, has the community a right or even an obligation to tax part of those gains for the community? And, in buying land compulsorily for public works, should it be required to pay values that in effect it has created?

In Europe, a century ago, nations like the Netherlands and Sweden resolved these dilemmas drastically, by buying up land for the community well in advance of demand; but even then, the pace of urban advance in cities like Amsterdam and Stockholm sometimes overwhelmed them. Other countries, like the UK half a century ago, sought to take a share of development value for the community, but these proposals brought fierce political controversy and no permanent solution. In the cities of the developing world today, of course, the challenge is far greater and the resources far fewer.

Guiding Physical Development

The Role of Planning

Historically, as planning has evolved in the cities of the developed world, it has commonly had certain clear aims and objectives: to increase the efficient working of the urban economy, to provide good-quality residential environments in attractive settings, to enhance the quality of urban society, to provide efficient systems for the movement of people and goods, to protect and enhance natural landscapes, and – an objective of greatly-increased importance recently – to guard the environment.

In pursuit of these aims, planners have adopted similar – though far from identical – policies in cities across the developed world. They have made zoning regulations to separate different land uses. They have imposed urban growth limits, either in the form of land-use restrictions or public land reservations, to limit or stop development in certain locations and to encourage it in others; they have developed satellite towns, or even completely independent new towns, to accommodate overspill of population and sometimes employment from the cities. Notable examples include London's green belt and new towns, Copenhagen's finger plan, Stockholm's satellite towns, the twin-axis plan for the Ile-de-France and the new towns policy in Hong Kong, Singapore and the Republic of Korea. Latterly, in the interests of sustainability, some cities have increasingly sought to restrict greenfield development and to encourage higher-density regeneration within existing urban envelopes.

A Basic Principle: Guiding the Trends

In market or mixed economies, which means most economies, planning regulations tend to work best when they are consistent with market behaviour. There are remarkably strong empirical regularities in market-based cities across countries. Urban areas develop forms that are functional for the location of industry and services, having regard to scale economies in production, lower transport costs, permissible densities for development, information-sharing and other linkages or networks across locations and agglomeration economies. Land-use regulations that ignore such market behavioural tendencies, as empirically observed and described by theory, are not likely to succeed. Policies that oppose normal human behaviour will often result in unexpected consequences and the creation of market inefficiencies.

Of course, planning sometimes has to work against trends too, when they become self-destructive and blind to the needs of the wider society. Good planning is a matter of balance. It is most effective when it seeks to shape and modify basic economic and social trends so as to make them operate more efficiently and more conveniently and more sustainably than they would do on their own. That is a lesson taught by basic common sense, but also by the experience of twentieth-century planning history. When Ebenezer Howard proposed the garden city solution in 1898, he did so in the sure knowledge that emerging new technologies, above all electricity, would free people and the factories in which they worked from

289

the dense nineteenth-century city. When Sven Markelius and Göran Sidenbladh designed the satellite towns around Stockholm in 1952, they did so in the knowledge that a new subway system would bring these places within a convenient travel time of the city centre, and that people living in the city's slums would flock to the new, well-designed, beautifully landscaped apartment blocks. When Jane Jacobs called for a return to traditional city street patterns in 1961, she did so from her deep personal knowledge of her neighbours' feelings about New York's Greenwich Village, where she lived. These ideas have stood the test of time. They provide lessons for shaping the new urban places of the twenty-first century, and for reshaping the older places that earlier eras have bequeathed to us.

As seen in Chapter II, the fundamental urban trend of the twentieth century was decentralization of people, and of the jobs they do, and of the services they use: decentralization from dense inner cities to less dense suburbs, and from larger cities to smaller ones. To this general rule, in any free market-economy society, there has scarcely been an exception. It was already observable in North America and Australasia, as well as Great Britain, from the beginning of the twentieth century; after World War II it spread to the Benelux countries and to Scandinavia, and later to all of Western Europe. In the developing world it is evident almost everywhere, from Latin America to Eastern Asia. Nor do we expect any change in the coming years.

But it is important to notice that the process and form of decentralization have varied considerably in detail. In some countries, particularly those in the Anglo-Saxon tradition, but also in Latin America, decentralization has resulted in low-to-medium-density suburbs of single-family homes with gardens, often outside the range of effective public transport. In others, particularly in mainland Europe, it has often taken the form of satellite towns planned around new rapid transit links, with pyramids of densities: higher around the transit stations, where shops and services are also clustered, lower away from them. Further, market trends and planning in the Anglo-Saxon tradition have often combined to encourage longer-distance decentralization from larger cities to smaller towns within their general commuter orbit, as around New York and Los Angeles and London; while in other countries, such as France, virtually all of the process has been housed in direct extensions of the city itself.

These variations seem to have worked satisfactorily enough, because they conformed to basic social and cultural preferences which differ from one country to another. What is to be avoided is planning that works against such preferences, which always gives rise to tell-tale signs of failure: above all, artificial housing shortages and artificially inflated house prices, combined with idiosyncratic building forms like high-rise blocks in rural villages, which are sure indications that something has gone wrong.

In the developing world, as noticed in Chapter I, decentralization has reached a new level and has produced a new form: the mega-city. This form, which has parallels and precursors in the developed world (London, New York, Los Angeles, San Francisco), consists of a series of anything between twenty and fifty towns, physically separate but functionally networked, clustered around one or more larger central cities, and drawing enormous economic strength from a new functional division of labour. These places exist both as separate entities, in which most residents work locally and most workers are local residents, and as parts of a wider functional urban region connected by dense flows of people and information along motorways, high-speed rail lines and telecommunications cables. It is no exaggeration to say that this was the emerging urban form at the end of the twentieth century, and that it will prove pervasive in the twenty-first.

However, as clearly seen, decentralization has its critics. For it appears to contradict the basic principle of sustainability, on which all observers are agreed. It appears to generate more trips, and to use more resources – including non-renewable ones – than more compact traditional forms of urban development. Therefore, there are widespread calls everywhere – in the United Kingdom, in Germany, in Australia – for a return to the compact city. Densities should be raised, these critics say; every possible opportunity should be taken to recycle brownfield land in preference to new greenfield development; living and working should be no longer separated, but placed in close juxtaposition; further decentralization from the city should be resisted.

There is a problem with this argument, simple and beguiling as it may seem: it does not capture the full complexity of what is happening. Indeed, the experts are disagreed as to prescription. While some call for compaction, others argue that decentralization produces quite sustainable results, because people and jobs re-equilibrate: both move out together, bringing a pattern of journeys shorter than before, hence more sustainable. (Two-earner households complicate this, but not entirely, because women tend to commute shorter distances than men.) But that still leaves considerable scope for different forms of decentralization: it may actually be preferable to encourage long-distance movements, as the British did with their new towns, so as to make the decentralized settlements as self-contained as possible.

Planning and Market Tools

Thus, planning does not and should not work on its own to shape urban areas. Urban policy-makers have other important instruments, and the clue is to make them work in concert, not in conflict. (The recent history of Eastern Europe, where the market economy has encountered a rigid planning system developed to serve an entirely different economic system, offers some salutary lessons – albeit negative ones.) There are three tools:

financial ones (taxes and subsidies), provision of infrastructure, and land-use controls.

Box IV.33. Plan and market in Kraków, Poland.

> In Kraków, the lack of spatial analysis when designing the zoning plan has resulted in an administrative distribution of land which both contradicts market trends and the master plan's own objectives. The plan will not result in a spatial modification of the city, in spite of its objectives. The resulting spatial organization will be less in conformity with objectives than the one that market forces would have produced if left alone.
>
> (Bertaud, 1997, p. 27)

Financial Methods

Property taxes and levies can have immense influence on development patterns if they are based on the benefit principle: investors should pay for public services, or provide them directly by taking over responsibility for access to the street system or other public networks.

The property tax should be seen as a standing compensation for the provision of a bundle of public services, including security. But cross-subsidization between housing and commercial investment, which is sometimes seen as an important element in progressive strategies for urban development, should be avoided. It makes good economic sense that some governments levy equal tax rates on commercial and residential property.

In many parts of the world local governments rely primarily on property taxes to fund municipal services. This motivates them to encourage the development of land uses that generate surplus revenues (manufacturing plants, warehouses, offices, retail facilities, and high-value luxury residential) and discourage land uses that generate deficits (low-value housing, especially high-density housing for poor people). Where local governments in addition receive special supplementary taxes on business property, but low taxes on residential property, the tendency to favour business developments can be even stronger. As local governments are mostly welfare maximizers for their local populations, balanced incentives for different types of development are more important than abstract obligations written into planning laws.

We earlier argued that cities need a property tax to finance important tasks. Well designed property taxes can improve the functioning of markets. Using market values of land as the tax base can increase the supply of land, especially where planning rations land for building purposes, resulting in rapidly increasing land values which again provide an incentive for hoarding land for speculative motives. A property/land value tax could counteract speculative land hoarding, since it forces land owners to pay taxes independently of use. As market value represents the optimal use for a developer on a particular site, the tax payment can be substantial and will have the effect of taxing underused land into this optimal use.

Land value taxation has effects rather like a leasing system, where the lessees have to pay a price for using the land. Taxes paid annually, based on market values of the land, or on the market value of annual use, increase competition on land markets and make land markets more flexible in adjusting to changing conditions. The double function of a land value tax, as both a source of revenue and an agent to bring forward the supply of land for development, makes it extremely useful as an urban tax: it will help simultaneously to increase the supply of land and to economize its use.

Planning creates planning gain. Planning gains should be used as a source of finance for infrastructure, since – as against profits on competitive markets – they have no function and represent pure windfall profits for owners. But taxing planning gain is difficult: very often, cities bargain with developers for special compensating favours whereby the developer provides public goods; a few countries have formal systems, in which development levies try to tax the precise gains which are a consequence of planning. Much easier are general capital gains taxes. But from a local point of view, they are not very attractive, since the revenue 'disappears' in the general national budget. Special local development levies which use simple calculation methods (x $ per square metre or per unit of housing) have the advantage that they are easy to administer and are a direct source of revenue to finance the spatial expansion of cities.

Providing Infrastructure

Infrastructure is the basic public input for urban development. Local authorities are responsible for providing it. They need adequate sources of finance to provide infrastructure of the right quality and in the right quantity. Experience shows that it is not necessary for public authorities to be the producers or organizers of specific infrastructure investments. Development contracts with private investors offer a flexible instrument to provide infrastructure, without detailed involvement of the public sector. There are different possible kinds of agreements. Special planning permissions may be accompanied by a development agreement whereby a private developer provides infrastructure investment for a large and complex project. Private investment in public infrastructure or buildings may be combined with leasing arrangements.

Land-use Controls

Zoning creates a predictable and rational – but also limited – framework for making development and land-use decisions, chiefly aiming to protect residential uses from the negative externalities of industrial and commercial developments. But it is too one-dimensional for the many different purposes it now has to serve. It works too much with exclusion rules which isolate certain uses from others. In reality, both now and in the future, we need more flexible planning to achieve desired objectives, whereby specific performance targets are set for new developments, and developers can themselves develop the means to get the desired results.

Very often, more important than density or height of buildings are the social, economic or other impacts. They include traffic counts, levels of pollution, noise, odours, vibrations, water runoff and open space preservation. Commentators have noted that 'Performance standards may be expressed in terms of minimum open space ratios, maximum trip generation rates, impervious surface area ratios, maximum emissions, storm water management capacities, and similar measures' (Duerksen *et al.*, 1995). By not being bound to rigid land-use separation, it is possible to develop mixed use projects and other innovative designs without creating negative externalities.

Cluster zoning provides for the construction of buildings in clusters that are not constrained by individual lot sizes and interval requirements, but that respect the overall average density restrictions on a subdivision tract. This device permits the design of larger areas for open space and other amenities while minimizing requirements for roads and utilities. Similar to the effects of both performance and cluster zoning is a more comprehensive American technique referred to as a Planned Unit Development (PUD): land development projects comprehensively planned as an entity via a unitary site plan which permits flexibility in building siting, mixtures of housing types and land uses, usable open spaces, and the preservation of significant natural features. This technique gives a developer broad flexibility to design large tract projects without being hampered by artificial rigidities built into zoning and subdivision regulations.

Flexibility can also be attained through a 'development agreement': a contract between a local government and a private land owner or developer. It allows the parties to agree to permitted uses, densities, maximum height and size of proposed buildings within such property, provisions for reservation or dedication of land for public purposes, provisions to protect environmentally sensitive lands and historically important structures. It also allows for the phasing or time of construction or development, requirements for public infrastructure and the financing of public infrastructure and any other matters relating to the development of the property. This contractual approach is a growing trend in many countries and mitigates some of the disadvantages of conventional zoning mechanisms.

Indeed, experience shows that planning has had limited positive effects in enhancing the quality of the urban environment. It has been able to achieve limited objectives but it has not in itself been able to guarantee good urban design. Conversely, many attractive urban areas have been built by private speculators whose middle and upper income clients demanded certain types of building or a well-accepted layout of buildings.

Of course, these are not general rules: comprehensive planning, as in the British new towns, has produced some very attractive neighbourhoods, while many down-market speculative developments have been poorly designed. Perhaps the real conclusion from long-term experience is that the best urban neighbourhoods have been produced by designers who had high standards of their own but were catering for a sympathetic public who confirmed their approval through the market. This is a better test by far than abstract exercises in design inflicted on clients (such as public housing tenants) who had no power of choice.

The Experience of the Developed World

Conflicts and Trade-offs

In practice, even in developed economies with a broad public acceptance of planning and with a well-developed and sophisticated professional bureaucracy, achieving different planning objectives is not at all easy. For it involves difficult conflicts and trade-offs. The most efficient location for industry and warehousing, in terms of single-floor operation for efficient assembly, may involve big rural land take and access to motorway interchanges, which will absorb valuable agricultural land and may encourage commuting by car. Major commercial developments will benefit from access to central train stations, which is sustainable, but they may then impinge on low-income housing areas and on historic areas which need conservation. New highways improve access, but they may affect established communities, bringing the threat of severance and pollution. New residential areas, whether on greenfield land or recycled brownfield land, may impinge on existing areas, such as exclusive inner-city residential areas or secluded rural villages, threatening their exclusivity. Higher-density urban development may appear 'sustainable', requiring less energy for travel by car, but may leave residents exposed to higher levels of pollution, especially from noise; it also increases the need for weekend travel to the countryside or ownership of weekend houses. Protecting natural landscapes may leave them in the hands of commercial farming which does not enhance the environment, and which may even use subsidies to leave the land unproductive. Often, it is not entirely clear which course of action would be best even in terms of achieving one objective, let alone trading off as between conflicting ones.

So it is not surprising that even in countries with a highly competent professional planning bureaucracy, planning has had mixed results. In the UK, researchers have found that London's green belt actually extended commuter journeys and also created land scarcities, raising the costs of housing. Decentralization strategies – green belts, new towns, growth corridors – may also entail longer commuting times and longer paths for freight logistics. Segregation of land uses has increased the length, time and cost of journeys to work, but a return to mixed-use planning – a major policy reversal – might bring incompatible uses again in juxtaposition, with homes next to noisy bars and discotheques.

Consequently, in spite of a plethora of academic and professional studies, there is no consensus on the management of spatial development. It comes as no surprise that recently, many of these traditional beliefs of planning – separation of different land uses, green belt and urban containment strategies, decentralization to new towns – have been challenged by reports that suggest it would more sustainable to mix land uses and to encourage higher-density brownfield redevelopment within cities.

Some forms of urban growth may be more efficient (and more sustainable) than others in this regard, though there has been little systematic comparison. All involve an element of trade-off: Los Angeles type sprawl reduces access to open landscape for many inhabitants, but increases the use of private gardens and private open spaces; Berlin apartment living gives a high density of population, easy access to open space or farmland, and effective use of public transport, but is too claustrophobic for some. London's typical form of development – the suburb in the city, celebrated sixty years ago by Steen Eiler Rasmussen – allows more everyday contact with green spaces, a more open and human, less monumental, urban environment. It is rejected by a latter-day generation of architects and planners as 'not urban enough', but it is far from clear that they represent the interests and tastes of ordinary Londoners, who will express their preferences in the market.

Despite the lack of agreement among experts, recent work in the UK and the USA strongly suggests that the optimum combination of policies, in terms of environmental sustainability and public acceptability, would consist not of a single solution but of what has been called a portfolio approach (Hall and Ward, 1998, p. 120): within the cities, medium-density urban brownfield redevelopment, combining residential and other uses, around public transport interchanges ('urban villages'), combined with similar greenfield small mixed-use units, all typically housing 20-30,000 people ('garden cities'), in linear clusters of up to about 200,000 people along public transport lines. The effect will be to create a highly polycentric pattern of development, both within and outside the city, allowing the city to grow progressively into a polycentric city region within which each part has a high degree of self-containment but each is highly networked to all the others through efficient public transport and high-quality ICT links. But the effects on traffic have not been rigorously tested, and there is vigorous debate as to key elements of such a policy, including the right proportions of greenfield and brownfield development, and the precise scale of decentralization, short- versus long-distance.

Clearly, within this broad rubric, different solutions are technically and economically viable. But they are quite different in their resulting atmosphere and lifestyle. They reflect cultural preferences and may not be readily transferable from one city to another: high-density apartment living in Paris, Berlin or Hong Kong may be suitable for those who care to live in those cities, but Los Angeles-type sprawl is equally acceptable to those who place a high premium on space in and around the home, even though it increases commuting costs and restricts public open space. The choice depends on historical traditions, on the surroundings and the quality of the landscape. It is a matter not only of the opportunity costs of different options, but also of different local preferences.

This is important, because in a democracy the planning system can only go so far to try to affect people's market preferences. It can and should do so wherever there are manifest and unambiguous negative externalities, and where it is clear that these are unacceptable. (Long commute times are an externality, but should be ignored if people are evidently willing to pay for them.) The most important imperative is the environmental one; but we must be quite clear about the effects, and of the results of policy changes (e.g. densification), before we embark on them.

Perhaps the best answer was the one given above: planners will not determine these questions; people and their preferences, expressed through markets and through political processes, will decide. This will not be easy, because politics may run up against markets: NIMBY politics will tend to set barriers against developments that change people's established and comfortable lifestyles, whether they are country or city people. The risk in developed countries is a kind of urban paralysis, in which it becomes almost impossible to change anything: BANANA (Build Absolutely Nothing Anywhere Near Anyone). In economies and societies characterized by rapid change, the resulting pressures may become almost impossible to manage.

Given all this, it becomes a delicate and difficult point as to how far, and in what ways, planning should intervene. Architects argue that it should seek to raise the quality of development. That is fine, as long as it does not become a device for forcing on people designs, including densities, that they do not want. In high-quality (meaning high-price) developments, the private sector will probably produce good design because people are willing to pay for it. But experience in the United Kingdom suggests that public intervention, through design guides, may be effective in the middle and lower ranges of the market.

Rules for Design

The key is to find ways of producing good quality urban environments, that people will be attracted to and will enjoy living in. Allan Jacobs and Donald Appleyard have suggested some of the qualities of such places: they should be liveable places, where everyone can live in relative comfort and security; they should have identity and control, in that people feel that they have some ownership and want to be involved; they should offer access to opportunity, imagination and excitement; they should give people a sense of authenticity and meaning, but not in too obvious a way; they should encourage a sense of community and participation; they should be as sustainable as possible; and they should offer a good level of environment to all (Jacobs and Appleyard, 1987, pp. 115-116). Jacobs and Appleyard go on to suggest what kind of an urban environment would meet those demands. They say there are five physical characteristics, all of which must be present:

The first is *liveable streets and neighbourhoods* with adequate sunshine, clean air, trees and vegetation and gardens and open space, pleasantly scaled and designed buildings, without offensive noise, and with cleanliness and physical safety. They stress that these qualities must be 'reasonable, though not excessive': sunlight standards must not result in buildings placed too far apart, or traffic safety must not produce over-wide streets and wide curves.

The second is *a certain minimum density*, which they say is about 15 dwelling units per acre (37 units per hectare) which translates to 30-60 people per acre (74-148/ha), typified by generous town houses. But, they point out, San Francisco achieves superb urban quality with 3-storey row houses above garages at densities as high as 48 units per acre (119/ha), translating to 96-192 people per acre (237-474/ha), yet offering separate entrances with direct access to the ground and either private or public open space at hand. Such densities are also characteristic of much of inner London, which also achieves great urban quality and liveability. But, they warn, at densities much more than 200 people per net residential acre – the highest planned density in Abercrombie's famous London plan – 'the concessions to less desirable living environments mount rapidly'. As well as density, there must be a certain intensity of use on the streets, and this is related to the density: both will be higher in central urban districts than in outer suburban areas.

The third necessary attribute is *integration of activities – living, working, shopping, public and spiritual and recreational activities – reasonably near each other*, though not necessarily all together everywhere. They say there is a lot to be said for 'living sanctuaries, consisting almost entirely of housing', but these should be fairly small, a few street blocks, and close to meeting places which should normally have housing in them.

Fourth, they say that *'buildings (and other objects that people place in the environment) should be arranged in such a way as to define and even enclose public space, rather than sit in space'*. Buildings along a street will do this so long as the street is not too wide in relation to them. The critical point is that the spaces, whether streets or squares, must not become too large. The spaces must also be primarily pedestrian spaces and they must be under public control.

Finally, they argue, *'many different buildings and spaces with complex arrangements and relationships are required'*. By this they mean a rather broken pattern of ownership, with small parcel sizes, producing a more public and lively city. Of course, there will need to be larger buildings, too; but these should be the exception, not the rule.

These principles, we would argue, provide an excellent guide to the design of good built urban environments. Of course, they do not cover the entire range of legitimate designs within cities; some parts, especially in the very centre and the very edge, will depart from them, and it should be no aim of the planner or urban designer to produce total uniformity across the city. But it is at least interesting, for instance, that though Jacobs and Appleyard question the Garden City ideal, their principles seem to conform pretty closely to Howard's original concept of 1898 – including his suggested density, which was right in the middle of their suggested density range. The key point is that the urban forms they recommend are not merely liveable; they are also sustainable. They provide the critical building blocks, which can then be combined into urban villages and country towns to constitute a sustainable city region.

These qualities will not come through market forces alone. As Jacobs and Appleyard argue, the problem is that commercial considerations will often suggest different arrangements – including large, monofunctional blocks or very low densities. Therefore, the planner will have to intervene on the basis that superior urban designs will be highly attractive once people can see them working. (San Francisco and inner London, cities which offer very high quality of urban life and are extremely fashionable living places with buoyant real estate markets, are examples.) This will require that planners are much better educated in urban design than many of them are today.

The Challenge in the Developing World

The Limits of Planning

All these problems are compounded, of course, in conditions of rapid growth and especially in the world's biggest cities. Half a century ago, a city like London placed draconian restrictions on its own growth, by means of a green belt and a series of new towns outside it, in order to reduce and hold its population to under 8 million. Today, the United Nations analysis suggests that there are already more than twenty cities in excess of that figure, and most of them are growing very much faster than London was then (see table I.2). This combination of huge size and rapid growth is the distinctively new feature, unprecedented in world history.

Further, as already seen in Chapter I, a new feature is that most of these cities – and many just below them – are in developing countries, many of them relatively poor. They compare unfavourably in this respect with the London or Paris or New York of 1900, let alone those cities in 1950.

This is significant, because it affects what planning can achieve. As already seen, some Latin American middle-income cities (Mexico City, São Paulo, Lima) have permitted uncontrolled growth of informal settlements; others in Eastern Asia (Seoul, Singapore, Hong Kong) have forbidden them, instead developing high-density public and industry-financed housing. It is not immediately clear which pattern has been optimal, and a pattern that is optimal at one stage (for instance where the majority of incomes are low) may not be optimal at another. Further, as in the developed world, cultural preferences enter into the equation: South East Asian people seem to have had a tradition of living at high densities, though that might reflect their poverty, while poor Latin Americans spread out like richer Californians. One important asset is flexibility: the ability of an urban settlement structure to adapt without too much strain to rapidly changing circumstances.

In many middle-income and all low-income cities, however, lack of resources has at least three consequences for the planning system.

First, planning is likely to command a low priority. Planning has to compete with a great many other national and local objectives – not least, economic growth. Because good planning is to some degree what the economist would call an income-elastic good, in early stages of development planning will not be seen as a high priority. Thus, if a large multinational investor proposes a major factory or office development, planning permission is likely to be forthcoming, however good the objections.

Second, arising from this fact, the system is likely to be weak. It will not command the best professionals, and in particular the routine administration of the system is not likely to work well. Rules can be bent, and corruption of low-paid officials is an ever-present danger. One particular problem is that, during the 1990s, decentralization policies often delegated functions to municipal authorities – but without a corresponding transfer of financial resources, leading to difficulties in supplying services to the poor, and compounded by a lack of know-how. In the worst cases, the lack of municipal administration, or its inefficiency, can lead to a power vacuum, filled by organizations that range from organized crime to fundamentalist terrorist groups, which force the urban poor into dependency on them (Network of GTZ Consultants on Municipal and Urban Development, 1997, pp. 17-18).

Third, and even more basically, the system may become physically impossible to enforce: throughout these poorer cities, a permanent feature is the illegal occupation of land by squatters, often living at the margin of existence. It could hardly be otherwise: in the early 1980s in low-income developing countries, nine new households were being formed for every permanent dwelling. The gap between demand and supply is huge and widening, typically between 1 or 2 per cent in Thailand to 20 per cent in Madras (Brennan, 1994, p. 240). So the authorities then have the unenviable choice of eliminating informal settlements and rendering the inhabitants homeless, with the certain expectation that they will go and settle somewhere else, or recognizing the reality and turning a blind eye to the illegality. (And indeed, in many of these countries the courts have eventually recognized some legal rights for squatters.)

The result, in many cases, is a system that generates elaborate paper plans that regularly get ignored and are then revised to fit reality. Even when plans are implemented – for instance, developing new satellite towns to rehouse the poor – all too often they do not work out as intended: they are occupied by richer people, or by commercial uses, while the poor return to the slums. The key in most cases is to help the people of the informal settlements to upgrade their own environment, using their own time and energies which they have rather than money resources which they do not have; but this demands some form of legalization of title as a prerequisite.

How Much Planning Can Poor Cities Afford ?

This poses a very basic and drastic question: *can poor cities afford effective planning?* Though comparisons are notoriously difficult, it appears that many cities in developing countries have per capita incomes no higher than their equivalents in the developed world a century ago, at the point when they were just tentatively beginning to accept the principle that planning could intervene in market decisions. Further, rather remarkably, most of them have many more people living in informal settlements than these cities did; the poor in 1900 mainly lived in overcrowded purpose-built tenements, and the main policy thrust in most of them in the first two-thirds of the century was to rehouse them in purpose-built public or cooperative housing, a programme which is quite beyond the capacity of many of these countries today. The brutal reality is that '. . . Staggering sums of investments would be required to provide adequate urban infrastructure and services' (Cheema 1994, p. 421): it was estimated that between US $10 billion and US $30 billion would have been needed during the 1990s to ensure adequate access to drinking water and sanitation.

Indeed, as already seen, over the past thirty years the conventional wisdom on housing policy has steadily shifted in favour of less intervention rather than more: until the early 1970s the standard solution was high-grade public housing using colonial models, coupled with clearance of slum housing; then, this was replaced by an acceptance of informal housing with site-and-service approaches, as an effective and efficient way whereby the urban poor could house themselves. But even these have been incapable of meeting more than a minority of demand. And so, around 1990, there came a further fundamental shift in the conventional wisdom: the experts concluded that upgrading of existing slums is more effective than new build, because it affects precisely the areas where the poor already live. Calcutta, one of the world's poorest cities, has been notably effective, improving conditions for nearly 2 million people; Jakarta's Kampung Improvement Programme has improved more than 500 of the city's notorious slum (*kampung*) areas and provided basic services to 3.8 million people (Brennan, 1994, pp. 240-242).

Planning as Enabling

In the last decade, therefore, authorities across the developing world have concentrated on 'enabling' policies: cities should withdraw from direct provision and concentrate on facilitating new private construction, both formal and informal, and creating an appropriate regulatory environment plus appropriate finance. This makes full use of self-help with cheap materials and local skills, using the private sector – including NGOs and community groups – and developing new kinds of housing finance. It also recognizes that an estimated 50 per cent of the labour force of the developing world is in the informal sector, and that these numbers could double between 1980 and 2000 (Brennan, 1994, p. 243; Cheema, 1994, pp. 421-423).

So the best conventional practice at the start of the new century is represented by slum upgrading schemes like those in Jakarta and Manila. They are based on fairly minimal standards that can subsequently be upgraded. German consultants have stressed this point: they argue that the key aim must be to help those living in absolute poverty. These people suffer from multiple disadvantages. They experience disproportionately high living costs for public transport, schooling, house rent, public services and food. They are more liable to experience environmental hazards, health risks and unhealthy or dangerous living conditions, missing or insufficient public services, and unhygienic, insufficient and climatically unsuitable homes. They are more vulnerable to sudden economic changes. They live in areas with heterogeneous social structures and often high criminality, where traditional social structures have collapsed, and where drug consumption and organized crime are endemic, especially among children and youth. They are open to indiscriminate attacks by officials and police, and an ever-present danger of eviction. And many of the households in these neighbourhoods are headed by poor females, who are most vulnerable of all. They comment:

The introduction of special areas with reduced urban planning standards, adaptation of road width, special minimum plot size and building regulations is often being prevented by traditional urban planners. University curricula neglect in many cases the informal city and produce architects, planners and engineers unprepared to work with and in poor neighbourhoods.

(Network of GTZ Consultants on Municipal and Urban Development, 1997, p. 18)

The public sector often is not, indeed never was, able to provide basic services, especially for the poor; so it is necessary to develop citizen bodies to fill the gap.

The key is to accept the built forms of the informal city, but to shape them in the direction of sustainability. Rather remarkably, it appears that this may not be too difficult. While formal high-rise solutions are impossibly expensive both to build and to maintain, it is possible to achieve remarkably high densities and compact developments with traditional housing which people build themselves and which they like living in because it has the traditional neighbourly qualities. The clue is to make plots of the right size available. Because most people are poor, these can be quite uniform and quite small. Later on, some people may become richer. But by that time, the built form will be set and difficult to alter.

Box IV.34. High-density, low-rise in Jakarta.

Jelinek suggests that in Jakarta, the predominant low-density urban form is incompatible with projected growth. Kampung housing is constantly destroyed near the centre to make way for business uses, and in fact more housing is being demolished in the central area than is being constructed, but it would be difficult to see how it could be otherwise. Yet up to now densities for four-storey walk-up apartments have been lower than for the kampungs they replaced. The fact is that low-rise high-density can rival densities of medium-rise apartment dwellings, and surveys show that the preferred way of living is low-rise, single- or two-storey houses with gardens and easy access to shops, schools and work. Present densities are typically 80-150 to the hectare, net, but if everyone were to be housed in this way, the residential area would increase by three times! He suggests that perfectly adequate low-rise housing can be developed at up to 800 persons per hectare or more, if the plot size is reduced to 26 or 30 square metres and if informal private initiatives, already responsible for 80 per cent of all shelter, are supported with infrastructure.

(Jelinek, 1992, pp. 10-14)

Universal Principles, Local Variants

So different are the experiences of citizens in the developed and the developing world, that the question poses itself: does planning have any fundamental, 'eternal', goals, valid for all places and all kinds? The answer might seem to be self-evidently 'no'. But we would argue the contrary: there are such fundamental goals, but their interpretation and application varies according to circumstances.

We can list eight such fundamental goals.

First, planning should promote the city's wealth-creating capacities, which alone can generate new employment for its people, including replacements for the jobs that are always being lost to globalization and technological change.

Second, it should seek to promote ways to provide adequate shelter for everyone, rich and poor alike.

Third, it should seek to produce an adequate and sustainable level of environment, in terms of air and water quality, drainage and noise, both in the immediate environment of the dwelling or workplace, and in the more general environment of the city and indeed the planet.

Fourth, it should seek to order land uses efficiently, so as to reduce unnecessary journeys for people, and to reduce demands on non-renewable resources.

Fifth, it should seek to protect the natural environment both within the city and in the countryside around it, by providing sufficient green spaces within the city and by protecting agricultural land around it, while providing sufficient space for the city's growth: a task that often will involve transformation into a polycentric urban region of networked cities.

Sixth, it should equally seek to conserve all that is best in the historic built patrimony, while promoting the capacity of the city to grow and change; not an easy trade-off.

Seventh, it should seek especially to protect the standards of the poorest and least fortunate, who lack the ability to guarantee these things for themselves.

Eighth, it can best do this by helping people help themselves, using their own skills and energies, which they have in abundance, rather than resources they do not have at all.

Having set those principles down, it is clear that their application will differ significantly from one city to another. Adequate shelter in a developed country is likely to mean a new house or apartment, comprehensively equipped; in a developing country, an informal self-build minimal structure capable of progressive extension. Adequate environment in a developed country is likely to mean protection from noise from a new highway or airport, or perhaps a late-night disco; in a developing country, it could be protection from a noxious chemical plant. Reducing unnecessary journeys in a developed-country context could mean more compact development on abandoned brownfield land, designed to woo people from their cars on to bicycles or good public transport; in the developing-country context, it is likely to mean reserving new rights of way for buses and bicycles to connect the latest informal development with the city.

Likewise, open space in the developed city means new parks and golf courses in the green belt; in the developing city, providing and keeping playing fields around the schools, which otherwise may fall prey to new land invasions. Conservation of the built environment in the developed city may entail the preservation of thousands of churches and literally hundreds of thousands of old houses; in the developing world, keeping a few score of buildings that have survived the numberless rebuildings of the last four decades. Equity in the developed world means for instance providing a certain proportion of affordable social housing in each and every development; in the developing world, where this would be a recipe for uncontrolled squatting, it means a priority to slum upgrading.

Even in the same city in the same part of the world, solutions that are good for some people may be thoroughly bad for others. High-rise solutions seem not to work for mothers with small children, even if they are perfectly satisfactory for singles or childless couples. American-style urban sprawl has created inefficiencies – such as unnecessarily long commuter journeys and high costs of service connection – that could have been avoided. (On the other hand, British urban containment policies also seem to have increased commuter journey lengths, because often people found homes outside the green belts while their jobs remained inside them.) Rationing of development land predictably raises its price, which bears especially hard on lower-income groups: everyone pays more for housing, and gets less than they would in the absence of such policies, but the poor lose out the most.

Again, mixed use is fine as a general principle, but some land uses may remain non-compatible, at least for some sections of the population: living over the shop may be fine if the shop closes at 6:30 in the evening but not if it stays open all night; it certainly will not be right if the shop turns into a late-night wine bar or early-morning night club. The answer to this contradiction may be to put different land uses close together, but to continue to separate any uses that may impose a nuisance on residents or other users.

Brownfield development is good as a general principle, but much brownfield land is contaminated to varying degrees: in the United States, contaminated brownfield sites are estimated between 400,000 and

700,000, in Europe, 750,000. Global remediation costs in 1997 were estimated at US$18 billion (Andersson, 1998). Brownfield regeneration can of course work, as dramatically illustrated by London's docklands. But even there, the problems were daunting. Canary Wharf, the huge Olympia & York development – 14 million square feet of commercial space on 93 acres of land, centred on a 50-storey tower designed by Cesar Pelli, the second tallest office building in Europe – went into receivership in May 1992, less than a year after opening of Phase One, though it has since proved a success and is being extended.

Box IV.35. London Docklands.

> **Urban Problem:** The London Docklands is in east London and consists of 8.5 square miles with approximately 55 miles of river and dock frontage. These docks at one time were the busiest in the world. As a result of labour unionization, mounting losses from pilferage during port handling, and technological changes such as containerization the docks were substantially abandoned in the 1960s and 1970s.
>
> **Best Practice Solution:** London Docklands Development Corporation (LDDC) was created in 1981 by Parliament to manage the regeneration of the Docklands. The agency was given broad powers and freed of local government accountability and from statutory service provision obligations. The agency was able to provide developers with property tax exemptions for ten years as well as other incentives.
>
> Initially the area was inadequately serviced by transportation modes. It was necessary to build the Limehouse Link, a 1.8 kilometre road tunnel from the City of London to Docklands that was completed May 1993. The cost was originally estimated at £141.5 million. A Comptroller and Auditor General reported indicated that the actual cost was £293.3 million to construct or 107 per cent more than the pre-tender estimate. An additional £155.3 million was paid by the LDDC to acquire land; rehousing local residents; and providing grants to the local authority for social, economic and community projects The limited capacity of the Docklands Light Railway and congested surface streets created problems for workers commuting to jobs at office development such as Canary Wharf. It was only at the end of 1999 that the Jubilee Underground Line connected Docklands to the rest of the London Underground system.
>
> From a planning and urban regeneration standpoint, Docklands represents a 'best practice.' By the end of March 31, 1996, there were 70,000 permanent jobs created, 20,000 homes were constructed and 7,900 local authority homes were refurbished or improved, 24.57 million square feet of commercial and industrial floorspace were built, and 1,800 acres of derelict land were reclaimed (London Docklands Development Corporation).
>
> (Ordway, 1998 pp. 20,21)

Forging an urban renaissance, in the blighted areas of many North American and some European cities, will not be an easy task. It will involve fairly drastic reconstruction in the worst-afflicted areas, with subsidies that may have to be generated through taxation of greenfield land, together with upgrading policies to stem the progressive decline of other areas. The justification lies not so much in the need to save rural land, since many parts of the world are burdened with huge agricultural surpluses, as in the argument that urban development is more sustainable in multiple ways – economically, socially, environmentally.

Not only the implementation strategies, but the implementation agencies, will be different from city to city. In the developed case, they will be professional bureaucracies mediated by democratically-elected politicians. In the developing case, they will be neighbourhood organizations and associations led by a few key activists, mediated if possible by mechanisms that ensure they do not fall into the hands of self-aggrandizing exploiters. There are parallels, of course: in the developed world, efforts should be made and are being made to involve poor people more actively in the design and the management of their own housing; in the developing world, planning will need to provide an overall structure of land uses and infrastructure, within which the poor can take control of their own lives. But the two experiences will remain very different.

In particular, financial incentives and disincentives, though important everywhere, may be more appropriate to poorer cities. In the cities of the developed world, remediating brownfield land, which is accessible and well-serviced but may be seriously contaminated by former industrialization, will often prove expensive and will fall on the public purse, since the private sector will prefer to locate on cheaper, easier greenfield land. There are possible ways of trying to enforce clean-up costs on owners, but few of them will prove effective, since invariably the original polluting agent has long since disappeared, and much of this land has effectively become derelict.

And so the major policy question here is how far, and in what ways, communities will be prepared to cross-subsidize such remediation by taxes on development of cheaper greenfield sites. If they are – and the urban development corporations, in the UK and USA, provide an interesting model – it is often possible through open bidding processes to recycle the land into new and productive uses: witness London Docklands.

But it is in the developing world, far more, that financial incentives can play an effective role. People can be offered money to improve their own local environments, based on local knowledge. Industrialists can be required to pay very large amounts to locate next to residential areas. Local groups can be subsidized to build a school and playing fields, and to guard them against invasion. But none of the above will be much use if the bureaucracy or judiciary can be corruptly influenced. For that reason, there should be a minimal bureaucracy but it should be highly professional and adequately paid. For all other functions, power should be devolved to local groups.

To come back to the central question: do universally-applicable principles lead to universally-applicable solutions? The answer again is yes and no: there is a broad good-practice solution that is applicable in virtually every city, North and South, rich and poor; but this solution will need to be tweaked in particular ways to suit local conditions, local constraints and local opportunities.

The overall strategy is to develop flexible planning strategies at different spatial scales, from the strategic to the local. The strategic plan for a metropolitan area would set out broad principles of development and would, above all, make clear where infrastructure investments were expected in the short-to-medium term. Within it, local design briefs would develop a simultaneous control of environmental standards and planning standards, set out transparently the proposals for infrastructure provision and upgrading, and develop policy solutions to control land speculation – including the radical solution that all development land should pass through public hands.

In particular, these plans should specify the areas on which – for good environmental reasons – no development, formal or informal, should be allowed. To enforce such prohibitions, it may be necessary for a public authority to acquire the land on which development was to be stopped, at least temporarily. The key, in the most difficult cases, would be to dispose of the land in such a way that it could never be developed; for instance, by dividing it into multiple small parcels and giving these away to members of the community, or to children, who could be expected to defend their tiny rural plots.

Within such a framework, the general solution would be to accommodate urban growth by progressively decentralizing it at the broad metropolitan scale while reconcentrating it at the more local scale. Employment and services should be encouraged by a variety of measures to decentralize as people move out to new homes on the periphery. To some extent, of course, this will happen naturally: local services will follow residences, and a little later other activities will migrate outwards in search of labour supplies and lower land costs. So the market will work with policy, but it may need encouragement.

The important point is not to permit an indeterminate sprawl, but to plan for decentralization into local communities of defined size, each with its own employment and services, clearly separated by green areas for agriculture and recreation, and connected by good quality public transport. Within these decentralized communities, further, there should be the maximum possible mixture of land uses subject to avoiding negative externalities (such as air, water or noise pollution). Densities should be medium-high, based for the most part on single-family homes with gardens on conventional streets, with occasional higher-density apartment complexes for single younger and older people, generally clustered close to shops and transport. Decaying and abandoned urban areas should be regenerated, and slums should be retrofitted with services, as far as possible on the self-help principle with appropriate assistance to local community groups.

Such a pattern is far from novel. On the contrary: it represents best planning practice from many countries over the last century, and it corresponds to the latest research about sustainable urban development. It has been tested and tried. And it fits powerful economic and social trends, expressed through real estate markets; it aims to bend these trends, not to try to break them, which would be neither possible nor advisable.

As said earlier, there may be local variations set above all by income, by social custom and by available resources, including human resources. Even as between developed countries, there are and will be distinctions in the proportions of houses and flats, in prevailing densities, in the pattern of service provision, and in the transport network. In the developing world the differences may be even greater, particularly as between those emerging middle-income countries well embarked on the development trajectory, and those faced with intractable problems towards the bottom end of the income scale. And even at any particular development level. Particularly striking, here, is the contrast between Curitiba and Singapore: both, starting as middle-income cities that have progressed into affluence, have planned on the basis of development corridors, but all the key details – the form of the urban transit system, the density variations, the development agencies – are radically different; and the differences depend very much on the social and political cultures of Latin America and Eastern Asia.

Generally, the ideal pattern is easier to achieve in more developed countries and cities, with plentiful resources and with well-developed and competent public administrations, than in developing ones. But it needs stressing that some middle-income cities – notably, though not exclusively, these two examples – have made themselves world leaders in urban innovation, having made a virtue out of necessity. As in Curitiba, bus rights of way may need to replace expensive metro rail systems, basic service plots may need to replace fully developed housing schemes, private farms and parks may need to replace green belts. Or maybe, as in Singapore, not so: the important point is to discover the solution that will work in the local circumstances. On that, only local people and their elected representatives will be able to judge.

The need above all is to learn from good practice in the successful cities, above all in these innovative middle-income cities, and translate it into the specific circumstances, never quite the same, in many other cities around the world. To that end, the first need is better and more accessible information systems. The United Nations have made a powerful start with their internet-based good practice database of sustainable urban development, prepared for the 1997 Istanbul conference; such databases need to be extended and regularly updated. And it matters very much that this information does not deal only with the success stories and the successful aspects; it must also chronicle the failures and the problems along the way. Cities need to learn by example, but in some ways the problems to avoid are as important as the successes to emulate, attractive as the latter may be.

Notes

1. Approved by 173 governments at the United Nations Conference on Environment and Development (UNCED), Agenda 21 is the UN's action plan for sustainable development in the twenty-first century. Adopted by the Plenary in Rio de Janeiro, on 14 June 1992 during the Earth Summit, Agenda 21 covers the issues referred to UNCED by the UN General Assembly in its Resolution 44/228 of 1989. It represents the current international consensus on actions necessary to move the world towards the goal of truly sustainable development.

    Agenda 21 deals extensively with actions that governments and international organizations, as well as industry and the community, can take to achieve lasting changes in the modes of human economic development. These actions recognize the impacts of human behaviours on the environment and on the sustainability of systems of production. The objective is the alleviation of poverty, hunger, sickness and illiteracy worldwide – while at the same time arresting the deterioration of the ecosystems on which humankind depends to sustain life.

2. The Grameen Bank was established in Bangladesh in 1984 and has helped over 450,000 poor rural families to build or upgrade their hosing through loans of between US$300 and US$620, with no collateral required, and repayable over ten years. There has been a 98 per cent recovery rate, and 7000 new loans are being made every month. The clue is that the title is vested in the woman of the family, giving her a source of independence and responsibility.

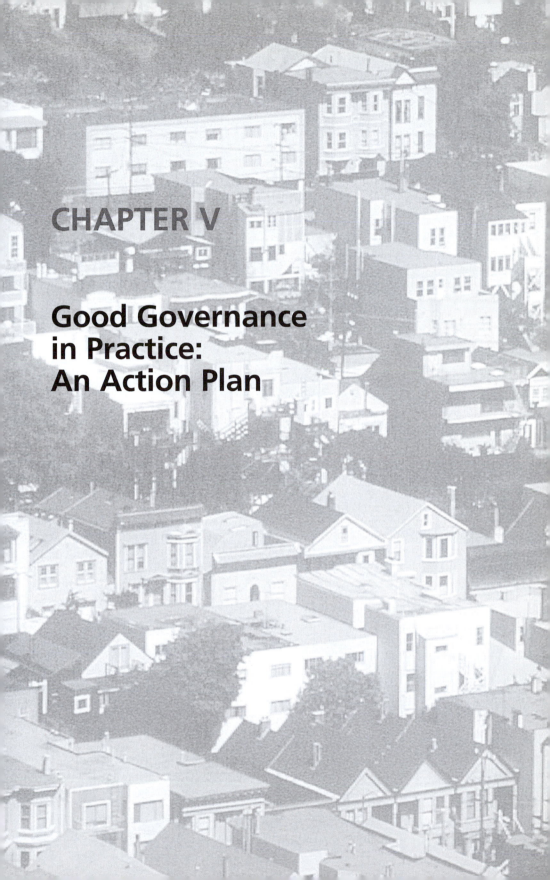

CHAPTER V

Good Governance
in Practice:
An Action Plan

V. Good Governance in Practice: An Action Plan

The Basic Principles: Strong Urban Government for Sustainable Urban Development

Local Government Matters: Local Tasks, Local Management

Strong national government and strong cities are not contradictory; they are actually complementary. In the past, most countries have been highly centralized; city governments have been weak. Centralization has brought many negative consequences in train: a distorted supply of public goods, waste or disempowerment of urban inhabitants. In contrast many examples demonstrate that in the long run local autonomy, based on adequate powers, will improve local economic and social development.

A strong democratic basis for local government can be successful especially in over-centralized political systems where cities tend to be understaffed because they lack resources. Democratic governments, directly confronted with local interests and also with the daily stress and suffering of their peoples, directly answering their demands for action, can release more resources and more direct local actions in response. As seen in Chapter IV, the late 1980s laid the foundations of a totally new approach across Africa, Asia and Latin America and the Caribbean, by focusing on the themes: *Accountability, Markets, Democratization and Decentralization*.

But the shift of power to local governments is unfinished. Financial and regulatory autonomy will remain on the urban agenda, and should be completed during the coming decade. This will increase the opportunity for local politics – in close cooperation both with national politics and with private companies, neighbourhoods and different action groups – to shape the future decisively over the next twenty to thirty years. Decisive local actions do matter. But decisive local government needs a clear urban policy framework.

Adequate Distribution of Responsibilities, Adequate and Fair Distribution of Revenues

Which Responsibilities?

The subsidiarity principle suggests that urban governments should be as autonomous as possible, but that they should be banded into regional bodies or cooperative networks for those tasks which can best be solved at the regional or the supra-urban level. Sustainable solutions need to avoid the traditional over-centralized or over-localized systems in which small suburban towns are free to maximize the welfare of their own electorates by exporting their problems to neighbouring towns and cities. Thus, an appropriate balance of power, a fair distribution of resources, and an effective cooperative framework must very often be guaranteed by central governments and parliaments, however reluctant they may be.

Cities lacking an adequate set of powers and responsibilities, with complementary independent financial resources, tend not to:

- Excite voters, mobilize adequate energies, inspire ideas and concepts. Democracy without substance invites petty quarrels or frustrations, and should be avoided.

- Attract strong independent entrepreneurial leaders who are the catalysts for urban development and for effective cooperation between the public and private sector, between government, NGOs, or neighbourhood organizations. Autonomous resources are the lifeblood of local politics, which is pumped through the urban system by strong leadership.

There is no universal set of powers which should be given to local authorities. But in successful decentralized political systems, the set of responsibilities typically comprises:

- Planning and financing of infrastructure, provision of land for building purposes and building permits, provision of water, sewer systems and treatment of waste;

- Schools and hospitals;

- Promotion of housing;

- Promotion of local economic development;

- Local public social services, welfare payments including health care;

- Traffic management and public transportation;

- Environmental monitoring and planning; control of pollution.

- Based on the right to tax the formal and informal sector and to demand fees from the user of public services.

The major transition – from traditional, centralized, rule-book administration to good, responsive, flexible, decentralized governance – will not happen overnight. The huge recent efforts, and the limited successes so far, show how difficult the process will be. Meanwhile, the need for independent local policies, tailored to the demands of the local situation and the local citizenry, continues to grow. In the developing world, greater local responsibilities cannot immediately overcome weaknesses in the tax base, administrative capacity and political participation. Local autonomy and development will go hand-in-hand, in a mutually-reinforcing process. Weak city administrations or utility companies need to be strengthened. Water and transportation, waste collection and other public services are candidates for outsourcing to independent private companies. A global market for utilities could overcome the inertia of overburdened local administrations. Standards for control and monitoring can guarantee better, more stable services. Benchmarking by international standards could strengthen local political control.

Nations should: Complete legislation to transfer an appropriate bundle of powers, including taxation, to local government.

Cities should: Upgrade their administrative capacities so that they are capable of taking over more responsibilities, decentralize and democratize their internal powers (as Johannesburg has already done in several stages), including devolution of all possible service delivery to outside contractors, with transparent systems of contracting and performance regulation.

Which Local Taxes?

Cities without adequate income from their own revenue base tend to lose their autonomy and become dependent on the central purse. The tax base should be as decentralized as the distribution of responsibilities. Fiscal autonomy is the basis of a strong sustainable democracy.

There is no universal set of taxes or revenues to finance the set of typical tasks; but again, successful local authorities tend to have typical sources of revenue.

- The queen of local taxes is the property tax with market value (or easy-to-assess substitutes) as the tax base. It is an expression of the benefit principle which should dominate the entire local tax system.

315

- Local services should also be financed according to the benefit approach, which sees cities as suppliers of goods which must be paid for by the user. This demands user fees for cost recovery, or taxes on cars or gasoline, or on specific economic activities which depend on inputs from the public urban sector.

- People's incomes should be another source of revenue. But local income taxes are difficult to administer. Simple taxes like taxes on automobiles or easy-to-measure business activities can be managed more easily. Taxes on retail transactions or turnover may be unavoidable, but they should be kept low, as they distort the efficient division of labour.

Nations should: provide cities with an adequate set of taxes which allows them to provide the services which voters demand. For basic services (education, health) equalization grants are necessary, since no tax system can finance minimum services in all cities.

Cities should: as a first priority, improve their financial management. Better collection of existing taxes is better than introducing new taxes, and in several cities like Porto Alegre, Brazil and Ahmedabad, India, effective tax collection has proved to be the starting point to the emergence of a healthier public sector.

The Environment

Environmental problems and solutions have a dual nature: they may originate locally but have global consequences, or they may start on global markets but have local effects, like car-based pollution. So solutions have to be found both globally and locally. The twentieth century was predominantly a century of labour-saving technologies. The twenty-first century needs a shift in priorities: it needs to become an eco-modernization century, a century of eco-saving innovations. Cities are the main pollutants of the world, as more and more activities are concentrated in them. And many cities in the developed world are the worst culprits, squandering energy and encouraging wasteful patterns of development. Higher urban density, in many cases, is a precondition for eco-efficiency. Setting and maintaining minimum densities, below which development should not fall, will produce energy savings, more recycling of materials or waste.

Cities depend for their success on overarching national and international policies. As long as world markets provide more than 50 million cars per year, production technologies fail to fulfil standards of sustainability, or manufactured goods cannot be recycled easily, cities are limited in their efforts and are bound to remain plagued by fleets of polluting cars, by polluting factories, by energy-intensive office blocks and by millions of dwellings which have to be heated or cooled. Only radical energy savings, or equally radical progress in developing eco-technologies, will allow cities to develop and demonstrate their strength in sustainable development, based on higher densities which will permit dense networks of short-distance contacts with large numbers of people.

For the most part, such eco-technologies will depend on research at national or even international levels. Yet cities, too, can play a role, encouraging universities and start-up companies to develop responses to local environmental problems and then to sell these to other cities and countries. By making themselves model demonstration cities for these technologies, they can market themselves and their companies.

Nations should: increase efforts for low-emission production, to reduce emissions from cars and later – but within measurable time – to develop the pollution-free car, to increase incentives for more recycling or to regulate the process of recycling, and – most urgent of all – to speed up the transition to an age of renewable energy. In market systems, incentives are the key to eco-efficiency: prices or taxes and cost recovering fees for public utilities must signal ecological scarcities or opportunities to make profits through new eco-friendly products. The entire system of economic incentives and disincentives needs to be stood on its head. Profits from pollution should be made impossible in the future. Cities will only partially be responsible for the eco-revolution which will inevitably happen in the years to come. But cities should lobby for radical changes and assist national governments in their massive task.

Nations should: Provide incentives and regulations for progress in eco-technologies and more sustainable consumption patterns, forming a supportive framework for cities to become effective in their environmental strategies.

Cities should: urge and assist national governments to develop and adopt such policies; seek to develop their own eco-technologies, to market these and to become model demonstration cities for them; become members of eco-networks, whereby they undertake mutually to stop competing to attract jobs and investment by offering low emission or pollution standards. They should accept common minimum standards – at least among cities of the same level of income or within a specific region of the world – to provide level playing-field conditions for individual companies which compete on communal markets. The continuing effort to reduce input and increase output can only be successful where and when cities, industry, national governments and international organizations work together.

Paradoxically, both poverty and wealth are enemies of the environment. Poverty reduces the ability to pay for cleaner technologies or for minimum standards. Wealth goes together with high-energy consumption and use of finite resources, based on vested interests and sunk capital. In both cases, ignorance is still a key factor. All types of cities, with different levels of resource, need to act for the same ends.

Cities should: concentrate on the Brown Agenda of reducing local pollution of the air, soil or water. If they prove successful in this, they can claim a huge reward: they will win a wider reputation, perhaps even worldwide, and will become even more motivated if their efforts result in eco-friendly goods and services for world markets – machines, cars, production processes, energy systems. Global and local progress can and should come together.

This communal task does not imply a common agenda for all cities, as the struggle for sustainability follows different paths and patterns. Economic conditions differ, and so do local preferences and sensitivities about environmental problems. Different types of cities have to develop a specific agenda, concentrating on their most urgent problems. Nearly everywhere, environmental education and information, linked to strategies involving the active participation of citizens (waste recycling, energy saving, reduction of pollution), will be helpful and should form part of a local agenda.

The City of Hypergrowth: Health and Lower Pollution

In the cities of hypergrowth, health hazards are still most urgent, as infant mortality remains stubbornly high, thus demanding improved water quality and better sanitation – but at low capital costs. In cases where the city's own administrative capacities are too limited, as they are in many (but not all) cases, private companies can take over responsibility for water, waste collection and even main sewer systems. Standard contracts and control mechanisms should prove relatively easy to develop.

Mobilizing neighbourhoods to organize local initiatives for better water quality and better sanitation should become a complementary common practice in the informal settlements with their large deficits in infrastructure. As their inhabitants will be unable to finance capital intensive formal solutions, informal solutions will have to be found: people and local organizations, based on technical assistance, should use their own funds and their own labour to provide sewerage lines, latrines or water pipes. Incentives are high, because private water delivery is often overpriced and investment in infrastructure increases the value of the buildings. Parallel to a resource-conserving strategy, cities need to develop a human-resource strategy to improve the environment.

Cities should: work to develop appropriate combinations of formal (usually capital-intensive) solutions and low-cost self-help communal mechanisms for environmental improvement; contract outside agencies to provide larger-scale trunk facilities while local supply will fill the gaps.

The City of Dynamism: Higher Standards

The middle-income high-growth cities have a wider agenda: fighting pollution from growing traffic, upgrading and integrating informal settlements into the mainstream urban fabric, better pricing of services and tougher regulations against polluting factories, are key elements of a broadening strategy which will progressively increase standards of environmental quality.

Increased awareness of environmental concerns is also important, as low awareness is still responsible for outcomes which lag behind the economic and technical potential of these high-growth cities.

Cities should: work to upgrade informal settlements and incorporate them in the mainstream urban fabric; promote urban awareness, especially among lower-income citizens, through imaginative schemes that harness their energies and enthusiasms and increase the percentage of local GDP used for local infrastructure and improved environmental quality.

The Mature City: Recycling and Renewable Energies

The mature cities have long ago solved their problems of water quality or adequate sewer systems. Their most urgent concern has to be to reduce their unacceptably high consumption of energy and of finite resources, or to find acceptable substitutes. They have to move into a new age of radically reduced fuel consumption and radical energy savings. The techniques are already known: energy and fuel should become more expensive, so as to increase incentives for savings and innovation.

This is a worldwide political task. The long-term sustainable solution – the transition to a world of recycling and renewable energies – should be the next and final stage. It will demand research, investment and new consumption patterns.

Cities should: pressure national governments and international agencies to take action; develop model projects which establish them as Best Practice cities on a global scale; and make the transition to renewable energies and a recycling economy into a key element of a national and local strategy.

The Competitive City: Promoting a Healthy Local Economy

Cities are engines of growth. They make people more productive. The urban share of output is invariably greater than the urban share of population. Urbanization is the precondition for successful development. Promoting urban economic development is always a carefully-balanced double task:

- Strengthening the local sectors of non-tradable goods where the majority of people earn their living and spend the majority of their income;
- Strengthening the competitive position of local suppliers on global markets.

Cities are in no position to create jobs directly, by running factories or service companies. Nor should they. But, working in parallel with national policies, they can and should improve the way markets function – especially in the way they generate jobs. Cities should see themselves as the first service and delivery organizations for the local economy. They should create an enabling environment where entrepreneurs with new initiatives do not have to embark on a long and exhausting march through bureaucratic jungles, or on a search for adequate infrastructure, before they can begin production.

Cities as permanent partners of private economic initiative have to provide a planning framework, especially zoning regulations, which reduces risks, negative external effects and uncertainty. As preconditions for private investment they have to provide infrastructure, urban services – in particular, licences and permits for new activities and buildings in due time and at low cost – based on effective management and on self-restraining bureaucratic practice.

Cities as complex organizations have to be able to deal simultaneously with world-class companies and high-street hawkers, local repair shops and central city department stores – in each case with appropriate methods. Being able to deal with the high-tech and the no-tech, the formal and the informal, the international and the backyard company alike, is essential for all cities, from New York to Nairobi.

Small businesses dominate the local economies of most cities, but urban bureaucracies tend to have difficulties in helping them. This is a permanent structural problem. It will become worse if cities do not react to the growing numbers of independent knowledge-oriented small or minibusinesses, which allow more and more people to work from home as independent self-employed suppliers of personal services, information, advice or information processing.

One key action for most economic activities is to improve access to urban land for all type of companies and investment. Thus reducing one of the most difficult hurdles for private investment: by developing low-cost schemes, such as covered public markets and workshops, to rent or for owner-occupation, in conjunction with the private sector; by ensuring that some of the development value, generated by urban infrastructure improvement, benefits the local community; and by trying to decentralize and democratize land-use policy and infrastructure decisions.

Cities are multi-task organizations. The range of their activities is still growing. They must be able to tax small informal self-employed firms in simple, informal, but effective ways. They have to manage technically complex systems of congestion pricing with high-tech methods. In this, they need to be as differentiated as are their local economy and their local workforce: their administrations have to mirror their economic structure and the needs of their people. The welfare of urban populations will depend both on the informal supplier and on high-tech modern products. So cities have to promote both.

Many cities, in a world of wealth and low mobility costs, will be the target of tourists who will grow in numbers. Making the cultural heritage, the local lifestyle or new expressions of modern art or architecture accessible to tourists will be a growing and rewarding task. Cities should understand that this is a subtle task: it means reconciling the needs of tourists with those of local workers or residents, catering for increases in traffic while maintaining the quality of the environment, and balancing pressures for new development against the need to conserve historic monuments and townscapes.

Cities should: understand the strengths and weaknesses of their local economy and their own potential to promote economic development. They should provide high quality inputs for all parts of the local economy. Promoting economic development means more than favours for private companies. It means, among other things, providing a competitive environment, effective urban planning, an educated workforce and calculable regulations which avoid unnecessary costs.

The City of Hypergrowth: Outreach and Efficiency

The city of informal hypergrowth has to deal with the most radical extremes. In informal areas where many people – especially women – work from home, providing low-cost but adequate infrastructure is the most urgent task. It has to be organized together with local community leaders. Security of tenure is a priority, for it reduces investment risks. Access to microcredit, or training in basic skills in credit management, should be possible in all cities; well-known examples (the Grameen Bank in Bangladesh or FINCA International in Latin America) have demonstrated that the high costs of processing loans can be reduced if peer groups are used for information and control. Small start-up subsidies, together with improvements in transportation, should help to increase productivity and to improve local capital accumulation.

At the other end of the spectrum, the few companies integrated into international markets are very often in a weak competitive position – in large measure because of a weak transportation network, the lack of an educated workforce, and the limited quality of local supplies. Urban policy has to help to overcome these weaknesses, which have their roots partly in a weak public sector.

Cities should: Create a supportive environment for different types of companies and labour markets; above all, develop ways of promoting small-scale enterprises, while simultaneously taxing them modestly but effectively.

The City of Dynamism: Balance and Stability

Strong but unstable growth potential, internal development stresses and an unbalanced physical or human capital stock are typical of cities of dynamic growth. Compared to the enormous deficits in public infrastructure, too many private jobs have been created. Weak planning, bottlenecks in regulation, poor supervision of pollution standards or lack of control of the almost continuous traffic congestion, deficits in safety regulations or banking standards: all these have to be rapidly overcome, as a more balanced development is economically affordable and will increase productivity and the welfare of the population.

The manufacturing sector is still growing. Barriers or bottlenecks should be reduced by specific measures. The most important include reducing licensing costs and speeding up licensing procedures, simplifying taxes, delivering good quality inputs and providing information.

Cities should: remove bottlenecks to the growth of the business sector, especially small businesses; develop simple but effective mechanisms to improve the operation of business; enforce necessary safety and environmental standards; and help to improve training, especially of high-class specialists for more sophisticated production.

The Mature City: Flexibility and Jobs

The overriding goal of mature cities is: jobs, jobs and more jobs, and an expansion of the workforce to be able to fund the financial needs of the growing number of economically dependent people. The solutions are similar to some extent to the solutions for the other types of city: in all of them, under-educated young people or outdated qualifications are an important reason for unemployment. But education by itself is not enough.

The more sophisticated the local economy, the more important are positive images and a high quality of life in cities. Together with the shift to the more subtle immaterial services, the demands for special urban quality have become more insistent. Cities which want to host high-tech or advanced-service companies have to provide an attractive environment for their employees. In a world of declining relevance of hard location factors, cities need a softer profile. What is good for the highly-skilled will be good for the economic development of the entire city.

Cities should: together with national governments, make markets – for labour, services and goods – more responsive to the changing demand and changing technologies. Integrating immigrant workers into the local labour markets will be especially relevant in cities with rapidly declining population. Reduced tax burdens and employment-oriented deregulation will be important elements of a strategy to improve competitiveness. Many mature cities already offer a high quality of life; an improved local environment, a higher urban quality are the key to attracting inward investment, thus decoupling their economic development from their shrinking demographic base.

Managing Social Change: The Problem of the Deprived Minorities

Since the beginning of systematic analysis of social conditions in industrial cities, poverty has been a core concern; it was then, and still is, the ugliest aspect of urban development. Even in mature wealthy cities, reducing poverty and inequality will be a key policy concern well into the century. It can be achieved only in the long run, through linked strategies which will enable unemployed or unskilled or isolated inhabitants to participate more effectively in urban labour markets.

After generations of programmes, it now seems clear that enabling strategies and capacity building are the only sustainable methods to this end. In both developed and developing cities, a sophisticated strategy will avoid both the bricks and mortar emphasis and the pure cash payments that have characterized all too many urban regeneration and welfare programmes, in favour of integrated social and physical strategies which do not treat their clients as carriers of entitlements, but as human beings with talents and capacities that can be developed, so as to take control of their own lives, or to integrate into a socio-economic system which demands greater education, more skills, more knowledge and more social qualities to achieve success. Poverty will be reduced only if labour and housing markets for people with low skills are made to function more effectively and people are enabled to use markets successfully.

The City of Hypergrowth: Enabling and Empowerment

Overcoming poverty in the informal sector means self-help. So improving opportunities for self-help must be in the centre of all activities: better education, especially for children of poorer families; growth policies that connect underemployed workers more effectively into informal or formal labour markets, generating higher demand for labour; more integrated urban planning; and provision of infrastructure. The overriding social problem is to provide adequate education for the still-growing number of children, and health services, especially for poorer people in the informal sector.

In the hypergrowth cities, skill-oriented policies and policies to improve the housing situation and infrastructure prove very productive. Poverty can only be overcome by winning the race between productivity growth, growth in the number of jobs, and population growth. So the best solution will consist in pushing productivity up as fast as possible, while reducing population growth. Education has a key function, as it improves labour market participation and reduces the number of children.

Cities should: work to promote setting up small business; as a priority, promote the quality of human capital through education. Informal areas need social capital and strong agents of a civil society much more than areas with strong formal institutions or administrative bodies. Cities should assist neighbourhood groups to provide local services to individual families or to groups. Where formal entitlements and public services are weak, a key task is promotion of supportive neighbourhoods through dense local networks of formal and informal services.

The City of Dynamism: Education and Overcoming Informality

High growth tends to increase inequality. But it should also generate resources to spend on education; there is no conflict between growth policies and investment in human capital. Additionally, more investment to upgrade and integrate informal areas and improve their integration into the mainstream economy (like the famous example of Villa El Salvador in Lima, Peru) will probably reduce inequality and improve economic development. Thoughtful policies can overcome any tendencies to greater inequality, as Asian cities in particular have demonstrated.

In these cities, the family and family networks continue to function as the dominant protective and supportive institution, forming the particular strength of informal neighbourhoods. But the recent dramatic drop in birth rates in many Asian cities (e.g. Bangkok) will reduce the traditional role of the family.

Cities should: continue to promote infrastructure and overcome bottlenecks; develop education as human infrastructure, especially through development of distance learning techniques; promote the family, which is threatened by rapid economic growth.

324

The Mature City: Re-enfranchizing Minorities, Welcoming Back the Family

Mature cities have developed elaborate systems of welfare assistance. But they have never overcome poverty. Social policy has to be combined with labour market policy and with the development or promotion of economic activities in deprived areas. Social welfare payments should be used to increase incentives to learn or as preparation for a new job.

In mature cities, families have been disadvantaged too often in the past. In future, urban environments should become family-oriented, more supportive to mothers and fathers. The twenty-first century needs to find a new balance between work and family life, so as to provide a better environment for the lives of urban families.

A parallel problem is the growing number of old people, especially those without family support, who will demand new forms of assistance, since traditional systems of pensions do not solve the problem of rising demands for personal care. Unemployed and older people should be encouraged into part-time work so as to deal with the rising burden of social security and pension payments.

Cities should: work to develop schemes to help the economically-dependent back into productive work; find ways of bringing older people back into part-time work, especially in the caring sector; promote, together with private companies, schemes of lifelong learning; promote supportive neighbourhoods where local capacities are used in informal networks to overcome shortages of personal services.

The Liveable City

The liveable city has multiple dimensions, all centrally concerned with the quality of life in cities: housing and the basic infrastructure of services to support it, urban transport, and the overall pattern of land uses and activities that go under the portmanteau title, urban form. Currently, and increasingly in this century, the Business as Usual scenarios suggest that this quality of life is deficient and could become more so. Nor is this just a problem for poor cities; it manifests itself across the range of urban development and urban wealth, as cities fail to cope in timely fashion with the challenges that are being thrown up before them.

Infrastructure and Housing

The City of Hypergrowth: Using Peoples' Resources

Infrastructure is crucial for economic growth and for a high quality of life; even for the reduction of inequality. Good urban infrastructure, the urban backbone, promotes stability and efficiency. Developing countries spend roughly 4 per cent of their GDP on infrastructure, and cities provide a growing proportion of this total. These cities, invariably with large informal sectors, need above all to find capital-saving solutions and to promote low-cost, labour-intensive production of infrastructure and housing through contractual arrangements with private developers. Provision of land and tenure will form the basis for strong investment in housing, which will be possible even if incomes do not grow.

Solutions can only be developed case-by-case, by assessing individual needs and deficiencies and finding a specific solution to each. Through a multitude of such projects, it will prove possible to develop forms of urban best practice and appropriate solutions which – with the help of international agencies – can potentially become export services, sold on global markets. The poor of these cities, who are the customers, need responsive institutions which understand and accept two key features: their limited ability to save and invest money, but their ability and enthusiasm to participate in the investment process through their own labour, which will allow them to fulfil their demand for gradual upgrading of services through a slow but steady process of improvement.

Cities should: use their scarce resources to reach as many people as possible, motivate groups and individuals to provide infrastructure; or to assist people and neighbourhoods to use their own resources – especially their labour – to launch a process of accumulation in housing and the necessary accompanying infrastructure.

The City of Dynamism: More Professional Investment, Reducing Informal Linkages

In the dynamic middle-income cities, rapidly growing demand for infrastructure and urban services allows the development of effective markets for water, sewerage and transportation. But markets for public services cannot take off autonomously without active involvement of cities. Cities should therefore become the creators of markets for all kinds of infrastructure, from use of streets to provision of water. They should develop standards of control and efficiency. Profits should be the result of effective high quality, never of monopoly positions or distorted pricing or corruption.

High private savings and growing incomes increase the demand for owner-occupied housing. Compared to traditional housing programmes, cities in the future can rely much more on supply-oriented strategies where they hold down land prices and costs of infrastructure in order to expand markets for individual housing. Targeted national and local programmes for housing should only be retained if they do not substitute for private efforts, but rather increase incentives for savings and for low-cost development. Upgrading programmes should not trigger gentrification processes; rather, they should adjust to peoples' needs and their ability to pay.

Cities need to involve themselves in other ways. Extreme growth and high land prices encourage more and more projects in redeveloped inner-city areas, threatening historically valuable buildings. High growth therefore demands effective policies for the protection of old neighbourhoods and of valuable old buildings.

Cities should: provide planning frameworks for high private investment and savings and reliable lending systems to allow easy access to loans for investment in housing; overcome bottlenecks in infrastructure as relics of past unbalanced growth.

The Mature City: Ensuring Efficiency and Flexibility

Mature cities, where the quantity of services is already sufficient, need to solve different problems: of quality, efficiency and flexibility. Quality means the quality of production processes and of output. Together with utility companies, cities have to promote innovative technologies (biological treatment of waste water, better measurement of individual consumption, simpler pricing methods). Organizational solutions have to be tested and applied in order to increase recycling and to build up markets for recycling material. Waste management and treatment have to become a growth industry.

Traditional social housing programmes are clearly outdated in cities with stable or even declining populations and with sufficient wealth for more and more people to become homeowners. Adequate land for building purposes will enable enough households to finance new owner-occupied housing. The number of tenants will therefore shrink quite rapidly. But it will remain an urgent task to assist low-income families, who may have to cope with discrimination, to find adequate housing which does not stigmatize and is affordable.

Cities should: develop more flexible and more demand-oriented systems of infrastructure and housing which allow effective private production and increase competition. The result will be lower prices and easier access to new supply of housing. Real estate can be distributed more evenly than in the past. Special policies and continuing efforts are needed to reduce segregation between different groups.

Promoting Sustainable Transport

Governments worldwide are already reacting to a crisis in urban sustainability, particularly in transport. Many are pursuing policies to restrict the growth of car use, or even to reverse it, through fiscal incentives and disincentives and physical traffic restraints. But cities are in a race with time. Local pollution and global warming have to be reduced through more use of renewable energy, particularly in transport. There is a medium-term solution. But there is also an urgent need for interim answers.

In the medium term, almost certainly by 2025, it seems clear that technological advances will create a new form of transport. As described in Chapter IV, it will consist of a fusion of several distinct developments: fuel cell technology, electronic traffic management and road pricing, physical priority to public transport and high-occupancy vehicles, and full vehicle automation. Together, by 2025, they will create an environmentally-benign successor to the present-day motor vehicle: the ecocar or supercar. It will represent a revolution in transport as great as that the car wrought a century ago, with fundamental effects on living and working in cities.

In the interim period, there are three clear parallel lines of action:

- To facilitate the research and development of the ecocar, and to give clear signals to the motor manufacturing industry to invest in the small city-based vehicle.

- To develop systems to manage scarce road space optimally, by a combination of regulation (e.g. bus lanes, bus priority, high-occupancy vehicle lanes, peak-hour loading bans) and fiscal measures (e.g. road charging and parking charges) to give priority and favoured fiscal treatment to those vehicles that use roadspace most effectively: buses, para-transit vehicles and high-occupancy vehicles. These corridors could be managed so as to embody technological developments, in particular vehicle automation, as they became available.

- In parallel, to develop a strong planning system at city and regional levels that will direct development to achieve larger, higher-density, mixed-use and accessible cities.

None of these policies contradicts the long-term objective. On the contrary: together, they will provide the vital foundations for the introduction and diffusion of the ecocar.

The City of Hypergrowth: The Superbike?

In the least developed cities, the supercar clearly has limited relevance for some years to come. Since the first stage of increasing affluence will give people the potential to acquire a bicycle, enhancing its potential should be the first aim of technical assistance.

However, many features of the intermediate strategy are highly relevant to less developed cities. Because of the extreme sprawl, sometimes at low densities, and because (in many, but by no means all, cities) of the poor state of the connecting highway infrastructure, the first essential is to develop ways of better optimizing traffic flows so as to eliminate obstacles and to prioritize more efficient vehicles such as buses, para-transit vehicles (minibuses or vans) and shared taxis. This is partly a matter of importing technology, including such basic elements as traffic lights, but also of more effective management and enforcement. In this respect, some low-income cities (for instance Chinese cities) are far more effective than many others. They should be used as examples of good practice and their lessons should be exported to other cities.

The City of Dynamism: Busways and Para-Transit

In the fast-growing middle-income cities, another element of the intermediate strategy is highly relevant: to improve the quality of urban public transport, particularly for low-income residents, through high-capacity dedicated bus (and para-transit) routes to city centres. Experience from Curitiba in Brazil shows that even without any technological revolution, main arteries, properly managed, can handle 30,000 passengers an hour by bus, producing a very high-quality mass transit system that operates without subsidy. Transit subsidies should be avoided, especially at earlier stages of development where scarce government resources are better spent on other programmes, such as education.

The optimal package, though it will differ from city to city, will involve three elements: fairly sensitive charging for the use of roadspace by private drivers, probably coupled with special priorities and dispensations for those prepared to share rides; reservation of dedicated routeways or corridors for the use of designated categories of vehicle, particularly light rail, buses, para-transit including taxis, high-occupancy vehicles, and bicycles (these last desirably segregated from the others); and zoning for selective higher-density development along these corridors, especially interchange points, where sub-centres of concentrated employment would be allowed and even encouraged to develop. These systems should be deliberately planned to accommodate the eco-bus of the future, a bus propelled by fuel cell and automatically guided. The development of such a vehicle should be a priority for middle-income countries with their own vehicle industries.

The Mature City: Preparing for the Ecocar

In the mature cities the key strategies should all facilitate the seamless introduction of the ecocar. In particular, systems of charging and control need to be evolved that will give priority to ecocars running on dedicated routeways equipped to handle them, particularly where they carry two or more people; these would be managed together with ecobuses on intensive urban corridors.

329

Nations should: together with the companies which are in search for sustainable markets, facilitate the development of the ecocar. This demands clear signals to the motor manufacturing industry to invest in the small city-based vehicle:

- To increase research and development budgets on the ecocar and associated technologies;

- To develop the necessary supporting infrastructure so that it can be used when available;

- To provide tax incentives for companies to invest in the appropriate technology and to take it to the production stage;

- To provide tax disincentives for purchasing large inefficient vehicles for city use;

- To phase out all forms of subsidy to the private car (e.g. company cars);

- At a later stage, to develop a scrappage programme to encourage people to purchase the ecocar.

The purpose of these actions will be to speed up the process of innovation, and to give clear signals to industry and people that the ecocar is the replacement technology for the current car stock. The main questions remaining are:

- The possible high cost of the ecocar;

- The role that the ecocar should play in low-income cities where people cannot afford expensive new technologies.

Simultaneously, we would develop a variety of top-down and bottom-up approaches to encourage more energy-efficient transport.

Nations should:

- Change the taxation system so that taxes are based primarily on consumption, rather than production (labour). A carbon tax in the transport sector would allow the price of petrol and diesel to be substantially raised to intensify the search for substitutes or at least for more savings.

- Give clear direction to industry to produce more fuel-efficient vehicles: tradable permits for zero-emission vehicles to meet targets for manufacturers to produce and sell a certain percentage of particular types of vehicles by certain dates (as in California).

- Make existing car fleets operate more efficiently, through testing, emissions regulations, the phasing out of old vehicles (scrappage programmes), the use of feebates to encourage change, efficiency targets for new vehicles, promotion of renewable energy sources and other forms of low carbon fuels.

Cities should:

- Give priority to the most efficient forms of travel – walking, cycling and public transport – with road space being reallocated to these modes, together with preference in demand management and traffic management. Elements should be: road pricing; smartcard technology to allow charges to relate to congestion and occupancy level; lower speed limits, taxation of parking, traffic calming and removal of all forms of subsidy to the car. (A notable example of such policies is Singapore.) Ideally, subsidies to public transport should also be eliminated on sustainability grounds; all travellers should pay the full costs of travel. But there may be grounds for subsidy to individual users of public transport for social reasons and for particular services. Public transport would be promoted through (public) investment, financed from road charging and revenues from parking fees.

- Take actions in the planning and development sectors to ensure that new development and redevelopment is located in mixed-use and high-density developments to minimize trip lengths.

- Develop trip reduction plans with employers, schools, hospitals and other public and private services.

- Limit availability of parking in the city.

Industry should: accept a clear set of responsibilities that permit innovation and technological development, so that companies participate in the process as equal partners seeking the same goals of more efficient management and use of city road space. With the switch from current technology to the new technology and the replacement of polluting vehicles, there is a tremendous opportunity – and self-interest – for the motor industry to develop sustainable markets.

The Vibrant and Attractive City

Cities are places to live in, and to feel at home in. Cities are seats of culture and therefore a unique stimulus for the intellectual and cultural life of a people. A city is built history; it represents the collective memory of society, a nation, or a region. With its buildings, streets, roads, squares and parks, the city reflects the cultural traditions and hence the character of the people who live in it. Towns and cities are more than mere collections of houses linked by traffic routes. They are more than mere functional systems whose linkages need to be optimized.

If well organized and well planned, the city can also provide a sense of security; it can convey a feeling of emotional well-being and social belonging. But that demands that its buildings and urban spaces are designed on a human scale and with architectural sensibility. The best examples of urban architecture in the world, be they in Europe, in Asia or elsewhere, combine these properties; they thus possess the *genius loci*, they are attractive and vibrant and they engender in their citizens a sense of identity.

The city is in a permanent state of flux, constantly renewing itself; and, if its development is healthy, it both conserves its valuable heritage and enhances it by adding equally good contemporary buildings. This is the ideal. But, throughout the world, in the rush for development the special properties of an urbane city are too often disregarded. And, in addition, in parallel with the globalization of markets, a 'globalization' of architectural expression is taking place; too often, national or regional cultural characteristics and forms are swept aside. Recognizing these forces of standardization, the challenge is to build vibrant and attractive cities that elicit a sense of identity from their citizens: a difficult but a vital art.

Not all cities can fulfil this ambitious goal. In many of them, time has been too short to develop an individual style of architectural expression, or the pace of development has been too rapid, or the city has lacked the means to invest adequately in its liveability. But the time to start is now.

To try to bring it about,

Nations should:

- Pursue an urban development policy with a view to ensuring, through general conditions and assistance measures, that

- The cultural heritage of historic spatial structures is maintained;

- And, in accordance with the principles of sustainability, these structures are added to and extended in such a way as to create urban spaces whose possible uses, scale, language of forms and cultural features provide the preconditions for a high quality of life for their citizens;

- Create political and structural preconditions for this (e.g. national policies on architecture, advisory councils on architecture, competitive procedures, educational and training policies) to ensure that national building measures satisfy high quality aspirations and, in general, develop a national consciousness about architectural quality.

Cities should:

- In drawing up land-use plans, take care to create an urban structure which permits the incorporation of attractive urban spaces and largely maintains the urban structures that have evolved over a long period of time, so as to preserve the unique character of the city;

- In preparing binding construction plans, ensure that spatial structures which typify urban areas are preserved and included, thus promoting urbane living. These plans should also ensure that buildings and building complexes fit into the existing urban spatial fabric and make a contribution to developing attractive urban spaces;

- Draw up a concept of urban design which – building on the existing urban development heritage – permits further development of high quality in the field of architecture and urban development. To deal with this task, the cities should set up advisory councils on urban development which should involve the general public as well as all social forces.

Guiding Urban Development

To make themselves more liveable and thus maintain their economies, almost all cities in the developed world, and most in the developing world, have tried through planning to produce a degree of certainty, allowing private agents to make their own plans in the knowledge that their immediate environment – including their sunk investments in real estate – is secure. All cities should have an effective planning system based on national laws, capable not only of making plans on paper, but of controlling and guiding development on the ground. Without this capacity, paper plans are useless.

However, in market or mixed economies, which means most economies, planning regulations tend to work best when they accord with market behaviour. Planning sometimes has to work against trends too, when they become wasteful of resources, self-destructive and blind to the needs of the wider society – particularly if they threaten sustainable development. But it is most effective when it seeks to shape and modify basic economic and social trends so as to make them operate more efficiently and more conveniently and more sustainably than they would on their own.

But this brings a problem: the fundamental urban trend of the twentieth century was physical deconcentration – of homes, people, jobs and services. It took various forms, from low-density sprawl to planned new high-density communities. Some of these (e.g. creating independent new towns) can be perfectly sustainable. Others (like endless low-density sprawl, difficult to serve by public transport) cannot. Some of these variations seem to reflect deep cultural preferences. Cities have to find forms of deconcentration that correspond to these preferences, are marketable and yet are sustainable: a difficult but by no means impossible task.

The answer is the portfolio approach outlined in Chapter IV: in the cities, 'urban villages'; outside them, 'garden cities' in linear clusters along public transport lines, together producing a polycentric pattern of development for entire city regions.

Nations should: promote research and publish guidelines on principles of sustainable urban development, adapted to their particular situation, including their level of economic development and the cultural preferences of their societies; support research (including reviews of best practice elsewhere) and its dissemination; develop appropriate tax incentive structures for the redevelopment and regeneration of brownfield land.

Cities should: develop integrated land-use and transport plans, which in the short term provide for forms and densities of development that will support conventional public transport as well as walking and cycling, and in the longer term will provide the necessary infrastructure for an ecocar system; develop portfolio strategies designed especially to ensure the speedy recycling of abandoned brownfield land.

Cities have to be liveable, and this has several dimensions: a decent home for every citizen, a high-quality built environment rich in urban design, with good-quality services, easy access and mobility, varied land use, cultural complexity and diversity, and the right mixture of vibrancy and tranquillity.

To achieve these subtle qualities,

Cities should:

- Guide private investment into an intelligible order, in which private investment decisions determine the purpose and function of buildings, while public planning prescribes building codes, infrastructure or land-use zoning in order to shape the basic urban structure, especially public spaces. At present far too many cities are dominated by urban sprawl: there is an uncanny similarity in the sprawl of the high-density informal settlements of the poor, and the low-density car-oriented sprawl of the wealthy suburbs, both of which inhibit public transport, increase pollution and are wasteful in terms of commuting time, use of energy, capital and human resources for building and maintaining the infrastructural networks. Further, because density tends to decline with rising incomes, this kind of development tends to grow unless checked. So cities need to plan to establish minimum densities to provide an economic base for public transportation and easy access to open landscape. In poorer cities, they also need to guarantee the adequate provision of land for housing. If they can get this right, there will be less need for costly tax subsidies.

- Ensure that they preserve what is most worth preserving, both of unique natural landscapes and of cultural urban landscapes, before development pressures overwhelm them. This is particularly important, because cities in rapid development tend to be particularly neglectful of such considerations, discovering their importance often when it is too late.

- Create a sense of urban identity in order to counteract the deurbanizing forces of mobility and separation, demonstrating that the city is a worthwhile place to live and work.

Planning is not the only way to achieve these objectives, and not even the most important way. Urban policy-makers have three important instruments to shape urban areas: financial ones (taxes and subsidies); provision of infrastructure; and land-use planning. The clue is to use them in the right balance, depending on the precise possibilities in each city, and to make them work in concert, not in conflict.

In every city, particularly fast-growing ones, planning creates land values and land profits, which can be huge. There is a strong case therefore for measures to capture at least part of these gains for the community whose actions have created them. As a basic principle, property taxes and levies should be based on the benefit principle: investors should pay for public services, or provide them directly by taking over responsibility for access to the street system or other public networks. On top of that, there is a strong case for the community to capture at least part of the windfall gains that come from urban extension.

Nations should: pass enabling legislation to allow local authorities to charge developers for the cost of providing basic public service infrastructure, and to capture some part of the windfall gains from development.

Cities should: negotiate with developers to ensure that these gains are used intelligently to promote investment in infrastructure, particularly in transport facilities.

Infrastructure is the basic public input for urban development. Local authorities are responsible for providing it, but it is not necessary for them to be the producers or organizers of specific infrastructure investments. Rather, as earlier explained, they should seek to coordinate and orchestrate the process. They may for instance negotiate with developers who themselves provide the necessary infrastructure to make new residential areas accessible by public transport.

Nations should: develop appropriate policies to give private investors appropriate incentives to develop infrastructure within an overall urban plan.

Cities should: use the powers thus given to negotiate appropriate packages of transport and service infrastructure as a basis for permission to develop new residential and other areas.

Land-use planning, the third tool, is often too one-dimensional for the many different purposes it now has to serve, especially in the cities of the developing world; they need new-style development strategies to achieve desired objectives, whereby cities set specific performance targets for new developments, but private developers can then develop the means to achieve them. A key instrument is the 'development agreement': a contract between local government and a private land owner or developer, with a contribution by the developer to the cost of providing public services.

Nations should: ensure that planning legislation is not based on rigid codification, but gives local authorities the power to develop innovative schemes; and publicize best practice.

Cities should: use these powers to compete in negotiating innovative package deals with developers.

In nearly all major urban areas, above all the fast-growing ones in the most dynamic economies, planning to guide development is beyond the capacity of individual municipalities – particularly if they are small and not well-staffed, as so many are. Here, there is an urgent need for a metropolitan-wide competence, both to provide the basic regional strategy, and to establish guidelines for local plans. Experience in the developed world suggests that this will not be easy: metro authorities are likely to conflict with more local administrations, especially on basic questions of the location of new development. It is vital to establish an effective division of powers and responsibilities; otherwise, there will be much wasted effort and contradictory policies.

Nations should: provide effective frameworks for metropolitan governance in large urban agglomerations, where it is important to provide overall strategic coordination.

Cities should: work to maximize the development opportunities for their own citizens, while recognizing the need for wide metropolitan-scale reconciliation of plans and proposals.

The City of Hypergrowth: What Kind of Planning Can Poor Cities Afford?

In the fast-growing low-income cities of the developing world, there is a very basic and drastic question: *what kind of planning can poor cities afford?* Cities everywhere are already providing the answer: they are reinventing the very idea of planning, in the form of 'enabling' policies within loose frameworks: they withdraw from direct provision and concentrate on facilitating new private construction, both formal and informal, and creating an appropriate regulatory framework plus appropriate finance. This best practice is seen in slum upgrading schemes like those in Jakarta and Manila, based on fairly minimal standards that can subsequently be upgraded. They accept the built forms of the informal city, but shape them in the direction of sustainability.

This leads to the question: do universally-applicable principles lead to universally-applicable solutions? The answer is yes and no: yes, there is a broad good-practice solution that is applicable in virtually every city, North and South, rich and poor; but no, in practice the hypergrowth city will always be a fragmented city, in which some areas are formally planned while others grow through informal decisions. That does not mean no planning; it means a very different form of planning, based on loose frameworks adapted to local circumstances.

The overall strategy everywhere must be to develop flexible planning strategies at different spatial scales, from the strategic to the local. The strategic plan for a metropolitan area will set out broad principles of development and will, above all, make clear where infrastructure investments are expected in the short-to-medium term. Within it, local design briefs will develop a simultaneous control of environmental standards and planning standards, set out transparently the proposals for infrastructure provision and upgrading, and develop policy solutions to control land speculation – including the radical solution that all development land should pass through public hands.

Strategically, the general solution will be to accommodate urban growth by progressively decentralizing it at the broad metropolitan scale but reconcentrating it at the more local scale. This is easier to achieve in more developed countries and cities, with plentiful resources and with well-developed and competent public administrations, than in developing ones. But low-income cities can and should learn from the experience of some middle-income cities which, making a virtue out of necessity, have become world leaders in urban innovation.

The City of Dynamism: Learning from the Best

The middle-income cities demonstrate a paradox. They include some of the worst examples of uncontrolled and apparently uncontrollable non-sustainable development: overgrowth at the centre, proliferation of low-density informal settlements at the periphery, rampant land speculation, failure of basic infrastructure provision, car dependence. But they also contain many of the examples of best urban practice – some on the part of cities that have also gone right through the development process, from poverty to wealth, in a generation.

The need above all is to learn from best practice in the successful cities, and translate it into the specific circumstances, never quite the same, in other cities around the world. The models are not by any means uniform:

some, especially in Eastern Asia, rely on tight controls on informal development and on provision of high-quality high-density public housing (which may later be privatized), coupled with high-density rail transit systems; others, especially in Latin America and the Caribbean, have adopted a more permissive approach based on bus corridors and density bonuses to cluster development along them. And this gives the possibility to develop a strategy appropriate to the particular cultural and social conditions in each city.

Nations should: develop general best-practice guidelines, based on experience at home and in other countries, for strategic metropolitan development: initiate fiscal policies that encourage cities to develop appropriate incentive structures.

Cities should: seek to develop local design briefs for both commercial developers and – especially in low-income cities – community-led developments.

The Mature City: Coping with Affluence

Superficially, it might appear that mature cities should have far fewer problems than their less developed counterparts. Not only do they have well-established and sophisticated systems of planning; they also face fewer of the basic problems, above all rapid population growth. But this ignores two features. First, increasing affluence appears invariably to produce increasing demands for more space per person and per household (and smaller ageing households may perversely exacerbate this trend). Those countries that have been affluent the longest (the United States and Canada, Australia) show the challenge in its starkest form. Second, even if effective powers exist on paper, they may be weakly enforced. A notable case is Italy, where the richest region, the Veneto, has become a case of uncontrolled hypergrowth and urban sprawl. One key is that few countries have truly effective regional planning organizations able to control development across the entire urban sphere of growth; in all too many, control is in the hands of small localities which may have a vested interest in encouraging further growth, whatever the cost in quality of life.

The key action here, therefore, has to be at national level: it is to raise consciousness to the need for more effective action to preserve and enhance quality of life, before it is too late. This does not presuppose a return to central power, although it may suggest the need for more effective regional organizations. Against this background, the precise prescription is bound to vary from country to country. In some, the need is to guard against restrictive Nimbyite policies that exclude newcomers and raise land values; in others, it is to control development more closely in the general interest.

Nations should: promote debate on promoting liveable urban growth; develop regional planning structures for larger urban areas where growth presents problems; develop incentives to local authorities, especially fiscal ones, to promote sustainable development.

Cities should: develop conscious debates based on scenarios for future sustainable development; join in cooperative regional structures to guide metropolitan growth on a wide spatial scale.

Appendix 1

Members of the Expert Group

Professor Hanns Adrian, Hannover

Professor David Banister, The Bartlett School of Planning, University College London

Diet von Broembsen, Director Settlement Policy, Department of Housing, Pretoria

Tim Campbell, Global Urban Unit, The World Bank, Washington D.C.

Michael Koh, Director Conservation and Urban Design, Urban Redevelopment Authority, Singapore

Stefaan de Rynck, European Commission, Brussels

Philip Gumuchdjian, Richard Rogers Partnership, London

Professor Sir Peter Hall, University College London

Professor Chris Hamnett, King's College London

Hogan Kirsti, EXPO 2000 GmbH, Hannover

Mauricio Lobo, Secretary for the Environment, Municipality of Rio de Janeiro

Dr Edda Müller, Wuppertal-Institut für Klima, Umwelt, Energie GmbH, Wuppertal

Estela Neves, Gerencia Educação Ambiental

Ulrich Pfeiffer, empirica GmbH, Bonn

Jonas Rabinovitch, UNDP Urban Development Team, New York

Roland Ziss, SUM-Consult, Wiesbaden

Representatives from German Federal Government Departments

Dr Peter Bote, Federal Ministry for Transport, Building and Housing, Berlin

Gerhard Eichhorn, Federal Ministry for Transport, Building and Housing, Bonn

Hans-Joachim Hermann, Deutsche Gesellschaft für Technische Zusammenarbeit, Eschborn

Dr Manfred Konukiewitz, Federal Ministry for Economic Cooperation and Development, Bonn

Professor Michael Krautzberger, Federal Ministry for Transport, Building and Housing, Bonn

Dr Wolfgang Preibisch, Federal Ministry for Transport, Building and Housing, Berlin

Hanno Spitzer, Federal Ministry for Economic Cooperation and Development, Bonn

Dr Karin Veith, Federal Office for Building and Regional Planning (BBR), Geschäftsstelle URBAN 21, Bonn

Dr Claudia Warning, Federal Ministry for Transport, Building and Housing, Bonn

Appendix 2

List of Reports

Sustainable Development and Transport by David Banister, Bartlett School of Planning, University College, London

Urban Social Change by Chris Hamnett, King's College, London

Urban Change from the Individual Standpoint by Peter Hall together with Stephen Day, Hoang Huu Phe, Judith Ryser and David Sloan, London

Living and Working in the Infomal Sector by Roland Ziss, Sum Consult, Wiesbaden together with Eva Dick, Hamburg and Joan McDonald, Santiago de Chile

Entwicklungen der technischen Infrastrukturen in den Städten und Siedlungsgebieten der Welt by Ute Schneider-Gräfin zu Lynar and Bärbel Winkler-Kühlken, Institut für Stadtforschung und Strukturpolitik (IfS), Berlin

Auswirkungen der Veränderung von Alters- und Haushaltsstrukturen auf die Städte in der Welt by Herbert Schubert, Institut für Entwicklungsplanung und Strukturforschung (IES), Hannover

Environment Protection as an Integral Part of Urban Sustainable Development by Christiane Beuermann, Wuppertal Institute for Climate, Environment and Energy, Wuppertal

Cities as Real Estate Markets

Paper 1: Fundamental Economic Trends and Their Consequences for Urban Real Estate Markets by Richard Barras, Property Market Analysis, London

Paper 2: Impact of Planning and Regulation on the Urban Real Estate Markets and Best Practice Models by Nicholas Ordway, University of Hawaii

Paper 3: Public Finance Aspects of Government Involvement Into Real Estate Markets and Best Practice Models by Louis Rose, University of Hawaii

Good Governance

Study 1: Good Governance and Urban Development in Manila by Dr. Rosario G. Manasan, Philippine Institute for Development Studies, Manila

Study 2: Good Governance and Urban Development in Johannesburg, Nairobi and Abidjan by Richard Tomlinson, Johannesburg, Davinder Lamba, Mazingira Institute, Nairobi, and Koffi Attahi, Abidjan

Study 3: Good Governance and Urban Development in Moscow and Vilnius Eastern Europe by Janina Urussowa, Moskau/Tübingen

Study 4: Good Governance and Urban Development in Hong Kong by Wong Kwok Chun, Department of Real Estate and Construction, University of Hong Kong, China

References

Albert, M. (1993) *Capitalism against Capitalism*. London: Whurr.

Alfaro, R. (1996) *Linkages Between Municipalities and Utilities: An Experience in Overcoming Urban Poverty* (Urban Environmental Sanitation Working Papers Series). Washington D.C.: The World Bank.

Andersson, R. (1998) Socio-spatial dynamics: ethnic divisions of mobility and housing in post-Palme Sweden. *Urban Studies*, 35, pp. 397-428.

Annis, S. (1988) What is not the same about the urban poor: the case of Mexico City, in Lewin, John P. (ed.) *Strengthening the Poor: What Have We Learned?* (U.S.-Third World Policy Perspectives Vol. 10). New Brunswick: Transaction Books, pp. 133-143.

Banister, D. (1999) Sustainable development and transport, in Bundesamt für Bauwesen und Raumordnung (BBR) (ed.) *Urban Future. Preparatory Expertises (Overviews) for the World Report on Urban Future for the Global Conference on the Urban Future Urban 21* (Forschungen 92). Bonn: BBR, pp. 41-59.

Bertaud, A. (1997*)* The Spatial Distribution of Population in Crakow. A City's Structure Under The Conflicting Influences of Land Markets, Zoning Regulations and 1st Socialist Past. Paper presented at the Lincoln Institute Conference: Land Prices, Land Information Systems and the Market for Land Information. Cambridge, MA, 14 November.

Bittner, A. (1997) Einwände gegen ein entwicklungspolitisches Chamäleon. *DED-Brief*, 3, pp. 6-11.

Bolade, T. (1993) Urban transport in Lagos. *Urban Age*, 2(1), pp. 7-8.

Boonyabancha, S. (1997) Community enablement, poverty alleviation and integrated savings and credit schemes in Bangkok, in Burgess, R., Carmona, M. and Kolstee, T. (eds.) *The Challenge of Sustainable Cities: Neoliberalism and Urban Strategies in Developing Countries*. London: Zed Books, pp. 215-229.

Booth, Ch. (1891) Labour and life of the people, in Court, W.H.B. (1965) *British Economic History 1870-1914. Commentary and Documents*. Cambridge: Cambridge University Press, pp. 288-298.

Brennan, E. (1994) Mega-city management and innovation strategies: regional views, in Fuchs, R.J., Brennan, E., Chamie, J., Lo, F. and Uitto, J.I. (eds.) *Mega-City Growth and the Future*. Tokyo, New York, Paris: United Nations University Press, pp. 233-255

Bromley, R. (1979) *The Urban Informal Sector; Critical Perspectives on Employment and Housing Policies*. Oxford: Pergamon Press.

Brooks, A. (1991) Omaha: thriving through both boom and bust. *New York Times*, July 21.

Buchheim, C. (1994) *Industrielle Revolutionen*. München: dtv.

Buck, N., Gordon, I., Young, K., Ermisch, J. amd Mills, L. (1986) *The London Employment Problem*. London: Oxford University Press.

Burki, S.J. and Perry, G.E. (1997) *The Long March. A Reform Agenda for Latin America and the Caribbean in the Next Decade*. Washington, D.C.: The International Bank for Reconstruction/ The World Bank.

Cairncross, F. (1997) *The Death of Distance: How the Communications Revolution will Change our Lives*. London: Orion.

Campbell, T. (1996) *Innovations and Risk Taking: The Engine of Reform in Local Government of LAC*. Washington, D.C.: The World Bank.

Castells, M. (1996) *The Information Age: Economy, Society, and Culture*. Vol. I, *The Rise of the Network Society*. Oxford: Blackwell.

Cervero, R. (1985) *Suburban Gridlock*. New Brunswick: Rutgers University Center for Urban Policy Studies.

Chatterjee, P. (1998) A new economic reality on Asian city streets. *Urban Age*, 5(4), pp. 5-9.

Cheema, G.S. (1994) Priority urban management issues in developing countries: the research agenda for the 1990s, in Fuchs, R.J., Brennan, E., Chamie, J., Lo, F. and Uitto, J.I. (eds.) *Mega-City Growth and the Future*. Tokyo, New York, Paris: United Nations University Press, pp. 412-428.

Cheshire, P.C. and Hay, D.G. (1989) *Urban Problems in Western Europe: An Economic Analysis*. London: Unwin Hyman.

Cheung, A.B.L. (1992) Financial, managerial and political dimensions of public sector reform. *Asian Journal of Public Administration*, 14, pp. 115-148.

Christaller, W. (1966, 1933) *Central Places in Southern Germany* (Translated by C.W. Baskin). Englewood Cliffs: Prentice-Hall.

Clark, C. (1951) Urban population densities. *Journal of the Royal Statistical Society A*, 114, pp. 490-496.

Clark, C. (1957) Transport: maker and breaker of cities. *Town Planning Review*, 28, pp. 237-250.

Cohen, S. and Zysman, J. (1987) *Manufacturing Matters: The Myth of the Post-Industrial Economy*. New York: Basic Books.

Crosland, A. (1956) *The Future of Socialism*. London: Cape.

Daniels, P.W. (1991) Technology, internationalisation of services and metropolitan areas, in Brochie, J., Batty, M., Hall, P. and Newton, P. (eds.) *Cities in the 21st Century: New Technologies and Spatial Systems*. Melbourne: Longman-Cheshire, pp. 215-228.

Davis, K. (1959) The origin and growth of urbanization in the world, in Mayer, H.M. and Kohn, C.F. (eds.) *Readings in Urban Geography*. Chicago: University of Chicago Press, pp. 59-68.

Dickens, Ch. (1854) Coketown (from: *Hard Times*) quoted in Clayre, A. (ed.) (1977) *Nature and Industrialization*. Oxford: Oxford University Press, pp. 124-126.

Dillinger, W. (1994) *Decentralization and Its Implications for Urban Service Delivery* (Urban Management Programme Discussion Paper 16). Washington, D.C.: The World Bank.

Dillon, D., Weiss, S. and Hait, P. (1989) Supersuburbs. *Planning,* 55, pp. 7-21.

Donnelly, S.B. (1991) The West: mixing business and faith. *Time*, July 29.

Drakakis-Smith, D (1995) Third world cities: sustainable urban development I. *Urban Studies*, 32, pp. 659-678.

Duerksen, C., Johnson, E. and Fricke, C. (1995) Colorado Growth Management Toolbox. (Appendix to Smart Growth and Development Summit White Paper, Clarion Associates, January).

Eveleigh, R. (2000) The 'Bill Gates of the Favelas': bringing the internet to Rio's poor children. *Financial Times*, 5 February.

Feder, B.J. (1991) Omaha: talk, talk, talk of telemarketing. *New York Times*, 20 July.

Figueroa, O. (1993) Transport and the environment in Santiago de Chile. *Urban Age,* 2(1), p. 11.

Fung, A. and Wright, E.O. (1998) Experiments in Deliberative Democracy. Draft.

Gakenheimer, R. (1994) Six strategic decisions for transportation in megacities, in Fuchs, R.J., Brennan, E., Chamie, J., Lo, F. and Uitto, J.I. (eds.) *Mega-City Growth and the Future*. Tokyo, New York, Paris: United Nations University Press, pp. 332-348.

Galeano, E. (1995) *Auto*cracy: an invisible dictatorship. *NACLA Report on The Americas*, 28(4), pp. 26-27.

Garreau, J. (1991) *Edge City: Life on the New Frontier*. New York: Doubleday.

Gillespie, A., Richardson, R. and Cornford, J. (1995) *Review of Telework in Britain: Implications for Public Policy*. (Prepared for the Parliamentary Office of Science and Technology). Newcastle upon Tyne: University, Centre for Urban and Regional Development Studies.

GTZ Consultants' Network (1997) Alleviation of Poverty. (A conceptual orientation based on results of the working group's meeting in Santos/Brazil 13 to 15 November 1996 and the discussion during the meeting of the KSE Network in June 1997).

Guldin, G.E. (1995) Towards a greater Guangdong: Hong Kong's sociocultural impact on the Pearl River Delta and beyond, in Kwok, R.Y.-W. and So, A.Y. (eds.) *The Hong Kong-Guangdong Link: Partnership in Flux*. London: M.E. Sharpe, pp. 89-118.

Hall, P. (1995) Towards a general urban theory, in Brotchie, J., Batty, M., Blakely, E., Hall, P. and Newton, P. (eds.) *Cities in Competition:*

Productive and Sustainable Cities for the 21st Century. Melbourne: Longman Australia, pp. 3-31.

Hall, P. (1999) Planning for the mega-city: a new Eastern Asian urban form, in Brotchie, J., Newton, P., Hall, P. and Dickey, J. (eds.) *East West Perspectives on 21st Century Urban Development: Sustainable Eastern and Western Cities in the New Millennium.* Aldershot: Ashgate, pp. 3-36.

Hall, P. and Hay, D. (1980) *Growth Centres in the European Urban System.* London: Heinemann.

Hall, P. and Ward, C. (1998) *Sociable Cities: The Legacy of Ebenezer Howard.* Chichester: Wiley.

Hoogvelt, A. (1997) *Globalization and the Postcolonial World: The New Political Economy of Development.* Baltimore: Johns Hopkins University Press.

ICLEI (1996) *The Local Agenda Planning Guide.* Toronto: ICLEI.

International Labour Office (ILO) (1995) *World Employment Report.* Geneva: ILO.

International Labour Office (ILO) (1998) *The Future of Urban Employment.* Geneva: ILO.

IUCN,UNEP (1991), *Caring for the Earth: A Strategy for Sustainable Living.* Gland, Switzerland: IUCN,UNEP.

Jacobs, A.B. and Appleyard, D. (1987) Toward an urban design manifesto. *Journal of the American Planning Association,* 53, pp. 112-120.

Jacobs, J. (1962) *The Death and Life of Great American Cities.* London: Jonathan Cape.

Jamal, V. and Weeks, J. (1993) *Africa Misunderstood, or, Whatever Happened to the Rural-Urban Gap?* Basingstoke: Macmillan.

Jelinek, G. (1992) Aspects of density in urban and residential planning for JaBoTaBek. (Urban Indonesia: New Developments). *Trialog,* No 32, pp. 8-14.

Johnson, D. (1991) Prosperity must make room for diversity in Utah. *New York Times,* 25 August.

Kasarda, J. (1997) The jobs-skills mismatch, in LeGates, R. T. and Stout, F. (eds.) *City Reader.* London: Routledge, pp. 305-310.

Kidokoro, Tetsuo (1992) Strategies for urban development and transport systems in Asian metropolises, focusing on Bangkok metropolitan area. *Regional Development Dialogue,* 13(13), pp. 74-86.

Koch-Weser, Caio (1996) The Urban Development Challenge: Putting People First. (Plenary Address Habitat II, 3 June). (http://www.worldbank.org/html/extdr/twurd/challeng.htm).

Koerner, B.I. (1998) Cities that work. *U.S. News and World Report,* 8 June, pp. 26-36.

Krabbe, G. (1994) Fremd am kalten Wasser: Nairobi, in Mönninger, M. (ed.) *Last Exit Downtown. Gefahr für die Stadt.* Basle: Birkhäuser, pp. 96-103.

Kusnetzoff, F. (1997) The state and housing policies in Chile: five regime types and strategies, in Gugler, Josef (ed.) *Cities in the Developing World: Issues, Theory, and Policy.* Oxford: Oxford University Press, pp. 291-304.

Lamba, D., Lee-Smith, D. (1998) Urban Development and Good Governance. Case Study of Nairobi. (Urban 21, Unpublished Survey).

Lee, Yok-shiu F. (1995) Intermediary Institutions, Community Organizations and Urban Environmental Management: The Case of Three Bangkok Slums. Working Paper 41. East-West Center, University of Hawaii.

Leman, E. (1995) The changing face of Shanghai. *Urban Age,* 3(2), pp. 8-10.

Levin, M.R. (1997) Goodbye Uglyville, Hello Paradise: Teleworking and Urban Development Patterns. Paper presented at the Urban Design, Telecommunication and Travel Forecasting Conference, August.

Levinson, M. (1998) To travel hopefully: a survey of commuting. *The Economist,* 18 September, Special Supplement.

Lewis, O. (1966) The culture of poverty, reprinted in LeGates, R. T. and Stout, F. (eds.) (1997) *City Reader.* London: Routledge, pp. 217-224.

Lin, G.C.S. and Ma, L.J.C. (1994) The role of towns in Chinese regional development – the case of Guangdong Province. *International Regional Science Review,* 1, pp. 75-97.

Lomnitz, L. (1997) The social and economic organization of a Mexican shanty town, in Gugler, J. (ed.) *Cities in the Developing World: Issues, Theory, and Policy.* New York/ Oxford: Oxford University Press, pp. 204-217.

Lösch, A. (1954) *The Economics of Location* (Translated by W.H. Woglom and W.F. Stopler). New Haven: Yale University Press.

MacDonald, J. and Ziss, R., (1999) Living and working informally in urban areas, in Bundesamt für Bauwesen und Raumordnung (BBR) (ed.) *Urban Future. Preparatory Expertises (Overviews) for the World Report on Urban Future for the Global Conference on the Urban Future Urban 21* (Forschungen 92). Bonn: BBR, pp. 81-100.

McGee, T.G. (1991) Asia's growing urban rings. *Work in Progress, United Nations University,* 13(3), p. 9.

McRae, H. (1994) *The World in 2020: Power, Culture and Prosperity : A Vision of the Future.* London: HarperCollins.

Manasan, R. (1998) Urban Development and Good Governance. Case Study of Metro Manila. (Urban 21, Unpublished Survey).

Maruya, T. (1994) The economy, in Yeung, Y.M. and Chu, D.K.Y. (eds.) (1994) *Guangdong: Survey of a Province Undergoing Rapid Change.* Hong Kong: The Chinese University Press, pp. 53-74.

Mehta, D. and Mehta, M. (1994) Privatization of municipal services in India. *Urban Age,* 2(4), pp. 9-10.

Migration News (1994) August, 1(8).

Mitchell, W.J. (1995) *City of Bits: Spaces, Place, and the Infobahn.* Cambridge, Mass.: MIT Press.

Mokhtarian, P.L. (1990) The state of telecommuting. *ITS Review,* **13**(4).

Mokhtarian P.L. (1991*a*) Telecommunications and travel behavior. *Transportation,* **18**, pp. 287-289.

Mokhtarian, P.L. (1991*b*) Telecommuting and travel: state of the practice, state of the art. *Transportation,* **18**, pp. 319-342.

Mokhtarian, P.L. (1992) Telecommuting in the United States, letting our fingers do the commuting. *TR News,* No. 153, pp. 2-7.

Mokhtarian, P.L., Handy S.L. and Salomon, I. (1995) Methodological issues in the estimation of the travel, energy, and air quality impacts of telecommuting. *Transportation Research, Part A: Policy and Practice,* **29**, pp. 283-302.

Mumford, L. (1961) *The City in History.* London: Secker and Warburg.

National Economic Research Associates (NERA) (1997) *Motor or Modem.* (Report prepared for the UK Royal Automobile Club). London: NERA.

Newman, P.W.G. and Kenworthy, J.R. (1989) *Cities and Automobile Dependence: A Sourcebook.* Aldershot and Brookfiled, Vt: Gower.

Noyelle, T. and Stanback, T. (1984) *The Economic Transformation of American Cities.* Ottawa: Rowman and Allanheld.

OECD/ECMT(1995) *Urban Travel and Sustainable Development.* Paris: OECD.

Olds, K. (1995) Globalization and the production of new urban spaces: Pacific Rim megaprojects in the late 20th century. *Environment and Planning A,* **27**, pp. 1713-1743.

Ordway, N. (1998) International Best Practices of Land Use Control in Formal and Informal Markets. (Urban 21 Unpublished Survey).

Pirez, P. (1994) Privatization: changing the nature of Buenos Aires. *Urban Age,* **2**(4), p. 7.

Potts, D. (1995) Shall we go home? Increasing urban poverty in African cities and migration processes. *The Geographical Journal,* **161**, pp. 245-264.

Putnam, R.D. (1993) *Making Democracy Work: Civic Traditions in Modern Italy.* Princeton: Princeton University Press.

Rabinovitch, J. and Hoehn, J. (1995) A Sustainable Urban Transportation System: The 'Surface Metro' in Curitiba, Brazil. EPAT/ MUCIA Working Paper.

Razzaz, O. (1997) Legality and stability in land and housing markets. *Land Lines,* **9**(3).

Rees, W. and Wackernagel, M. (1994) Ecological footprints and appropriated carrying capacity: measuring the natural capital requirements of the human economy, in Jannsson, A.M. *et al.* (eds.) *Investing in Natural Capital: The Ecological Economics Approach to Sustainability.* Washington, D.C.: Island Press.

Reichert, C. and Boschmann, N. (1995) *Förderung von Kleingewerbe und Handwerk.* Eschborn: GTZ.

Renaud, B. (1989) Compounding financial repression with rigid urban regulations: lessons of the Korean housing market. *Review of Urban and Regional Development Studies*, 1, pp. 3-22.

Renaud, B., Zhang, M. and Koeberle, S. (1998) How the Thai Real Estate Boom undid Financial Institutions – What can be done? (Paper presented at the Seminar on Thailand's Recovery and Competitiveness, Bangkok, 20 May).

Rondinelli, D. A. (1998) Background Note on Centralization and Decentralization in Developing Countries. (Paper prepared for the World Bank, *World Development Report 1999*).

Salomon, I. and Mokhtarian, P. (1997) Coping with congestion: understanding the gap between policy assumptions and behavior. *Transportation Research Part D – Transport and Environment*, 2, pp. 107-123.

Schneider-Barthold, W. *et al.* (1995) *Die Organisationsfähigkeit des informellen Sektors. Der Beitrag des Kleingewerbes zur Reform des Wirtschafts- und Rechtssystems in Entwicklungsländern*. Köln: Weltforum Verlag.

Schreiber, J.-J.S. (1967) *Le défi americain*. Paris: Denoël.

Schumpeter, J.A. (1942) *Capitalism, Socialism and Democracy*. New York: Harper.

Seabrook, J. (1996) *In the Cities of the South: Scenes from a Developing World*. London: Verso.

Sellers, P. (1990) The best cities for business. *Fortune*, 22 October.

Sen, A.K. (1970) *Collective Choice and Social Welfare*. San Francisco: Holden-Day.

Shatkin, G. (1998) 'Fourth World' cities in the global economy: the case of Phnom Penh, Cambodia. *International Journal of Urban and Regional Research*, 22, pp. 378-391.

Sivaramakrishnan, K.C. (1994) Is urban politics unique? *Urban Age*, 2(4), pp. 10-11.

Simone, A. (1997) Urban development in South Afrika: Some critical issues from Johannesburg, in Burgess, R., Carmona, M. and Kolstee, T. (eds.) *The Challenge of Sustainable Cities: Neoliberalism and Urban Strategies in Developing Countries*, London: Zed Books. pp. 245-260.

Simone, A., Hecht, D. (1994) *Invisible Governance: The Art of African Micro-Politics*. Brooklyn, N.Y.: Autonomedia.

Sinha, S.B.K. (undated) *Making Cities Manageable – State of the Art*. Ahmedabad.

Sit, V.F.S. and Yang, C. (1997) Foreign-investment-induced exo-urbanisation in the Pearl River Delta, China. *Urban Studies*, 33, pp. 647-677.

So, A.Y. and Kwok, R.Y.-W. (eds.) (1995a) *The Hong Kong-Guangdong Link: Partnership in Flux*. London: M.E. Sharpe.

So, A.Y. and Kwok, R.Y.-W. (1995*b*) Socioeconomic center, political periphery: Hong Kong's uncertain transition toward the twenty-first century, in Kwok, R.Y.-W. and So, A.Y. (eds.) *The Hong Kong-Guangdong Link: Partnership in Flux*. London: M.E. Sharpe, pp. 251-257.

Soja, E. W. (1995) Postmodern urbanization: the six restructurings of Los Angeles, in Watson, S. and Gibson, K. (eds.) *Postmodern Cities and Spaces*. Oxford: Blackwell, pp. 125-137.

Solow, R.M. (1957) Technical change and the aggregate production function. *Review of Economics and Statistics*, **39**, pp. 312-320

Stanback, T. (1985) The changing fortunes of metropolitan economies, in Castells, M. (ed.) *High Technology, Space and Society* (Urban Affairs Annual Reviews, 28). Beverly Hills: Sage, pp. 122-142.

Stickland, R. (1993) Bangkok's urban transport crisis. *Urban Age*, **2**(1), pp. 1-5.

Tapales, P.D. (1996) The Philippines, in McCarney, P.L. (ed.) *The Changing Nature of Local Government in Developing Countries*. Toronto: Centre for Urban & Community Studies, University of Toronto, pp. 197-219.

Taschner, S. Pasternak (1992) Changes in the process of self-help housing production in São Paulo, in Mathéy, K. (ed.) *Beyond Self-Help Housing*. London: Mansell, pp. 145-155.

Ter-Minassian, T. (ed.) (1997) *Fiscal Federalism in Theory and Practice*. Washington: IMF.

The Economist (1995) Turn up the lights: a survey of cities. 29 July.

The Economist (1998) To travel hopefully: a survey of commuting. 18 September, Special Supplement.

Thomson, J.M. (1977) *Great Cities and their Traffic*. London: Gollancz.

Thurow, L.C. (1992) *Head to Head. The Coming Economic Battle among Japan, Europe, and America*. New York: Warner Books.

Thurow, L.C. (1996) *The Future of Capitalism: How Today's Economic Forces Will Shape Tomorrow's World*. New York: Morrow.

Tinker, I. (1998) Feeding the megacities. *Urban Age*, **5**(3), pp. 4-9.

Tocqueville, A. de (1835) Manchester (from *Journeys to England and Ireland*), in Clayre, A. (ed.) (1977) *Nature and Industrialization*. Oxford: Oxford University Press, pp. 122-123.

Toffler, A. (1980) *The Third Wave*. New York: Bantam Books.

Tomlinson, R. (1998) Urban Development and Good Governance. Case Study of Johannesburg. (Urban 21, Unpublished Survey.)

UN Best Practices Database: www.bestpractices.org

UNEP, World Bank, NEPA, CNCPC (eds.) (1996) *Cleaner Production in China*. New York: United Nations.

United Nations Centre for Human Settlements (UNCHS) (HABITAT) (1996*a*) *The Habitat Agenda* (including Istanbul Declaration). Nairobi: UNCHS.

United Nations Centre for Human Settlements (UNCHS) (HABITAT) (1996*b*) *An Urbanizing World: Global Report on Human Settlements 1996.* New York/ Oxford: Oxford University Press.

United Nations Development Programme (UNDP) (1995) *Gender and Human Development.* (Human Development Report 1995). New York/ Oxford: Oxford University Press.

United Nations Development Programme (UNDP) (1998) *Government for Sustainable Growth and Equity.* Report of International Conference, United Nations, New York, 28-30 July 1997. NewYork: UNDP.

United Nations Population Fund (UNFPA) (1998) *The State of World Population 1998. The New Generations.* New York: UNFPA.

United Nations, Economic Commission for Europe (1997*) Human Settlements Trends in Central and Eastern Europe.* New York, Geneva: United Nations.

Urussowa, Janina (1998) Urban Development and Good Governance. Case Study of Moscow. (Urban 21, Unpublished Survey).

Vanderschueren, F. (1995) Rol de las municipalidades en el apoyo al sector informal de la economía, in Assoziazione Volontari per il Servizio Internazionale (AVSI) *et al.* (ed.) *Challenges of the Informal Town. Rules towards the Integration of Peri-Urban Settlements.* (Conference reader prepared by AVSI for Preparatory Event for the Habitat II Conference, Belo Horizonte, Brazil 1995), pp. 231-239

von Weizsäcker, E.U., Lovins, A.B. and Lovins L.H. (1998) *Factor Four: Doubling Wealth – Halving Resource Use.* London: Earthscan.

Wallerstein, I. (1976) *The Modern World System.* San Francisco: Academic Press.

Wong, K.C. (1998) Urban Development and Good Governance. Case Study of Hong Kong. (Urban 21, Unpublished Survey.)

World Bank (1996) *Sustainable Transport: Priorities for Policy Reform.* Washington D.C.: The World Bank.

World Bank (1997) *The State in a Changing World.* (World Development Report 1997). New York, Oxford: Oxford University Press.

World Bank (1998) *Fortifying Rio's Resurgence: A Report to the Mayor.* Washington D.C.: The World Bank (unpublished).

World Commission on Environment and Development (1987) *Our Common Future* (The Brundtland Report). Oxford: Oxford University Press.

World Resources Institute (WRI), The United Nations Environment Programme (UNEP), The United Nations Development Programme (UNDP) and The World Bank (1996) *The Urban Environment. World Resources 1996-97.* Oxford: Oxford University Press.

World Resources Institute (WRI), United Nations Environment Programme (UNEP), United Nations Development Programme (UNDP) and World Bank (1998) *World Resources 1998-99. A Guide to the Global Environment. Environmental Change and Human Health.* Oxford: Oxford University Press.

Yeung, Y.M. (1994) Introduction, in Yeung, Y.M. and Chu, D.K.Y. (eds.) *Guangdong: Survey of a Province Undergoing Rapid Change.* Hong Kong: The Chinese University Press, pp. 1-17.

Yeung, Y.M. (1996) An Asian perspective on the global city. *International Social Science Journal,* **147**, pp. 25-31.

Index

Illustrations

The photographs on pages 142, 161 and 162 are reproduced with the kind permission of Bartle Frere. Other photographs were provided by the Federal Ministry of Transport, Building and Housing.